APR 98

POISONING
FOR PROFIT

POISONING FOR PROFIT

The Mafia and
Toxic Waste in America

ALAN A. BLOCK and
FRANK R. SCARPITTI

WILLIAM MORROW AND COMPANY, INC.
New York

This book is dedicated to

JEREMIAH B. McKENNA,

a combination of Frank Hogan and Harold Lasswell.

Foreword

THE POISONING OF AMERICA by the illegal and indiscriminate disposal of toxic and hazardous waste is a problem of enormous magnitude. Industrial poisons are seeping their way into the food chain and the drinking water supply in ways that make it unlikely if not impossible to stop. Among the many reasons why this is so is that organized crime is involved in the illegal and dangerous disposal of the most deadly wastes known to humans.

By "organized crime," we mean certain major criminal syndicates that are lumped together and called by law enforcement the "Mafia" or "La Cosa Nostra." These criminal syndicates are loosely structured, the bonds among members often quite tenuous, and the relations usually competitive not cooperative. And, it is these traditional organized crime gangs, known collectively as the "Mafia," which are involved in the waste industry. In the chapters that follow, we shall detail the ways in which these syndicates and their many helpers in business, politics, and law enforcement are poisoning all of us for profit.

There is little doubt that part of the waste industry has been penetrated, dominated, and controlled by organized crime. Our contention, however, is that organized crime's waste racket is larger and more dangerous to the public welfare than anyone has yet recognized. One of the differences between the waste racket and other businesses run by organized crime is that in matters of waste there are potentially vast numbers of unknowing victims. Unlike gambling, for instance, the public has no choice of participation. No one can simply decide not to be a victim of industrial poisons that have been dumped in landfills, on highways, into sewers, rivers, and streams by organized crime.

Organized crime is not the only culprit involved in this extraordinarily dangerous development. Responsibility for the situation also rests with many of the generators of toxic and hazardous waste. Some of the largest and most prestigious companies in the petrochemical industry knowingly deal with organized crime disposal firms because they provide a cheap way of getting rid of their most harmful wastes. Government, too, has failed in its protection of the public welfare. The laws passed to regulate the toxic and hazardous waste disposal industry have enough loopholes in them to allow the biggest tankers through. And if that isn't enough encouragement for organized crime and its industrial partners, the almost total lack of meaningful enforcement is.

This work could never have been done without a great deal of help from many people. New York State Senator Ralph Marino, the chairman of the New York State Senate Select Committee on Crime, most generously permitted our active participation in his committee's work. Members of the staff gave unstintingly of their time and expertise. We thank Jim Poulos who, year after year, combines intelligence, compassion, and tenacity in his work as the committee's chief investigator. In the same category is Jerry Wendelken, a walking repository of information on New York and New Jersey politics. Both men have worked long and hard combating the toxic waste menace. The other members of the staff, Lorraine Burns, Frank Reay, and Harriet Sasso, have been good friends and extraordinarily helpful in countless ways. The committee's counsel, Jeremiah B. McKenna, simply embodies the highest qualities of citizenship and scholarship, and we respectfully dedicate this book to him.

Outside the confines of the committee, we acknowledge the fidelity of purpose of Detective Richard "Dirk" Ottens, who will someday be given the recognition and thanks for public service that he so richly deserves. In the same vein, this book has greatly benefited from the work of Detective John Guslavage, and the support of his chief, Joseph Brennan.

Others who have aided us in understanding are Ben Smethhurst and Dick Frandsen, staff counsels on the Congressional Oversight Subcommittee. Everyone owes a debt to Hugh Kaufman of the EPA, and Michael Brown, author of the path-breaking book *Laying Waste*. Both men contributed to our knowledge in significant areas. Interviews with Detectives Bill Grogan and Stan Greenberg from Yonkers and Rockland County, respectively, were exceptionally revealing, and we thank them for taking the time to help us. The repentant William Carracino afforded us an in-depth education in all phases of toxic waste disposal. Also very helpful was Harold Kaufman, now in the Federal Witness Protection Program. Certain detectives from Brooklyn, especially the recently retired Thomas Fitzgerald, gave us the benefit of their experience in dealing with organized crime. Joining Fitzgerald in this sometimes laborious task of education was Detective Kenny McCabe.

Many journalists were helpful and encouraging in our work. We gratefully thank Ben Franklin and Ralph Blumenthal of *The New York Times*, the incomparable Herb Jaffe of the Newark *Star-Ledger*, Victoria Churchville of the Orlando (Florida) *Sentinel*, and Peter Arnett of Cable News Network. Three other reporters, Joe Trento of Cable News Network, John Toth of KYW-TV (Philadelphia), and Bob Windrem of NBC, have done splendid work on toxic waste dumping and organized crime and have also been very helpful. Windrem generously assisted us in understanding the inner workings of the Teamsters. And all who are affected by the horror of indiscriminate toxic waste dumping are indebted to John Fine.

There are many others who provided insight and material but who cannot be mentioned for obvious reasons. We haven't forgotten them, and will thank them privately.

Naturally, without support from our university this work would have been much more difficult. Many assistants tackled arduous research assignments during the course of this project. For their hard work we thank Maureen Feeney Roser, Charles Schleich, Sharyn Rosenblum, and Patricia Bulger. Our families displayed courage and patience with us and our constant traveling. We are grateful to Marcia Block and Ellen Scarpitti for taking on so many extra burdens which we escaped.

None of the above is, of course, responsible for any errors or misinterpretations we have made.

Newark, Delaware
May, 1984

A.A.B.
F.R.S.

Contents

1

"Fear Death by Water"

AUGUST 2, 1979, was a typical summer workday, and few people noticed the activities in the yard of the Duane Marine Corporation or in the parking lot of the adjacent industrial park. The Duane Marine Salvage Corporation was located in the city of Perth Amboy, on the north central New Jersey coast. Perth Amboy is one of many small but old cities in this part of the Garden State; like its neighbors to the north, south, and west, it is principally an industrial city that has experienced recent population changes, physical deterioration, and economic depression. The eastern edge of the city, along the waterfront, is pocked by industrial parks, warehouses, truck depots, and oil storage terminals. A grimness lays over everything, the residue of years of industrial production. The air smells like a combination of oil, gasoline, smoke, and seawater. On any given weekday, the Duane Marine yard is in motion, with workers and vehicles—especially trucks—moving along the avenues and in and out of industrial establishments.

Outside the Duane Marine building, amid 55-gallon drums stacked helter-skelter, a worker stood on top of a mound of garbage which filled a roll-off (an open-top container much like a dump truck body). Into the center of this mound the worker was pushing a metal drum with dozens of holes punched in it. Once the drum was firmly wedged into the garbage heap, the workman climbed down and picked up a 2-inch hose running out of the bottom of an 8,000-gallon tanker parked next to the roll-off. Scrambling back on top of the container full of various solid wastes, he placed the hose in the perforated drum and opened the release valve. For some time thereafter, a liquid flowed from the truck into the drum, slowly seeping through the garbage in the container. When the

13

truck was empty, the hose was removed, as was the drum, and a heavy tarpaulin was placed over the top of the roll-off and tied down securely. The liquid was toxic waste, and the truck was headed for a nearby landfill.

In a neighboring lot, some distance away but within sight of the activity in the Duane Marine yard, a well-used two-door Chevy Impala was parked. Inside, a tall, husky man with light brown hair and a heavy mustache sat holding a 35mm camera with a 100-200 zoom lens. Over and over he snapped pictures of the transfer operation, smiling to himself as he recorded the tank truck being drained of its contents. New Jersey State Police Detective Sergeant Richard "Dirk" Ottens knew he was observing a crime in progress. What Ottens didn't know, at that time, was that his discovery would cost him far more than it would those who ran Duane Marine.

In 1980, a citizen from New Jersey wrote a letter to the head of the state's Division of Criminal Justice thanking him for a raid on an oil company. "As an individual struggling to operate a legitimate oil company," he said, "I would like to pass on some information, but because of the type of people dealing in the illegitimate sector of the oil business today, I feel that I must remain anonymous." The writer described the operations going on at several companies: the Noble Refinery in central New Jersey; an old terminal called Wellan's in Jersey City which was then owned by Eastern Oil Co.; a terminal in Newark apparently owned by a company called Northern Oil; the R.K.D. Oil operation at Little Ferry, New Jersey; and Key Oil of Cliffwood Beach, New Jersey. He charged that all these companies were both mixing fuel oil with toxic wastes and selling the conglomeration as pure fuel oil, and selling fuel oil with a much higher sulphur content than allowable.

What he wanted Criminal Justice to do was simply stop the "illegitimate companies from putting legitimate companies in a no compete position." With enforcement and publicity, he stated what he hoped would happen:

1. Companies that are buying off spec material will know who is operating outside the law and they will stop their purchases.

2. Legitimate company prices will not look out of line to their customers.
3. The public will not have to breathe pollution just so certain companies can make high profits.
4. The public will be informed and back your office in the efforts to put certain companies out of business.
5. Companies that are found guilty should be banned from bidding on City, State and Federal business.
6. Once the public finds out who these companies are, they should demand a refund for their purchases and they should be supported by the proper authorities.

The citizen obviously believed the raid reported in the newspapers was the harbinger of more to come. He believed that, at long last, the Division of Criminal Justice was ready to put an end to the toxic fuel mixers who were selling their brew both in and out of state, forcing him, and others like him, into bankruptcy. Unfortunately, his six points still remain unfulfilled.

Also in 1980, a reporter wrote a letter to a New York State investigator, checking into a landfill in Warwick, New York. She enclosed an affidavit from the landfill owner's son, who told of midnight dumping and other highly suspicious activities witnessed by him. She also sent copies of manifests filed with the New Jersey Department of Environmental Protection, which indicated that toxic waste from New Jersey was taken to a transfer station on Route 94 in Warwick and from there shipped on to Saugerties, New York, to be recycled. But, she noted, "No one ever saw a transfer station" in Warwick.

At least ten months earlier, an investigator had sent a memorandum to one of New Jersey's deputy attorney generals (DAGs) charged with prosecuting toxic waste dumpers. The investigator had an informant or two and told the DAG that "the chemical industry is currently serviced by a large group of small contractors with a great percentage of the eventual disposals being violations of State laws." Examples followed: Global Landfill, partially owned by Arthur Sills, had numerous chemical violations; Duane Marine had twenty-nine drums of assorted chemicals in a roll-off which were destined for an illegal dump in Edison Township. Two organized crime figures were dumping chemicals, one into the Egan

Landfill, the other under a bridge in Newark. Coastal Service was pumping chemicals on the ground in their yard and also directly into the bay. The Earthline Company was storing drums of chemicals at a New York farm. And finally, the investigator reported, the Newark Municipal Landfill was accepting toxic chemicals which had been placed in garbage roll-offs.

The one common lesson the detective, the reporter, the citizen, and the investigator had to learn was that those who were poisoning for profit were not about to be stopped. For every moment of optimism each one experienced as he or she took pictures, checked out leads, gathered compelling information, and read news accounts of raids that spurred them, perhaps foolishly, to volunteer information at some risk to their personal safety, there were many more moments of despair, frustration, futility, and, indeed, danger. The reasons for this are quite complicated, but they can be disassembled and explained. To do so, one must start with that time when it seemed the issue was under control, safely in the hands of Congress and the Environmental Protection Agency (EPA).

False Promises

During the mid-1970s the problem of toxic waste disposal was being addressed. Congress and the Environmental Protection Agency were carving out legislation and regulations which were supposed to deal adequately with this form of pollution. At the same time, however, certain law enforcement officers were beginning to realize that organized crime figures who controlled the solid waste or garbage industry in general were also deeply involved in the disposal of toxic wastes. For the few detectives who recognized the fact, this meant more trouble than satisfaction as they quickly found out how deeply political this new business was. While they were learning this difficult lesson, the governmental authorities in charge of protecting the public from toxic waste confidently went about their business.

In order to canvass public opinion and to gather information on the subject of toxic waste, the EPA held a series of public meetings on toxic waste issues under the direction of the Office of Solid

Waste Management Programs. The EPA program, announced in the *Federal Register* on September 17, 1975, gave notice that four public meetings would be held "as to the scope and nature of the hazardous waste management problem and related topics." Within the first two weeks of December, public meetings took place in Newark, New Jersey; Rosemount, Illinois; Houston, Texas; and San Francisco, California.

With the hindsight of almost nine years, it is instructive to note some of the comments presented in those halcyon days when it seemed the EPA and others in both state and national government were in control and seriously interested in arresting a national problem of large dimension. They all saw the toxic waste disposal issue as primarily a technological problem and were confident of their ability to handle it. They were whistling in the dark.

Here's the problem, they said. Here are some solutions at hand, they added. And then came the public relations message: Reasonable people working together from different sections of the country and different sectors of the economy will find reasonable solutions to the problem. Have confidence in the government, in the Environmental Protection Agency, in industry, and everything will be managed efficiently and effectively.

On Tuesday, December 2, 1975, John P. Lehman, the director of the Hazardous Waste Management Division of the Office of Solid Waste Management Programs of the EPA, called the first public meeting to order at the Gateway Downtowner Motor Inn in Newark, New Jersey. The date marked the fifth birthday of the EPA. Lehman began the meeting with a definition of hazardous wastes: "the non-radioactive discards of our technology based society . . . [which] include the toxic, chemical, biological, flammable and explosive byproducts of the nation's extractive, conversion and process industries." He claimed that the purpose of the meeting was "to solicit input . . . as to the extent of mismanagement of hazardous wastes and the available or anticipated systems and technologies to abate this problem."

Lehman then introduced Conrad Simon, director of the Environmental Programs Division for Region II of the EPA, who opened his talk by referring to the EPA's Report to Congress in 1973. This report estimated the amount of non-radioactive hazardous wastes generated in the United States to be about 10 million tons a year, or about 10 percent of all industrial wastes. Simon acknowledged the "high potential for growing water contamination, by leachate from landfills, surface water contamination by run off from landfills, air pollution by open burning and evaporation," and other dangers. He recognized that expansion of industrial production meant an increase in the amount of hazardous waste generated. And finally, he noted that the new air-water pollution controls, including controls on ocean dumping, would mean a growth of hazardous waste generation in the years to come of about 5 to 10 percent each year.

Simon then offered both some good news and some bad news. He asserted that current technology was adequate for the treatment of most hazardous wastes. And "for those few wastes to which current treatment and disposal technology does not apply, there are secure storage facilities available." Presumably, more storage would be created to fill the needs of expanding technology and the corresponding increase in toxic waste. The bad news was that the use of even the available technology was expensive and there was a decided lack of economic incentives to inspire corporations to make use of the technology. He maintained that "as long as the economic pressures tilt the balance toward improper disposal, as long as no consistent and uniform rules exist for public and private operation, as long as offending sites cannot be closed because no alternatives exist," then the improper management of hazardous wastes would remain the rule.

It wasn't that Simon's caution simply fell on deaf ears at the Newark meeting that morning. Most of the participants understood the environmental hazards posed by toxic wastes. But many of them were not focusing so much on the problem of industrial responsibility as they were on the opportunity for the disposal companies. Toxic waste treatment was clearly a new growth industry. One representative, William B. Philipbar from Rollins Environmental Services, presented the first statement from industry. "The management of hazardous wastes in regional treatment plants," he held, "has passed from the sound concept stage to proven, practical, available technology." The Rollins Company had been a pioneer in this business starting in 1969, he added, and then noted that it is a wholly owned subsidiary of RLC Corporation, which is worth $180 million and is traded on the American Stock Exchange.

Philipbar stated how much Rollins had already invested in technology development and in the construction of three hazardous waste treatment plants located in New Jersey, Louisiana, and Texas. He pointed out, however, that Rollins faced several critical problems, which all boiled down to the simple fact that Rollins needed more business. (Despite the overall rosy picture painted, two years later Rollins would face a much more severe problem when its New Jersey facility blew up, killing six people.)

As the EPA constructed a regulated industry, then, of course, firms like Rollins would have all the revenue needed. The prospects may be described in the following manner: Proper toxic waste management is an expensive operation. With legislation and enforcement to prevent the cheap and dirty disposal of toxic wastes, the necessary capital investment in high-tech facilities would be more than worthwhile. Without legislation and enforcement, private capital will not be forthcoming. Obviously, for the new disposal companies, the ticket to success was to be the increased prices brought about by federal regulation of toxic waste.

For the purposes of enforcement, Rollins's man then proposed a manifest system: "for each load of waste, the generator initiates a manifest [a form] describing the waste, the hauler and the disposer. The hauler fills in the portion of the manifest outlining that he has completed his job and the disposer completes this document outlining treatment and disposal procedures and dates. These are all funneled back to the state for control purposes."

And there you have it—the fully-found system that would both regulate and control the toxic waste problem. Turn it over to the EPA and the various state environmental agencies, call in representatives of the major new high-tech toxic waste disposal companies, implement a manifest system . . . and relax. With the costs of disposal sufficiently raised, disposal companies would be able to process the hazardous waste and make their money.

Somewhat less enthusiastic about proposed regulations were the voices of the generating industry. A solid waste management consultant for the Engineering Service Division of the DuPont Company suggested a different approach to the issue of responsibility. "There has been a desire on the part of the State regulatory agencies in recent years to fix the responsibility for transport and ultimate disposal of a waste on the waste generator," he maintained. This was undoubtedly a serious error, he implied. Indeed, while the generator has some responsibility, it is in no way equal to that of the waste hauler and disposer. In fact, to concentrate on the generator and not the disposer is to invite irresponsible action.

To make sure that the DuPont Company's position was clear, the representative stated its waste disposal contracts "pass ownership of the waste to the waste disposer when it is acquired by him for disposal." Summarizing the DuPont position, he held that "we believe that only a disposal permit system is needed," although "a system for reporting the transportation of the hazardous wastes would be beneficial." That was all that was necessary, he concluded, to be certain that toxic wastes would be disposed of in a safe and orderly manner.

Finally, another representative of the disposers was heard from: Al Gathman, employed by an outfit called Scientific, Inc., which had interests in many aspects of the waste recycling and disposal business. It was an established concern. Gathman's idea was to urge public education to short-cut what he saw as one of the big problems in toxic waste disposal: individual carelessness, rather than industrial responsibility. "On clean-up days, the citizen who is cleaning up his cellar comes across a can. He says, 'I think it might be turpentine or it might be lacicin, or it might be something, oh the heck with it, I'll throw it in the garbage,' and this winds up in a compactor and the compactor doesn't break it and a bulldozer runs over it and breaks it and flashes on the man or it might even set a fire going." If someone whose company not only was in the recycling business but also owned and operated several landfills in New Jersey could define the problem in terms of safety consciousness, then surely the problem was manageable and about to be solved. When a voice from the audience asked Gathman whether he believed that toxic materials could and should be disposed of along with municipal garbage in the same facility, he replied, "Yes."

One might think that the remarks at the meeting were confined to chummy interplay between the EPA and the various industry representatives, all agreeing that regulation was important, with only slight squabbling over how much was really necessary and who should be liable for both past and possibly future mistakes. So it was for the most part. But there were some spoilers. Blakeman Early, a lobbyist for Environmental Action, (a Washington, D.C.–based environmental group), described some of the hazards associated with improper toxic waste disposal, focusing first on the established links between cancer and a poisoned environment. He then recounted some specific examples of the damage created by the "inadequate lagooning of hazardous wastes." He cited two incidents in Pennsylvania where companies abandoned industrial waste storage lagoons (one containing 3.5 million gallons of toxic wastes) when faced with having to clean them up. From Pennsylvania to Newfield, New Jersey, to Long Island, New York, to Hollywood and Hewlick, Maryland, his examples were plentiful. Nearly every state in the country had sustained some waste damage from illegal and indiscriminate dumping. "Here in New Jersey approximately one hundred fifty wells were condemned and rendered useless for decades, when over four thousand drums of petrochemical wastes were dumped at an abandoned chicken farm in Dover Township."

Early went on to cite from an unreleased "preliminary" study done for the EPA's Office of Research and Monitoring. This study "found samples of air in the community near the Kin-Buc Landfill to contain vinyl chloride, a carcinogen, in amounts alarmingly close to the Occupational Safety & Health Administration's occupational limits." Early also pointed out how New Jersey received toxic wastes from states such as Ohio and Virginia because the limited enforcement of state regulations meant lower costs for haulers and disposers. When Early finished his statement, the EPA representative, Lehman, announced that Early had requested that Volume I of the *Hazardous Waste Disposal Management Report* (June, 1975) be entered into the record. It was done, and one portion of the report was most illuminating. It concerned this Kin-Buc Landfill in Edison Township, New Jersey.

The section was dated March 7, 1975, and in twelve paragraphs told how a bulldozer operator had been killed in an explosion at Kin-Buc the preceding October. The operator was bulldozing "from one to five 55-gallon drums of unidentified chemicals" from "unknown industrial origin," which exploded as he was burying and compacting them. The landfill remains active, the report noted, and "management has agreed to make every effort to keep out unknown chemical wastes." The last paragraph, entitled "Remarks," offered the following information: "The Kin-Buc Landfill, located on 30 acres adjacent to the Raritan River, has received both municipal and industrial wastes for about twelve years. It is owned by Kin-Buc, Inc., a subsidiary of Scientific, Inc., of Scotch Plains, N.J."

Scientific, Inc., was, of course, represented at the meeting by Al Gathman. Interestingly in the light of what Early had to say about Kin-Buc and what the *Hazardous Waste Disposal Report* contained, no one bothered to reconsider Gathman's ideas about the desirability of mixing toxic and municipal waste in the same facility. Indeed, no one even referred back to Gathman's presentation at all.

The Problem in Yonkers

In mid-December, 1975, just about the same time as the EPA-sponsored public meetings, William Grogan, a first-grade lieutenant in the Yonkers, New York, Police Department, assigned to intelligence work on organized crime, received a phone call from another agency asking for information about a man named Joseph Zingaro. The call came from the Westchester County Parkway Police (which would soon be merged with the Sheriff's Office and renamed the Westchester County Department of Public Safety). The Parkway Police were interested in establishing whether or not Zingaro was, in police parlance, "an organized crime figure." Grogan relayed to them public source information confirming Zingaro's organized crime status. Toward the end of the conversation, the officer asked Grogan if he was aware that one of Zingaro's companies had just signed a contract with the city of Yonkers. He didn't remember the exact name of the company, but he told Grogan it was hauling the city's garbage.

The news that Yonkers was doing business with an organized crime figure was no surprise to Grogan, who through the years had described Yonkers as a city of hills where nothing is on the level. He remembered that Dutch Schultz had run his bootleg beer operation in Yonkers right through the city's sewer system. That thought usually brought a smile to Grogan's face. Most often the very tall, blue-eyed detective was a funny, relaxed guy, ready with a quip. But Grogan was not aware of this new development and so decided to investigate. He was not in a laughing mood.

Joe Zingaro had been named in some FBI tapes which recorded numerous conversations made at the business office of Sam De-Calvacante, a highly placed New Jersey mob figure. In fact, when the DeCalvacante material was published by the Bureau in the early 1970s, Zingaro's name came up in a discussion dealing with both garbage and murder. An FBI analyst wrote that the wiretaps show that DeCalvacante and several of his associates murdered someone, and that Carlo Gambino was advised of the killing beforehand. Gambino, one of the most notorious organized crime figures in the nation until his death in the mid-1970s, apparently had to approve the murder. The analyst then tried to figure out who the victim was, using both informants and wiretaps.

One informant reported that Gambino and several other organized crime people, including Joe Zingaro and Jimmy Failla, were partners in a garbage business in Mount Vernon, New York. One of the others was a fellow aptly named Joseph "Joey Surprise" Feola. The informant stated that DeCalvacante was somewhat upset with so many Gambino men involved, because his own mob was under-represented. DeCalvacante, apparently, had some financial interest in the Mount Vernon business and was afraid his profit would be too small. Next, DeCalvacante was told that Feola had contacted one of DeCalvacante's men and requested they go into business together in New Jersey. In particular, the informant said, Feola had contacted the Ford Motor Company in Metuchen, New Jersey, and attempted to get their garbage contract. In return, Feola wanted DeCalvacante's man to locate and secure a dumping site.

Feola had made his move before getting either permission or his proposed partnership. DeCalvacante told his associate to stall Feola while he consulted Feola's boss, Gambino. DeCalvacante added that he believed Feola was already in trouble with Gambino for stealing garbage stops from another major organized crime figure, Joe Colombo. Given the information gathered, the FBI figured the victim had to have been Feola. He had angered Gambino and DeCalvacante. And he was incontestably dead. The FBI's last thought on the matter was that Feola had been, no doubt, in the Gambino crime syndicate reporting to Joe Zingaro.

Grogan was familiar enough with the murder of Joseph "Joey Surprise" Feola in 1967 to realize that the FBI's information had been on target. Zingaro, as far as Grogan was concerned, was without doubt an organized crime figure associated with the Gambino crime syndicate especially prominent in various aspects of the garbage industry. In fact, the New York State Senate Select Committee on Crime in its 1970 report on organized crime had stated that

Zingaro was believed to be one of the "most important men in Carlo Gambino's garbage removal operations in New York City." It was also suspected that Zingaro worked very closely with James "Jimmy Brown" Failla, who in 1970 was a "Delegate to Association of Trade Waste Associations" and a member of the Gambino crime syndicate, serving as "Gambino's personal representative in his dealings with DeCalvacante concerning Gambino's use of a New Jersey dump." The DeCalvacante material also showed that Zingaro, along with Failla, to some degree controlled landfills or dumps and, most importantly, had the power to determine who from New York would be allowed to go to New Jersey and dump.

The first move Grogan made was to find out exactly who had contracted with the city of Yonkers. It didn't take long. Yonkers had gone into business with the Cimino Contracting Corporation. The deal called for Cimino to haul incinerated garbage out of the city. He also knew that Raymond Cimino and Joseph Zingaro were linked together in a number of activities. Grogan's next step was to obtain a copy of the contract. He went to his commanding officer with his information and request. Grogan took this mildly circuitous route because there was a standing order in his unit issued by his commander that no one but the commander goes to City Hall. At this time, Grogan's boss was willing to obtain a copy of the agreement for Grogan—it would never again be so easy.

Instead of a contract, Grogan found the city had merely signed a rather open-ended memorandum, and it was immediately apparent that the city and organized crime had cut quite a deal. There were also special transfer clauses in the agreement that allowed payment to be made to several different corporations. The Municipal Code called for bids on jobs where payment was in excess of $3,500 but Grogan learned there were no bids except for Cimino's. This violation suggested that someone at City Hall was on the take. Another clause in the agreement gave Cimino the option of transferring the operation to something called the Route 59-30 Development Corporation, located across the Hudson River in the town of West Nyack, New York.

Grogan went back to his boss and asked him to initiate a fullscale investigation. He told him the police would look like fools if they didn't follow this case. Eventually the newspapers would pick up the scent and the story would get out—"Yonkers Signs Open-Ended Agreement with Mob Company to Haul City Garbage, No

Police Action," would be a likely headline. Grogan's commander, however, was more a political cop than a professional one; promotions came to those who did not investigate City Hall. There was to be no investigation. Grogan, in response, pointed out they had no idea where the garbage was going; at least they should determine what dump was being used. No investigation, he was told again. The garbage was going across the river and it was out of Yonkers' jurisdiction. It was not their responsibility.

One last time Grogan tried to get the department to back an investigation. He asked permission to look into the Route 59-30 Development Corporation, but was once more turned down. Yet the constant claim of "It's across the river, not our responsibility," instead of turning Grogan off, made him angry and even more determined. He decided to call up a friend, Deputy Sheriff Stanley Greenberg of the Rockland County Sheriff's Office, whose jurisdiction included West Nyack, New York. Grogan explained the interesting circumstances to Greenberg, and asked him to check out 59-30 and find out what was going on.

What they found was most intriguing. By the early spring of 1976, Grogan and Greenberg had discovered that the Yonkers garbage was going into an illegal landfill, or at least what they thought at the time was an illegal one, in Clarkstown, Rockland County, New York. To the best of their knowledge, the landfill had no current New York State Department of Environmental Conservation permit, and clearly violated a New York State statute known as the Wetlands Act.

Greenberg and Grogan, unofficially working together, established that Zingaro and Cimino were meeting at the illegal dump. Greenberg did reverse tails, following vehicles from the dump back to Yonkers. He also set up observation points to check on the traffic into the dump, and soon noticed tankers moving onto the dump. Watching these tankers unload their waste, both detectives wondered what besides garbage was being flushed onto the ground. At first they thought it might be a nighttime dumping operation of septic sewerage; then it occurred to them it might be some combination of toxic wastes. In any case, there was enough mysterious activity going on involving important organized crime people for Greenberg to move for an official investigation by the authorities in Rockland County. He was about as successful in Rockland as Grogan had been in Yonkers.

Greenberg received no support from the county district attorney, Kenneth Gribetz, nor from officials in the State Department of Environmental Conservation (DEC). Greenberg, who is of medium height and heavily muscled, grew up as a very tough street kid in New York. He is pugnacious by nature, even though graced with an almost pretty face. Like Grogan, no one pushed Stan Greenberg around or could ease him off an investigation. He moved ahead with his own investigation, reaching out for informants, checking with other working detectives who had knowledge about Rockland County's organized crime syndicates, and pushing leads into the activities of Zingaro and Cimino. Grogan and Greenberg had begun what was probably the first covert intelligence operation into the illegal dumping of toxic wastes in the nation.

One of the first signs that Rockland County officials, or more appropriately Clarkstown politicos, were less than forthright in this matter was revealed to Greenberg that spring. He learned the landfill which both he and Grogan believed to be illegal was operating with a special permit granted at a unique meeting of the Clarkstown Town Board convened on New Year's Eve—December 31, 1975, at 10 P.M. In fact, the property had been rezoned the same night at that private meeting.

While Greenberg received no support from the district attorney, and Grogan none from his department, they had yet to face much overt opposition. But in June, 1976, the local Yonkers newspaper, *The Herald Statesman*, published the Cimino story. Reporter Jennie Britten noted the Yonkers contract (the news story did not mention that the contract was actually a rather informal memorandum of agreement) with Cimino Contracting was "awarded without competitive bidding," which state law mandates for public works jobs expected to exceed $3,500. So far, she added, Yonkers has paid Cimino $53,000. Other reported irregularities included the fact no performance bond was required of Cimino; the City Council did not approve the contract; the city's Board of Contract and Supply did not approve the contract; and no background check of Cimino Contracting was conducted by Yonkers police, "a routine procedure established by former City Manager Seymour Scher for firms doing business with the city."

Having established the irregularities, Britten then identified those responsible. On December 10, 1975, City Manager J. Emmett Casey signed the Cimino contract, which had been negotiated by Casey's deputy manager, Vincent R. Castaldo. Cimino had been recommended to the administration, Britten reported, by Mayor Angelo R. Martinelli and Councilman Charles A. Cola while he was chairman of the council's Public Works Committee.

The newspaper's own background check on Raymond Cimino and his associates was most interesting. In 1973, for example, Cimino was vice president of a firm called Cross-County Landfill. That year Cross-County was fined by Westchester County "for illegal dumping on property owned by the Sisters of Saint Francis." (We must add that current intelligence reports indicate the illegal dumping of toxic wastes on the same site by many of these same principals is still going on.) The president of Cross-County was Richard Gizzi, who "has a record of arrests—but no convictions—on charges of bookmaking and gambling." Gizzi also associated with alleged organized crime figures such as "Lawrence Centore of Yonkers, whom law enforcement records list as an upper echelon member of organized crime."

The disclosure of alleged criminal enterprises and associates went on. Raymond Cimino's partner who signed the contract with Yonkers was Dario Cioti. Both men were also partners in the Route 59-30 Development Corporation over in West Nyack. And Cioti was the "president of the DeFoe Corp. of the Bronx, which bid for a $1.9 million contract with Westchester County this year [1976] to haul fill dirt to the Croton Dump." The DeFoe Corp. notified the county it would get the fill from a Dutchess County business called Route 55, Inc. The president of this last company was Joseph Zingaro.

Finally, reporter Britten turned to the Clarkstown dump. This private landfill was not approved, she noted, until New Year's Eve. But even then, after the extraordinary town board meeting, the "approval hinged on several conditions, one of which was the posting of a bond by the owner of the landfill site, Thomas Dexter, who formerly owned a printing firm adjacent to the site." This condition was simply unfulfilled until "three weeks ago"—after *The Herald Statesman* began asking embarrassing questions.

The Herald Statesman's story was politically explosive. And, apparently, Yonkers officials believed that Grogan had leaked a great deal of his information to the press. He hadn't, but now the pressure on Grogan and especially on his friend Greenberg increased dramatically. Eventually, the opposition would crystallize into a series of dramatic confrontations, which we will detail later, with Greenberg on one side and the district attorney and various Rockland County politicians on the other. So strong was the pressure at times that both men tried to figure out what they were doing that was causing so much turmoil. Who was involved, they wondered? What must it be worth? Millions, hundreds of millions? They searched their past experience to find something, anything, that was commensurate. Even when they realized one of the sources pressuring them to hold back, to divert, to ease up, was coming from Governor Hugh Carey's office—which through a series of actions (or non-actions) did its best to prevent the investigation from progressing—they still could not understand exactly why.

In any case, once the Cimino story broke in the Yonkers paper, the town officials had to act. They decided the Cimino job must now be officially, legally, bid. No longer would that quiet memorandum of agreement suffice. The job was advertised and two bids came in. One was from the Cimino Contracting Corporation; the other from a company which, interestingly enough, had an officer associated with the Route 59-30 Development Corporation. Not surprisingly, Cimino offered the low bid and was awarded the contract. When Grogan suggested to his superiors that there may have been collusion in the bidding process, he was told by town officials that "we don't want to get into that."

Unable to move the politicians on the question of bid rigging, Grogan took another tack. He set out to investigate the proposed disposal site. The Dexter landfill which had received such remarkably special treatment by the Clarkstown politicos was no longer in operation. Cimino Contracting indicated they would take the waste to the Kin-Buc Landfill in Edison Township, New Jersey. Grogan, of course, had no knowledge of the recent unhappy history of Kin-Buc. When he called New Jersey officials, he received a quick education and was told that Kin-Buc was closing down in ten days. Grogan conveyed this news to Yonkers officials who passed the word to Cimino. Another disposal site, the Al Turi landfill in Goshen, New York, was then proposed by Cimino. Grogan was back on the phone with Goshen officials who told him the site was almost totally exhausted. Next, Grogan wrote a report which said that unless the New York State Department of Environmental Conservation granted a special dispensation, the Al Turi landfill could not be used. Yonkers officials were furious with him and what they considered his constant meddling in town business.

Confirmation

About three years later, a great deal of what Grogan and Greenberg uncovered, and indeed feared, was finally confirmed and brought to public attention. A Special Grand Jury for Investigations into Organized Criminal Activities of the County of Rockland issued a lengthy and damning report in the summer of 1979. Among the items discussed were some seventeen private wells in West Nyack that had been contaminated by trichloroethylene (TCE), an industrial degreasing agent and solvent. The grand jury noted TCE "has grossly contaminated the groundwater which provides drinking water to a neighborhood in West Nyack"; TCE is "known to have adverse effects on the human nervous system, the cardiovascular system, the liver and the kidney"; and TCE is "related to vinyl chloride, a known carcinogen in man." Laboratory analysis conducted on kitchen taps in West Nyack disclosed the water "posed an average lifetime exposure risk of cancer one thousand times greater than that of the maximum recommended concentration." In addition, a DEC official testified the dump's chemical contents were probably contaminating not only nearby groundwater but also the Hackensack River.

To make sure no one missed the connection between the contaminated wells and the detective work of Greenberg and Grogan, the report concluded its section on contamination with the following: "As early as 1976, detectives . . . conducted surveillances of a private dump site . . . not far from the neighborhood where 17 private wells were contaminated." It was noted that the site operator had only a building permit allowing him to dispose of the debris from construction, such as concrete, wood, and plaster. So ended the mystery of what actually was granted on New Year's Eve. The rezoning never did, never could, make it legal for Cimino to dump incinerated garbage in Clarkstown, which borders West Nyack. Now we know why none of the interested politicians was anxious to let either Grogan or Greenberg find out what was going on. Just as clearly, however, it was not only incinerated garbage that was illegally dumped. The tank trucks Greenberg had watched dump unknown liquids directly onto the ground at the dump had found their mark—somewhere in that witches' brew someone had dumped the TCE.

The 1979 Grand Jury Report also observed that despite the detectives' investigation, no legal action was taken by county officials. It was not until late 1976 that the Department of Environmental Conservation ordered the private landfill closed. Unfortunately, the grand jury did not elaborate on why the detectives were unsuccessful, or why the DEC waited until almost the end of 1976 to officially close the dump. Thus, although the 1979 Grand Jury Report vindicated the work done by Grogan and Greenberg, this justification was small consolation. They knew that the dumpers and their political cronies had, without doubt, gotten away with it.

Political Talk

The events in Yonkers and Rockland County revealed both solid and toxic waste disposal were criminal problems of great magnitude, involving individuals and companies associated with organized crime syndicates, yet they still received no mention in the continuing EPA meetings and forums devoted to hazardous wastes. The first public meeting sponsored by the EPA had occurred almost simultaneously with Detective Grogan's call from the Parkway Police. Another was held about fifteen months later, in February, 1977.

These two meetings neatly bracketed the period when at least the outline of the organized crime problem in the New York metropolitan region was being brought to public attention through the efforts of Grogan, Greenberg, and *The Herald Statesman*. True, no one could claim that their efforts did more than alert the corrupt, and force the closing of one private landfill in 1976. But one should not imagine that officials from the metropolitan region's environmental agencies were unaware of what had transpired that year.

Of course, the entire issue of regulating toxic wastes had changed during the course of that year with the passage of the federal Resource Conservation and Recovery Act (RCRA), to be discussed at some length shortly. It was toward that end that the original public meetings had been held. So, naturally, the primary topic of discussion concerned the act and its implications in all the areas of toxic waste management. Yet for all that was offered at this meeting—and some of the talk was enlightening—there was nothing which even hinted that one of the root problems might be more criminological than technological.

The second EPA meeting took place in New York City, at the Americana City Squire Inn, and was sponsored by the Scientists' Committee for Public Information, Inc., which "is part of EPA's continuing efforts to educate and involve the public on the Federal solid waste management programs." Funding for the meeting came from the EPA's Office of Solid Waste. The first speaker was Eric Outwater, the EPA's deputy administrator for Region II, which includes New York, New Jersey, Puerto Rico, and the Virgin Islands. Somewhat prophetically, Outwater began his presentation by telling his audience that, as of yet, they didn't "look too hostile because we haven't done anything to make you mad yet. I am just hoping that you will love me in September like you love me in the spring, as the saying goes." He went on to describe "the pretty good progress" of the EPA in its six years of existence, and to note with the passage of RCRA together with the Safe Drinking Water Act and the Toxic Substances Control Act, the EPA had "all the arrows in our quiver that we need." Remarkably, he complained of the growth of EPA personnel—"I take no particular pride in Region II, in my region, that we have gone from two hundred twenty-five people to almost six hundred," and exhorted the representatives from industry and state regulatory bodies to step in and help out in order to halt this "growth of government." The largest problem facing the EPA was not the management of toxic wastes, the deputy administrator informed his audience, but the growth of the Agency itself. This was the EPA's official analysis of the toxic waste problem.

The New York Department of Environmental Conservation (DEC) also volunteered its accomplishments. Its deputy director of solid waste management, William Wilkie, gave a smooth rundown of their programs dealing with hazardous waste management. The state had legislation requiring annual registration of all industrial waste collectors, and requiring DEC approval (whatever that meant) of processing and disposal facilities. On this second point, he added, the DEC was asking the state for the power to require permits to operate, rather than just approvals. Oh yes, Wilkie noted, the DEC is also busily surveying industrial waste generators.

Yonkers, Rockland County, Joe Zingaro, Raymond Cimino, the Clarkstown Town Board, private deals and arrangements, investigations thwarted and diverted, corruption in municipal garbage bidding, control of landfills, the mixing of toxics and garbage, organized crime—none of this apparently entered the EPA's or DEC's consciousness or was thought important enough to discuss at a public meeting. Was Wilkie, supposedly the DEC's best informed expert on hazardous waste problems, simply uninformed or unconcerned with the preceding year's scandal and what it implied for toxic waste management? Could these officials actually believe such situations were controllable by legislation which fundamentally relied upon the good faith of all those in the industry?

A Dissenting View

Among the crush of pollyanna statements offered in the winter of 1977, one participant sounded a less cheery note. His remarks didn't deal with organized crime's heavy involvement in the toxic waste field, but they certainly provided a vivid picture of the rampant confusion and impotence in New Jersey's Department of Environmental Protection. Peter Preuss, of the New Jersey DEP, spoke up:

> I am sort of a little puzzled, I must admit, by what has gone on today so far, and I am not sure if this is a perception that is shared by others in this room, or this is simply my perception, but the feeling that I get, and that I have gotten listening to what is going on is that we are doing pretty well in hazardous wastes, and it is not that much of a problem.

Preuss noted that if others had the same impression as he had, then they were being misled. "I think we are in terrible shape. I don't—I really don't understand this easy feeling that I have heard all day." Many spoke about the available technologies, but they really weren't generally available. Many spoke about the new regulations and guidelines, "but I am not sure to what extent they are actually being followed in many parts of this country."

Clearly, an elementary analysis of the budgets allocated to deal with the hazardous waste problem revealed how little would actually get done. The reasons for this were apparent, Preuss went on. "Most people do not see dumps, most people do not see hazardous waste leaching out of a landfill, or whatever, so that there has really never been a very strong constituency that has been built up for this." Government unfortunately doesn't act, Preuss pointed out, until there is a major crisis, until there is a widely shared perception that a crisis is upon us. Today, "we are finally aware that a problem does exist," and that puts us at "square one."

As for New Jersey in particular, Preuss stated it was not in very good shape at all. In fact, the DEP really didn't know what was happening: "At this point in time, I don't think we know who generates hazardous wastes, I don't think we know who transports them, I don't think we know where they are going, I don't think we know the environmental effects of these wastes." It was clearly impossible, he observed, to build a serious management program in ignorance.

Special Assistant Preuss then provided a short history of regulation in New Jersey which detailed, he thought, why the state was in its present, perilous situation.

We promulgated a set of rules. I guess it must be two and a half years ago that they were—that they went into effect, in July of 1974, which contained provisions as to what was needed to be done with hazardous waste.

Certain of these provisions with regard to hazardous wastes were to go into effect in March of 1970 [sic], and these provisions were stayed at the last minute because we really did not know what would happen if these were to go into effect.

At the same time, or very shortly thereafter, we proposed new regulations which everybody dumped on. It was unbelievable. I mean, I had just come to the Department, I had never seen anything like it. I mean, everybody picked on them, we really did not do too much with those regulations either.

Preuss also related that another set of regulations had been proposed in September, 1975, which were also not adopted. This set contained a list of materials the DEP considered toxic or hazardous. The one major New Jersey success which Preuss could point to was the closing down of "the very large number . . . I mean maybe in the order of magnitude of about a hundred landfills that were accepting chemical and industrial wastes without differentiation, whether it was hazardous or not, and that this year the last such public landfill was closed in New Jersey."

While good in itself, however, this raised the question of what to do about all the known hazardous wastes dumped in the landfills for the past fifty years. This was, Preuss claimed, the "Achilles heel" of the current program, with little attention being directed at the toxic wastes working their way into the environment. The worthwhileness of closing down the contaminated landfills also begged the question of how to enforce the closing, and determine where toxic waste would then go. While Preuss did not pose these questions, his rather passionate statement clearly indicated neither enforcement nor the securing of new, safe sites was very likely.

Indeed, if the activities in New York over the past year or so were any indication, then dumpers would still find their way into both the closed landfills, and even more insidious and environmentally damaging locations. Peter Preuss was one of the most candid environmental officers to appear at these public meetings in 1975 and 1977. His despair matched, it seems, that felt by Detectives Grogan and Greenberg. He realized and stated, as they had, there was simply no reason at all to feel confident about the government's ability to control toxic waste. What Preuss didn't know or tell, however, was that one major reason for the confusion and impotence was corruption: the heavy political influence enjoyed by organized crime syndicates in the waste industry. Yet his short history of failed regulation in New Jersey, where standards "were dumped on by everybody," was an inevitable expression of that kind of influence.

When Detective Ottens sat in his car photographing one of the multitude of crimes at Duane Marine that hot August day in Perth Amboy, he couldn't have realized he would soon join with Grogan and Greenberg in the battle of their professional lives. And little could the others who had reported illegal dumping and the mixing of toxic waste with fuel oil comprehend they were tilting at windmills. All of them would have many unfortunate lessons to learn about the power exercised by the entrepreneurs of toxic waste.

2

The Environmental Time Bomb

By MID-1977, Peter Preuss's gloomy assessment of the toxic waste situation in the United States was based on his knowledge of both current conditions and the history of disposal practices in this country. Concern with the dangerous effects of industrial by-products was, of course, not new. More than two thousand years ago the ancient Greeks exhibited concern about asbestos fibers breathed by slaves as they made cloth. Many members of the Roman aristocracy were inadvertently poisoned by the lead used to line their wine jugs and to pipe water into their homes. For hundreds of years thereafter, examples may be found of human harm resulting from the use of one substance or another.

In those early years of limited and crude technology, the harmful wastes produced by the few available craftsmen were often unrecognized and their potential danger unappreciated. Although hatters might suffer from the effects of mercuric nitrate and printers from the effects of lead, their use posed little danger to others, and even when hatters and printers disposed of these harmful substances in a reckless and haphazard manner, the quantities were not sufficient to cause significant harm to the general population.

All this began to change with the Industrial Revolution. As the new industrialism demanded unprecedented amounts of fossil fuels, mining soon became a major source of toxic waste. Now, not only did the dust of the mines eat away the lungs of the miners, but when the heaps of unused coal spoils combined with rainwater, they formed acids that poisoned streams and rivers used by whole communities. In Great Britain, Europe, and the United States, the advances in technology took a toll, as ever-increasing amounts of toxic industrial by-products were generated and flushed into the earth and its water. Coal tar dyes used in the textile industry, acids used to strip corrosive materials from iron and steel, lead used in batteries, sulphuric acid used as an electrolyte, and nitrates produced by the manufacturing of high explosives—all became new industrial wastes generated in unprecedented quantities which now had to be disposed of. And yet this was only the beginning.

In the second half of the nineteenth century, the rapidly developing technology of the industrialized nations produced scientific and manufacturing advances that would set the stage for an era of enormous economic growth. Crude oil suddenly became an important natural resource and new chemical techniques were developed to exploit its various hydrocarbon chains. New methods of distilling petroleum required the use of toxic metal catalysts, which were used even more extensively as the need for gasoline grew. When it was discovered that gasoline performed more effectively as a motor fuel after tetraethyl lead was added to reduce premature combustion, large amounts of lead waste were subsequently created. Waste flouride was created when the process of extracting aluminum from its ore by electrical methods was developed in 1889. Each technological advance seemed to come accompanied by an unwanted toxic by-product. In all phases of these new industries, from mining to processing to production, dangerous waste materials were being created and disposed of.

The use of petroleum as the basis for the production of a wide range of synthetic organic chemicals created an extraordinary variety of dangerous industrial by-products. Although limited amounts of organic chemicals were developed during the nineteenth century, the use of petroleum as a basic feedstock allowed the synthesis of organic chemicals in quantities that were nearly limitless. As Samuel Epstein has remarked in his revealing book *The Politics of Cancer,* "petrochemicals are the quintessence of a 'process industry,' in which a small number of primary constitutents from crude oil are converted into a large number of intermediate chemicals in a still larger number of large scale end products." Consumer goods such as synthetic fabrics, paints, plastics, pesticides, and even drugs soon resulted from this process. Whereas the United States produced about 1 billion pounds of synthetic organic chemicals in 1940, this had increased to some 30 billion in 1950, and to an astronomical 300 billion pounds in 1976. Synthetic materials such as polyester have substituted increasingly for natural material and have been used to provide consumers with a range of new goods that were not previously available to the mass market.

This explosion in the chemical industry and the resulting bonanza of new products, oftentimes cheaper for the consumer, was, of course, a mixed blessing. As Americans bought more commodities such as cars, gasoline, and polyester clothing, manufacturing increased and so did the amount of hazardous by-products of that process. Within the decade of the 1970s alone, it is estimated that the production of toxic wastes increased five times. Many of these artificial, synthetic materials were not biodegradable. That is, unlike cotton, wood, and other natural fibers, these products could not be broken down into their organic components, or elements that could be used again in nature, or at least not quickly enough to avoid, in some way, damaging or poisoning other natural cycles occurring in the environment.

By 1977, when Peter Preuss voiced his concerns at the EPA's open meeting, the ways in which some waste generators and disposers were handling the problem had already become known. In 1971, Union Carbide's Bound Brook, New Jersey, plant had contracted with a waste hauler named Nicholas Fernicola to dispose of over four thousand 55-gallon drums of waste. Fernicola rented a former chicken farm near Toms River and, telling the owners that he wanted the land to store empty drums, proceeded to place drums full of toxic chemicals on it. When the owners investigated complaints of unusual smells coming from their farm, they discovered Fernicola's work, which by now included many leaking drums of chemicals.

As a result of legal action, Union Carbide was forced to remove the drums and clean up the dump site. The drums and the contaminated soil were removed to the Rollins Environmental Services facility in Bridgeport, New Jersey, and to the Kin-Buc Landfill in Edison. Ironically, within just a few years the Kin-Buc site would be closed by the state of New Jersey because toxic chemicals dumped there were leaching into the Raritan River and contaminating that important source of drinking water for a number of New Jersey and New York communities.

Unfortunately, removal of the drums did not solve the problems created by the improper dumping of the toxic waste at the one-time chicken farm. By 1974, area residents noticed that the odor and taste of their well water was becoming offensive. Tests indicated the presence of petrochemicals, resulting in the local board of health's condemning some 148 private wells and ordering that they be capped with cement.

John Miserlis, a chemical engineer and former college professor, once had the idea of salvaging, reprocessing, and neutralizing hazardous waste material. Founding a company to which he gave his own name spelled backward, Silresim Chemical Corporation, he accepted thousands of drums of waste at his 5.2-acre plant in Lowell, Massachusetts. Unfortunately, he never got around to the worthwhile goals of his business, and instead stacked the drums without disposing of them. Soon the ground became saturated with chemicals leaking from broken and unlabeled drums. When the state finally investigated the site, they found a cauldron of highly toxic chemicals capable of endangering thousands of city residents. The Silresim Chemical Corporation declared bankruptcy, leaving behind more than a million gallons of dangerous chemicals for state and federal officials to clean up.

And there was more. Apart from the 1975 explosion at the Kin-Buc Landfill that had killed the bulldozer driver, investigators were dismayed to discover that about a quarter of the waste being dumped at this landfill was hazardous in nature. In 1976, an Indiana family learned that milk produced by their cows contained twice the maximum concentration of polychlorinated biphenyls (PCBs) considered to be safe. Apparently, the cows had been grazing in a pasture fertilized with sewerage sludge from the city of Bloomington which had been contaminated by PCBs from a local manufacturing plant. About twenty-five miles south of Louisville, Kentucky, seventeen thousand drums were found scattered over a seven-acre site which came to be known as the Valley of the Drums. Thousands of the drums had rusted and were leaking their deadly contents onto the ground and into streams that flowed through the site. Eventually, the EPA identified about two hundred toxic chemicals and thirty metals in the soil and surface water. In 1972, hexachlorobenzene (HCB), a toxic organic compound containing chlorine, was found in a landfill near Darrow and Geismar, Louisiana. HCB apparently vaporized and accumulated in cattle spread over a hundred-square-mile area. The cattle, of course, had to be destroyed—costing local residents over $380,000. Worse yet, elevated levels of HCB were also found in the blood plasma of some residents. And, until the practice was halted in 1972, over

1,500 drums of waste from metal finishing operations were buried near Byron, Illinois. By that time, however, both water and ground were so thoroughly poisoned that wildlife and vegetation were destroyed and the soil rendered barren.

These are but a few examples of the information about hazardous waste disposal that was coming to public attention in the 1970s. From north to south and east to west, discoveries of toxic landfills, of contaminated wells, of poisoned livestock, and of ruined soil were coming to light so frequently as to be more than just random occurrences. Perhaps the traditional, sometimes haphazard ways of disposing of industrial waste by-products were also more dangerous, capable of environmental and human harm, than anyone ever before realized. The tragic answers to these and related questions would soon be revealed to the entire nation in a series of discoveries and events that began in 1977.

"While I Was Fishing in the Dull Canal"

Before the turn of this century, William T. Love attempted to connect two branches of the Niagara River with a canal. Love's dream was to build a model city along the canal, with industry using the hydroelectric power generated by the abundant supply of water. Digging commenced, but before long Love's plans collapsed when alternating current was developed, making it possible to transfer electricity over long distances. With the need for a canal and model city rendered obsolete by advancing technology, it was abandoned, leaving behind a partially dug excavation just southeast of Niagara Falls.

Over the years, the Love Canal filled with water and was used by local residents as a swimming hole. By 1942, however, the canal's owner, the Niagara Power & Development Corporation, decided to put its property to better use and allowed the city of Niagara Falls to lease it as a garbage dump. More importantly, they also signed an agreement with Hooker Chemical & Plastics Corporation (then known as the Hooker Electrochemical Corporation) allowing them to dump industrial wastes on this site. Four years later, Hooker purchased the property and converted its use exclusively to the disposal of chemical wastes resulting from the production of various industrial chemicals, especially chlorine, plastics, and fertilizers.

Between 1947 and 1952, over 43 million pounds of chemical wastes were dumped into Love Canal by Hooker. According to some sources, this amount was in addition to unknown quantities of toxic chemicals dumped at the site earlier by the United States Army, a charge which the Army denies. Among Hooker's wastes were over 13 million pounds of Lindane, a pesticide known to be highly toxic and carcinogenic; over 4 million pounds of chlorobenzenes, derivatives of benzene, an industrial solvent known to induce leukemia and aplastic anemia; and some 400,000 pounds of trichlorophenol (TCP), a highly toxic chemical used to manufacture herbicides and caustics. Even worse, the TCP was mixed with hundreds of pounds of TCDD, a deadly by-product of overheating TCP during the manufacturing process. It is estimated that just three ounces of TCDD could kill the entire population of New York City. In addition, dozens of other chemicals known to cause genetic damage, birth defects, respiratory ailments, and various types of cancers were also disposed of in the Love Canal.

Under pressure from the city of Niagara Falls and the Board of Education, which wanted the property for residential development and a new elementary school to accommodate an expanding population, Hooker sold the land to the School Board in April, 1953. Soon, new homes and an accompanying school were constructed along the banks of the swampy field with its high grass and undulating terrain. As one might expect, neighborhood children often chose to play in the canal, fascinated by its protruding drums of chemicals and pools of black sludge that often hissed and smoked. Sometimes they were burned by the chemicals and parents would call the company to inquire about proper treatment. Although Hooker claims to have warned the School Board about restricting the access of children to the areas of exposed chemicals, it issued no public statement of what was buried in the canal or its potential danger to human life and health.

Throughout the 1960s and early 1970s, residents of the area experienced increasingly offensive odors and the invasion of their homes and property by liquids obviously originating in the canal area. Basements began to flood with black sludge, sump pumps would corrode and be rendered useless, holes would appear in yards and fill with foul-smelling ooze, and cultivating plant life became nearly impossible. The complaints of residents finally forced the city of Niagara Falls to employ a Buffalo engineering firm to investigate the cause of these problems. In its final report, the firm concluded that a number of drums close to the surface of the canal had corroded and were leaking their contents into the ground and subsequently into the basements and sewers of nearby homes. Groundwater and surface water were both found to be contaminated with many highly toxic chemicals known to be, among other things, carcinogenic.

The report was disquieting news for the parents of children in the local elementary school. When the School Board refused to allow pupil transfers, a number of parents started a petition drive to close the school completely. As the drive picked up steam, residents began to voice their concerns about health problems which they also related to the proximity to Love Canal.

Once neighbors began to talk about their concerns, they discovered that others shared illnesses of unexplained origin. Some children had been born with multiple birth defects; others had severe asthma; while still more were hyperactive, had lost clumps of hair, or suffered from skin rashes. Among the adults, a number of the women had had miscarriages or had given birth to stillborn babies. Their understandable alarm and the growing public concern prompted the State Department of Health to begin a health survey of local residents and the State Department of Environmental Conservation to determine the extent of local contamination.

The surveys found that the air, water, and soil of the area around the canal were greatly contaminated with toxic and carcinogenic agents coming from the former dump site. Contaminated air was found in local homes, particularly in basements. Women between the ages of thirty and thirty-four in the surveyed area were found to experience miscarriages four times more often than would normally be expected. These data finally prompted State Health Commissioner Robert Whalen to announce that the local elementary school would be closed and that a number of families closest to the canal and most affected by its contaminants would be evacuated and their homes purchased by the state. But despite this dramatic, unprecedented action, the tragedy of Love Canal was far from over.

Hundreds of area residents were convinced that the state's action simply did not go far enough. Since informal health data for those living outside of the evacuation zone indicated that they too suffered from an excess of chronic disease and other effects of toxic chemicals, they wondered why they were being left behind. Some families went so far as to send their children away, while others abandoned their homesteads for fear of what staying behind might mean. Class action suits and personal injury claims filed against the city contributed to the rising tension between local residents and government officials. Finally, out of desperation, the residents left behind decided to conduct their own health survey with the help of a Buffalo area cancer researcher.

Although this study was not conducted in a scientifically pure manner, it did reveal that those residents who lived on former streambeds and marshy areas had higher rates of miscarriage, birth defects, asthma, and urinary tract diseases than those who lived in other areas. Even more frightening, though, were the results relating to birth defects. The study concluded that women living in the vulnerable areas had a 56 percent chance of giving birth to children with defects. When the State Health Department reviewed the results of the homeowners' study, they recommended that all pregnant women and children under the age of two evacuate the canal area, at least on a temporary basis. Although it seemed to agree with much of what the homeowners' study concluded, the state continued to refuse to authorize the general relocation of over two hundred families that remained in the vulnerable locations.

In the ensuing months the state attempted to clean up the site, or at least to prevent further leakage. But the construction work caused even more problems, necessitating the development of an emergency evacuation plan involving some thirty buses that stood by during the spring and summer of 1979 in case a disaster should occur. By August, the state agreed to relocate on a temporary basis in hotel rooms those who could get a doctor to certify that remaining in the area during the canal clean-up posed an immediate danger to their health. Making matters even worse was the decision of the federal government to halt action on all Federal Housing Administration (FHA)–insured loans for homes being purchased in the area. Now, left behind in a place known to have exceedingly high rates of debilitating and deadly illnesses, feeling abandoned by local and federal officials who refused to assume responsibility for their plight, and seeing no possibility of escaping without abandoning their homes and possessions, the remaining residents of Love Canal were frustrated, angry, and frightened. Through the fall and winter of 1979 and 1980 they endured, believing that they were incapable of bearing any more setbacks. But there would be one more.

In May, 1980, the EPA released a study which indicated that nearly one-third of a sample of canal residents had suffered chromosome damage. Although these results could not definitely link the chemicals in the canal with the chromosomal changes, that conclusion was drawn by most observers. Needless to say, residents of the canal area responded with alarm and new demands for the relocation of all families that could possibly be affected by Love Canal's poisonous contents. Although much controversy surrounded this chromosome study, its results were conclusive enough to convince the federal government that the time had come for decisive action. On May 21, 1980, the EPA announced that all remaining residents would be evacuated. By the end of 1980, the federal government had purchased over five hundred homes within a thirty-square-block area around the dump, offering local residents an opportunity to flee the horrors they had been suffering and start life anew where breathing the air and drinking the water would once again be safe.

The Problem and Its Disposal

Love Canal, Valley of the Drums, contaminated milk, drums stored on farm land, poisoned wells, landfill workers killed by explosions—these are but a few of the products of hazardous waste disposal that were turning up all over the country throughout the 1970s. Ironically, at the beginning of the decade, hazardous waste was not even considered a health or environmental problem. In fact, the 1970 Report of the Council on Environmental Quality contains no mention of hazardous waste, nor did the EPA say anything about it in the early years of that Agency's existence. It appears that both official and private concern for the environment centered upon air and water pollution, but not on the potentially dangerous by-products of industrial production. That, of course, would change over the next ten years.

For some, hazardous waste disposal and the health and environmental damage which it caused represented the price our society had to pay for achieving the world's loftiest economic and commercial goals. Chemical breakthroughs and the accompanying industrial production helped us to achieve a standard of living un-precedented in the entire history of mankind. From toothpaste that works more effectively against cavities to vegetables and fruits that are questionably lusher and more plentiful, we enjoyed the comforts derived from the wonders of chemistry. But, for all of this, greater and greater quantities of deadly waste was the result. Some people called this our gross national by-product.

As health and environmental problems associated with the dis-posal of hazardous waste were discovered during the 1970s, more concern was expressed and controls called for. Although the words "hazardous waste" were commonly used to refer to those sub-stances placed in locations where they fouled the air, land, and water, no official definition existed until the latter part of the dec-ade. Even though a number of private agencies and consulting firms offered their own definitions of hazardous waste, it was left to the EPA to determine what was officially meant by the phrase. Deciding upon a definition of the term turned out to be a terribly complex issue. Generally, hazardous waste may be thought of as the organic and inorganic residues that are the by-products of com-mercial production and the sludges and solutions produced by heavy industry. Federal legislation now defines a hazardous waste as "one that may cause or significantly contribute to serious illness or death, or that poses a substantial threat to human health or the environment when improperly managed."

The EPA has established four characteristics that may be used to determine whether or not a waste should be classified as haz-ardous. Three of these characteristics produce acute effects that cause immediate damage, and the fourth creates effects that gener-ally appear over a longer period of time. According to a recent EPA publication, *Everybody's Problem: Hazardous Waste*, the characteristics that determine the hazardous nature of a waste are:

Ignitability, which identifies wastes that pose a fire hazard dur-ing routine management. Fires not only present immediate dangers of heat and smoke but also can spread harmful particles over wide areas.

Corrosivity, which identifies wastes requiring special containers because of their ability to corrode standard materials, or requir-ing segregation from the other wastes because of their ability to dissolve toxic contaminants.

Reactivity (or explosiveness), which identifies wastes that, during routine management, tend to react spontaneously, to react vigorously with air or water, to be unstable to shock or heat, to generate toxic gases, or to explode.

Toxicity, which identifies wastes that, when improperly managed, may release toxicants in sufficient quantities to pose a substantial hazard to human health or the environment.

A conventional way of classifying hazardous wastes is to divide them into the categories of radioactives, flammables, heavy metals, asbestos, acids and bases, and synthetic organic chemicals. *Radioactives* are those elements which give off energy as they decay, and thus may cause death, burns, or various diseases. They currently enjoy a wide range of industrial uses and pose an increasing danger because of their expanding use and the amount of time it generally takes to render them inactive. *Flammables* are chemicals which give off great quantities of heat when they react with oxygen. Petroleum and natural gas by-products constitute the largest group of flammables. *Heavy metals,* such as arsenic, cadmium, copper, lead, mercury and zinc, continue to be a source of hazardous waste. From their mining to various uses, their by-products may contribute to a number of health problems and environmental deterioration. Because some of the original uses of the heavy metals have been rendered obsolete by advancing technology, it is surprising to learn that their production has nonetheless increased quite dramatically since World War II.

Asbestos, whose threadlike fibers and resistance to heat and electricity give it a number of beneficial uses, is dangerous because it resists biological degradation and chemical change. When its tiny fibers and fibrils enter the body to penetrate the surfaces of the lungs or to be carried in the blood- or lymph streams, a variety of illnesses may result. *Acids and bases* are dangerous primarily in large concentrations when they may pose a considerable environmental hazard. The increasing use of corrosive acids and bases for industrial production in recent years has made this a more difficult category of waste to confront and control than was the case previously.

Synthetic organic chemicals constitute the newest category of hazardous waste. The chemical industry revolution, due largely to the use of petroleum as a basic feedstock in the synthesis of organic chemicals, has created a group of compounds that are highly complex and often incapable of being handled by the processes of nature. The halogenated hydrocarbons, for example, created by adding atoms of chlorine, iodine, or bromine to basic hydrocarbon chains, are insoluble in water but soluble in fats. Hence, when pesticides, a leading product of halogenated hydrocarbons, are washed into rivers or streams, they do not break down into less toxic substances. Instead, they find their way into the bodies of fish, where they are stored in the fat cells and subsequently ingested by whatever eats the fish. If consumed by man, they accumulate in his fat cells and may induce a variety of illnesses, including cancer. Although numerous benefits, such as the greater availability of many consumer goods at less cost, are derived from synthetic organic chemicals, there is little doubt that they constitute a mixed blessing.

Because precise and accurate statements regarding the amount of harmful by-products of industrial production are difficult to obtain, government officials have admitted that only approximations of levels of hazardous chemical wastes are available. Shortly after World War II, it is estimated that we were producing about 1 billion pounds of hazardous waste each year. According to figures published in the *Federal Register,* this rate has increased about 10 percent each year since that time. By 1980, depending upon which report one reads, estimates ranged from 77 to 125 billion pounds a year, with one study attributing 10 billion pounds of that total to the state of New Jersey alone. The official EPA estimate in 1980 was about 80 billion pounds of hazardous waste generated each year, or, as one observer noted, "about 350 pounds of hazardous waste for every inhabitant of the United States."

If these figures are not startling enough, a more recent survey produced even more frightening revelations. In 1983, the EPA announced the results of a statistical survey of hazardous waste generators and treatment, storage and disposal facilities that are regulated by that Agency. For the year 1981, it was discovered that the amount of hazardous waste generated was four times higher than the EPA's previous official estimate. The survey revealed that 150 million metric tons of hazardous waste was generated that year, a far cry from the Agency's previous estimate of 40 million tons. Despite the revelation that the actual amount of harmful waste generated by industry was at least four times greater than previously thought, an EPA spokesperson, Dr. John Skinner, assured the nation that there was no cause for alarm and that there was no evidence that "we are about to be overwhelmed by these quantities of waste," especially since most of it was being managed properly.

Nevertheless, a closer look at the EPA data seems to indicate that the problem may be even greater than the revised estimates predict. For one thing, the survey showed that only 14,100 regulated manufacturers generated hazardous waste in 1981, even though some 60,000 companies had previously notified the Agency that they intended to engage in operations that would generate hazardous waste by-products. Despite the fact that 1981 was a recession year, which saw diminished levels of industrial production, it seems unrealistic that nearly 46,000 companies that had previously declared their intentions to generate harmful waste did not do so. In addition, the survey did not include hazardous waste produced by small manufacturers generating less than 2,000 pounds each year, since they are not controlled under existing federal regulations. Of course, the study also had no way of determining how much waste was disposed of by illegal haulers who have become increasingly active in the industry. Hence, it is no wonder that several EPA officials said privately, even while Dr. Skinner was assuring the public that everything was under control, that the actual amount of hazardous waste generated in the United States was probably far in excess of the 150 million metric tons revealed by the study.

This most recent survey of waste producers shows that 71 percent is generated by the chemical industry. No other industry even comes close to this amount; machinery and transportation equipment producers rank next, each with a mere 6 percent of the total. The remainder of the list of toxic waste generators includes industries dealing with motor freight transportation, petroleum refining, primary metals, fabricated metal, electrical machinery, and electric, gas and sanitary services, as well as a number of other small and diverse manufacturers. All of these industries generated enough toxic waste in 1981 to fill New Orlean's mammoth Superdome from floor to ceiling nearly three times every day of the year.

With some 750,000 firms producing wastes in the United States, it is difficult to know precisely how many are engaged in activities that generate hazardous substances. In 1980, approximately 60,000 firms registered with the EPA as hazardous waste producers. Since the EPA has virtually no way of monitoring the waste produced by the hundreds of thousands of potential producers in the country, the figure may well be a gross understatement. That conclusion is more likely when one realizes that the state of New Jersey itself contains approximately 10,000 known hazardous waste producers. Hence, like the amount of waste generated annually, it is almost impossible to know exactly how many firms are producing by-products.

Although hazardous waste is produced all over the country, it tends to be concentrated in certain regions. The highly industrial Midwest and Northeast, with their traditional industries, have the greatest problem. The newly industrialized South and the state of California, however, are also areas where the problem has been growing rapidly in recent years. About 60 percent of the nation's hazardous waste is generated in only ten states: New Jersey, Illinois, Ohio, California, Pennsylvania, Texas, New York, Michigan, Tennessee, and Indiana. Of these, New Jersey is the leader, accounting for 8 percent of the total amount of waste. Not far behind the ten leaders, though, are states such as Florida, Louisiana, Virginia, North Carolina, South Carolina, Massachusetts, Wisconsin, and Missouri. To no one's surprise, these are also the states which have had the greatest problem with disposal.

Disposing of so much hazardous waste would be a frightening problem under the best of conditions. But the best of conditions have never prevailed among those industries generating harmful wastes. The EPA, typically conservative and protective of industry, indicates that most hazardous waste is disposed of by environmentally unsound methods. In fact, some 90 percent of the total hazardous waste in the United States is placed in unlined surface impoundments, dumped in land disposal sites, burned by uncontrolled incineration, or managed in other equally unsafe ways. The remaining 10 percent is burned by controlled incineration, deposited in secure landfills, or recovered so that the compounds may be salvaged for further use. Of the generators producing hazardous waste in 1981, only 16 percent managed their waste completely on their own sites, while another 22 percent managed some on their property and shipped a portion of it elsewhere for disposal. The remaining 62 percent of the generators disposed of their waste somewhere other than on the site of their manufacturing operation.

With so many generators using off-site waste management facilities, one would expect to find a large number of such operations existing across the country. Unfortunately, that simply is not the case. There are only about two hundred licensed secure dumps existing nationwide and even fewer facilities designed to dispose of hazardous materials through incineration or reclamation. Obviously, the bulk of our hazardous waste goes elsewhere—principally to disposal sites that are unprepared to hold dangerous liquids. Again, knowing how many of these sites there are around the United States is a virtual guessing game. One EPA-sponsored study estimated the number of disposal sites containing some hazardous waste at between 30,000 and 50,000. This study warned that as many as 2,000 of these sites may pose an "imminent hazard" to public health and the environment. Other estimates have placed the number of unapproved sites at over 100,000, and at least one writer states that over 400,000 such locations may exist in the nation. Without question, monitoring all of these is a herculean task.

The Risks of Waste

What chemicals are being disposed of at these sites in such an unsafe manner? In many cases, determination is difficult. Labels may be faded or deliberately obliterated, barrels old or corroded. Chemical analysis is expensive; prevailing charges may exceed $500 per sample. What is known, however, is not cheering news. In general, these chemicals are non-degradable, without benefit of natural breakdown. They can be highly flammable and explosive. There is one waste so volatile it combusts and explodes when exposed to air. Some are so highly corrosive that they eat through all varieties of metal containers. When this occurs, the soil becomes permeated.

In a report on hazardous waste management, the congressional Subcommittee on Oversight of Government Management concluded that among the wastes it found at sites around the country were highly toxic dioxin, C5-6 (hexachlorocyclopentadiene), trichlorophenol, trichloroethylene, as well as other organic and inorganic contaminants. The report states further that "such wastes can produce toxic effects in humans and animals including poisoning, carcinogenicity, mutagenicity, and teratogenicity (fetus-deforming qualities)."

But these are only a few of the most dangerous chemicals found in our land and water. Other studies have found benzene, chloroform, and carbon tetrachloride. Each of these has known detrimental effects on human health. Some chemicals found in dump sites retain their chemical identity and toxicity for astonishingly long periods of time. PCBs, for one, may be active toxic agents for centuries. These are only a few examples. By the early 1980s, the EPA's list of hazardous chemicals exceeded 55,000 substances posing a substantial or potential hazard to human health.

People living in close proximity to hazardous waste disposal sites run a substantial risk of health damage if the sites are not properly managed. Residents near a disposal site, either on or off the grounds of a manufacturing facility, may be exposed to the harmful effects of chemical wastes by breathing airborne pollutants, by drinking or bathing in contaminated water, or by living, playing, or working on contaminated soil. A recent study has shown that many playgrounds have been built on sites containing soil laden with toxic chemicals, thereby posing a serious health threat to children playing in these parks.

Because a hazardous waste is one that can cause or contribute to serious, often irreversible illnesses, the health problems associated with exposure to toxic chemicals are many, both acute and chronic, mild and severe. Short-term effects usually involve high levels of exposure and can be related directly to specific chemicals. When TCDD-contaminated oil was spread as a dust control agent on Missouri race tracks and a farm road, sixty-three horses and numerous other animals died and a child playing on the road required treatment for severe bladder pain and urinary bleeding. At the Love Canal site, both children and adults coming into contact with substances leaching from the dump developed skin irritations—probably chloracne, a chronic skin disease. The short-term effects may also be deadly, as it was for a Louisiana truck driver asphyxiated while pumping waste into a disposal pit.

The long-term effects are more difficult to link with specific chemicals and generally involve exposure to low levels of toxic chemicals over a considerable period of time. The relationship between exposure and its consequences is difficult to establish, however. Long-term effects may include respiratory illness, miscarriages, birth defects, kidney failure, chromosomal damage, and several forms of cancer. These effects may also include behavioral and personality changes and neurological problems. In all cases, the long-term effects of contact with hazardous waste components are chronic, sometimes subtle, and always difficult to confirm.

In addition to human health hazards, the EPA has documented a number of ways in which hazardous wastes affect the environment. In a study of some 350 hazardous waste disposal sites, the Agency determined that waste dumping had ruined groundwater and water supplies. Thus not only were drinking water wells rendered useless, but natural habitats such as rivers, streams, or fields were made unfit for indigenous species, and soil contaminated. In addition, the study reported fish killed by the chronic release of hazardous material from dump sites, livestock and wildlife lost as a result of eating poisoned vegetation or drinking spoiled water, and sewer systems and water treatment works made unsafe or inoperable. Further, the study maintained, some toxic chemicals create greater problems because they build up in living organisms, progressing through the food chain at ever-increasing levels until they end up with man.

Perhaps the most serious threat to the environment caused by unsound waste disposal practices has been the actual and threatened contamination of groundwater. Over 100 million Americans depend on this water from beneath the surface of the earth. Despite the fact that so many of us use it to drink or to bathe or to irrigate our crops, it is becoming increasingly contaminated by the poisonous leachate seeping out of disposal sites. Another recent government report revealed that private and public water supplies have been contaminated in at least twenty-five states. It notes that the situation has become critical in some areas, particularly where industrialization is the heaviest. The report declares:

Toxic chemical contamination of ground water supplies in several areas of the country has reached alarming proportions. Over 200 wells in California have been contaminated by toxic wastes. In Jackson Township, N.J., 100 drinking water wells have been closed as a result of contamination from a local landfill. On Long Island, N.Y., where 100 percent of the population is dependent on ground water, 36 public water supplies and dozens of private wells have been closed because of synthetic organic chemical contamination. The water supplies of nearly 2 million Long Island residents have been affected. In the state of Massachusetts at least one-third of the Commonwealth's communities have been affected to some degree by chemical contamination. More than 16 municipal wells have been closed in the past few years as a result. In Michigan, officals have been faced with a "virtual explosion" in the discovery of ground water contamination problems; in 1979, 278 sites were identified as being already contaminated, and 381 additional sites were classified as "suspect" contamination areas.

Not only are toxic wastes contaminating our food chain, affecting our crops, livestock, and fish, and poisoning our soil; but, more consequentially, toxics are now leaching into subterranean water flows, spoiling drinking water far from the initial source of disposal. We have only recently begun to comprehend the widespread nature of groundwater contamination from toxic leachate. Special problems are created by synthetic organic chemicals, which are not broken down before they reach groundwater supplies. Since huge quantities of these chemicals are used and disposed of all over the country, it is not surprising that they are now turning up more and more in our supplies of groundwater.

The greatest threat to the nation's underground water supply comes from the improper use of landfills, although surface impoundments, such as ponds and lagoons, and waste injection wells, where waste is buried below all water levels, may also contribute to contamination. Landfills, impoundments, or injection wells located in or on permeable soils are particularly dangerous and may contribute to the contamination of water supplies that have taken thousands of years to develop. Major aquifers (significant supplies of underground water that have filled zones of rock strata) may be located at varying depths below the earth's surface and are the source of water for thousands of communities and millions of private wells. When liquid wastes seep out of landfills, impoundments, or injection wells in the form of highly toxic leachate and find their way into our underground water supply, aquifers may be *permanently* contaminated. Because groundwater moves through the soil very slowly, such contamination may not be discovered for many years—thus making the source of contamination extremely difficult to locate. Although it travels slowly, groundwater has the potential for moving considerable distances. This means, of course, that wastes in such water may also travel great distances over time. In one such example, arsenic and other compounds discharged in a pharmaceutical firm's landfill were found fifty miles away from the source of contamination.

Once groundwater is polluted, rehabilitation is almost impossible. Offending chemicals may be trapped by rock formations and stay in the same locations for considerable periods of time, never evaporating nor breaking down under the rays of the sun. In fact, one government report speculates that aquifers may hold contaminants for hundreds of thousands of years, during which time they may continually spoil the groundwater that flows through the area. Such is the nature of this environmental time bomb.

Of the 90 percent of the nation's hazardous waste that is disposed of in an unsound and dangerous manner, a large portion is dumped in landfills. Few of the estimated 75,000 industrial landfills and 15,000 municipal landfills were constructed to hold toxic substances without their leaching into the surrounding earth and water or evaporating into the atmosphere. Chemical contamination was found in 80 percent of the landfill sites studied by the EPA in 1977, with as many as 34,000 landfills causing significant health and environmental problems. A 1979 study further showed that between 1950 and 1979, about 1.5 trillion pounds of industrial wastes were dumped into some 3,300 landfill sites by just 53 chemical companies. At the time of the study, nearly one-third of these landfills were inactive and abandoned, but leaching can continue long after a dumper has finished with a disposal site. In fact, it is estimated that tens of thousands of inactive landfill sites may be taking their toll on unsuspecting men, women, and children who, like the residents of Love Canal area, now live and play near dangerous sources of toxic chemicals. In his important book, *Laying Waste*, Michael Brown discusses landfills and their often lingering effects:

The Environmental Protection Agency Office of Solid Waste has estimated that an average land disposal site, 17 acres in size, with an annual infiltration of 10 inches of water, can generate 4.6 million gallons of leachate a year, and can maintain this impressive productivity for 50 to 100 years. A large landfill in New Castle County, Delaware, was found to be depositing 170,000 gallons of polluted water a day into an important aquifer, while in Islip, Long Island, a thirty-nine-year-old landfill had developed an underground plume that extended 1,300 feet wide, 170 feet deep, and one mile long, accounting for the destruction of one billion gallons of water.

Recent federal legislation no longer permits the use of unsecure landfills for the disposal of toxics. Instead, federal guidelines specify that their disposal must take place in "secure" sites, although a great deal of debate continues about how much security there is in so-called secure landfills. At the present time, licensed hazardous waste landfills must be fully lined with an impermeable soil such as clay as well as with impermeable artificial liners like asphalt, rubber, or plastic. In addition, the site must be underlaid with a leachate collection system so that the drainage may be collected and treated before contaminating the soil and underground water. Each day the landfill must be covered, and when the site is closed, it must be capped with an artificial liner and another layer of clay. Even after closing, the landfill must be monitored regularly to make certain that leaching is not occurring. At least in the short run, a secure landfill may be the soundest and cheapest way of legitimately disposing of the most hazardous waste. Unfortunately, such sites as do exist in the United States are few and far between.

The Laws That Govern

Federal legislation designed to control one or another phase of waste management has been evolving since 1965. In that year, the government entered the field when the Congress passed the Solid Waste Disposal Act, a modest effort authorizing funding for research and planning to develop a solution for solid waste problems. The act called for the government to play an advisory, not a regulatory role, and failed to make any mention of hazardous or toxic waste. It was not until five years later, in 1970, that Congress called for a study of hazardous waste disposal practices.

The Environmental Protection Agency was created this same year and assumed all responsibility for the federal role in solid waste management, including its very limited responsibility for hazardous waste. Unfortunately, the EPA failed to grasp the legitimacy or the urgency of waste management concerns, and relegated them to a priority well below that given to air and water pollution issues. Perhaps for that reason, the report called for by the Congress in 1970 was not issued until 1975, and then with little publicity. But Congress had not been completely inactive in the meantime. In 1972, it had passed the Federal Water Pollution Control Act Amendments, then the most comprehensive and extensive environmental legislation in the nation's history. The purpose of this bill was to limit pollutant discharges into the country's waters and set strict water quality standards. In the same year, the Marine Protection, Research, and Sanctuary Act was also passed, limiting the ocean dumping of materials that could adversely affect human health and the environment. After various studies which showed the poor quality of drinking water in a number of cities across the nation, Congress passed the Safe Drinking Water Act in 1974, authorizing the EPA to set national standards for such water. This bill gave the government, for the first time, regulatory authority to monitor drinking water contaminants suspected of causing chemical poisoning or non-communicable diseases.

The problem of waste disposal, including hazardous waste disposal, arose again in the Congress in 1974. After a great deal of debate in both Senate and House hearings, no action was taken on either solid or hazardous waste. The next year, however, the Hazardous Materials Transportation Act was passed, establishing criteria for labeling, shipping, and handling hazardous materials. Its major objective was to protect the public against risks connected with the transportation of dangerous materials, a need that was becoming more apparent with the increasing number of train and truck accidents resulting in dangerous chemical spills.

Although hazardous waste was an element, albeit minor, in some legislation, and even the focus of the Hazardous Materials Transportation Act, it is safe to say that Congress was more concerned with solid waste and its management, at least until 1976. Late in that year, two acts became law virtually within days of each other which have served as the foundation for efforts to manage the generation and disposal of hazardous wastes. The Toxic Substances Control Act (TSCA) allows the federal government to regulate the manufacture and distribution of new chemicals that have the po-

tential to harm the environment or public health. The act also allows the EPA, the Agency responsible for its implementation, to
monitor currently used chemical substances that may be deemed
hazardous. Most significantly, the EPA administrator has the authority to prohibit the use of chemicals suspected or proved to be
dangerous. For the first time, the EPA was given the authority to
regulate thousands of chemicals by controlling those already in use
and by preventing new substances from entering the market if they
are shown to be dangerous. As one reviewer points out, "the passage and implementation of TSCA constitutes the first attempt to
subject the entire chemical industry to comprehensive federal regulations."

How the EPA has used the authority granted to it by Congress
in 1976 is another story. Very few new or old chemical compounds
have been banned and the EPA has had neither the manpower nor
the enthusiasm to evaluate and review the thousands of potentially
dangerous chemicals available on the market. Even more astound-
ing is the fact that TSCA explicitly prohibits the consideration of
wastes generated by the use of either old or new chemicals. Although this important piece of legislation does provide the mechanism by which chemicals that attack human health and destroy the
physical environment may be banned from all use, it has so far
proved to be a weak and ineffective tool in the hands of those public officials charged with its implementation.

The second law promulgated in 1976 was intended to protect
society from improper and illegal dumping of toxic wastes. This
was the Resource Conservation and Recovery Act (RCRA). The objective was to establish a minimum set of standards and regulations
for the control of hazardous wastes that would be applicable
throughout the nation. States were free to adopt more stringent
standards, but in their absence, the RCRA standards and guidelines would apply. Provisions of the RCRA were placed in the Environmental Protection Agency for implementation and enforcement.

RCRA's objectives are comprehensive and designed to regulate
toxic waste disposal by: (1) mandating the identification by EPA of
specific hazardous wastes and the development of criteria for identifying wastes as hazardous; (2) establishing a manifest system designed to follow the life of such wastes from the generator to the
disposer; (3) promulgating minimum standards for disposing of haz-

ardous wastes and enforcing the standards through a system of permits for disposal facilities; and (4) encouraging states to develop and implement waste control systems of their own. In addition, the act made certain administrative changes within the EPA necessary, having the effect of elevating the waste disposal problem to the same level as air and water pollution.

In other words, once identified, the act envisioned the control of toxic waste by a manifest system that would track the waste from the generator, through the carting agent, to its final disposal site. Through this technique, the present location and/or ultimate destination of identified waste is known and monitored. Regulation is enhanced by a permit system, requiring waste generators, transporters, treaters, storers, or dump operators to obtain authorization for their operations. Each operator qualifies for a permit by meeting standards specified in the act or in accompanying regulations developed by the EPA. Although RCRA establishes a federal system of permit granting and regulation enforcing, it allows transfer of these responsibilities to the state if it enacts laws at least as effective—the assumption here being that more effective enforcement will result from state rather than federal control.

In any case, the act clearly creates a process for the supposedly safe disposal of hazardous waste by requiring that both transporters and disposal sites be known, licensed, and subject to state enforcement standards. Transporters are required to obtain an identification number from the EPA, haul only waste accompanied by a signed manifest, and transport their cargo to known and licensed facilities. Operators of disposal facilities must sign the manifest and return it to the generator within thirty days, noting any discrepancy between the manifest and what is actually deposited at their sites. The use of the manifest—or what is sometimes known as the cradle to grave tracking system—is intended to prevent illegal practices by transporters who may find it more profitable to get rid of their cargo in an unauthorized fashion. Now, generators of hazardous waste were to be aware of the final destination of their shipment and were required to notify authorities if the cargo did not arrive at the designated facility.

At the same time, performance standards for owners and operators of hazardous waste facilities were to be enforced by the EPA, including standards regarding the manifest system, treatment, storage or disposal of waste, and location of disposal sites. The statute also required the preparation of plans to cover accidents and emergencies at the facilities, standards regarding personnel and financial responsibility, and compliance with the requirements of operating permits. Operating permits could, of course, be revoked if noncompliance can be demonstrated. As analyst Georgina Wilheim summarizes, ". . . the EPA believes that through the use of the manifest system, record-keeping and reporting requirements, and the training, inspection, and contingency plan requirements, the agency will begin to bring under control environmentally disastrous practices that have previously gone unregulated."

It is interesting to note that the statute has placed the primary focus of reform on waste disposal rather than waste generation. Instead of inhibiting the production of commodities that generate hazardous wastes or demanding new technology that might control such by-products, the system of permits, licenses, manifests, inspection, and ultimately, "good faith" compliance by waste generators may well have compounded and complicated waste regulation. Unscrupulous generators may cope with their need to dispose of toxic wastes by assigning all such activity to disposers whose methods of disposal are not questioned or probed. In addition, a system based on licenses and inspections is susceptible to corruption of various sorts and might serve more to facilitate the illegal exchange of money than to attack the problem at hand.

The structural deficiencies of RCRA have been magnified by the history of its implementation since 1976. From the time of its passage, this act has been something of an EPA stepchild, languishing in unfulfilled promises, never being permitted to reach its admittedly limited potential. Many observers have been highly critical of EPA for long delays in identifying hazardous wastes and their characteristics, as well as its delay in creating and issuing new standards for the safe disposal of toxics. Not only has this permitted the dumping of dangerous waste to continue virtually uncontrolled; it has also inhibited the enactment of regulatory statutes in many states. Not knowing what the federal regulations might be, most states simply waited until federal action was taken so as not to be in conflict with EPA standards.

This was not always possible in those states with serious hazardous waste problems, since the EPA took years to publish its RCRA-mandated guidelines. The important manifest system did not go into effect until late 1980, with all of the act's standards finally completed only in mid-1983. A number of states did take the lead without EPA assistance and put a set of regulations in place. At a minimum, such states ordinarily have developed a manifest system for tracking toxic wastes and a program of licenses and permits to do business as haulers and site operators. To meet RCRA standards, however, state legislation will have to go much further and include provisions for identifying waste, establishing guidelines for sites, long-term care of waste facilities, and financing various components of compliance with federal standards. Few states have enacted such comprehensive regulatory legislation. By early 1984, in fact, only one state, Delaware, had received full authorization from the EPA to operate its own hazardous waste management program.

Manifest systems, whether on the national or state level, generate enormous quantities of paper which serve little purpose unless they are periodically reviewed by responsible agencies. Unfortunately, few if any, government regulatory agencies concerned with environmental protection are funded and staffed to permit that type of necessary auditing. Even when audited, though, detection is difficult, unless field investigators are prepared to trace truckloads of waste leaving tens of thousands of manufacturing plants bound for disposal sites. Hence, laws of this type in most states have been forced to rely upon the voluntary compliance of generators, transporters, and site operators.

The last piece of federal legislation currently making an important contribution in the area of hazardous waste management is the Comprehensive Environmental Response, Compensation, and Liability Act of 1980, commonly known as the Superfund Act. The purpose of the Superfund is to provide revenue for the clean-up of hazardous waste disposal sites or other places where the presence of toxics may be considered dangerous. The act makes responsible parties liable for clean-up operations. In the case of a dangerous landfill, for example, responsible parties may include the generator of the disposed wastes, the owner and operator of the site, and the transporter who selected the site and actually deposited the chemicals in that location. Through a tax on crude oil and chemical feedstocks, and a small contribution from the U.S. Treasury, a $1.6 billion fund has been established to clean toxic landfills when responsible parties cannot be identified or fail to meet their obligation. Responsible parties who refuse to clean up designated dump sites may be sued for reimbursement and assessed damages of up to three times the cost of the clean-up. Even though the threat of triple damages may deter some individuals from disposing of their waste in an irresponsible manner, the act's main purpose is to begin the process of righting dangerous past wrongs.

Enter the Hauler

Prior to 1976, 80 percent of the nation's toxic wastes were managed on site by the industries that generated them, while the remaining 20 percent required the services of haulers to perform the disposal task for the producer. Toxic waste haulers had been around for some time, performing this important task for both large and small industries. A few of these haulers were national corporations, but most were small, local, independent entrepreneurs, operating only a few trucks and servicing a limited number of industries. A number were also in the solid waste business, but branched out to include the removal of toxics as the demand for such service grew with the increase in the generation of hazardous wastes. Prior to the new federal and state legislation in the 1970s, it is quite apparent that a significant portion of these haulers disposed of their cargoes in an irresponsible manner. In fact, irresponsibility has characterized most toxic waste disposal until very recently. But, while much on-site and off-site disposal was reckless and dangerous, it was not necessarily illegal.

In 1976, the Resource Conservation and Recovery Act and similar legislation in a number of states changed all of that. Generators who once took care of their own waste now found it cumbersome and prohibitively expensive to do so. Increasingly, they turned to waste haulers to provide the service they once provided for themselves. As the need increased, so did the number of available transporters, as more and more of them entered the field from the allied solid waste industry. Although proper dump sites were scarce, these new haulers seemed to have no trouble getting rid of their loads and generators soon learned to ask no questions about the ultimate destination of their waste.

With new legislation creating more rigorous standards and guidelines for the disposal of toxic chemical wastes, generators found their costs rising rather dramatically. Chemical neutralization, incineration, or burial in sealed, ecologically safe areas became expensive means of disposal. Depending upon the nature of the waste, it could cost a generator as much as $100 to have a 55-gallon drum of chemicals removed from his property. A tank truck of common solvents and degreasers could run as much as $10,000 to dispose of in a safe manner. Even today the cost of incinerators is so high, with a commercial-scale facility costing possibly in excess of $30 million, that this means of disposing of toxic chemicals may cost an average of $110 per ton for some materials, while more toxic wastes can cost several hundred dollars per ton. Quite simply, disposing of waste in a safe and sound fashion came to cost generators a great deal more than they had been accustomed to paying.

Faced with seemingly prohibitive costs for disposing of their wastes in a non-hazardous manner, some generators contracted the services of illegal haulers and site operators, whose fees, although high, were more acceptable. Illegal disposal by "midnight dumpers" of great sophistication and guile came to represent a relatively inexpensive alternative, thus keeping the costs of production competitively low. As one EPA official explained, "If somebody offers to take it off your hands for a tenth of the cost, you can see how some people would be tempted." At the Valley of the Drums in Kentucky, barrels of caustic chemicals were dumped at a cost of 75 cents each. Although this was probably an extreme case, illegal haulers were often able to outbid competitors because of their relatively low overhead, which did not include costly processing or licensed storage facilities. Nevertheless, with 150 million metric tons of toxic waste being produced in the United States each year, one can readily see that illegal haulers and site operators are capable of earning huge profits by not complying with federal and state regulations.

"Midnight dumpers" have used every means imaginable to get rid of the waste they collect. Chemicals known to be deadly to all living things have been pumped directly into streams and rivers, often turning up in the water supplies of downstream communities. Flushing waste onto city streets or into sewers has also been a popular method of illegal disposal. The marshlands of New Jersey and the bayous of Louisiana are saturated with toxic wastes, as are countless farms all over the country. Sometimes, illegal waste haulers store their deadly drums in abandoned houses, rented warehouses, or simply on the grounds of their property.

In eastern Pennsylvania, toxic chemicals have been poured down abandoned coal mines, and into ravines and valleys of the Pocono Mountains. Drums have been thrown on the side of highways and tank trucks have deliberately leaked their contents as they travel. An Associated Press report described the latter technique in this way:

> One operation that allegedly runs out of Hartford, Connecticut only works in foul weather. A driver watches the forecast for rain or snow, then picks up a tanker load of chemicals. With the discharge valve open he drives on an interstate until 6,800 gallons of hot cargo have dribbled out. "About 60 miles is all it takes to get rid of a load," boasted the driver, "and the only way I can get caught is if the windshield wipers or the tires of the car behind me start melting."

In another North Carolina incident, transformer fluid loaded with PCB was splashed over some 270 miles of state highways.

Mixing waste oil and fuel oil with chemical wastes is another method that has been used to get rid of the chemicals while enhancing profits. Placing waste oil on dirt roads to suppress the dust has been done for a long time and in itself is a dangerous practice, since most waste oil contains additives such as detergents, heavy metals, and pollutants from the machinery for which it is used. When that oil is mixed with deadly chemical wastes, the danger is magnified and the public welfare is threatened. This is precisely what happened in Times Beach, Missouri. An equally lucrative practice for the irresponsible hauler is mixing fuel oil with chemical wastes and selling the fuel to customers for wintertime heating. The effects of this practice on human health are not yet known, but one can well imagine what might happen to those who breathe air contaminated by the discharges from this mixture.

By far the most prevalent technique of illegal disposal is to dump hazardous materials into landfills meant to accommodate only solid waste. Although this practice has been illegal since 1976, there is a great deal of evidence that it continues to be a frequently used method of disposal. It also continues to be very dangerous, since about 75 percent of all landfill sites are located in wetlands, on floodplains, and over aquifers, all quite susceptible to contamination. Although dangerous dumping has occurred in many of these landfills for some time, continued illegal disposal will simply exacerbate serious public health problems and environmental deterioration.

As the need to dispose of hazardous waste became more acute in the 1970s, and the concomitant potential for profits created new carting opportunities for solid waste haulers, a number of these carters simply expanded their activities and carried on "business as usual." Under these conditions, it is not surprising to find that organized crime figures who have long been associated with the solid waste carting industry became involved in practically every aspect of hazardous waste disposal. The outline of this problem has been stated by Congressman John D. Dingell of the House Subcommittee on Oversight and Investigations:

> It is appalling enough when disposers of hazardous waste, through inadvertence or ignorance, recklessly poison the environment and endanger the public health. But it is considerably more disturbing when generators, haulers and disposers—in order to avoid the cost of legitimate disposal—engage in the practice of illicit dumping for profit. In the course of the inquiries of the Subcommittee, we have developed information linking organized crime to the illegitimate dumping of toxic wastes. This comes as no surprise. In fact, it was predictable, given the lucrative nature of this activity.

No one should assume, of course, that all hazardous waste disposers are members of or affiliated with organized crime syndicates. That is not the case. Even among those haulers who engage in illegal disposal practices, a significant portion are independent operators without organized crime ties, but who engage in unlawful practices in order to make an easy profit. Nevertheless, on the basis of available evidence it appears safe to conclude that known organized crime figures play a prominent role in the hazardous waste industry, especially in the most industrialized states. This is so despite attempts to regulate the disposal business by enforcing various codes and standards. While a number of such figures own waste disposal companies and dump sites, either directly or indirectly, others serve as officers of such companies or related enterprises. In addition to illegally dumping hazardous wastes into landfills, sewers, rivers, on farms, and elsewhere, companies controlled by organized crime figures are known to forge manifests, mislabel containers, rig bids, engage in restraint of trade, and corrupt state agents charged with safeguarding the public welfare. These and other charges will be explored in more detail in the following chapters.

Organized crime has traditionally been perceived as racketeering and vice-related activities, dominated by ethnically similar gangs or "families." Such groups are often thought to be characterized by their hierarchical structure, dependence upon violence, monopolistic control and influence, and immunity from the law. To a certain extent all of this is true, but organized crime is really more than that. Today, it is increasingly viewed as activity which provides services that cannot be supplied as efficiently or as cheaply by legitimate enterprises. Most importantly, its activities are based on the same market processes as legal businesses, and according to criminologist Dwight Smith, it should be viewed as "the extension of legitimate market activities into areas normally proscribed, for the pursuit of profit and in response to latent illicit demand." As a result, organized crime has now come to be thought of as a series of mutually beneficial relationships among professional criminals, upper world clients, and politicians.

Hence, in the United States, there are recognizable groups of individuals who provide these unpleasant services for willing customers with the implicit or explicit cooperation of public officials. These organized crime groups—known as families, syndicates, or mobs—are loosely structured and made up of individuals who are often engaged in a number of criminal activities, even though they may have legitimate occupations as well. Those organized crime figures involved with the disposal of hazardous waste share these characteristics and seem to view their waste disposal activities as simply another opportunity to make large sums of money.

This is the nature of our environmental time bomb. Because of past ignorance and irresponsibility, our present burdens would be enormous even if recent federal and state legislation designed to protect the public interest worked. Available evidence indicates that this has not yet been the case, as illegal disposal of hazardous chemical waste products has in recent years increased dramatically, and continues to escalate. The power of the state to control a practice undeniably threatening the public welfare appears to have failed. Part of this is due to the entry into the hazardous waste disposal field of organized crime figures whose blatant disregard for the law may now have possibly irreversible and horrific consequences for large portions of the population. The consequences of illegal disposal practices result in far more unknowing and involuntary "victims" than all of the mob's past criminal operations combined.

3

When Garbage Was Garbage

As the production of toxic wastes increased during the 1970s, and as new legislation designed to control its dangerous disposal grew, chemical companies and other generators were in a quandary. On-site disposal, by the companies themselves, was becoming too cumbersome and expensive, and specialized disposal companies, trained and experienced in hazardous waste disposal, were few and far between. Clearly, industry growth had outstripped the growth of the necessary ancillary business of getting rid of the waste generated in the production of mass consumer goods.

An alternative was available, however. Thousands of solid waste or garbage companies across the country had been operating for years, collecting and disposing of other people's trash by dumping it into landfills or incinerating it. Many of these companies had the equipment necessary to haul 55-gallon drums and claimed that they had access to safe and secure disposal sites. Since they were professional and experienced solid waste haulers, why not assume that they could get rid of the toxic stuff, especially since their price was right? In addition, many of them had licenses to haul hazardous wastes, given to them by the official regulatory agencies in a number of states. With unbelievable ease and virtually no concern from either the public or the private sectors, private garbage haulers, especially in the populous Northeast, moved into the hazardous waste business and began operations.

Had the toxic generators or the government regulatory agencies been more diligent about checking into the backgrounds of many of these companies and their owners, they would have found that, in many locations, the waste industry appears to have become something of a subcategory of organized crime. In various metropolitan areas across the country, a significant number of garbage companies are enterprises owned, operated, or controlled by organized crime figures. Through outright ownership, labor union influence, control of trade associations, and the use of organized crime's traditional tactics of fear and intimidation, syndicated racketeers had come to virtually control the garbage disposal business. From the mid-1950s to the present, evidence detailing the role of organized crime in the solid waste disposal business has come to light periodically.

Traditionally, New York City has been the hub of organized crime activity in this country, thus more investigations of its involvement in the waste business have occurred there than elsewhere. In one of the few scientific studies available of racketeer involvement in the waste industry, Peter Reuter of the Rand Corporation identified fourteen different investigations of this relationship since 1956. In his unpublished paper, "The Value of a Bad Reputation," he comments:

> Every level of government has been involved in these investigations: local, state and federal. Some investigations have been initiated by specific complaints, others have resulted from law enforcement concern with possible racketeering in the industry. Some have produced convictions, while others have led to nothing more than newspaper articles. A great variety of investigative and legal tactics have been used. At least two of the investigations were based on undercover operations, while others have focused on tax evasion as the point of vulnerability in the industry. . . . Law enforcement efforts may have been unsuccessful but they have certainly not lacked number or variety.

The long list of New York investigations began in 1956 when Mayor Robert Wagner appointed a special committee to look into alleged abuses, including monopolistic practices, among private carters servicing commercial establishments. The committee recommended that the industry be regulated through a price ceiling and a review of each service contract by a city agency. In addition, the committee also recommended that free waste collection for businesses located in residential blocks be discontinued. This had the effect of adding some 52,000 customers to those being served by private carters. Later that year, three grand juries began investigations into "monopolistic practices" among the carters. None of these grand juries managed to produce any indictments.

The McClellan Committee Investigation

The entire nation became aware of problems in the garbage industry the next year when the Senate Select Committee on Improper Activities in the Labor or Management Field, chaired by Senator John McClellan, began its famous 1957 hearings in Washington. These hearings soon became one of the most important and comprehensive presentations of the relationship between organized crime and the waste industry which we have witnessed in the United States. The committee focused much of its attention on the private sanitation industry in suburban New York—approximately $50 million worth of business annually, serving 122,000 individual businesses and around 500,000 private homeowners. The intent of the hearings was to show that organized crime was constructing a highly profitable business in the private carting industry through a monopoly enforced by trade associations and friendly labor unions. Principally, the New York hearings focused on the activities of particular organized crime figures and their associates in the garbage business, including Vincent J. "Jimmie" Squillante, Bernard Adelstein, Joseph Parisi (who, though dead in 1957, had been important in the organized crime conspiracy under investigation), and Nick Ratteni.

Much of the testimony concerned Teamster Locals 27 and 813. These unions were under the thumb of organized crime. The committee concentrated on activities in Yonkers, New York, and Nassau County, Long Island. In Yonkers, the focus was on Westchester Carting Co., which had been directed by Nick Ratteni since 1949. Ratteni had an arrest record stretching back to 1926, having served a considerable amount of time in Sing Sing Prison. Among Ratteni's associates, it was pointed out, were the notorious Frank Costello, Anthony "Little Augie" Carfano, John Dioguardi, John Biello, and Joseph "Stretch" Stracci.

Although Teamsters Local 456 represented the Yonkers private garbage workers, Westchester Carting abruptly switched to Local 27 soon after Ratteni assumed the company's presidency. Local 27 was headed by a convicted rapist who immediately began to assist Ratteni in expanding business by intimidating customers and competitors alike. Secondary boycotts were called against chain stores in the New York area, principally with the help of Bernard Adelstein, head of Teamster Local 813, which soon took over Local 27. When Local 456 protested this expansion, the president was killed and objections ceased. Not long after, when Westchester Carting grew to dominate the waste collection business in Yonkers, it set up a company union and severed its ties with Local 813.

The committee then shifted its attention from Westchester County to Nassau County on Long Island, and narrowed in on the dealings of Adelstein, of Local 813, and Vincent J. Squillante, who was the leader of the Greater New York Cartmen's Association. The committee documented the ways in which both Adelstein and Squillante extended their influence into Nassau County. In 1953, Nassau County carters had formed an association which included most of the larger carting firms servicing the area. Apparently, the Association did not become particularly active until early in 1955 when the contract with Local 813 expired. Surprised that the union hired lawyers to negotiate the new contract, Association officers, obviously feeling intimidated, also sought outside help.

At the suggestion of other members of the Association, the president approached Jimmie Squillante of the Greater New York Cartmen's Association and invited him to come out to Long Island to help them deal with the union. Squillante did just that, and more. Within a short time he had taken charge of the Association, bringing in his brother Nunzio and nephew, Jerry Mancuso, to play key roles in the takeover.

Chairman McClellan summarized this portion of the hearings by stating, "Not only does Vincent J. Squillante, a hoodlum labor relations man, play a part, but we find that garbage collection industry men banded together in associations which eventually, under Squillante, invoked monopoly and restraint of trade arrangements with a system of punishments for nonconforming members through the use of whip companies." McClellan added that Bernard Adelstein, who was the secretary-treasurer and business agent for Local 813, worked together with Squillante in the scheme. Adelstein compelled private sanitation firms to join Squillante's association of company owners, while Squillante induced those who worked on the trucks, many of whom were the owners of companies, or partners, or family members, to join the employees' union or face the unpleasant consequences. Thus, Adelstein supported Squillante and Squillante supported Adelstein, and both increased their power and wealth. The big losers were the legitimate members of the union, whose wages and benefits suffered as a result of the collusion.

Under the questioning of Committee Chief Counsel Robert F. Kennedy, John Montesano, a member of a family-owned and -run carting business and president of the association when Squillante was invited in from Westchester, explained what union membership meant:

> *Mr. Kennedy:* . . . Did he [Squillante] suggest you become members of the union?
>
> *Mr. John Montesano:* That was the first thing, sir.
>
> *Mr. Kennedy:* Why was it necessary to become members of the union?
>
> *Mr. John Montesano:* Because he claimed that he could get us a blanket contract with the union, and in so doing he would get us a much better deal if he had every cartman in the association in the union. That was even though some of us didn't need the union at all, because in some instances there was a father and 2 or 3 sons, and he didn't need the union. So Jimmie said, "Well, if we can get you all in the union, in the long run you will all make money, because if you all have to go out and raise your customers, you can always fall back on the union, and say due to the fact you have to pay union scale, then you can turn around and say you can raise your customers. No one would take your customers due to the fact that the union would always step in."

To help his friend Squillante, Adelstein conceived of the security deposit to dissuade cartmen from dropping out of the Association. Garbage companies that were not members of Squillante's trade association had to post a security deposit of $300 per employee with the union to guarantee their paying a living wage. Eventually, member firms were also compelled to put up a deposit with the union, but only $50 per business. The favoritism shown to Association members made it quite worthwhile to join the group and remain a member in good standing. To do otherwise was costly, not only because a carter might be forced to have a substantial sum of money tied up with the union for some period of time, but also because Adelstein enforced the terms of the contract with great zeal and inflexibility against non-members.

Soon after the taking control of the Nassau County association, Squillante suggested that the local carters implement a practice known as "property rights," a feature that other trade associations had apparently found profitable. Again, in response to Robert Kennedy's questions, John Montesano explained "property rights."

Mr. Kennedy: Could you describe some of the things that he said should be put into effect as far as the association was concerned?

Mr. John Montesano: Yes sir. He brought out the point of what we call property rights. In the event a man has a customer or a stop, and another customer—and that customer moves from that stop, that man claims that empty store and his customer. No matter what customer shall move back into the store, that man has the property rights. No other cartman can go in there and solicit the stop. This was one of the basic things brought up to us.

Mr. Kennedy: In other words, it would be a monopoly.

Mr. John. Montesano: If a man had a stop, it was his customer, and no one could take it from him. The only way he could take the stop from him was if the board of directors decided that the man was in arrears, or he was a delinquent association member, and they would throw him out and then his work would become open work for everyone.

Mr. Kennedy: To go one step further, what if someone did jump someone else, and did take his property rights, then what did happen?

Mr. John Montesano: We would have meetings at the board of directors in New York, and we would penalize the man in some cases, $10 for every dollar collected from the customer. For instance, if the customer was paying $10 a month, the cartman who took the stop had to pay to the cartman who previously had it, $100.

Mr. Kennedy: So there was this penalty clause of 10 to 1.

Mr. John Montesano: Yes, sir.

Mr. Kennedy: Who made the decision regarding this?

Mr. John Montesano: It was brought up at the board of directors' meeting, but the last say-so had to be through Jimmie.

[Montesano, a star witness in these 1957 hearings, later claimed he was a marked man as a result of his testimony. He was eventually murdered.]

In addition to the union discrimination and coercion, a second means of enforcing decisions made by Squillante's association was the "whip" company. Apparently, this was a device conceived by Squillante earlier, after he had assumed control of the New York City Cartmen's Association. The whip's mission was simple: Raid the customers of those firms that stepped out of line. In some cases, it would offer to pick up a customer's garbage for practically nothing in order to whip the uncooperative cartman back into line. The whip company in the city was Corsair Carting, owned by Squillante's nephew, Jerry Mancuso. In Nassau County, Squillante set up the General Sanitation Co., run by his brother Nunzio. General Sanitation was more than just a whip, however, since it built a pick-up list of its own with the help of the union, which actually picketed customers until they agreed to sign on with this Squillante family enterprise. General Sanitation, of course, was a non-union firm.

In his concluding statement, McClellan pointed out that more than forty-six known organized crime figures were found to be associated, in one way or another, with the private waste hauling business in just these two suburban New York counties. Returning to Squillante, he remarked that he was the "self-styled godson of gangland executioner Albert Anastasia," and that he had no previous experience in anything except "policy rackets and as a pusher of narcotics." Reiterating the evidence presented, McClellan pointed out how Squillante had used his associations with the underworld and the union to (a) "Establish himself as the executive director of three separate employer associations; (b) Force individuals into the various associations and into Local 813, IBT; (c) Create a monopoly with respect to the collection of garbage and refuse in the Greater New York area; (d) Uphold and enforce the principle of territorial rights; and (e) Trick the members of these associations into paying his back income taxes."

Among the firms owned by organized crime figures identified in this limited investigation were: Sanitary Haulage Corp. (Anthony Ricci); Sunrise Sanitation (Carmine Tramanti and Anthony "Tony Ducks" Corallo); General Sanitation Co. (Nunzio and Vincent Squillante); Corsair Carting Co. (Nunzio and Vincent Squillante); Westchester Carting Co. (Nicholas Ratteni); Carter Landfill, Inc. (Vincent Squillante, James Licari, and Joseph "Joey Surprise" Feola); and Jamaica Sanitation Co., Inc. (Gennaro "Jerry" Mancuso, Alfred "Pogy" Torielle, Joseph Feola, Anthony "Little Auggie" Carfano, and Frank Caruso).

By describing Squillante's accomplishments at the conclusion of his committee's hearings, Senator McClellan also gave an idea of the scope and potential for racketeering in waste. In almost all cases of industrial racketeering, one finds both corrupt trade associations and trade unions. Control of both employers and workers allows for innumerable methods of enrichment, ranging from restraint of trade and price fixing to the misappropriation of union funds. When one adds to that the fact that organized crime families also own firms in the waste industry, it is not difficult to imagine the power and leverage available to them. In the waste industry, not only are firms organized around trade associations and workers around trade unions but, as McClellan noted in his summary, the entire industry could be structured around the principle of territorial rights. One of the key tasks performed by organized crime was the enforcement of this principle. This meant, naturally, that disputes over territory could be adjudicated by organized crime, using its traditional methods of threats, coercion, and violence.

The publicity generated by the McClellan Committee Hearings required some type of official response. That response came in the latter part of 1957, when New York State Attorney General Louis J. Lefkowitz went to court seeking an injunction against some four hundred individuals and corporations engaged in the business of garbage collections and hauling in New York City and Nassau, Suffolk, and Westchester counties. Also named by Lefkowitz in his court action were the three corporate trade associations headed by Jimmie Squillante, as well as Bernie Adelstein's Local 813.

Lefkowitz asked the court to prevent all of the defendants from engaging in violations of Article 22 of the General Business Law, which prohibited anti-competitive practices in business dealings. More specifically, the injunction sought by the state of New York asked that all of the defendants—virtually the entire private carting business in the city and the three neighboring counties—be prevented from joining associations which restrained competition, fixed prices, rigged bids, joined in collusive agreements with trade unions, and generally engaged in the illegal practices that had characterized the garbage industry trade associations in the past. After prolonged court action, injunctive relief was finally awarded in 1959. Yet many of the same companies and their owners, as well as labor union officials and organized crime figures, soon were engaged in the same practices prohibited by the court action. There was little or no enforcement to prevent them from doing so.

As a result of the McClellan Committee Hearings, several local New York district attorneys initiated independent investigations of racketeers involved in this business. Shortly thereafter, criminal convictions were obtained in a number of cases, usually on relatively minor charges and without very serious consequences. Ironically, though, the one person for whom that was not true was Jimmie Squillante. In late 1957, he was arrested on charges of extortion and attempted extortion in connection with his many illegal activities in the New York Cartmen's Association. Squillante's case dragged on for nearly three years, during which time he was the subject of wide publicity and notoriety and the object of numerous official investigations. Perhaps because of his increasing visibility in the official and public eye, he became too great a liability for his organized crime associates. Squillante disappeared on September 30, 1960, never to be seen again. Later, testimony before the U.S. Senate Investigations Subcommittee revealed that he had been kidnapped and murdered on that September day three years earlier.

The continuing involvement of the Squillante family in organized crime and the waste industry did not, however, end with the disappearance of Jimmie in 1960. Nunzio, Jimmie's brother, continued to be active in waste hauling, becoming a principal with Anthony D'Agostino in D & S Service Company. Along with D'Agostino, Nunzio organized a second firm called Flannary Towing Corporation, which owned a tugboat and three steel barges used to burn trash at sea. Still later, the two of them operated the New England Carting Company, Inc., of Hartford, Connecticut.

Just as the Squillante family continued to influence the waste industry, so did Nick Ratteni, who turned up once again in 1972 when the Newburg (New York) *Evening News* reported that he was one of the principal organized crime figures attempting to extend racketeer influence into Rockland County. Not surprisingly, the object of the racketeer influence was the sanitation business, in particular, the private garbage haulers. The newspaper reported that a Teamster official, Theodore G. Dailey, was convinced that his life was in danger as the result of racketeers attempting to take over the waste hauling operations at a number of construction sites. Dailey indicated that the $1.5 billion worth of construction going on in the area made this a potentially lucrative operation for illegal operators.

Basically, the situation in the Newburg area concerned an attempt by Teamster Local 531 under the direction of Carmine Valenti, and with the backing of Samuel Provenzano (brother of Anthony "Tony Pro" Provenzano), and Ratteni to take over Dailey's Teamster Local 445. Apparently, Dailey had led an insurgent move-ment in the Teamsters Union in the mid-1950s which successfully ousted an earlier racketeer regime. The 1959 New York injunction obviously had not prevented Nick Ratteni from continuing his in-volvement with organized crime figures in the garbage collection business.

Corruption in New Jersey

Although the U.S. Senate Committee concentrated its energies on the waste industry in New York, a similar situation existed in New Jersey. In 1959, the New Jersey State Senate Committee, chaired by Senator Walter H. Jones, held hearings on the waste industry in the Garden State. The committee was concerned prin-cipally with the allocation of territories and how that worked in the bidding on municipal contracts. Three overlapping themes ap-peared in the testimony: charges of rigged bids, bribed municipal politicians, and violent struggles for territorial control among waste disposal firms. In addition, the committee heard evidence of collu-sion between the North Jersey Municipal Garbage Contractors As-sociation and Teamsters Local 945 in their effort to monopolize the garbage business in New Jersey. At that time, the Garbage Con-tractors Association was the largest of its kind in New Jersey, rep-resenting twenty-nine municipal garbage collectors. According to figures supplied by the state attorney general, members of this as-sociation controlled nearly 93 percent of the funds appropriated for municipal garbage collections and serviced two-thirds of the New Jersey population.

Rigging bids to haul municipal garbage and bribing public officials also appeared to have been common business practices for members of the Garbage Contractors Association. Vincent Ippolito, a member of a family that had been in the garbage business in New Jersey for several decades, testified that he was aware of several instances of garbage haulers not bidding against each other and paying off public officials. Ippolito stated that payoffs to municipal officials were absolutely customary in Hoboken. He acknowledged that Frank Stamato, a large waste entrepreneur, whose family controlled a variety of garbage enterprises, had spent about $100,000 in payoffs to secure a Hoboken municipal contract several years before. Apparently, Stamato even factored the payoffs into his estimate bids, which meant that corruption costs were passed on to the residents of the city. In addition to questions about these payoffs, counsel for the committee also raised the issue of territories with Ippolito.

Q. Did Stamato give you any impression that payoffs were something that were part of the activities of the group, or the Association?

A. Well, he said that they had to give up jobs. . . .

Q. And he said that members of the Association had to give up jobs because the people who were running the Association were assigning the jobs to certain Association members. Isn't that right?

A. Yes, it is.

Q. So that he told you that there was a complete system associated with bidding, which system included—which system involved the selection of bidder to get the job by the Association and complimentary bids by the other members of the Association.

A. That is right.

Ippolito went on to state that Crescent Roselle, one of the major waste operators in northern New Jersey (and, again, part of what was a family business), once offered him money if he would not bid on a job in East Paterson, New Jersey. The job had been fixed for another garbage hauler and the Association did not want

Ippolito involved. Roselle offered Ippolito $500 to stay out of the bidding, stating that the favored hauler would arrange for a complimentary bid higher than his own so as to assure himself of getting the contract.

A similar incident occurred when a three-year contract for the city of Elizabeth was to be bid in January 1955. When garbage contractor Joe Cassini was questioned about his role in the bidding, he denied any involvement in posting a complimentary bid. Following Cassini to the witness table was Frank Miele, Jr., who told a different story, however. Miele testified about a conversation he had with Cassini concerning the Elizabeth job. Cassini allegedly told him that everything had been worked out with Alfred Lippman of Fareday & Myer, the firm that was supposed to get the Elizabeth contract. Miele testified that Cassini told him he was going to receive $25,000 not to offer a serious bid for the job, but instead, to post a higher bid to assure the job's going to Fareday & Myer. Indeed, that is exactly what happened. Fareday & Myer offered a winning bid of $1,215,000 as opposed to Cassini's posted bid of $1,250,000.

Some of the most revealing testimony was offered on the eighth day of the hearings when A. J. Maitilasso, a private scavenger who was not a member of the Association, testified about the plight of private operators who had to compete with the unfair competition of members of the trade group. Not only were the privateers excluded from much business as a result of prearranged and fixed bidding, but they also suffered from the threat of violence when they became too aggressive in recruiting and keeping customers. The Association demanded that they keep a low profile or face the possibility of being run out of business altogether.

When independents like Maitilasso did bid on jobs that were fixed, the response of the Association members was usually swift and to the point. On one occasion, Maitilasso testified that he was stopped on a road by two enforcers working for Mike Signorelle, the owner of at least two Association firms, and a rival for a contract being offered by the town of Rockaway. Signorelle's men informed him that he was not expected to offer a bid and if he did he would have no access to dump sites. On another occasion, when the grapevine identified Maitilasso as a bidder for a contract in Mine Hill, Signorelle again sent his men to inform Maitilasso that Signorelle would see that he would not be able to secure a bond.

Maitilasso, however, went to a neighboring town to secure his bond just prior to the time of bidding. Even the bidding process had to be done in a devious way in order to protect himself, as he explained to committee members.

> Q. How as it arranged that you didn't attend bidding, but put in a bid?
> A. I sent my wife's brother, none of them knew him and I felt that if they saw me there they would do the job for nothing to beat me out.
> Q.They would shoot the job?
> A. They would shoot the job.

Maitilasso also explained how the same people often owned two companies that would compete against each other. Under this arrangement, one bid would be submitted under the name of one firm and another under the name of the other firm, each knowing in advance what the supposedly rival bid would be. Companies often had high and low bids ready to submit for a job, depending upon which competitor showed up at the time of the bidding. All in all, the independent carters didn't have much of a chance to win the more lucrative contracts when competing against members of the Garbage Contractors Association.

When Maitilasso was asked if Signorelle ever told him the purpose of the organization and how it operated to protect its members, he replied:

> A. They had it set up so all the contractors would get the right price, what they considered the right price at the right town so that nobody would be working cheap, they'd all get the right price.
> Q. And that was all by agreement before the bid, wasn't it?
> A. That is right. Senator, these guys don't want to tell you, but I'll tell you that there is not a contract in the State that is not rigged. I want to tell you now, and I know that. And any contractor in here, I dare them to defy it, defy me. Every job is rigged before it goes to the board. They know it. They are just playing coy.

New Jersey in the late 1950s had in addition to the Association an equivalent to New York's Local 813. This was Local 945 of the

Teamsters Union, authorized to represent warehousemen, industrial and sanitation workers in northern New Jersey. According to a profile of this local written by Bob Windrem, it has always been responsible for organizing the garbage industry and has had links to organized crime from its very inception. At the time of the hearing, the local's business manager was John Serratelli, who witnesses testified forced industry members of the trade waste association to contribute money each year to buy him a new Cadillac. As far back as 1939 and 1940 he had begun organizing garbage workers and forcing companies to comply with his demands through threat and intimidation. On one occasion, he allegedly threw a lead pipe on the desk of a company owner and informed him that the pipe was his "credentials."

During the hearings, witnesses constantly made reference to Serratelli and to his control over the garbage industry and contractors in North Jersey. His power was reflected in a statement made by Crescent Roselle, who said, "I often granted favors to Serratelli to keep on his good side. . . ." When asked what could be gained by Serratelli's friendship, Frank Miele, Jr., replied, "He said that if any major problems that we could not solve ourselves, go to him, he would help us straighten it out—that he could pick up a telephone and he could have anybody stopped from dumping. . . ." Serratelli also seems to have been intimately involved in deciding which companies would make bids on jobs being offered and how much they could bid on a contract. Using the power of Local 945 in this way made Serratelli inordinately powerful within the garbage hauling association. Often he coerced contractors into buying products from his friends. In one incident, he got members of the Association to purchase a large number of tires from Metropolitan Tire Company in return for a percentage of the sale. Metropolitan Tire was owned by George Katz, a large garbage contractor and, according to Robert Greene in his book *The Sting Man*, "a known bag man for corrupt officials" and a friend of two underworld figures, Meyer Lansky and Peter LaPlaca. In fact, Greene reports that Katz once told Mel Weinberg, the infamous ABSCAM figure, that he had paid bribes to a number of elected officials in order to achieve his municipal garbage contracts. Serratelli had a number of business relationships with Katz, including partnerships in several municipal garbage hauling jobs.

Another common practice of Serratelli's was to discriminate among contractors in terms of labor costs, a practice which he shared with Bernie Adelstein across the river in New York. Friendly contractors were allowed to pay their workers much less than the wages unfriendly contractors were forced to pay. An example of these rate differences occurred in the contract bid for Elizabeth in 1958. Alfred Lippman, who had had the Elizabeth job for twenty-four years but lost it to Crescent Roselle, charged that Roselle was able to underbid him because he was paying lower wages. While the union's labor rate for Lippman was $114 for drivers and $104 for helpers, Roselle got away with paying much less, $88 and $80, according to rumor. Although Roselle's favored position won him the contract, he was not immune from Serratelli's dictatorial and strong-arm tactics. On one occasion, when he was having trouble with the union over the signing of contracts, he reported that he received a telephone call from an unknown man who told him to sign the union contract or something would happen to his two children. Needless to say, he signed the contract.

Questioning by the committee also revealed another area of organized crime's control of the waste industry. Waste firms not only need customers with waste to purchase their services; they also need locations in which to dump the waste. Access to sites is an indispensable element: to control dump sites such as landfills is to control the industry. Firms that couldn't get dumping permits couldn't bid for jobs. Control of the dumps was in the hands of the Association—testimony showed—which included firms owned by Crescent Roselle, Thomas Viola, Frank Stamato, and Chester Iommetti, among others. Again, John Serratelli collaborated with members of the Association to make dump sites a precious commodity available only to those who were in good standing with both the Association and the union.

One private hauler who felt the sting of the Association and the union over the issue of dump sites was Frank Miele, Jr. Serratelli and the Association had control over the dump in Kearny, New Jersey, which Miele had been paying to use for some time. One day the rate to dump was raised by a large amount. Miele and several other people he was affiliated with went to North Arlington to get a dump of their own so that they could escape the Association's control over them and their businesses. Within only a few days, however, Miele was summoned to a meeting at the union office. His father Frank, Sr., also a private garbage hauler, was also summoned after receiving a phone call telling him that he could no longer dump in Kearny even though he had been using it as his main disposal site for quite some time. Both father and son assumed that Serratelli was behind this maneuver and that it was the penalty being imposed for Frank, Jr.'s, having the audacity to search for a new dump site rather than pay the higher rates.

Present at the meeting in addition to the Mieles were Crescent Roselle, Joe Cassini, and Mike Signorelle, along with Serratelli, who strangely remained silent throughout the session. While Frank, Sr., wanted to find out why he could no longer dump in Kearny, the others were more interested in questioning Frank, Jr., about his plans to acquire a new dump. Soon the purpose of the meeting became obvious when they told young Frank that if he and his independent associates attempted to open a dump, they would drive them completely out of the garbage business. Although they didn't specify how they would do this, they indicated in no uncertain terms that they would find a way to eliminate them and their businesses. In addition, they advised him that he had better give up his position as leader of the independent haulers and come to terms with the Garbage Contractors Association. After the meeting, the quest for a new dump ended and Frank Miele, Jr., abandoned his attempt to fight the Association.

Independent hauler A. J. Maitilasso summed up the findings of the committee in a series of answers he provided to questions posed to him on the eighth day of the hearing. Maitilasso started the exchange by stating: "Serratelli started the whole thing and they knew it, I don't give a damn where he is; he can be right around the corner from me. He went out and organized labor first, then he organized all of these contractors in an Association."

Q. You mean, the big fellows?
A. The big guys. Then he controlled all the dumps, and he got a complete monopoly on the entire industry, and after he did that he set up jobs, and they all know it, and he set up jobs for certain contractors—"this is your job and that is yours, and you get the figure you want on it,"—and these other guys go in and give complimentary bids, and that is going on all over the state of New Jersey.
Q. And how long has it been going on?

A. It has been going on the last three years that I know of and it has been going on before that.

Q. And you heard Signorelle talk about this on frequent occasions?

A. Yes, and I hear not only Signorelle but all of them.

Q. You heard them all talk?

A. Yes, they all talk and they all know what they are doing.

Q. When they set a town and set a bid, the price is always either very high or excessive, isn't it?

A. It is exorbitant.

Q. And from your experience in the business, you know that the price that they set has no relation to the cost of doing the job; isn't that right?

A. That's right.

Q. They don't sit down and be competitive from the point of view from what it is going to cost to make a fair profit; they sit down there to give the town away to a specific contractor and he makes an exorbitant profit, is that right?

A. That is right. And these other guys all hang around for the hand out. You are going to get so much to put in a complimentary bid, and you get so much for laying off the job.

Q. Now, are you talking about money?

A. Money.

Q. And is that why the contractor's association was so disturbed about the development of an independent association?

A. That's right, they felt that we were all going to get together and give them trouble.

Q. And they felt that you would be able to find a place to dump; right? And that they wouldn't be able to control you any more?

A. That is correct. As long as they kept us small, they can call their cards the way they want them.

Q. Is that why they knocked off young Miele?

A. That is right. They did a good job on him, too. And they'll continue to knock us off until they get a complete monopoly.

Q. You don't think they are particularly concerned about the developments and the attendant publicity that has—

A. No, they're not even worried about you yet. They're not worried about your investigation yet.

Q. They're not worrying yet?

A. They're still laughing.
Q. You think that they are that brazen?
A. Yes sir.

Although a number of indictments resulted from these hearings, none resulted in convictions. One of those indicted by the state of New Jersey was John Serratelli, on charges that he accepted $4,000 in bribes from a garbage contractor to guarantee labor peace. This indictment was swiftly followed by a second one charging that Serratelli and others in the Association arranged to rig the bids on a garbage collection contract for the town of Belleville, New Jersey. Unfortunately for Serratelli, he disappeared and was presumably murdered, according to a congressional report, "for failing to go along with the directions of organized crime leaders who warned him against cooperating with authorities in any way." It seems that Serratelli, like Vincent Squillante in New York, had become too great a burden for organized crime; both men had served their purpose and were now expendable.

It is disheartening to realize, however, that the primary consequences of both the McClellan and the New Jersey State Senate investigations were the murders of Squillante and Serratelli. There were no structural changes made within the waste industry. In fact, there was not even a pattern of serious prosecutions indicating that law enforcement was conscientiously monitoring the industry.

Local 945, IBT

Among other things, the New Jersey State Senate Hearings showed the intimate ways in which Local 945, International Brotherhood of Teamsters (IBT), was involved in the entire garbage carting industry in northern New Jersey. Even after the disappearance of John Serratelli, the racketeer influence in the union continued to grow.

With Serratelli gone, Teamster president Jimmy Hoffa placed the local into a trusteeship with control being assumed by the International union. Justifying the trusteeship on the need for stability and security, Hoffa appointed Anthony "Tony Pro" Provenzano, the president of Local 560 in New Jersey and of Joint Council 73, as the trustee responsible for Local 945. Ironically,

Provenzano had been identified as a member of the Genovese organized crime syndicate and during the period of trusteeship was indicted for taking bribes to ensure labor peace. Provenzano's trusteeship lasted until March 1, 1961, when the presidency of the local was assumed by Michael Ardis, who also had connections with organized crime. Ardis soon appointed John "Johnnie Coca-Cola" Lardiere as the union's business agent. Not surprisingly, Lardiere, too, was a member of the Genovese mob. Under the leadership of Ardis and Lardiere, the conduct of the local remained the same and its influence on the garbage carting industry continued to be profound. In fact, there is no evidence that the charges made before the State Senate Committee regarding the illegal and corrupt activities of the industry and the union were not equally valid during the decade of the 1960s.

Ardis's leadership lasted until June 18, 1971, when he mysteriously disappeared while under investigation by the Internal Revenue Service. His automobile and eyeglasses were found in the union hall parking lot in West Paterson. Two months later, Johnnie Coca-Cola was imprisoned for refusing to cooperate with the New Jersey State Commission of Investigation. While he was serving his sentence, his wife, Carolyn, was poisoned by an arsenic-laced bottle of diet soda. Twenty-four hours after his release, in April of 1976, Johnnie was gunned down in Bridgewater, New Jersey, gangland style.

Once Ardis and Lardiere were out of the way, leadership passed to the new business agent and director of the local's Sanitation Division, Ernest Palmeri. Palmeri had succeeded Lardiere as business agent in 1969 after a checkered career in the restaurant business and on the fringe of the syndicate. His father, Paul Palmeri, had been described in Senate testimony as a hoodlum and his brother Frank was an associate of the Catenas in various scams and frauds. After assuming his union position in 1969, Ernest became increasingly powerful in both union and organized crime circles. In fact, during the 1977 trial of Robert Prodan, former president of the Bank of Bloomfield, New Jersey, who was involved with Palmeri in a multi-million-dollar bank fraud, a government witness testified that Prodan once described Palmeri as one of New Jersey's most powerful men. "He told me that nothing ever goes on in the State, in the garbage industry, without his blessing one way or another."

In testimony presented to a congressional committee, New Jersey State Police Colonel Justin Dintino asserted that Palmeri was responsible only to New Jersey organized crime boss Peter LaPlaca, who allegedly represented the Genovese family in the Garden State. Dintino believed that LaPlaca's primary function in the state of New Jersey was to "control the garbage industry for the mob." If this was the case, as so many law enforcement and labor officials believed, then it is no wonder that Palmeri's term of office was characterized by violence and corruption. Dintino's testimony linked Palmeri to two murders. The victim in one case, George Franconero, a New Jersey attorney (and brother of singer Connie Francis) had provided information against Palmeri to the FBI, only to be shot down in the driveway of his home.

During Palmeri's reign over Local 945, he enriched himself and his associates, while corrupting or coercing those who stood in his way, often legitimate businessmen or public officials. Compared with other unions of its size, the officials of 945 made very handsome salaries, supplemented by generous expense accounts and fringe benefits. Pensions, life and health insurance plans, severence pay, and other benefits were set up for the exclusive use of union officials and employees. Not surprisingly, these benefits became so expensive in 1976 that the union had to borrow $20,000 to meet expenses. At the same time, the salaries and fringe benefits of rank-and-file members of the local were lower than those of comparable workers in unions located in other parts of the country.

Palmeri also used his power to arrange favorable loans for friends and family members, to make or break companies which he favored or disliked, to extort money from legitimate businesses, and to manipulate fringe benefit funds, one of the most common activities of corrupt union officials. Palmeri and his mob associates even began using union funds in an attempt to take over several small New Jersey banks.

The most lucrative scheme of this nature involved the purchase by Palmeri of certificates of deposit. A short-term form of security used by many banks to raise capital, the certificate of deposit was a relatively easy way for many of New Jersey's small banks to increase their assets quickly. Money raised through the sale of certificates of deposit was then used by the banks to finance their investments in profit-making mortages and loans. On large certificate investments, the rate of interest paid by the bank to the de-

positor was negotiable, with the two sides working out a rate that
was mutually beneficial. Union locals, especially small ones without professional investment counselors on their staffs, often used
the certificate of deposit as a stable and secure form of investment,
certain to generate a reasonable rate of interest with little or no
risk. When used properly, this form of investment can benefit both
the union local and the bank.

Taking advantage of the leverage that investments in certificates gave him over small banks in need of cash, Palmeri was able
to work out deals that were of no benefit to the union and of considerable risk to the banks themselves. Union money was invested
in banks, often at an unfavorable rate of interest, in return for kickbacks and other considerations given to the union officers and their
friends. One important consideration extracted from cooperating
bank executives was the promise of low-interest or even no-interest
loans made by the bank to union officials. In an exposé of Local 945
published by a congressional subcommittee, the consequences of
this practice are described in this way:

> What often happened was that the fund lost valuable interest
> and the bank eventually came laden with bad loans. Since the
> CD can be pulled at any time—at a loss of interest to the
> fund—sweeter deals could be worked by the fund official using
> the threat of no more money. A bank president dependent on
> fund deposit would promote more in terms of low interest
> loans, under/or uncollaterized loans, or forgive past loans for
> fund officials, and their friends.

As a result of such corrupt arrangements between Palmeri and
the president of the Bank of Bloomfield, Robert Prodan, a number
of America's most notorious organized criminals received loans
from this bank. In fact, some $3.8 million was loaned by the Bank
of Bloomfield to organized crime boss Carmine Galente; Detroit's
Raffaele Quasarano and Peter Vitale, identified heroin importers;
Jimmy Fiorillo, an associate of Genovese syndicate members;
Thomas Milo, a garbage hauler from Westchester, New York,
whose father and uncle were cited as Genovese family soldiers involved in gambling, loan sharking, and narcotics; and Anthony
Ferro, another Genovese soldier. Loans to this group and to others
equally as notorious were never repaid and became part of the

price that Prodan and the Bank of Bloomfield had to pay for Local 945's business.

In the winter of 1976, the bubble burst as the effects of the bad loans began to be felt by the banks. Four banks collapsed, and millions of dollars were lost in uncollected loans to union officials and organized crime figures. No one knows, however, how much was lost by the men and women of Local 945 whose dues and pension and welfare payments were mismanaged by Palmeri and his henchmen. Eventually, Palmeri was convicted and sentenced to seven years of imprisonment for violation of the Racketeer Influenced and Corrupt Organization (RICO) statutes. His replacement as business agent of Local 945 was Anthony Rizzo, a former garbageman who was also the nephew of organized crime figure Joseph Schiapani, an alleged member of the Genovese crime family. Palmeri's old associate and body guard, Flen Chestnut, took Palmeri's place as president of 945. The reign of organized crime's influence remained unbroken.

Little Changes in New Jersey

In 1969, the New Jersey State Legislature once again became concerned with the issue of garbage and created a special legislative commission to investigate certain problems relating to solid waste disposal. Among the garbage haulers who appeared before the committee were Crescent Roselle and Alfred Lippman. Although Roselle had been indicted for bid rigging nearly a decade earlier with John Serratelli, and Lippman had been accused of paying Serratelli a bribe, each now maintained that the high cost of their services was due to legitimate business expenses and that they had no knowledge of illegal or improper activities among members of their trade association. In fact, Lippman self-righteously proclaimed that "we have seen comments in the press about either the lack of bidders or the small number of bidders on many jobs, with the implication that there might be some sinister reason for this condition. Within the field of my knowledge of municipal contracting for the collection and disposal of solid waste, this is wholly without foundation. The question lies entirely in the field of economics, geography, and availability of equipment and labor."

Such testimony and the complaints of the municipalities brought little light to the underlying workings of waste disposal. From the pages of testimony of this nature, only one thing becomes clear—the decade had brought little change to the private refuse collection industry in the state. The trade associations continued to be powerful, dump sites remained scarce and valuable coercive weapons, and many of the same owners and operators cited a decade earlier for questionable and even outright illegal activity were still prominent in the industry. Shortly after the conclusion of the committee's work, the New Jersey Legislature passed legislation which placed the solid waste collection industry under the regulatory authority of the Public Utility Commission (PUC). This action gave the PUC the right to set prices and even allocate territories as well as refuse licenses to persons of questionable or bad character. In addition, the legislature also passed its first anti-trust act. Potentially, this was a valuable weapon in controlling the collusion between the solid waste trade associations.

Controlling Garbage in New York

New York, too, remained unchanged by the revelations growing out of the hearings held in the late fifties and sixties. In 1967, Charles Grutzner of *The New York Times* reported that "an investigation directed by United States Attorney Robert M. Morgenthau has found that 90 percent of the trade-waste disposal in Westchester County is handled by members of the Genovese and Gambino families of the Mafia." Grutzner wrote that Morgenthau began his investigation following the presumed murder of Joseph "Joey Surprise" Feola, who had taken the job of hauling waste from a large Ford Motor Company plant in Mahwah, New Jersey, away from a waste removal company controlled by the Gambino family. Also identified in this report as still active in Westchester waste was Nick Ratteni who, along with Sabato Milo, allegedly headed the Genovese crime syndicate operations there.

About six months later, *The New York Times* added more detail to the story, reporting the arrest of Sabato Milo's son, Thomas, on charges of trying to intimidate a competitor in the garbage hauling business. In addition, it was pointed out that the private carting industry in Westchester County (as in New York City) had undergone a process of extraordinary consolidation. The newspaper found that most of the profitable contracts had been going to four large companies and that the county seemed to have been divided into four sections over which each had exclusive control. The four companies identified were Queen City Refuse Collectors, a Milo operation; Greeley Sanitation Service, run by Joseph and Robert Liquori; Westchester Carting, operated by Ratteni; and Valley Carting Company, which was operated by Tobias DeMicco and Nicholas Melillo who, the *Times* reported, were identified by law enforcement agencies as representing the interests of the Gambino family in Westchester County.

In the early 1970s the focus of attention shifted to Brooklyn and the Brooklyn Trade Waste Association. Because evidence against garbage carters was so difficult to get and because state officials had such a miserable record in prosecuting those who had previously been indicted for illegal activities in the waste hauling business, Brooklyn District Attorney Eugene Gold initiated an undercover investigation in 1972. Purchasing a garbage truck and obtaining a license to operate from the Department of Consumer Affairs, the district attorney's office set up its own small garbage company staffed by police officers.

The first job of this new entry into the field of Brooklyn waste haulers was to solicit customers. That was not very easily done, however. Even though many businessmen offered support and encouraged the representatives of the new company, only a few merchants actually retained its services. Of some two thousand solicited, nineteen signed up. Some merchants were threatened when they attempted to give their business to the new firm and others were dissuaded by their old haulers' use of threats followed by vandalism. Not surprisingly, the undercover firm was denied membership in the Brooklyn Trade Waste Association and was soon labeled by the other garbage carters as a threat to their business and general welfare.

On March 28, 1974, District Attorney Gold revealed that fifty-five private carting companies and nine other persons associated with the industry had been indicted for restraint of trade and perjury. The district attorney stated at that time that "the carting industry in this borough was controlled by organized crime through the Brooklyn Trade Waste Association." Gold pointed out that organized crime controlled a $60 million a year industry, which included approximately $20 million a year in over-charges resulting from "collusive practices in the industry." In fact, the indictment alleged that overcharging customers by as much as 500 percent occurred regularly. Further, the Brooklyn Trade Waste Association itself had "taken in fees of $100,000 or more for assigning private carters their territories in the borough."

In addition to the usual practice of protecting the property rights of the carters, the Association also acted as the exclusive agent for carters in their dealings with merchants and in their trading and exchanging stops among themselves. Of course, this practice eliminated any semblance of competitive bidding and excluded the customer from any freedom in choosing whom he wanted to do business with. One merchant was threatened with having his business blown up because he bought a garbage compacting machine, but the far more common practice was simply to refuse to service those customers who complained or wished to switch to another contractor. Eventually, all dissatisfied customers either returned to the carter who "owned" the stop or faced the possibility of having their establishment overrun by waste.

The Brooklyn Trade Waste Association officials indicted were the president, Patsy D'Avanzo; vice president Sam Galasso; Joseph Schipani, identified as a soldier in the Genovese organized crime syndicate and only recently released from prison; Joseph Dantuoro, who was said to be a member of the Colombo organized crime syndicate; and five other men—Salvatore Sindone, Sabino Colluci, Dominick Colluci, Michael Russo, and John Cassillo— who apparently did the bidding of the mob in its control of the Brooklyn Trade Waste Association and in structuring the trash collection business in that borough of New York City.

Most of the fifty-five indicted carters, representing over 60 percent of the trash haulers in Brooklyn, pleaded guilty to the restraint of trade and were given light fines by the court. Those who did not cop a plea fared better, since the charges against them were thrown out because of a technical error made by the officials in building their case. Still, the Brooklyn Trade Waste Association was ordered dissolved by the judge.

Because the waste industry is regulated in New York City by the Division of Consumer Affairs (DCA), it was hoped that this agency would impose sanctions against those who had pleaded guilty. Severe and meaningful penalties might have served as a deterrent for members of the Association and for others who might think of engaging in similar restraint of trade activities. This was not to happen, however, as the DCA imposed fines of only $500 per truck owned by those who entered guilty pleas.

The Rand Corporation's Peter Reuter pointed out that the DCA response was totally inadequate, serving neither as punishment nor deterrent. A fine of $500 per truck represented less than 1 percent of the extortion revenues calculated by the district attorney's office. Reuter concludes in his unpublished paper that "the renewal of licenses and failure to determine whether prices had changed or whether customers were less constrained in their choice surely signaled carters that they faced only minor costs in continuation of the customer allocation agreement." And, as one might imagine, the Brooklyn Trade Waste Association was dissolved only to reappear as the Kings County Trade Waste Association. In August, 1974, before the indictments against the fifty-five carters had been resolved, the Commissioner of Consumer Affairs, Elinor C. Guggenheimer, maintained that her agency was not doing a very good job in policing and controlling the activities of the city garbage haulers. Some fifteen months later, she seemed to change her mind. While the reconstituted Brooklyn Trade Waste Association was deeply involved in negotiations with the city over a strike in the private carting industry called by Local 813 (still headed by Bernie Adelstein), Commissioner Guggenheimer was quoted in *The New York Times* as saying, "We have no evidence now that the industry is ridden with crime. Commercial firms and customers of the carting industry now seem to be able to change companies fairly easily. If there was a persistent crime situation that might be different." Both she and Leo Pollack, the head of the Consumer Affairs Trade Waste Division, were satisfied that there was "no evidence that strong arm tactics were now being used in normal operations." Brooklyn District Attorney Gold disagreed, but the resurrection of the Brooklyn Trade Waste Association continued as the DCA stood by and did nothing.

If the DCA believed that monitoring the industry meant waiting for complaints to be brought in, it was, perhaps unknowingly, guaranteeing the failure of its effort. Given the violence associated with the waste business and the sordid reputation it has, this waiting for complaints is not a very effective method of policing the industry. Anyone familiar with the industry during the last two decades or so would know of the murders of Vincent Squillante, John Serratelli, and a number of others associated with waste hauling. In fact, John Montesano—one of the major witnesses for the Senate Committee back in 1957, killed in 1981—asked reporters several times before his murder, "You know there is a contract on me? You are the third one to tell me about it. Because I testified [in the Senate Hearings], I was the heavy, I did the right thing . . . Now, I hear they're going to whack me out . . . leave my brains on the street." Thus it was hardly realistic to expect witnesses to come forward with information or charges of illegal behavior. Nevertheless, waiting for complaints seemed to characterize the Consumer Affairs agency's strategy.

Before the Brooklyn Trade Waste cases could be forgotten, another scandal occurred within the New York garbage industry. This time the target of a federal investigation was Joseph Gambino, an illegal alien and cousin of the notorious organized crime godfather Carlo Gambino. In an attempt to show that Gambino was monopolizing garbage collection in a neighborhood of the Bronx containing a very large public housing project, federal agents set up an undercover carting firm to compete with Gambino for local business. Not surprisingly, the undercover garbage company was threatened and an FBI agent posing as an owner was physically assaulted by a close friend and associate of Gambino's, Carlo Conti. Both Gambino and Conti were indicted and convicted of restraint of trade and extortion; they were sentenced to ten and eight years of imprisonment, respectively. In addition, Gambino was convicted of tax evasion.

About the same time, New York Carting, owned and operated by brothers Charles and Robert Macaluso, was also being investigated by undercover police agents. Posing as a purchasing agent for a hotel, an undercover policeman had no difficulty soliciting a bribe from the vice president of New York Carting, Robert Macaluso, who admitted to overbilling the hotel. The investigation revealed that a previous purchasing agent had been threatened and had fled New York after attempting to verify the bills submitted by New York Carting. The company and Macaluso were convicted of extortion and bribery, and Macaluso was sentenced to a one-year jail term. In this case, the Division of Consumer Affairs actually stripped the company of its license to do business in the city.

In recent years, the situation has hardly changed in the Greater New York area. When Peter Reuter interviewed the staff of the Division of Consumer Affairs in 1982, he found that "almost everyone was willing to admit that racketeers were involved and that customers were allocated and improperly treated as a property of a particular carter." The staff, it appeared, had little faith in the existing regulatory system and did not believe that significant change would come about in the near future. They blamed this on the lack of serious political interest in controlling the garbage industry and on the leniency of the courts, both factors undermining what little effort was made by their agency to police waste hauling companies. Reuter found that the sale of customers continued, sometimes for as much as fifty times the monthly revenues; it has not diminished over the last thirty years of investigation and public exposure.

Recent New Jersey Scandals

The same pattern of conspiracy and corruption was also continuing across the Hudson River in New Jersey. In July, 1976, the New Jersey Trade Waste Association (NJTWA) was formed by a combination of organized crime figures, garbage carters, and union officials. It is alleged that another prominent organizer of this new Association was James Failla, also known as Jimmy Brown, who at the time was the head of the New York Trade Waste Association and considered by law enforcement people to be a Capo in the Gambino crime family. Within a short time, the Association, located in South Hackensack, consisted of some 140 members providing garbage collection services in Somerset, Bergen, Essex, Middlesex, Monmouth, Morris, Passaic, and Union counties. Hudson County was not included because it was already controlled by the Hudson County Sanitation Association (HCSA). Together these two groups controlled approximately 35 percent of the total garbage collection revenues in the entire state of New Jersey, or about $46 million annually.

Under the leadership of Carmine Franco, who was elected president of the New Jersey Trade Waste Association, members of the group had to agree not to take customers away from each other. In fact, according to Edwin H. Stier, the director of the

State Division of Criminal Justice, the Association was actually formed to "affect and enforce [this] agreement among garbage collectors in all counties except Hudson." To enforce this policy of property rights, the officers and "friends" of the NJTWA met weekly at the Crows Nest Restaurant in South Hackensack or at Snuffy's II Restaurant in Somerville. Here they heard grievances, resolved differences, and made policy that would be carried out by thugs supplied by the Association. As president, Franco assumed complete control of the Association's activities and over all of its members. For a period of time he became something of the garbage king of northern and central New Jersey, presiding over practically every detail of the business in the area.

On October 17, 1980, a statewide grand jury indicted NJTWA and the HCSA along with twenty-four corporations and twenty-eight individuals associated with the solid waste disposal business. The indictments charged, as usual, that the two associations and their members were illegally monopolizing the garbage industry. Most of the individuals and firms were indicted on charges of price fixing, illegally dividing up territories, using threats of violence to deter competition, and policing these illegal arrangements through the two trade associations.

The indictments came about as a result of a three-year federal and state investigation that went to the grand jury only after the FBI made a key witness available to the state. The key witness turned out to be an inside informant named Harold Kaufman, a one-time bank robber and convicted felon. After being released from Atlanta Federal Penitentiary, Kaufman went to work for Teamsters Local 813 as executive assistant to the president, Bernie Adelstein. Once he served his New York apprenticeship, Kaufman moved to New Jersey where he went to work for Charles Macaluso at Statewide Environmental Contractors. While working for Macaluso, Kaufman had a first-hand opportunity to observe and participate in a variety of illegal activities associated with waste hauling.

After a falling out with his boss, he left Statewide and went to work for Duane Marine Salvage Corporation, the chemical waste disposal company located in Perth Amboy, New Jersey. Before leaving Macaluso, however, Kaufman claimed that his conscience began to bother him and that he became remorseful about the corruption he saw in the waste industry. Since he was also aware of the illegal dumping of toxic chemical wastes, he decided to do something good for once in his life and reveal what he knew about these operations. Whether or not Kaufman was motivated by such altruism or by vengeance toward Macaluso is unknown. What is known, however, is that Harold Kaufman approached the Federal Bureau of Investigation and volunteered to provide them with whatever information they desired. For some time thereafter, Kaufman was an inside informant for the Bureau, sometimes attending meetings and conferences with a hidden microphone strapped to his body to record threats being made and bribes being offered. Now, after a year and a half of undercover work, Kaufman became one of the most important witnesses that the state of New Jersey had ever used against the mob and its activities.

Several of those indicted were well connected with organized crime. Tino Fiumara was a waterfront mobster before being sent to prison in 1979 and was alleged to have supplied much of the muscle to enforce decisions made by the trade waste associations. He, and his associates, Michael Copolla and Lawrence Ricci, were charged with attempting to shake down another waste hauler by forcing him to clear the sale of his business with Carmine Franco and by taking a percentage of the sale price as a kickback. Another organized crime figure, John Albert, a soldier in the Tieri (formerly Genovese) crime family, ran Jersey Sanitation, a garbage hauling firm in East Brunswick accused of participating in the price-fixing conspiracy. Also indicted for price fixing was Anthony Scaffidi, vice president of Metro Disposal and identified as another associate of the Tieri family. Others thought to have organized crime ties were Carmine Franco, the president of the NJTWA; Louis Mongelli, the president of I.S.A. in New Jersey, Inc.; Charles Macaluso and the secretary-treasurer of his Statewide Environmental Contractors, Frank J. Latano; and Ed Lecarreaux, Harold Kaufman's former boss at Duane Marine Salvage Corporation.

Before the trial of those indicted could start, Harold Kaufman testified before the Subcommittee on Oversight and Investigations of the Committee on Interstate and Foreign Commerce, the congressional body looking into the links between organized crime and the garbage industry. Here Kaufman repeated many of his charges, asserting that organized crime was deeply involved in the New Jersey garbage industry and was able to control it through fear and intimidation. As an example of the intimidation that racketeers could use, he cited the SCA Services, Inc., a firm he claimed was linked to organized crime and involved in the murder of Alfred DiNardi in 1976 because DiNardi's Custom Disposal Company violated SCA's property rights. Needless to say, this was a significant charge given that SCA was the third largest waste hauler in the United States, with stock traded on the New York Stock Exchange and a board of directors made up of a number of prominent American businessmen.

Trials growing out of the fifty-nine indictments were scheduled for September, 1982, in Somerville, New Jersey, before Superior Court Judge Arthur Meredith. Meredith decided first, however, that the defendants would be tried in small groups of manageable size. For technical reasons, Charles Macaluso was granted a separate trial and Tino Fiumara's case was dismissed because it did not conform to the state's statute of limitations.

Finally, after a great deal of legal haggling, postponements, and extensions, the initial trial began. The first five to stand trial were Frank Arace, Carmine Franco, Anthony Scaffidi, Anthony Rizzo, and Michael Grillo. Asserting that the trial would probably last four or five months, Judge Meredith was obviously surprised when, on the seventh day of jury selection, all the defendants pleaded guilty to the reduced charge of conspiring to monopolize industrial garbage collections in New Jersey. The New Jersey Trade Waste Association also pleaded guilty to the same charge.

The guilty pleas of the NJTWA and the five individual defendants were the result of a plea bargain arrangement worked out with the State Attorney General's Office. Originally charged with violation of the State Anti-Trust Act, each agreed to plead guilty to violating a more lenient statute of the Public Utilities Act. Had they been convicted of the original charge, they might well have been prohibited from owning any kind of business in New Jersey and have faced a prison sentence of up to eighteen months and a fine of possibly $50,000. In addition, their companies might have been liable for a corporate fine of up to $100,000. The Public Utilities Act subjected the defendants to much lesser penalties.

With the plea of guilty, all of the defendants agreed to pay personal and corporate fines ranging from $10,000 to $75,000. Franco, Scaffidi, and Rizzo were each sentenced to six months in jail and placed on three years probation. Each was also sentenced to one thousand hours of community service by Judge Meredith. A fine of $50,000 was also imposed upon Franco, while Rizzo and

Scaffidi were assessed at $40,000 each. Franco's company was fined $75,000, while lesser fines were meted out to Rizzo's company and to Arace and Grillo. Faced with a $100,000 fine, the New Jersey Trade Waste Association agreed to dissolve.

All but five of the remaining defendants pleaded guilty to reduced charges and were fined or given short suspended sentences. Besides Macaluso, who would be tried separately, the group left to be tried consisted of John Gentempo of Browning-Ferris Industries, Anthony Scioscia of Home Industrial Disposal Service, Louis Mongelli of I.S.A., and Louis Spiegel of Inter-County Refuse Service, Inc. Each was accused of violating the state's anti-trust law by conspiring to restrict competition in the garbage industry.

Early in 1983, the next trial began. For the first time, the state of New Jersey had an opportunity to use its star witness in an open courtroom, and use him it did. Although no mention of organized crime was allowed before the jury in order to protect the rights of the four defendants, the six-week trial exposed the history of the New Jersey Trade Waste Association and the corrupt practices of its members. The packed courtroom listened intently as Kaufman explained how bids were rigged and inflated, how territories were distributed, and how decisions were enforced by the Association. He explained that before the NJTWA was formed, rival garbage companies competed for customers and undercut each other in the marketplace. This was defined as unprofitable for the firms, even though it kept the cost of service reasonable for the customer. Kaufman gave the court some idea of the violence that characterized this industry by explaining that his former trash hauling firm did not bid on a 1977 Newark garbage contract "because we were told that if we didn't get out of Newark somebody's head would be blown off." These remarks, like others pertaining to violence, were made in the absence of the jury since Judge Meredith felt that hearing of such instances would not enable the jury to remain unbiased.

Under cross-examination, Kaufman revealed that his own participation was hardly innocent. The same year that Maculuso was having Kaufman bribe officials and politicians, he acted as co-host of the 1976 Democratic Convention in Madison Square Garden.

The defense attorneys tried to discredit Kaufman by inferring that a shunt implanted in his head to relieve water on his brain had impaired his memory and by dredging up an affair he once had with an English prostitute. They called him a liar who had sold a good story to the FBI for $32,000, though Kaufman's story was often corroborated by evidence or other witnesses. In the face of repeated requests for a mistrial because of the unreliability of the key witness, Judge Meredith finally decided that the jury and not the court would make the ultimate determination of Kaufman's credibility.

Throughout the trial, the state tried to show that the defendants had prior knowledge of the conspiracy and had actually taken part in grievance hearings where disputes over territorial rights were settled. This, of course, would make them guilty of violating the state's anti-trust laws. The defense, on the other hand, argued that their clients either did not participate in such meetings or were unaware that they were participating in illegal sessions. After seven days of deliberation, the jury finally returned a verdict of guilty against Spiegel and Scioscia, but were unable to reach a decision on Gentempo and Mongelli and their companies. Because of this, Judge Meredith declared a mistrial for the latter two.

The last trial, of Charles Macaluso, began in Paterson, New Jersey, in late April, 1983. Although Macaluso was named in five separate indictments, he went on trial first for allegedly bribing city officials of the borough of Wanaque. The state charged that Macaluso used cash payoffs to get members of the borough council to change the Wanaque sanitation contract to exclude refuse collections for businesses. This, of course, would have enabled Macaluso's company, Statewide Environmental Contractors, to charge the businesses separately and enhance its profit.

Once again the star witness of the trial was Harold Kaufman who, as a former employee of Macaluso's, had had many intimate conversations with his boss about political corruption and the payoff of public officials. Unknown to Macaluso, of course, Kaufman was wired during several of these conversations, with interesting results. Prior to one meeting in Macaluso's home with two officials and a candidate for township council, Macaluso is heard suggesting that the three guests be searched for hidden microphones. He asked, "Who's gonna shake 'em down, make sure they're not wired? It may sound silly. We got three guys that could send us on vacation for a long time." Kaufman finally dissuaded Macaluso from conducting the search. Although Macaluso contended that the money paid to these officials was a campaign contribution and not a bribe, the jury convicted him of bribery and attempting to illegally influence elected officials. He was sentenced to a two-year prison term.

The outcome of this investigation and of the subsequent trials was the dissolution of both the New Jersey Trade Waste Association and the Hudson County Sanitation Association, and the conviction of a number of solid waste disposal firms and their operators. Once again, it established that the racketeer influence in the trade waste associations in the northeastern part of the United States remained strong. The testimony of Harold Kaufman, often reinforced by other witnesses, showed the firm linkage between a number of waste operators and their companies and well-known organized crime figures in New York and New Jersey. However, like the investigations, indictments, trials, convictions, and sentences that occurred in 1957, 1959, 1969, and throughout the 1970s, there is no reason to believe that these most recent dissolutions will have much of an effect on the garbage industry.

Calculating the Costs

Although it is not possible to say exactly how typical the involvement of organized crime in solid waste collection is in cities around the country, the fact that organized crime is so persistent in the Northeast leads us to believe that the relationship may be found elsewhere as well. Perhaps more is known about the New York–New Jersey area because of the magnitude of the problem there and because law enforcement officials have been particularly active in investigating organized crime and its activities. Allegations about organized crime involvement in the garbage carting and disposal industry have been made however, for a number of other cities—including Los Angeles, Philadelphia, Detroit, Cleveland, and Chicago. In fact, the original 1957 McClellan hearings revealed a pattern of corruption and illegality in the Los Angeles garbage business similar to that found on the East Coast. In 1980, the Anti-Trust Division of the U.S. Justice Department again investigated the Los Angeles Carters Association and found anti-competitive practices similar to those that existed in the 1950s. The same division of the Justice Department also convicted the carters association in Philadelphia of engaging in the practice of customer allocation. In 1971, the Chicago area carters were ordered by the Illinois State Attorney General to cease their illegal practices.

Additionally, since many organized crime figures have illegal enterprises in different cities and states around the country, it is logical to assume that they do what is profitable wherever they are. The nature of the garbage industry is essentially similar in most urban areas, so that organized crime can provide the same services in the South or the Midwest as it provides in New York, New Jersey, or Philadelphia. Finally, the ties between organized crime and the Teamsters Union have been well documented on the national level and in specific locations around the nation where locals are dominated by racketeers and mob figures. Since this relationship serves as a vehicle for racketeer influence in several trucking-related industries, including garbage collection, one may assume that similar conditions exist outside the Northeast. Unfortunately, more precise knowledge of the extent of organized crime involvement in and domination of the solid waste industry across the country will have to await future study by investigative journalists; one has less hope for government-sponsored investigations.

The cost of allowing organized crime to structure and dominate the waste disposal business can be measured in two ways. First, the illegal nature of the business has raised costs of waste collection and disposal for all customers victimized by garbage company conspiracies. It is estimated that the customer allocation agreement which operates in New York City raises the cost of collection for industrial establishments by some 35 percent, or about $45 million a year. It is more difficult to determine the extent to which practices such as bid rigging and excess billings also inflate collection costs for taxpayers and private customers. Nevertheless, the second cost may be even greater than the first.

There is, of course, a more significant cost to be computed. The tradition of illegality that developed in the solid waste industry in the last thirty years has blurred all distinctions between right and wrong, good or bad. This tradition was fostered by the unique needs of the industry and by the entry into it of racketeers and syndicated criminals whose sole desire was to make as much money as possible. Through fraud, extortion, restraint of trade, rigging bids, corrupting public officials, and outright violence, their desire was fulfilled. Until recently, however, cost was only material except, perhaps, for those involved in the dirty business itself.

When, during the 1970s, these same garbage haulers and their organized crime affiliates expanded their operation from solid waste disposal to the field of toxic waste control and added to their criminal repertoire the practice of illegal dumping in unsafe places, the nature of the cost changed greatly—shared now by untold millions of men, women, and children across the nation.

It was this transformation that would create a crisis situation from a merely criminal one.

4

Organized Crime
Moves In

ORGANIZED CRIME CONTROLLED the solid waste disposal industry through the major trade associations, the relevant Teamster locals, and the connivance of political cronies. Year after year, decade after decade, this dominance has been chronicled. But what of the toxic waste disposal industry? Simply put, much toxic waste disposal is dangerously and illegally carried out by many of the same carting firms which operate in the more traditional garbage industry, the same firms which are either controlled or owned outright by organized crime figures.

It is only common sense to assume the generation and build-up of toxic waste preceded by decades the crafting of both state and federal environmental legislation. Chemical firms and others that generated toxic waste contracted with private carting companies to dispose of their waste long before the Resource Conservation and Recovery Act (RCRA). And given that organized crime basically controlled the private carting disposal industry, it is quite obvious organized crime was already in the business of toxic waste disposal by the time RCRA was conceived.

But several things changed in the 1970s. First of all, there was the dramatic increase in the generation of toxic waste. And second, there was the growing demand that both state and federal environmental agencies step in to regulate the toxic waste disposal industry in order to protect the public welfare. Concern, of course, was heightened by the environmental movement and by the periodic reports of one environmental disaster after another. Stories claiming the imminent death of Lake Erie, poisoned by countless tons of toxic waste, for instance, were only part of the growing picture of general environmental decay.

It slowly dawned on an ever wider public that American industry had no idea what to do with the toxic by-products of the many goods considered now as necessities of modern life. Few, if any, thought to argue that perhaps the goods were not so essential. Fewer still argued that industry should be prohibited from producing goods whose wastes were harmful, unless they could safely dispose of them. As for the generating industries, they claimed the problem wasn't theirs, that the blame belonged with the disposal companies. In fact, industry has not been forced to handle its own toxic waste. And the behavior of Hooker Chemical in the Love Canal area of Niagara Falls should make everyone nervous about the ways in which the generators do handle their own waste when left alone.

The organized crime problem is probably among the most vexing in this environmental quagmire. Imagine an EPA inspector or state regulatory agent trying to deal with firms controlled by members of the most powerful crime syndicates in the country, crime syndicates which can and do buy public officials with ease. Naturally, the problem is much greater than the relative impotence of regulatory agents. In the mid- and late 1970s, those officials trained to deal with organized crime in its many manifestations were almost completely lost when it came to environmental issues—especially those involving the arcane chemistry of toxic waste. On the one hand, then, were the regulatory agents with no experience in investigating organized crime; and on the other, police with no experience in environmental work and little knowledge of what toxic chemicals were or how to recognize them. Mediating between these agents and officers were the environmental policymakers and certain politicians whose task, it appears, was to keep the lid on the whole mess.

The first to realize just what was going on were law enforcement officers who were drawn by chance into the toxic waste disposal field. If the Westchester Parkway Police hadn't called Detective Grogan in Yonkers and he hadn't called Detective Greenberg in Rockland County, what we do know, certainly about New York State, might never have come to light.

As both the toxic waste disposal business and organized crime involved interstate connections, the problems that confronted the New York detectives were soon enough mirrored in New Jersey. The New Jersey response was, however, quite different, though no more successful. The Garden State created a special law enforcement task force to deal with the increasing menace of toxic waste dumping. Of all the states with these hideous problems, New Jersey took the most innovative approach. Unfortunately, the potential was never realized. The complex power of organized crime thwarted New Jersey's handful of dedicated police in much the same manner as it did across the border.

Given the scope of the problem and the seriousness of the danger, the activities of the very few law enforcement officers working such cases eventually sparked some state and federal attention. Among the many bits and pieces of intelligence first gathered on organized crime and toxic waste after the passage of RCRA was one from a confidential informant (CI) to the New Jersey Division of Criminal Justice:

> The undersigned was contacted by a reliable, confidential source of information who has previously supplied this investigator with information relative to the illicit disposal of chemical waste in New Jersey and other states. This informant has long been associated with both solid and chemical waste pickup and disposal. He has personal knowledge of cartage and disposal procedures as well as people employed or associated with the industry.
>
> The CI advised in November of 1976 he and others became aware that "organized crime" was beginning to attempt a "take over" of this state's lucrative chemical pickup and disposal industry. The CI advised the first attempts came from the New Jersey Trade Waste Association. The presiding association president is Carmen [sic] Franco, "Tony Pro's boy."

What was happening in the latter part of 1976 and on into 1977 was a strong-armed attempt by organized crime to structure the newly regulated toxic waste industry on the same lines as the solid waste business. It wanted to run the industry through a new trade association, and the heavyset, tattooed Carmine Franco was the man to do the job.

One obvious reason for this call to structure the toxic waste disposal industry in the same manner as the garbage industry was the new legislation designed to eliminate the haphazard and dangerous disposal of these wastes. Organized crime responded by securing the necessary permits and licenses called for under the new legislation.

In fact, for quite a long period there were no formal licenses or permits to secure. The EPA did not issue its mandated guidelines on many of the toxic waste issues for some years. This placed state regulatory bodies in a quandary, and finally forced several to sue the EPA in order to speed the development of its program on toxic waste disposal. Few states were willing or able to pioneer in this field, especially when their programs might well become subject to expensive and time-consuming revisions after the EPA published its own guidelines. Most state regulatory action was basically suspended in the period following the passage of RCRA. Not suspended, however, was the stockpiling of toxic wastes. This went on at an ever-increasing pace, mocking the slow motion of the regulatory agencies.

Rockland County

The activities of Detectives Grogan and Greenberg in Westchester and Rockland counties had not stopped with the passage of RCRA, nor, indeed, with the closing of the Dexter dump in Clarkstown by New York State's Department of Environmental Conservation. But what happened in Rockland County to Greenberg's investigation was in many ways a failure. The more he and those who joined with him probed organized crime's toxic waste dumping, the more obstacles were thrown in their path. The investigation in Rockland County, New York, soon centered more and more on the activities and associates of Carmine Franco, the head of the New Jersey Trade Waste Association, the man supposedly picked to run the mob's new toxic waste disposal enterprise. There was no bureaucratic means of cooperation between Detective Greenberg, working in New York on Carmine Franco, and New Jersey's Division of Criminal Justice, which had been conducting a large-scale investigation into the New Jersey Trade Waste Assocciation and the activities of Carmine Franco and his associates. The small Sheriff's Department in Rockland County was hardly able to conduct major investigations, as it had no official intelligence or organized crime units. It was far more logical for the larger and more specialized Rockland County District Attorney's

Office to take over the case and pursue the investigation. The DA wasn't interested, however, so Greenberg and several fellow deputies stepped up their work.

On October 12, 1976, Greenberg and Deputy John Liguori held a meeting with officials of the Department of Environmental Conservation at which the entire investigation of the Dexter dump was reviewed. Movies of dumping taken in June by Greenberg and Liguori were shown. The meeting concluded with the DEC officials stating that a summary order closing down the dump would be issued by Larry Vernon, regional counsel for the DEC, on Friday, October 15. The day before the order was supposed to be issued, the two detectives went to the dump and took motion pictures of several trucks emptying material picked up at the Yonkers incinerator. Among the materials deposited were plasterboard, wood, tar paper, metal drums, filled plastic bags, black incinerated garbage, and construction debris. The firms identified from markings on the trucks were Cimino's, and two from an outfit called I.S.A. in New Jersey, Inc.

Again on the day that the New York Department of Environmental Conservation ordered the Clarkstown dump closed, Greenberg and others from the Sheriff's Department watched a large tanker from an organized crime toxic waste hauler spread a clear liquid on top of the burned garbage which had come from Yonkers. Four days later, on October 19, Greenberg and Liguori were on their way to a prearranged meeting with Yonkers police officers. They stopped at the "closed" landfill and watched as a tanker marked "ALL COUNTY LIQUID WASTE DISPOSAL" entered the Dexter property and backed into the dumping area. Once in position, the driver attached a hose to the tanker and emptied its contents onto the garbage.

While Greenberg centered his efforts on the Dexter dump and the machinations of Cimino, Zingaro, and others, events just a few miles west in Ramapo, New York, were heating up. There were clear signs of an organized crime move to control the solid waste industry in Rockland County, which meant that the Dexter dump was only a detail in a much broader problem. The first major indication came on March 2, 1976, when several garbage trucks owned by Natale Schettino, a solid waste hauler in Rockland County, were torched. Three months later, Schettino's seventy-eight-year-old mother-in-law was murdered by a shotgun blast in the face when she opened the door of his house. Shortly after this Schettino reported to the police and district attorney that both the arson and the murder had occurred because he refused to join a Rockland trade waste group being formed by mobsters from New York City.

Around the time of these incidents, Greenberg learned Raymond Cimino had entered a bid to operate the town of Ramapo's municipal dump, which was being franchised out through public bidding. For Greenberg and the other stalwarts in the Sheriff's Department, it was becoming clear that Ramapo was the main theater of action. Nevertheless, they were unable actively to investigate the Ramapo dump until the fall of 1976 because their total force of two or three men was still working on the problem of the Dexter landfill.

Later on that summer, the Ramapo contract was finally awarded. The winner was a building contractor named Eugene Sorgine, who lived in Mahwah, New Jersey, just across the New York–New Jersey border from Ramapo. Apparently, Sorgine was not supposed to have the contract. Someone had made a mistake. Prior to his winning bid on the Ramapo contract, Sorgine had been negotiating to sell the business. But the price offered was too low and he decided not to sell. The individual attempting to buy out Sorgine was Carmine Franco. On the day the bid was awarded, Sorgine's house was set on fire. Although his wife and children were in the house at the time, they managed to get out without any injuries. The next day—according to Greenberg, who interviewed Sorgine—Carmine Franco called Sorgine and asked whether he was now ready to sell his business. Sorgine relented and Franco bought him out. Beginning in either September or October, 1976, the Ramapo landfill was operated by Franco.

The arson investigation that followed the torching of Sorgine's house makes an interesting coda. The chief investigator was James Cotrell, fire inspector at the time in Mahwah, New Jersey. Cotrell, it turned out, not only investigated the fire but was there that night in his capacity as a fireman with an engine company. While the fire was still going on, Cotrell began to collect various floor samples for laboratory examination because he was suspicious. On August 13, 1976, Cotrell's lab analysis came back indicating the high likelihood that the fire had resulted from arson. Cotrell then turned his information over to the local police for criminal investigation.

One week later, he inquired about the investigation's status and was told that it had been taken over by the Bergen County Prosecutor's Office. Cotrell heard nothing else about this until the winter of 1979, when he was contacted by Greenberg who asked him if he would meet with him and Assistant Attorney General Richard Stavin. Greenberg and others had convinced Stavin to investigate the fire. Meeting with them, Cotrell learned that his original reports on the fire, supposedly on file in Mahwah's Fire Prevention Bureau Office, were missing. During this period of renewed interest in the Sorgine fire (brought about because outside agencies were investigating), Cotrell learned the Mahwah Police Department's official report listed the fire as accidental. However, he had no official way of knowing that, since he left the Fire Prevention Bureau in 1977 when he was not reappointed by the town. He also had a towing business and was under contract with the Mahwah Police. After his testimony before a grand jury inquiring into the Sorgine fire as well as illegal toxic waste dumping, this contract was suspended. Cotrell moved out of town.

Long before any of this came to light, Greenberg and Liguori had begun to watch the Ramapo landfill. Almost immediately, they noticed the first of several irregularities. Garbage trucks would follow a set routine upon arrival at the landfill, first going to the scales to be weighed, then moving to the dump to deposit their load. They would return to the scales and the difference in weight would be entered and the haulers billed for that quantity of garbage by the town of Ramapo. This held true for all the local garbage haulers from Ramapo. But those trucks belonging to Carmine Franco's businesses bypassed the scales and proceeded directly to the dump. They were never weighed, and, therefore, never billed.

With this information, Detectives Greenberg and Liguori met with Kenneth Gribetz, the Rockland County District Attorney, on October 17, 1977. According to the detectives, Gribetz said: "Didn't you learn your lesson on the last one? What are you messing with garbage for?" Stubbornly, Greenberg requested that a grand jury be convened. He also pointed out to the district attorney that in addition to Franco's trucks not being billed, other companies using the site were receiving preferential treatment. Very early in the morning, before the landfill opened for business, garbage trucks with the name Valley Carting, from Ossining, New York, unloaded. Greenberg, accompanied by a local radio reporter, had watched as Valley Carting drove in and unloaded at the unopened landfill which, however, had an operating bulldozer at the ready to move and bury the garbage. On checking out Valley Carting, Greenberg learned it was owned by Tobias DeMicco, a well-known organized crime figure.

The reporter accompanying Greenberg was from the Rockland County radio station WKRL. The station decided to go with the story but Greenberg asked them to wait until the investigation was finished. The station was reluctant at first, then agreed to wait until Greenberg met, once again, with District Attorney Gribetz. And still Gribetz stalled. Greenberg got back to the station with the news that there was no hope for prosecution as there was little likelihood of continuing the investigation. He added laconically that if the station wanted to release the story, it should do what it had to do. WKRL then called Gribetz and told him they were going to release a story on the dumping.

Gribetz immediately called a meeting with Sheriff Raymond Linderman, Greenberg, and Chief Clark Hill of the Sheriff's Department. He told them that the DA's Office wanted to work with them on the investigation, that it "could be the biggest thing that ever hit Rockland County." The only problem was that the radio station was going to short-circuit the investigation by going public. The point to Greenberg was obvious—if they could get the station to hold off, then the DA would move forward. Greenberg tried, but the station finally broadcast the story.

With the story now out, the district attorney let loose a blast at the Sheriff's Department. The local paper quoted him as saying that the sheriff had nothing and couldn't lock up "Joe Schmo." This outraged the sheriff, who retaliated by calling the local newspapers in and letting them know exactly what was happening. So, the day after the DA's statement, the papers followed with the sheriff's version of what was going on at the Ramapo landfill.

This battle between the DA and sheriff fought through the local media clearly could not continue. Gribetz called the sheriff and proposed they straighten out their problems through the U.S. Department of Justice in Newark, New Jersey. This was done to no great success. The Justice Department saw no violation of federal laws in the dumping going on by Valley Carting. The following day, Greenberg and a member of Gribetz's staff tried the White Plains Regional Office of the New York State Organized Crime Task Force. Again, Greenberg presented his case. This time, probably much to the surprise and perhaps the unhappiness of the DA, the Assistant Attorney General in charge of the White Plains office, John Fine, was very interested. He took the case, and soon Fine and Greenberg were working full blast on the investigation.

John Fine Investigates

Tall, thin, almost gaunt in appearance, John Fine looked to some like a very intense Ivy League lawyer. In fact, he was educated at Notre Dame Law School and served as an assistant district attorney in Manhattan for a short time before moving to the Organized Crime Task Force. In addition to his legal training, Fine had studied biology as an undergraduate and was an accomplished marine biologist, photographer, and writer. He came to the investigation, therefore, with a background in both science and law. John Fine understood better than most the environmental dangers of toxic waste dumping.

In the summer of 1979, Fine sent a memorandum to Ralph W. Smith, Jr., Acting Deputy Attorney General in charge of the Organized Crime Task Force. Fine summarized some of the conclusions and many of the leads he had been pursuing. He noted work had begun in October 1977, attempting to determine the extent of criminal activities in the operation of landfill sites in Rockland County. Subsequently, the investigation had moved to other New York counties and also to certain sections of New Jersey.

Fine first reported on the status of the Penaluma landfill in Warwick, New York. Several witnesses, he wrote, had seen toxic wastes dumped at Penaluma, which was only licensed to accept solid waste. Confirmation of these reports came from interviews with both a landfill employee and the owner of the property itself. An investigation of the manifests filed by many of the owners and managers of the tankers revealed an interesting pattern of deception at the Penaluma site. The vast majority of toxic waste dumped at this New York landfill was generated in New Jersey. On the Jersey manifests it was indicated that disposal would be made in Warwick, New York. Yet the same haulers filed papers with the

New York State Department of Environmental Conservation stating that disposal would be made at approved sites—Penaluma, of course, not being one. The reason for the discrepancy was clear. As far as New York State was concerned, there was no approved toxic waste landfill in Warwick. As far as New Jersey knew or perhaps cared, the toxic wastes were being disposed of out of state, beyond their jurisdiction.

The principal carters dumping toxic materials at the Penaluma landfill were All County Environmental Service Corporation and several affiliated companies, including All County Service Corporation, All County Industrial Waste Disposal, Round Lake Sanitation, I.S.A. in New Jersey Inc., Tri-State Carting Corporation, and L-J-M Enterprises, Inc. It was, of course, an All County tanker that Greenberg and Liguori had watched disposing of some liquid back at the Dexter dump several days after it was closed. The parent company, All County Environmental Service Corporation, was owned by Louis J. Mongelli, Frank Cappola, and John Cappola; the letters L-J-M were Louis J. Mongelli's initials. The Penaluma landfill itself was leased by the town to an outfit called Grace Disposal and Leasing, Ltd., whose principals were also the Cappolas and Mongelli. They leased the landfill, falsified New Jersey manifests and New York DEC documents, and simply poured toxic wastes into Penaluma.

In order to show Smith the way in which these men, supposedly key members of organized crime syndicates, operated, Fine recounted an interview conducted by the Organized Crime Task Force investigators. They had interviewed Larry Capasso, owner of Capasso Sanitation, which had recently won the bid on a contract to service the Mid Hudson Psychiatric Center, a state institution in Orange County. In a story reminiscent of the Sorgine affair, Fine stated that Capasso had underbid three other carting companies for the contract. One of the losing companies was Round Lake Sanitation, also one of the toxic dumpers at Penaluma. Capasso was soon visited by Robert Mongelli, who worked at the Penaluma landfill and, according to Fine, was the son of Louis Mongelli. The purpose of the visit was to threaten Capasso and his family in the interests of Round Lake Sanitation. Fine added: "Larry Capasso also indicated that he had sought to purchase the entire business of Hathaway Sanitation, but was told by Mr. Hathaway that he did not want to sell. Shortly thereafter, Mr.

Hathaway sold the business to Round Lake Sanitation for a price that was reportedly substantially less than the value of just his two trucks."

Fine then turned to the situation in Goshen, Orange County, New York. Again he found dumps owned by and receiving toxic wastes from organized crime companies. This time the cast of characters included Thomas Milo, Nicholas Milo, Vincent Milo, Alfred DeMarco, and Vincent DeVito. The Milos and DeVito operated the Al Turi landfill, and, along with DeMarco, several carting companies, including Suburban Carting out of Westchester County and DV Waste Control. This last firm was linked, by Fine, to another company known as Dutchess Sanitation Service, owned and operated by Matthew Ianniello and Joseph, Michael, and Vincent Fiorillo, all reportedly organized crime figures.

One other sanitary landfill located in Goshen which Fine investigated was owned by the county. Operating this landfill was Victor B. Bucksted, the county engineer. Bucksted, together with a man named Dewey Parr who owned the Merion Blue Grass Sod Farm in Orange County, had started a company called the Nutrient Uptake Corporation. This company, for a fee, accepted septic and sludge wastes that were to be land-spread and then used as fertilizer at the sod farm. The New York Department of Environmental Conservation gave permits to several municipalities and to DV Waste Control to haul septic waste and sludge to Nutrient Uptake which, of course, was on the same property as the sod farm. Fine wrote: "Recent observations of the Merion Blue Grass Sod Farm by OCTF investigators revealed numerous tank trucks from All County Environmental Services Corp., as well as other marked and unmarked tank trucks, have disposed of their contents at the sod farm." Much of the obviously toxic waste was dumped into a canal alongside the property that flows into the Warkill River. Fine added that All County was not one of the firms with a DEC permit to operate at the sod farm.

In the final section of his memorandum, Fine discussed the criminal background of some of the principals operating in Orange County. Thomas Milo was associated with the Genovese–Tieri gang. Milo, he stated, had been directly involved in illegally influencing the awarding of private carting contracts. Milo's partner in the Al Turi operation, Vincent DeVito, was also reportedly involved in organized criminal activities, and had been previously convicted of loan sharking. Fine pointed out that Matthew Ian-niello had long been associated with organized crime activities, and that in the 1960s he had conspired to bribe police officers and of-ficials of the State Liquor Authority. Police intelligence held that Ianniello had interests in a plethora of concerns—Manhattan bars and restaurants in the midtown area, the cigarette vending and jukebox industries, a talent agency providing topless and nude dancers, as well as a hidden interest in two gambling casinos and the largest loan-sharking operation in New York City. Ianniello's partner in Dutchess Sanitation, Joseph Fiorillo, had a number of arrests for felonious assault, including one against a state police officer.

According to an earlier police intelligence survey of Ianniello's activities, it appears that Dutchess Sanitation was also the part-owner of a firm called Consolidated Carting Corporation, which was incorporated in the winter of 1975 and located in midtown Manhattan. Dutchess Sanitation owned 100 percent of the stock of Rodan Industries, which in turn held 100 percent of the stock in Consolidated. The president of Dutchess Sanitation was Vincent Fiorillo, and the other stockholders and members of the board of directors included three other Fiorillos and Matthew Ianniello. Im-mediately after Consolidated was formed, several midtown topless bars changed carters from a firm called Two Star Carting to Consol-idated Carting and paid approximately four times more per month for the service.

When all was said and done on this part of the investigation, Fine had linked together about a dozen major organized crime fig-ures and seventeen carting and landfill companies. From Yonkers stretched the influence of the notorious Nicholas Ratteni, the orga-nized crime garbage czar from Westchester County first identified by the McClellan committee back in the 1950s, a partner with Thomas Michael Milo in another local garbage business. Ratteni's grasp extended from Yonkers into Mamaroneck, New York, to the Al Turi Landfill Corp., and a number of related ventures in the overwhelmed Goshen, New York, and finally to a disposal outfit with offices in both Carmel, New York, and Danbury, Connecti-cut. Tied in with these Ratteni interests were several of the Milos and their brother-in-law Vincent DeVito. Also joining up at various points and in various firms were Joseph Zingaro who, unknowingly of course, had set the inquiry into motion, Matthew Ianniello, and the Fiorillos. Police intelligence also firmly believed that the notorious Mario Gigante, whose brother some thought was the current leader of the Genovese–Tieri crime syndicate, was behind the activities of the Mongellis and their companies such as All County Environmental and Round Lake Sanitation. Clearly, the top leadership of New York organized crime was directing the industry, just as it had been doing for decades.

In investigating toxic waste disposal, John Fine had run into many of the major New York mob figures. He had discovered this particular cabal had spread its control from Yonkers, just north of New York City, to an area bounded roughly on the north by Interstate Highway 84, on the south by the New Jersey border, and on the east by Danbury, Connecticut. Running through the heart of this arc is the Hudson River. Organized crime was indiscriminately dumping toxic wastes in and around the countryside in one of the loveliest sections of the Northeast—part of the celebrated river and mountain land so vividly described by the marvelous early American writer, Washington Irving.

Return to Ramapo

Even though Ramapo had drawn so much attention, the state regulatory agency reponsible for monitoring environmental problems was not, by any means, working full tilt to make sure the public health was protected. Greenberg made many requests to the Department of Environmental Conservation that went unheeded. He did, finally, get one of their engineers, Richard Gardineer, to go with him to the dump. Upon arrival, he instructed Gardineer to take samples of the leachate running out of the dump into a brook feeding into the Ramapo River, water which eventually became part of the drinking supply for northern New Jersey. Gardineer refused, saying it didn't appear as though the leachate was causing any problems. Yet when Greenberg provided several jars in which to take samples of the run-off, Gardineer refused to put his hands in the water. Faced with Gardineer's squeamishness, Greenberg took the samples himself and gave the sealed jars to the engineer. Later, when Greenberg asked for the test results, he was told, somewhat disingenuously, that since neither preservatives nor refrigeration was used to protect the samples from contamination, they could not be tested.

The investigators did try to keep close watch on Carmine Franco. They noted that "large quantities of garbage were going into the Ramapo dump, and that New Jersey trucks were on the site almost all the time." This was contrary to the town's contract, which allowed only Ramapo garbage to be dumped at the landfill. Carmine Franco had at least two garbage hauling companies feeding the dump: Sal-Car Carting, and Carmine Franco, Inc., which was located in Hillsdale, New Jersey, just a few miles east of the Garden State Parkway, which directly connects with the New York State Thruway and Route 17. It is a short ride from Hillsdale to Ramapo.

The Franco operation in Hillsdale was something known as a waste transfer station, which means that garbage trucks from different garbage companies come to the site to dump. Scavengers then go through the material, removing whatever may have value. What remains is compacted and compressed to be made smaller and placed on another truck. Among the trucks seen by Greenberg and the other investigators at Ramapo were those that picked up the compacted garbage from New Jersey. Law enforcement officials became convinced that toxic waste was being compacted and disposed of as compressed solid waste.

Carmine Franco and his operation in Ramapo was the center of a pinwheel in which various points on the wheel's edge represented many organized crime interests. Unfortunately for Franco, he was ultimately unable to deliver what the other organized crime figures involved in toxic waste disposal needed at that time. The point was to secure a large landfill to take the place of Kin-Buc after its closure in 1976. Ramapo was to be the new Kin-Buc. But with all the heat brought to Ramapo, it simply couldn't function in the wide-open manner necessary. Hence, the dispersal to small, often private landfills or sod farms in Rockland and Orange counties became necessary.

This dispersal of effort in the illicit dumping of toxic wastes was not only seen in the New York State operations of the Mongellis, Milos, and others; it was also happening in New Jersey, and Carmine Franco and his New Jersey organized crime associates were right in the middle. Not that there was a great distinction between New York's organized crime and New Jersey's. The principals for the most part operated within the entire metropolitan region. Indeed, some extended their reach throughout the country. But

Franco was, at the time of his takeover in Ramapo, the president of the New Jersey Trade Waste Association. Thus, while the 1980 New Jersey investigation into the Association named Franco and many others as conspirators in the solid waste industry, John Fine and the New York Organized Crime Task Force investigation showed that many of them were also major handlers of toxic waste.

Carmine Franco, incongruously tattooed on his left bicep with a picture of two hearts and the saying, "Love Mom & Dad," put a man named Anthony Rizzo in charge of daily operations at Ramapo. Rizzo was also a carter working out of Wayne, New Jersey, using the corporate name of A. Rizzo Carting, Inc. By tailing Rizzo, John Fine learned he was connected to a toxic waste hauling firm called Sampson Tank. Further surveillance of Rizzo and Sampson Tank led to the discovery of major toxic waste dumping by an outfit named Chelsea Terminal on Staten Island, New York. All this took a fair amount of time and a great deal of effort as the information was laboriously gathered through surveillances and the checking and cross-checking of corporation papers, police intelligence reports, toxic waste manifests, and so on.

It may well be that if Franco could have secured Ramapo without any untoward publicity, then Rizzo and other organized crime toxic waste dumpers might not have needed Chelsea Terminal and several other so-called toxic waste facilities located along the Arthur Kill—a body of incredibly polluted water which separates New Jersey from Staten Island. Indeed, if it hadn't been for the publicity and corresponding effort of Greenberg and Fine, organized crime would probably have put together the toxic waste trade association they had planned for in 1977.

Given, then, the very tenuous nature of the New York–based investigation, it is extremely interesting and important to note that around the same time Ramapo was becoming an issue, about September, 1977, New Jersey was receiving information that organized crime figures were involved in the chemical hauling industry. The material came during the tail end of an undercover operation in the port area of Newark, New Jersey, called Project Alpha. This operation had been going on since December, 1974, and lasted almost three years. Perhaps the most interesting part of Project Alpha was its growing concentration on the man to whom Carmine Franco supposedly reported—Tino Fiumara. Born in 1941, the handsome and exceptionally strong Fiumara was a rising power in organized

crime. Where Project Alpha led after the rather remarkable prosecution of Fiumara and some of his associates was to the 1980 New
Jersey Trade Waste Association investigation. Where it might have
gone, however, was to the heart of organized crime's involvement in
toxic waste.

Project Alpha and the Case of Tino Fiumara

Alpha began when Patrick Kelly, a successful, well-to-do businessman with interests in real estate and construction, came to the
attention of law enforcement for some very shady business deals.
Kelly was given the choice of prosecution or becoming an informant. He chose the latter, and began working first with the New
Jersey State Police and then with the FBI. Kelly was the key to
Project Alpha because he was personally close to several organized
criminals in the Newark Port area. Among his friends were Dominick DiNorscio and members of his branch or "crew" from Angelo
Bruno's Philadelphia-based crime syndicate, including DiNorscio's
son Giacomo (Jack). With an introduction from Kelly, the New
Jersey State Police were able to infiltrate the Newark underworld
and place a detective, Robert Delaney, undercover.

Not only did Kelly have close friends in organized crime, but
more importantly for Alpha, the DiNorscios were in prison while
the operation was going on. Dominick DiNorscio was serving a
relatively short sentence (two to three years) in the federal prison
in Lewisburg, Pennsylvania, for the interstate transportation of
stolen property, while Jack was in the New Jersey State Prison at
Rahway serving eight years for bookmaking. The DiNorscios had
requested that Pat Kelly manage their criminal affairs in their behalf while they were away. But management of the DiNorscios'
activities was not left solely to Kelly's direction. He had to report
on a regular basis to another organized crime figure named John
Simone, one of the leaders of the Bruno syndicate. Simone's major
responsibilities, though, were in South Florida and he himself
lived in Hollywood, Florida. It was obviously difficult for Kelly and
Simone to get together, so Simone asked Tino Fiumara to watch
Kelly and the management of the DiNorscios' interests.

According to testimony presented by undercover Detective
Robert Delaney, Tino Fiumara was at that time a member of the

Vito Genovese crime syndicate, primarily based in New York. The fact that the Bruno syndicate members turned to a Genovese member indicates, Delaney testified, that crime syndicates are not nearly as highly structured as popular writers and the media have suggested. Syndicate lines are constantly crossed in the pursuit of profit, and partnerships between members of different syndicates are often the case. It is also true that Tino Fiumara enjoyed a great deal of esteem then, and had a well-earned reputation for ruthlessness.

The first phase of Project Alpha started with the undercover operatives, Detective Delaney and Pat Kelly, engaged in the operation of a small trucking business in the Newark area. Soon, it became apparent a larger enterprise was both possible and necessary. Delaney testified: "As long as we were perceived as small time operators, that was the kind of criminal behavior we would be exposed to." Therefore, they started the Alamo Transportation Company in December, 1976, which was located in Jersey City, less than ten miles from the Port of Newark.

With Alamo on line, the operation expanded and soon involved another group or crew from the Genovese syndicate headed by John DiGilio. The contact developed through an introduction of the undercover operators to Anthony Pacilio, who was a member of DiGilio's crew. The importance of this contact became evident when Alamo Transportation was chosen as the "house trucker" for the Frigid Express Company, which shipped high-quality frozen foods. Frigid was itself controlled by a major organized crime figure named Pasquale "Patty Mack" Macciarole, one of the leaders of the Genovese syndicate. Sometime, then, in the spring of 1977, Alamo was working with the DiGilio crew from the Genovese syndicate, the Fiumara crew from the same syndicate, and, from the beginning, with the DiNorscios from Angelo Bruno's syndicate.

The entire run of Alamo Transportation lasted less than a year. As part of the investigative procedure, Kelly—whose undercover role was central because he was Alamo's manager—would summarize activities at Alamo on almost a daily basis. His summaries would often be corroborated by wiretaps and other forms of electronic surveillance. What follows are snatches of summaries:

February 12, 1977: Tony Tomay of A. Tomay and Sons stopped by the office. We went over the cinders and the Nigerian and

Ghana project. Also a project that he is bidding on concerning the removal of garbage from the Parsipanny area and Tony was telling me that in the specs that bid this job, they had a specific location to dump the garbage and a price set in the bid. This would also, according to Tony, figure that somebody writing specs had made the deal with the Dump It people. . . . The gimmick was proposed to me down in Florida at Johnny Key's office, that's Johnny Simone, the captain in Angelo Bruno's outfit, approximately a year and a half ago. You'll find that this has been done in Florida, Chicago and St. Louis area plus the Philadelphia area and other parts of New Jersey.

February 28, 1977: Arrived at the Alamo office approximately 7:30 AM. Received a phone call from Tino Fiumara stating that he would be over. . . . Tino arrived at approximately 9 AM. Along with him was Larry Coppola. Tino asked me to get an insurance certificate for a demolition project in Newark on 108 Walnut Street. The company is taking the building down and the company owned and negotiated with Tino Fiumara. The company's name is T & J Landfill.

March 8, 1977: Approximately 8:45 Joey A. and Richie Mazziotti arrived. General discussion of this goes in on the 9th for the State Valley Sewerage job removal of garbage. Tino has a man known to me only as Teddy [who] has a landfill. We are joint venture in this with Mazziotti, Tino and Joey A. This is the removal of garbage from the Passaic Valley Sewerage Authority to Lansdale on Doremus Avenue. This again, the Alamo will actually act as a conduit for funnelling the money to the joint venture. The trucks we will rent from Joe Ryan and Roy Stocker out of Pennsylvania. They are with Russ Buffalino. The loading of the material will be done by the general contractor. The dump area will be with Tino's man so our position will actually be for some credibility and funneling of the money. . . . The various companies we've bidded the project to are in the file. To name a few, A. Tomay and Sons, connected with Louie Larasso; Wigglesworth, connected with Andy Gerard; Gadon, connected to Tumak; so we have some good in here besides dealing with some of the larger contractors . . . we will be in a position to follow the misappropriation of federal funds. Also with a couple of projects coming up in Jersey, the same position far as the councilman, Henry Martinez, he is a councilman in Newark. . . . Also Martinez claims according to Pacilio he is in the position of controlling some of the dumping areas in Newark and also in a position to get some HUD work.

March 10, 1977: Received a call from Tino about 7:45 AM requesting that they needed a 977 track loader on the 108 Walnut Street demolition job, T & J Landfill. . . . While in my office, one of the garbage men known to me as Joey came around noontime and him and Johnny DiGilio went outside for a few minutes alone. . . . Tom Shear and Jack Bernstein came from meeting with the Lehigh Valley people in New York and the Pennsylvania railroad. . . . The persons attending this meeting were Bob Hess, myself, Joey A., Richie Mazziotti, Tom Shear and Jack Bernstein. They came back with some answers on Lehigh Valley, the state property down at the power plant, the landfill on Doremus Avenue also asked us if we were interested in taking a landfill in the Bronx. This project in the Bronx, although might not be of interest directly to our project but is certainly controlled by somebody in oc [organized crime].

March 16, 1977: Joey A. and Richie Mazziotti arrived. Tom Shear was in the office. They had an appointment with Mr. Boham who is in the real estate department of Conrail and works under Clark. The purpose of the meeting was to look at the landfill that Clark wants us to take over in the Bronx and to arrange to take the landfill on Doremus Avenue in Newark. Joey A. proposed to Boham that we would work a joint venture with him and whoever was on his side make them a partner on a per yard or per ton basis of any items that were brought into the landfill. . . . Joey suggested we have somebody to handle the payoffs to Boham because I seemed a little wishy washy.

March 23, 1977: I received a call from Tino Fiumara to see if I could get a couple of dump trailers for Walnut Street. I spoke to Teddy Fiore. He's Tino's man at T & J.

March 28, 1977: Received a phone call from Tino . . . he was at T & J landfill. . . . Joe arrived with Mike Coppola . . . Joey A. arrived . . . Neil Pacilio and Anthony Pacilio stopped in to join this meeting. We called Jack Bernstein in reference to the fill of the Lehigh Valley and the Doremus Avenue landfill. Also the Oak Island project. Tom Shear called a couple times. Joey A. suggested that Bernstein and Shear were trying to go around our back . . . Tino made the suggestion that maybe a gash in the back of Bernstein's head would straighten him out.

March 30, 1977: Tino stated that so far with the landfill operation on Port Street, that they've done over $200,000 worth of business.

April 6, 1977: Shear also stated that Joe Barber is now the head of the Environmental Protection and is a close friend of John Molineri from William's office. Joe Barber is quite a mover. He was one of the directors of the Heritage Bank, Morristown, also a director of Chatham State Bank in Chatham.

April 19, 1977: Went over to Brooklyn, Bernie Panton from Blanford Construction. This is the contractor that is doing one of the smaller jobs in Passaic County Sewerage Authority. . . . From there I met Dom Mirabelli . . . and proceeded to Trenton. There we had a meeting with Joe Barber, head of the EPA concerning the T & J landfill. We also had a meeting with [the] head of the PUC. Meetings went pretty good . . . the person that called Barber was a guy named Lamb that works for Williams.

May 11, 1977: I left the Alamo about 8:15 and went up to the Bella Vita Restaurant for a meeting with Pat D'Amore from Falcon. . . . While we were there we met Bucky Jones and Robert Caravaggio [ph.] and his brother Emil. . . . Bucky is looking to get us some accounts out of Mennen and Faberge and a few places around the Morristown area. Bucky also approached me on pulling some chemicals in a few of the plants up there. He said he was approached. They will pay $50 a barrel. That will be approximately $8000 a trailerload.

May 12, 1977: Chemical material that was pulled out by Fiore with our truck and his trailer came from a plastic factory. Further details on that.

Unfortunately, there were no further details on this or any other toxic waste matter connected to Fiumara. The issue of Fiumara's involvement in waste, both solid and toxic, did come up, however, several years later following his trial for extortion and racketeering which stemmed directly from Project Alpha. In the fall of 1979, at the U.S. District Court in Newark, New Jersey, Judge Herbert Stern conducted the sentencing hearing for Fiumara and the other Alpha defendants—Michael Copolla, Jerry Copolla, and Larry Ricci.

Mark J. Malone, the Assistant U.S. Attorney, questioned Patrick Kelly about Fiumara's arrangement with public officials in Newark to remove fill and dump garbage. Kelly testified that a deal had been worked in August or September, 1977, with the Housing Authority in Newark whereby clean fill was to be removed and replaced with decomposed garbage from the Passaic Valley Sewerage Authority. Fiumara's representative in this was Larry Ricci.

This particular deal led to another one equally as lucrative. The clean fill from the Newark site fit the need of a "builder or contractor, Malanga, who was doing an extension of Route 280, I believe, in Harrison." This arrangement was negotiated by Larry Ricci, Michael Copolla, and Patrick Kelly representing Fiumara and two other organized crime figures, Joe Pulverino and James Palmieri. At a meeting in the Plaza Diner in Secaucus, New Jersey, Pulverino and Palmieri were offered a "third of the profits if they would get Malanga to go along." They did, and the deal was set at a tavern with Fiumara and Malanga meeting to iron out details. The only subsequent hitch developed when one of Malanga's supervisors responsible for the fill objected to what was going on, and was beaten up at the construction site. The beating was carried out by one of John DiGilio's associates, Johnny "Moose" Marone, and succeeded in silencing the supervisor.

Patrick Kelly also related the story of Anthony Tomae, who wanted to sell his garbage route. Kelly testified he was instructed to tell Tomae to contact Carmine Franco about the sale of his garbage route and to remind him they were aware he had joined the New Jersey Trade Waste Association, "controlled by Mr. Fiumara for the purpose of building up a route and getting a price for it." There were several meetings over Tomae's route, at least one of which was held in Carmine Franco's Bergen County office and attended by, among others, Ernie Palmeri, business agent of Local 945.

After discussing the Tomae matter, Prosecutor Malone asked a series of illuminating questions which brought together Fiumara's activities in both solid and toxic waste.

Q. Mr. Kelly, in addition to the incident involving the sale of the garbage route by Anthony Tomae, did the defendant Fiumara have any other active participation in the solid waste disposal industry?

A. Yes, sir. . . . He controlled the dumping sites for garbage waste.

Q. How did he control those dumping sites?

A. Through the garbage association and other associates of his.

Q. Were they able to set prices or inflate prices for the cost of dumping?

A. Yes, sir.

Q. Also did they eliminate competition in the garbage industry?

A. Yes, sir.

Q. Was Mr. Fiumara in any way involved in chemical dumping?

A. Yes, sir.

Q. Would you tell us his involvement in chemical dumping?

A. Through T & J Landfill and Theodore Fiore. . . . Dumping illegal chemicals at T & J Landfill.

Q. During the period you were associated with Airport Landfill was there any discussion about using Airport Landfill for illegal chemical dumping?

A. Yes, sir. . . . That once [the] landfill was properly graded and had enough material, where it could be concealed, it was considered dumping chemicals there.

No one could conceivably fault the detective work on Project Alpha. Difficult, extremely demanding, carried out faultlessly, the operation was a police triumph. New Jersey State Police officers Delaney and the Alpha tactician, Richard "Dirk" Ottens, executed one of the most brazen and productive penetrations of organized crime in recent times. The activities of Fiumara and his friends, the Copollas, Ricci, and others, were closed down—no small accomplishment.

But lying there in raw form was the matter of toxic waste disposal. Running through the hidden microphones and onto the
tapes placed around Alamo and sometimes worn by Patrick Kelly,
contained in the summaries recorded and transcribed, was the undeniable case that mobsters were in the lucrative business of toxic
waste disposal. This was the message hidden, undeveloped,
missed, misunderstood, or deliberately avoided in Project Alpha.
It was directly stated on May 11, 1977, when Kelly reported that
Bucky Jones (Emil Caravaggio's nickname) had approached him
"on pulling some chemicals" out of the Morristown area. Most intriguingly, Kelly said that Jones was approached, we may presume
by generators, who would pay $50 a barrel, about $8,000 a trailer,
to get rid of the stuff. The real question is why that intelligence
material was allowed to be ignored by those in positions of responsibility. No one involved in Project Alpha—with the shining exception of Detective Dirk Ottens—followed the Alpha leads into toxic
waste matters.

Yes, New Jersey's Division of Criminal Justice did set up various special units to investigate both the solid waste and toxic waste
industries, with exceptionally heavy funding from both the EPA
and the Department of Justice's Law Enforcement Assistance Administration. And they did investigate, indict, and ultimately prosecute people involved in both solid and toxic waste disposal. But
what they didn't do, unless they were dragged into it by media
publicity and/or congressional pressure, was to follow those leads
which could have revealed how organized crime operated in toxic
wastes, how much toxic waste was being illegally dumped by organized crime haulers, how many phony toxic waste facilities were
run by organized crime people, and how many public officials were
partners in these matters. Who was Joe Barber, after all? Did those
in charge of the Division of Criminal Justice know that one of the
state's allegedly key environmental officials had been named in the
Alpha investigation and appeared to be in bed with racketeers?
Perhaps they did and responded to it by stating—as Edwin Stier,
the head of Criminal Justice, reportedly did—they were not in
business to investigate sister agencies, which meant the Department of Environmental Protection and the Public Utilities Commission.

For New Jersey, the full scope of the many problems associated
with toxic waste disposal would not become apparent until well

after the end of the Alpha probe. Before it was absolutely clear New Jersey's official agencies needed scrutiny, it was already obvious that New York was in deep trouble. The years of ultimate revelation would begin in 1979, when those first pioneers— Grogan, Greenberg, and Fine, shortly to be joined by Detective Ottens—would find out precisely how tough it was to know too much about organized crime's involvement in toxic waste disposal.

Cooper Funding and the FBI

In the meantime, however, there was one other law enforcement agency developing pertinent information on how organized crime operated in the waste industry. Again, ironically enough, this investigation began on January 19, 1976, barely a month after Grogan was first alerted to look into the affairs of Cimino and Zingaro. On that day, a confidential source advised Special Agent Albert L. McGinty of the FBI that "Cooper Funding, Ltd. and its subsidiary companies are engaged in arranging fraudulent leases for several LCN affiliated companies." In FBI terminology, LCN stands for La Cosa Nostra, one of the more popular terms to describe some of the major organized crime syndicates. The Cooper leases of interest to the FBI were, in essence, rental agreements on equipment primarily used in the waste industry, including trucks of various types and sizes. It was the first day of summer, 1976, when subpoenas were issued to Bankers Trust Company and Chemical Bank for their records of any leases arranged by Cooper Funding since the end of 1973. Another subpoena was issued to the National Bank of North America in October, 1976, asking for the same type of material.

In between the two subpoenas, a list of some of the leases arranged by Cooper Funding was provided to FBI agents by another source. Among the companies working with Cooper Funding from just this first list were the following:

American Disposal, Inc., Elizabeth, New Jersey
Stamford Carting Co., Cos Cob, Connecticut
Sanitary Haulage, Inc., Brooklyn, New York
P.G.S. Carting Co., Inc., Amityville, New York
C.G.I. Sanitation, Corp., Amityville, New York

Capital Contractors Container Service, Little Ferry, New Jersey

Rapid Disposal Service, Inc., Middlesex, New Jersey

Peter U.S.A. and Son (doing business as Industrial Disposal Service), Elizabeth, New Jersey

Middlesex Carting Co., Inc. Boundbrook, New Jersey

Continental Carting Co., Inc. New York City

V and V Carting Co., Inc., Parisppany, New Jersey

Carmine Franco and Co., Inc., Hillsdale, New Jersey

Rutigliano Carting, Brooklyn, New York

Schaper Disposal Works, Inc., Midland Park, New Jersey

G and R Carting Corp., Brooklyn, New York

Marangi Brothers, Inc., Spring Valley, New York

C. Pyskaty and Sons, Inc., Secaucus, New Jersey

Michael Morea (trading as Coney Island Rubbish Removal), Brooklyn, New York

Middlesex Carting Co., Inc., New Brunswick, New Jersey

Rosedale Carting Corp., Brooklyn, New York

Gary Corigliano (doing business originally as Limited Carting Co., then United Carting), New Rochelle, New York.

According to records on file with the County Clerk's Office in Brooklyn, Cooper Funding Ltd.—located at 215 Moore Street in Brooklyn—was in business to manufacture, sell, lease, or purchase refuse containers, trucks, truck chassis, compacting equipment, and other items relating to the waste industry. The articles of incorporation were signed by Mel Cooper, living in Lawrence, New York. Also occupying the same premises were Cooper Tank & Welding Co., and the Kleen-Tainer Corporation.

The nature of Cooper Funding's operations, stated an assistant vice president of Banker's Trust Company, was to act as a "lease broker," which "entered into equipment leases with companies in need of financing and then arranged financing for the purchase of the equipment with banks or other lending institutions by selling the lease paper at a discounted rate." If things went right, the bank received the lease payments directly from the company and Cooper Funding took a commission on the deal. However, Banker's Trust notified the FBI it would not deal with the Cooper Funding Ltd. lease paper, although it would do business with

Cooper Tank & Welding. Apparently, someone at Banker's Trust, at last, had grown wary of Cooper Funding paper.

Nevertheless, Banker's Trust had already arranged financing for many disposal companies based on equipment leases that companies from Connecticut, New York, and New Jersey held with Cooper Funding or Cooper Tank & Welding. An officer in the installment loan division of Banker's Trust stated that loans from the bank to or through Cooper Funding were backed by these leases. Astonishing as it may seem, certainly in retrospect, the method used by the bank to verify real equipment was received was to call up the companies on the phone.

The fact that Cooper was dealing in phony equipment was graphically described to FBI agents in the fall of 1976, when the owner of a New York firm told of the cushy arrangements between Cooper Funding and the National Bank of North America. Desperately in need of capital for his business, the owner, through the advice of his accountant, ended up dealing with one of Cooper Funding's salesmen, Joseph Gluck. The upshot of the arrangement ultimately worked out was the owner's receiving a loan for equipment which he would then be able to use as security for the loan. The owner was given an invoice, written on the letterhead of Galaxy Industry, reflecting the order of a jet brine injector costing $25,000. The Cooper salesman told him the bank officer handling the loan knew no equipment ever changed hands. And, indeed, no such equipment existed.

Cooper Funding was primarily but not exclusively in the business of loan sharking, according to the investigators. Basing the operation on either totally false leases of nonexistent equipment or leases based on wildly overvalued and usually unnecessary machinery, money was put on the street. Exactly one year after the FBI's initial probe began, it received information that Mel Cooper had another subsidiary company operating out of the same address. This one was Cooper Equities, run by Mel's nephew, Vick Goldfarb, which handled second mortgages and equipment liens.

This same informant also relayed information on Cooper's "advanced payment" schemes with various companies located from New York to California. One example concerned "a lease arranged by Phil Gentile, Cooper Funding, between George Briggerman, Briggerman Sanitation, Los Alamitos, California (Seal Beach Section), and an unknown bank for 10 garbage trucks on November 1975." Briggerman was told that the bank had approved the leases (one for each truck) and he then made the "initial advance payments to Cooper Funding." In fact, the bank had turned down the leases, and Cooper Funding basically told Briggerman to forget the money he had advanced.

Late in the spring of 1977, the FBI through a former employee of Cooper Funding learned a bit more about the organized crime connections running rampant through the various Cooper companies. The source reported that Mel Cooper and other members of the Cooper family associated in the Cooper businesses worked with Joe Lombardo and Sal Sindone, an officer in the Brooklyn Trade Waste Association, in putting together "shylock" loans for a number of garbage companies. Both Lombardo and Sindone were reportedly two notorious organized crime figures. Others involved in what was undoubtedly a tremendous loan-sharking enterprise included Tommy Lombardi, whose restaurant on Avenue X in Brooklyn played host to almost monthly meetings of metropolitan area organized crime figures, among them Tino Fiumara and the undercover informant Patrick Kelly.

Even before finding out about Lombardi (who it appears brought Cooper together with Sindone and other organized crime members and was related to the notorious Carmine Persico), the FBI agents presented their evidence to an Assistant United States Attorney. The U.S. Attorney stated the facts available at the time indicated bank fraud and possibly mail fraud on the part of Cooper Funding. The Bureau was also confident that Sindone; Andrew G. Mannarino, former president of Intercontinental Leasing; and Jerry D. Fillippo, formerly of Domler Leasing and currently with a business known only as P.F.R.D., were in the loan-shark conspiracy.

Interestingly enough, although the FBI had no idea what P.F.R.D. was back in 1977, it turns out that the company acted as a consultant for firms in the toxic waste disposal business. About four years after the loan-shark conspiracy was presented to the U.S. Attorney, an indictment was returned in Newark charging the Taylor Pumping Service and P.F.R.D. with obstruction of justice, conspiracy, and perjury. Two Taylor officers and the head of P.F.R.D. had allegedly burned, buried, and destroyed documents subpoenaed by a federal grand jury investigating the illegal disposal of chemical, industrial, toxic, and hazardous wastes at the Lone Pine Landfill in Freehold, New Jersey, by Taylor. Taylor Pumping had been dumping at Lone Pine since the mid-1970s, and company officials hastily destroyed the records in 1981 when New Jersey's Hazardous Waste Task Force and federal authorities finally moved against them. The head of P.F.R.D. was Francis J. Perno, who was charged with directing at least some of the record burning, and with perjury. There was no mention of Jerry D. Fillippo, but it is clear that P.F.R.D. was involved in "consulting work" with toxic waste disposal firms. This means, of course, that those racketeers allegedly behind the massive Cooper loan-sharking conspiracy must have had their hands on other toxic waste disposal companies.

By August 9, 1977, the FBI had collected information on 453 leases involving Cooper Funding or one of the other Cooper companies. The overwhelming majority were for firms in the private sanitation industry, including a large number of licensed toxic waste haulers. So many were known or suspected organized crime companies that it would be pointless to list them all. They reached from the Northeast to southern California to Florida, although the bulk came from New York and New Jersey. One might imagine, in fact, that those carting firms involved with Cooper in southern California and Florida represented the long reach of Northeastern organized crime figures to control private carting and the seemingly inevitable toxic waste hauling associated with it through loan sharking.

Some of the leases do deserve comment, nevertheless. For instance, the Duane Marine Salvage Corporation, located in Perth Amboy—that enticing toxic waste facility watched by John Fine and later by Detective Dirk Ottens—had lease number 75103, which had been vended by Oil Truck Tanks from Patterson, New Jersey. Solid Waste Management Systems, Inc., from Bayside, Long Island, was the vendor of several Cooper leases to private carting firms such as Central Salvage in the Bronx. Others that showed up in the Cooper list were Anthony Rizzo Carting, with the vendor being Telstar Sanitation out of Brooklyn; Round Lake Sanitation, the vendor for a lease held by the Di Bella Sanitation Company of Park Ridge, New Jersey. Carmine Franco & Co. had two leases, one less than Miele Brothers with theirs running through a Springfield, New Jersey, firm called Quality Products,

Mel Cooper's own Kleen-Tainer Corp., and American Sanitation Equipment. Not to be left out, Andrew Fiore & Sons (which included Fiumara's man Teddy Fiore) out of Kearny, New Jersey, held two leases, while the Mongelli Carting Co. in the Bronx had one, the vendor being the King Con Trucking Corporation in Elmont, New York.

There is hardly a significant carting firm linked to organized crime through the many investigations noted in the preceding chapters that did not do business with Mel Cooper. Indeed, there is hardly one which didn't have its hands in the toxic waste business so far reviewed that wasn't a Cooper client or partner. Put all that together, and one wonders why the FBI investigation into the affairs of Mel Cooper was put into an almost interminable holding pattern. And this despite the intelligence which kept coming in, some as recently as the summer of 1983. Current information logged in by the FBI tags Cooper as an organized crime loan shark still working out of Cooper Funding along with other figures such as John "Sonny" Franzese, Joseph Schipani, and Carmine Lombardozzi. By 1983, the Bureau had learned that Franzese and Schipani were what they called "business associates" of Cooper Funding, while Lombardozzi reportedly owned a partial interest in the company. In addition, Mel Cooper at some point had started yet another lending business called Resource Capital Group. (At long last, Cooper was indicted by federal authorities in New York in the summer of 1984, charged with loan sharking.)

Closing the Circle

The Mel Cooper operation was strongly reminiscent of earlier banking and lending scams of organized crime. Cooper's activities followed—although not quite directly—the severe problems experienced by four New Jersey banks, including the State Bank of Chatham and the Bank of Bloomfield discussed earlier. In the case of the Bank of Bloomfield, its use by organized crime started in 1974, when Robert Prodan became president. Almost from the day that Prodan took office, he started embezzling funds through a complicated plan involving fraudulent lease loans, a deal he worked with a man called Arnold Daner, who ran his own finance companies.

It is in the deals between Prodan and Daner that the antecedents of Mel Cooper's unique contributions to organized crime truly lie. Prodan and Daner had worked together in the past when both were accountants with an obscure commercial finance firm. As soon as Prodan took over at the Bank of Bloomfield, the two men and several organized crime associates planned to "loot the bank" in the following way: "Criminal elements obtained $6 million worth of leases from Daner's firms, which in turn the Bloomfield Bank bought for $4.7 million in cash, for the right to collect the remainder and the interest. But millions of dollars in equipment the leases supposedly purchased didn't exist and what did was inflated in value." For the bank, it was absolutely disastrous. The loans defaulted and there was no property to foreclose on. The result was a takeover by the Federal Deposit Insurance Corporation.

Mel Cooper ran a more diversified, and therefore more sophisticated, operation. He worked his many deals with a variety of banks, never intending to loot any. His deal wasn't a bust-out, but an ongoing loan-sharking scam for just about the same customers formerly counting on both Chatham and Bloomfield. Cooper Funding and its subsidiaries did basically what Daner and Prodan had been doing: phony lease deals for organized crime figures prominent in the waste industry. But by not tying himself to one or even two banks, by spreading his paper around, Cooper protected both the operation and its legitimate agents in the banking world.

From the State Bank of Chatham and the Bank of Bloomfield to the many interests of Mel Cooper lies one of the least known routes of organized crime's financial control over the waste industry. And if Patrick Kelly's summaries are correct, there is even a figure who may symbolize many of the disparate links that allow organized crime to poison and prosper. On April 6, 1977, Kelly reported his meeting with Joe Barber, "head of the Environmental Protection." Barber, politically connected, was quite a mover, wrote Kelly, a "director of Chatham State Bank," the same bank busted by Ernie Palmeri's certificates of deposit secured by his union's pension and welfare fund.

From the political law firms, the regulatory agencies, the banks, and those financial intermediaries in the shadowy world of lending and leasing firms, came men delighted to serve and prosper with the Fiumaras and Francos and Lombardis and Lombardozzis and Mongellis, who saw the waste industry as one large ripe, if not rotting, plum. Arrayed against them in one of the most unlikely one-sided battles were men like Grogan, Greenberg, and Fine, whose stubbornness even in the face of increasing hostility from their own was not always sufficient. In his despair of running alone, John Fine, with some help from Hugh Kaufman, the EPA maverick, turned to Congress and the New York State Senate Select Committee on Crime.

5

Problems in the Northeast

FROM THE RELATIVE OBSCURITY of Rockland County, the issue of toxic waste and organized crime slowly came to Congressional attention. In the fall of 1978, John Fine, casting about for support in what was now a lonely battle, contacted Hugh Kaufman, the manager of the Assessment Program in the Hazardous Waste Management Division, EPA. Kaufman had testified on October 30, 1978, before the Subcommittee on Oversight and Investigations of the Committee on Interstate and Foreign Commerce. Fine, reading the news stories of the hearing, felt Kaufman might be able to help.

Kaufman's testimony was something of a revelation. He described the EPA's bungling, if not subversion, of RCRA, and the Agency's apparent disregard of the public health and welfare. The House subcommittee had met to explore why the EPA delayed promulgating RCRA regulations and what action it had taken on known dangerous toxic waste sites. It was clear congressional impatience with the EPA was rising. Congressman Albert Gore, Jr., of Tennessee pointed out that the deputy administrator of EPA, Barbara Blum, had in the spring assured a House Appropriations Subcommittee that the EPA was right on schedule with its regulations. That claim, of course, was utter nonsense and brought the entire issue of the EPA's priorities into serious question. Gore asked: "What has EPA been doing since the RCRA was enacted?"

Kaufman had some answers. First, he reported he had no budget and a staff of one. Yet he was responsible for managing the Assessment Program, acting as the "agency focal point and lead office in assessing the environmental and public health damages caused by hazardous waste management practices," and assuring

133

that the public and responsible officials were notified of imminent or potential damages from hazardous waste sites. He stated, unequivocally, that EPA policy was to refrain from discovering new hazardous waste sites that threatened the public health, and to minimize the dangers of hazardous waste disposals. The following is an exchange between Gore and Kaufman.

> *Gore:* How many sites such as Toone, Tenn., Love Canal, the other sites that have been mentioned, how many of them are there in the country? Do you have any way to estimate?
>
> *Kaufman:* To be honest with you, there have to be thousands when you look at the amount of hazardous wastes that have been generated every year. But without going and doing assessments and going through regional files and working with the States, I have no way to make even a close estimate of how many thousands.
>
> *Gore:* And you have been ordered not to look closely?
>
> *Kaufman:* Yes, sir.

The Toone, Tennessee, situation, which was especially important to Congressman Gore, was further illuminated by several memos introduced into the record. The first came from Kaufman and told of well contamination, which area residents were convinced came from a nearby dumping ground—"the "burial site of drums containing thousands of gallons of chemical pesticide wastes from the Vesicol [sic] Chemical Corporation in Memphis." Kaufman called for a vigorous and immediate EPA investigation. It was not to be. Kaufman's staff of one, Virginia R. Thompson, reported her attempt to gather information on the problem from Jim Scarborough, the EPA officer in Region IV that covered Tennessee, was thwarted. Scarborough told her, in effect, to butt out.

Thereafter Kaufman received a memo from John P. Lehman, director of the Hazardous Waste Management Division, which chided him for seemingly bypassing Lehman, then informed Kaufman that "a direct link to the Velsicol hazardous waste disposal site apparently has not yet been established," and stated finally it was EPA policy to wait for the results of a study of the problem conducted by a firm hired by Velsicol. In questioning Kaufman about these matters, Congressman Gore stressed: "I want to avoid using language that is too harsh. But when you have 16 million pounds of exotic chemicals a quarter of a mile from wells that have the same chemicals in them, it would seem not too difficult a task to make that connection." Kaufman replied that he agreed, which was why he had attempted to bring pressure on the region.

Reading about Kaufman's forthrightness, and the issues raised by the subcommittee, John Fine went to Washington seeking an ally. While knowing nothing in particular about organized crime, Kaufman as well as others in Washington had suspected mob involvement because of the garbage connection to the toxic waste disposal industry. Kaufman and Fine met and talked of their common problems in investigating toxic wastes, and of their suspicions of corruption. The result was that Kaufman agreed to alert, as best he could, the appropriate congressional committees to the link between organized crime and toxic waste disposal. Through the many subtle undergrounds of Washington life, information steering would begin.

Congress Gears Up

About five months after Fine and Kaufman met, the first tentative fruits of their collaboration appeared. The Subcommittee on Oversight and Investigations, now chaired by Representative Bob Eckhardt of Texas, held a mammoth hearing on hazardous waste disposal stretching from March 21 through June 19, 1979. Eckhardt opened the hearing by referring back to the October session when the subcommittee learned that the EPA would be very late in promulgating its mandated regulations, that the EPA had been very tardy in its actions concerning imminent health hazards caused by improper toxic waste disposal, and that RCRA did not address abandoned or inactive dump sites. Finally, even though the hearing record was almost two thousand pages long, very little of it was devoted to organized crime.

Throughout the long new sessions on Hooker Chemical and Love Canal, on the Valley of Drums in Kentucky, on Browning-Ferris and the appalling mess it had created by mixing toxics and waste oil in Texas, the theme of EPA failure and corporate mismanagement in hazardous waste disposal was constantly in the foreground. Lurking in the background, at least when the subcommittee turned to New Jersey, was the question of organized crime.

During the first week of April, 1979, attention focused on the problems experienced by New Jersey and Pennsylvania. Congressman Gore, while pursuing information about a site in Elizabeth, New Jersey, asked Dr. Ronald Buchanan, the chief of the Bureau of Hazardous Wastes in New Jersey's Department of Environmental Protection, whether the DEP found organized crime involved in the management of the site. Buchanan's reply was that current investigations were being conducted by the New Jersey Attorney General's Office along those lines, but that he was not aware of all the details. Gore pressed him: "But it is your understanding that there are some significant connections between organized crime and at least some of the people who have been responsible for this site." The answer was "It appears that way."

Taking over from Buchanan at this moment in the hearing was Dr. Glenn Paulson, the Assistant Commissioner for Science and Research of the DEP, who said the possibility of organized crime involvement was being "aggressively investigated" by New Jersey's Division of Criminal Justice and the U.S. Attorney for the state. Gore pressed once more: "But to what extent has organized crime become involved in the disposal of chemical waste within New Jersey?" The most that Paulson could offer to this was "some involvement."

A little more than a month later the subcommittee called James W. Moorman, an Assistant Attorney General in the U.S. Department of Justice working out of the Division of Land and Natural Resources, to testify about how the staff of his Department saw their legal authority in the enforcement of disposal laws. After reviewing some of the statutes, he went on to add that the major problem EPA had was a serious lack of trained investigators. Serious, indeed, he added, because the Department of Justice simply deferred to EPA as the primary investigative agency. "Tough law enforcement investigators" were needed by the EPA, Moorman pointed out, because they may well be dealing with organized crime, which is "involved with the midnight dumping of hazardous waste and toxic substances into our rivers, our lakes, our wetlands, our sewers or any other convenient location." Moorman was only partially correct when he placed organized crime within the orbit of midnight dumping. Nevertheless, a Justice Department official stated on the record that one of the problems associated with the policing of toxic waste dumping was the presence of organized crime.

The questioning of Moorman on the issue of organized crime was not over with his statement. When committee member Matthew J. Rinaldo of New Jersey had his turn, he brought up once again the Elizabeth toxic waste facility, Chemical Control Corporation. Rinaldo noted that the previous month Dr. Paulson from the DEP had admitted some organized crime influence at the Elizabeth dump site. Yet, he added, the current director of Criminal Justice in New Jersey, Edwin Stier, had "denied that organized crime played any significant role in the illegal disposal of hazardous wastes." The questions Rinaldo had for Moorman were the following: "Is organized crime involved in that site? Is there going to be an intensive probe by the Department of Justice, or are they going to rely on the State?"

In responding, Moorman reported this particular site was "one that is so dangerous that we had a ridiculous moment in which one EPA official prohibited anyone [from going] on the property to sample it because it was too dangerous for any human being to step on it." Nevertheless, he had no knowledge of organized crime's involvement there because that was not his jurisdiction. Moorman also could not answer what action, if any, the Department of Justice was planning for that site. He advised the subcommittee members to turn for their answers to the Criminal Division of the Justice Department and the U.S. Attorney in Newark.

It wasn't that Moorman was unconcerned. Far from it. His answers reflected the uncertainty and confusion in federal law enforcement circles when it came to toxic waste disposal. He described the sporadic efforts of the Department of Justice and the rather incredible catch-22 situation represented by Justice's deferring to the EPA when the EPA had virtually no investigators capable of handling serious crime matters, especially when powerful crime syndicates were involved. Moorman's testimony was remarkably similar, in fact, to the statement given several years before by Peter Preuss of New Jersey's DEP when the EPA was canvassing public opinion. From the vantage point of the Land and Natural Resources Division of the Justice Department, the problem—as Moorman saw it—was either the first or second most serious environmental issue in the nation. Like Preuss before him, he added: "We really do not know what the dimensions of the problem are. . . . We do not know where the millions of tons of stuff is going. . . . We do not have the capacity at this time really to find out what is actually happening."

The Jersey Scene

Congressional probing of organized crime involvement in New Jersey raised the issue of just exactly what was going on in the Garden State at that time. Certainly Representatives Albert Gore and Matthew Rinaldo had information that criminal syndicates were operating some of the toxic waste facilities in New Jersey, and their questions about the Elizabeth site indicated rather specific knowledge. The most interesting response to this line of inquiry, however, came from Edwin Stier, New Jersey's director of Criminal Justice, who had earlier downplayed organized crime influence and involvement.

Stier, of course, was more than well aware of organized crime's domination of the solid waste industry in New Jersey, but he seemed very hesitant to make that same claim for toxic waste disposal. However, only a few months after the congressional hearing, he was ready to admit the possibility of organized crime's involvement in toxic waste disposal was much more likely than he had either thought or reported in the spring. In the fall of 1979, Stier gave a talk at a conference in Arizona where he admitted that unless something was done quickly, "traditional organized crime elements" would for all intents and purposes control the hazardous waste industry.

From not playing any significant role in the industry in the spring to imminent takeover by the fall, it seems either organized crime had moved with incredible rapidity or Stier had learned a great deal more in the few months between the hearing and the conference. But whatever new knowledge Stier had gathered over the course of 1979, it was, with the exception of the Arizona meeting, always presented in such a manner as to minimize organized crime's significance. The Arizona remarks were wildly out of character for Stier, who soon after picked up where he had left off in the spring. As far as toxic waste was concerned, Stier, it seems, played the role of a damage control officer. The unwritten but clear policies of the Division of Criminal Justice during his tenure were to concentrate on the midnight dumpers, play down the role of organized crime, prosecute minimally, and especially avoid investigating allegations of corruption in sister agencies—which in New Jersey meant the DEP and Public Utilities Commission.

The changing, indeed contradictory, statements made by Stier in 1979 probably stemmed, in part at least, from the actions and activities of a state trooper investigating toxic waste disposal in New Jersey. Playing somewhat the same role in New Jersey that John Fine did in New York was New Jersey State Police Detective Sergeant Dirk Ottens. Unlike the New York officers Grogan, Greenberg, and Fine, however, Ottens was something of a latecomer to the field of toxic waste disposal. It wasn't until 1979 that he began to investigate actively. But what he turned up in a very short period of time deeply worried many people in New Jersey. Until Ottens's findings could be understood, there was both confusion and fear among New Jersey officials.

Ottens had enjoyed a distinguished career with the state police when he became involved in investigating toxic waste disposal. During the early 1970s he had coordinated an organized crime investigation in Bergen County which was extremely successful, and was then placed into Project Alpha. So strong were his administrative skills and presumably his judgment that Ottens was effectively put in charge of the operation. He set up a fake engineering consultant firm in downtown Newark which allowed undercover detectives like Bob Delaney to avoid reporting to any police station. From this vantage point, Ottens supervised the daily operations of the investigation, determining, in addition, its overall direction and ultimate outcome. Following the wind-up of the undercover phase of Alpha, Ottens still managed the many spin-off investigations generated by Alpha intelligence. In fact, it is likely that information generated by Alpha concerning U.S. Senator Harrison Williams was one of the major reasons why Williams was targeted in ABSCAM. For his work on the Alpha project, Ottens was given a meritorious service award.

The intelligence gathered by Patrick Kelly in the last phase of Alpha concerning chemical dumping and landfills did not escape Ottens's notice. He realized Fiumara and his associates were trying to control the landfills, and he believed an anti-trust case based on the monopolization of landfills might have been constructed. Ottens was also aware that the organized crime figures working through Alamo claimed to have people placed in both the Public Utilities Commission (PUC) and DEP. What Ottens didn't know, however, was the Division of Criminal Justice was conducting its own investigation into the solid waste industry. As soon as word got out about what Project Alpha was generating in the way of intelligence, representatives from the Division of Criminal Justice came in and took away all the information concerning waste matters. This neither bothered nor seemed strange to Ottens at the time. He subsequently learned that Criminal Justice had two task forces working on waste matters. The first and primary one was working the garbage industry, the New Jersey Trade Waste Association, Carmine Franco and the others. The other one was directed toward toxic waste. The Division of Criminal Justice kept these two task forces separated from each other for quite some time.

For Ottens, the toxic waste problem appeared in the somewhat squat form of William Carracino, former president of Chemical Control Corporation, the infamous toxic waste disposal site in Elizabeth, New Jersey, which had sparked the congressional questions about organized crime. When Ottens met Carracino, the ex-president of Chemical Control had been convicted of toxic waste dumping and was awaiting the outcome of an appeal of his conviction. Carracino claimed he had been framed and there was corruption in the DEP. As a result of these charges, the state police had directed Ottens to interrogate Carracino.

At the initial interview, there was a great deal of mutual suspicion. On Ottens's part, it was hardly novel that a convicted criminal claimed innocence; nevertheless, some of what Carracino was saying intrigued him. Ottens also realized he needed an education on the whole subject of toxic waste and the various regulatory and Criminal Justice activities and relationships in the field. Even though he had some rough ideas coming out of Project Alpha, Ottens knew he was far from well prepared. With the help of Carracino, he began to learn what was going on. At that time, Ottens was not attached to any particular state police field office nor to any particular investigation, so he had the rare luxury of conducting a free-lance investigation.

Carracino took Ottens to a number of toxic waste facilities, including landfills and companies like Chemical Control, and pointed out the many methods used by toxic waste dumpers. Also, Carracino reported almost all his facts and suspicions about corruption and collusion between the industry and the regulatory agencies to Ottens. It wasn't long before Ottens centered his attention on one particular facility, Duane Marine, out of the many illegal ones around. His selection came partly from working with Carracino and partly because he had already begun to develop other informants in the field. He learned, for instance, the business agent for Duane Marine Salvage Corporation in Perth Amboy had a brother who was the chief of investigators for the Division of Criminal Justice. Moreover, Ottens discovered Duane Marine's legal affairs were handled by the Wilentz law office, a very powerful and prestigious Newark firm headed by David Wilentz, who would be described by *New Jersey Monthly* in September, 1981, as "the legendary 86-year-old former attorney general, former Middlesex County Democratic chairman, and father of Supreme Court Chief Justice Robert Wilentz."

There were several reasons for Ottens to target Duane Marine. He had found out from informants other than Carracino that Duane Marine was picking up hazardous materials from the Ford Motor Company's assembly plants in Mahwah and Metuchen, New Jersey. And even though he had an informant who told him to be careful in speaking with Ford's environmentalist, he went to the plant hoping to learn something. He met with the environmentalist, who was very gracious and apparently open. While discussing toxic waste matters with him, Ottens was also allowed to go through some of Ford's files dealing with their garbage contracts. One item in particular caught his attention: a letter which stated that Ford's Mahwah plant had six categories of waste, five of which were toxic. The letter went on to state that Ford Mahwah had contracted with the Louis Mongelli firm—I.S.A. in New Jersey, Inc.—to haul all of its waste. Furthermore, it was clear in the communication that Mongelli had subcontracted some parts of the job to, among others, Duane Marine. In some detail, the letter noted Duane Marine would haul the paint sludge and other flammable toxic waste from Ford to its site for incineration. But Ottens knew Duane Marine did not have an incinerator, that it was nothing more than a transfer site.

Trying not to arouse the suspicions of anyone at Ford, Ottens took copious notes on the material from the files dealing with the volume of waste generated by Ford and supposedly handled by Duane Marine. He then requested permission to take some of the material back with him to the state police barracks. The environmentalist asked instead for a more formal request and they parted on friendly terms. Leaving Ford, Ottens knew one thing that substantiated some of Carracino's allegations: Duane Marine was a phony outfit with heavy political clout and a fat contract from Ford which it could never legally fulfill.

He then went to the Division of Criminal Justice to report on what he had found and to suggest a plan for proceeding. Rather surprisingly, he was told that there was no need for him to work the corruption angle. The Division of Criminal Justice would assign a Deputy Attorney General and one of its own investigators to probe any possible official corruption in the Duane Marine case. Nevertheless, Ottens still tried to get a formal request from Criminal Justice to secure the Ford–Mongelli letter and the rest of the pertinent documents. It was during this time, around May, 1979, Ottens finally learned that New Jersey had a special toxic waste task force. The Deputy Attorney General who ran most of the toxic waste investigations was Gregory Sackowicz, and he was targeting Duane Marine. Also that spring, Ottens became aware that one of Duane Marine's officers was Harold Kaufman, who came out of Statewide Environmental, a Macaluso outfit which, for Ottens, meant probable organized crime involvement. Ottens had no idea that Kaufman was then an FBI informant.

Even though he was told not to bother investigating corruption in the toxic waste industry, especially if it went to the DEP, Ottens still pushed to get a subpoena from Criminal Justice for the Ford material. He kept after Sackowicz for it, and finally, after three months of trying, succeeded. By this time he had a partner, Detective Jack Penney, assigned by the state police to work with him. Ottens and Penney trooped up to Ford's Mahwah assembly plant with their subpoena expecting, at last, to secure the Mongelli letter and other significant documents. Once again they were graciously received by Ford's environmentalist and the files were opened. But there was no Mongelli letter, and the Ford man swore there never had been one. However, while going through the cabinet where it had originally been, Ottens saw a note indicating a very recent phone call from a Deputy Attorney General. Asked what that referred to, the Ford official stated that he had been called the day before by a Deputy Attorney General who said that two state troopers would be in the next day with a subpoena. The call was placed, they were told, to make sure that Criminal Justice had the right address.

Ottens and Penney continued to work Duane Marine, keeping a written record of the strange mishaps. Both detectives were also scrupulous in reporting to their superiors in the state police. Sometime in the summer of 1979, though, another curious event occurred. Ottens reported to his major, Anthony DiMassi, almost in passing, that he was convinced organized crime was into toxic waste. The major virtually exploded in rage, screaming at Ottens that he was wrong. Meanwhile, the information on organized crime and corruption kept rolling in through surveillances and informants from truck drivers to corporate officials in the petrochemical industry who told them, "in the dark," that it was too big, too powerful to stop. With the major's outburst in mind, Ottens and Penney wisely decided to play it very close to the chest and wait until they had a complete case. Then, they would walk in to the major and the task force people from Criminal Justice and hand it over.

Ottens's surveillance of Duane Marine had taken several different directions even before Penney joined him. He learned early on, for instance, that Sackowicz and his team had already been conducting an on-site investigation and had supposedly photographed operations at Duane. Ottens requested the pictures and after a long wait was given permission to look at them. What he found was dismaying, to say the least. The pictures revealed nothing; they were taken from such a distance that it was impossible even to make out license plate numbers on any of the vehicles. In addition, no tails had been set up to follow trucks and cars leaving the grounds. Naturally enough, Ottens went to work himself. With a zoom lens on his camera, he took pictures of toxic waste dumping and of cars and trucks on the grounds with all the identifying marks clearly visible.

At one point in this earlier phase of his work, Ottens observed and photographed a tanker pumping liquid waste into a roll-off filled with garbage. Not knowing exactly what to do beyond documenting this exercise, Ottens watched the roll-off being loaded onto a truck, which started down the road from Duane Marine and headed for a nearby landfill, called the Edgeboro Landfill, located in East Brunswick, New Jersey. Ottens followed and was surprised to see the police from East Brunswick stopping the truck for a motor vehicle inspection. It turned out that one of the local officers, Jerry Greenley, was deeply troubled by what he believed was toxic waste dumping at the landfill, so he and a local fire inspector were checking entering trucks. Ottens pulled off to the side and identified himself to Greenley. He told Greenley what he had seen going on at Duane Marine and they both decided to call the DEP and have them inspect the truck's contents.

Before Greenley called, Ottens noticed liquid dripping from the roll-off. Finding a clean container, he collected a sample, although he had no clear idea yet of who would do an analysis. Ottens next decided to play it both safe and cagey. He told Greenley that he was going to disappear from the scene before the DEP arrived. Greenley agreed not to mention his presence, and Ottens moved to a point where he could watch what happened. Sure enough, the DEP arrived and one of the inspectors went around the truck looking here and there. After both the truck and DEP left, Ottens asked Greenley what went on. It turned out the DEP inspector had ordered the truck back to Duane Marine and told Greenley that an accident in loading had taken place. That was all.

Meanwhile, Ottens had his sample—about three ounces of a foul-smelling liquid. He then called Sackowicz, told him what he had done, and indicated he was interested in having the sample analyzed. Sackowicz replied that he would get back to him. Soon, Sackowicz called to say that the DEP had advised that the sample was too small, they weren't interested. Not satisfied with this and already suspicious of the DEP, Ottens took the sample to the Shell Oil Company, which agreed to run various tests in one of its New Jersey laboratories and even sent part of the sample to Houston for further analysis. The results were absolutely conclusive, indicating the presence of toluene, ether, and numerous other toxic substances. Before leaving Shell, Ottens also was able to scrutinize the company's files on oil spills and related matters. With permission from the plant manager, he found in the very detailed records only a few minor spills and that Shell had never contracted with Duane Marine to handle them. This last point would become important a bit later, when Ottens saw that Dr.

Ronald Buchanan, the DEP hazardous waste chief, had given written permission to Duane Marine to dump into the Edgeboro Landfill twenty cubic yards of oily sludge supposedly picked up from Shell.

Slowly but surely Ottens was building a case on Duane Marine. Eventually he put all his data in order and went to Criminal Justice requesting a search warrant. Ottens knew they had to get Duane Marine's records on what was coming in and where it was going. Furthermore, he stated that informants were telling him Duane Marine was protected by the DEP, that when inspectors from DEP went to Duane Marine, it was warned in advance, and Duane Marine would take out the hose it had running into the sewer system and put it into a 250,000-gallon tank on the site.

Reluctantly, Criminal Justice agreed to work up a search warrant. Early on the morning it was to be served, Ottens interviewed the president of Duane Marine and accompanied him to the facility. The president told Ottens he was out of his league, that he wouldn't get anywhere, it was too big. By the time they reached the site, Criminal Justice had moved in with the search warrant. Walking through the grounds, Ottens now noticed several leaking drums whose contents were flowing into a waterway. This, he knew, was a definite violation of the Water Pollution Control Act and he insisted that DEP be notified immediately.

Having worked on this problem for a while now, Ottens had come to know some of the DEP field inspectors, and four of them quickly arrived. They put on their protective gear and walked through the site noting numerous violations, including the storage of flammable material on the second floor. (A finding that became more significant later when Duane Marine burned to the ground.) It was primarily the records that Ottens wanted—and there were plenty of them. Criminal Justice, however, didn't appear to be nearly as interested, and initially made no attempt to seize them. So, Ottens told the inspectors he would call for a state police van and take them himself. Criminal Justice quickly changed its mind and the records were carted off. Ottens was promised that Criminal Justice accountants would review the material, conduct an audit, and give him a copy of everything relevant.

The very next day, Ottens received a call from one of the DEP inspectors who had been at Duane on the raid. The caller told him that when they returned to their Trenton headquarters, they were ordered by their supervisor, Karl Birns, never to go back to Duane Marine.

The summer and early fall of 1979 proved to be one of those peculiar and revealing times when a number of disparate events finally begin to draw together. Ottens was contacted by one of the staff investigators from Congressman Eckhardt's Oversight Subcommittee. The subcommittee wanted Ottens to provide some assistance; he said he would be pleased to do so but the subcommittee would have to make its request to his superiors in the state police. On the last day of July, John Fine sent his memorandum on organized crime dumping toxic wastes in Orange and Rockland counties to his boss, Ralph Smith, Jr. In the first week of August, the special grand jury investigating organized crime's activities in Rockland County issued its report, which was extraordinarily damning of the ineptitude of the regulatory agencies, but unfortunately thin when it came to organized crime.

Dirk Ottens also met with the New York Organized Crime Task Force people, led by John Fine, around this time. It wasn't that the embattled finally sat down, compared notes and bruises, and reached some ultimate conclusion. They were—as law enforcement officers always are—wary of one another, careful about revealing too much of their own investigations, and professionally unwilling to share informants. Nevertheless, they were able to pass to one another some very important information and leads. They also were glad to know someone else was working organized crime and toxic waste, even when they figured out what the political costs for their careers might be. In one sense it appeared to them uncanny that the Yonkers and Rockland County investigation led to Chemical Control and Duane Marine while Ottens, beginning from another angle entirely, ended up at the same places. In another sense, however, they were all experienced in working organized crime cases, and they were not at all surprised to find just how tight the web of syndicate control was woven between the two states.

In the midst of these developments, one of Ottens's informants from Duane Marine called him. In essence, the informant said his cover was blown and he was leaving the state before he got killed. Ottens told him it was impossible, that he had protected him; the only thing Duane Marine had was the search warrant, which revealed nothing. The sole document which could have led to the informant was Ottens's affidavit, given before a judge in complete privacy and, Ottens believed, disseminated to no one. As he tried to console the very worried informant, he thought to himself that the man was obviously becoming paranoid.

Less than two months later, Ottens learned to his horror that the informant had been right. While executing a search warrant on the New Brunswick office of a notorious toxic waste dumper and organized crime figure, one of the officers looking through a brief-case turned to Ottens and handed him a copy of his Duane Marine affidavit. Ottens immediately confronted Deputy Attorney General Gregory Sackowicz, who angrily stated he was going to call the deputy director of Criminal Justice and demand an internal investigation. Right then and there, Sackowicz called the deputy director, talked for a short time, and hung up. Ottens asked him what the story was. Sackowicz looked at him and quietly said: "Bob Winter gave it out." Robert Winter was the assistant director of Criminal Justice. Winter—for reasons never adequately explained—apparently gave a copy to Duane Marine's legal representative from the Wilentz firm.

The investigation of Duane Marine was by no means over, however. In fact, more and more information on its criminal activities would surface in several different contexts. Harold Kaufman would report on Duane Marine before the Congressional subcommittee; John Fine would report on Duane Marine before a New York State Legislative Committee also probing organized crime's activities in the toxic waste field; and the state of New Jersey would indict Duane Marine and several of its officers for conspiracy, creating a nuisance, and violation of the Water Pollution Control Act. But before all this took place, in 1980 and 1981, several other important events were to transpire, which brought even more disturbing revelations about the links between organized crime and the disposal of toxic waste.

The End of the Line in Rockland County

While Detective Sergeant Dirk Ottens was just entering his years of turmoil, John Fine and the OCTF investigation were reaching the end of the line. The special grand jury's report of

August, 1979, merely brushed the issue of organized crime. It emphasized, instead, the politics of pollution, and the incredible failures of both the EPA and the state's Department of Environmental Conservation. The design of this report was intentional, guided by a strategy which called for the special grand jury to report first and foremost on the regulatory horror in the state. For those who didn't know the full extent of gross ineptitude in the state of New York, the report was a potential revelation. Unfortunately, its impact was very limited. Simply put, those in positions of responsibility were not moved to act much more vigorously in the field of toxic waste than before. With the exception of the New York State Senate Select Committee on Crime, chaired by State Senator Ralph Marino, no other state body seemed to care very much.

The special grand jury did more than report, of course. The main job of a grand jury is to indict, and under the direction of John Fine, the grand jury returned indictments against Albert Franco, Howard Stevens, Carmine Franco, Salvatore Franco, Tobias DeMicco, Jr., Anthony Rizzo, James Hickey, Matthew Hickey, and two of the Franco companies—Sal-Car Transfer Systems and Sorgine Construction Services of New York, Inc. The second company was, of course, bought from Eugene Sorgine under very exceptional circumstances right after the torching of Sorgine's house. On January 17, 1980, in the Rockland County Court, Judge Harry Edelstein, having heard various defense motions to dismiss the indictments, agreed. Judge Edelstein found almost all the grand jury testimony was inflammatory, and the charges against the defendants incorrect for the most part. In one example, the court found the state had "misapplied the New York forgery statute." And in another, concerning the use of the Ramapo landfill without payment by Carmine Franco and the others, Judge Edelstein decided the state's charge of grand larceny was wrong, that "such conduct on the part of defendants, if proved beyond a reasonable doubt, constitutes the crime of theft of services." The indictments were dismissed, although not without a great deal of talk, according to later testimony given before the New York State Senate Select Committee on Crime on July 8, 1980, concerning Judge Edelstein's alleged friendships with key Ramapo officials and off-the-record conversations with District Attorney Gribetz.

Within six months John Fine was fired. His last word on toxic waste and organized crime while still Assistant Attorney General in charge of the White Plains OCTF office came on March 14, 1980, in front of the Subcommittee on Toxic and Hazardous Substances of the New York State Standing Committee on Environmental Conservation. (Even here, there were rumors claiming that Fine's testimony was delayed until after Anthony Scotto, the organized crime leader of the Brooklyn waterfront who conspired along with Tino Fiumara and Michael Clemente to control waterfront businesses, was tried. Some have speculated that the major reason for the suspected delay in calling Fine before the subcommittee came from Governor Hugh Carey's office, which wanted some time to elapse between the trial and any new discussion about Scotto's organized crime associates, especially Fiumara. Astonishing as it may seem, Governor Carey had appeared as a character witness for Scotto.) Fine began his testimony by noting that many of the individuals and companies that he would comment on were the same as those involved in the ABSCAM corruption investigation. In particular, he pointed out that George Katz, an associate of Senator Harrison Williams and Newark Mayor Kenneth Gibson, was a partner with John Albert and Patsy and Frank Stamato in several companies that specialized in toxic waste dumping. Fine testified that these individuals and others turned up in his investigation into Chelsea Terminal on Staten Island.

Fine initially was drawn to Chelsea Terminal by tailing Anthony Rizzo from Ramapo. The trail led from the Ramapo landfill to an outfit called Sampson Tank to Chelsea. Now, Fine also told the state subcommittee there were other reasons to look at Chelsea. It seems in December, 1978, a conservation officer driving to work on Staten Island noticed some strange activities going on at a site owned by Texaco Oil and leased to the Positive Chemical Company. Further investigation by the officer uncovered a terrible problem of dumping. This, in turn, prompted the Department of Environmental Conservation to issue an abatement order. Noxious wastes were flowing into the adjacent marshland and Arthur Kill waterway. When the abatement order came through in 1978, Positive Chemical merely changed its name to Chelsea Terminal, Inc., and continued to receive millions of gallons of toxic waste. It is important to note that Positive Chemical and its successor company, Chelsea Terminal, were only permitted to act as a transfer station for pure chemicals destined for overseas shipment—not chemical waste. Among the individuals associated with Positive Chemical and Chelsea Terminal were John A. Lynch, Jr., the mayor of New Brunswick, New Jersey, and John Albert, who had a history of arrests for organized crime matters. Just the week before, Fine stated, John Albert, Bernard Gordon, and Joseph Lemmo, Jr., had been arrested in Middlesex County, New Jersey, "for crimes arising out of a massive organized gambling and narcotic ring."

Albert and Bernard Gordon also owned the Sampson Tank Cleaning Company, located in Bayonne, New Jersey, which had another corporate name—101 East 21st Street Corporation. Sampson Tank, according to Fine, hauled tens of thousands of gallons of toxic wastes to the Staten Island site. The trucks used by Sampson to haul the toxic waste were leased from another firm named Jersey Sanitation, Inc., owned by George Katz and other members of his family, Frank Stamato, and Patsy Stamato. Not only did Jersey Sanitation lease trucks to Sampson Tank, it also owned the Edgeboro dump, one of the favorite sites used by Duane Marine and other large-scale toxic waste dumpers.

Fine then pointed out that Jersey Sanitation and another company, J & B Disposal, were "for all intents and purposes" the same. The directors and officers of J & B were John Albert, the Stamatos, George Katz, and Eugene Conlon. Next, Fine introduced a 1974 newspaper article headlined "FBI Tapes Link Scavenger Operation to Reputed Mobster." The article stated, "Frank Stamato, Sr., a one quarter owner of the largest garbage combine in Middlesex County, has been linked in Federal Bureau of Investigation tapes to Geraldo Catena, reportedly a top figure in the Cosa Nostra." The report also mentioned both Jersey Sanitation and J & B Disposal, and added that information on these companies came from the part-owners and managers, John Albert and Eugene Conlon. That wasn't all, however. It turned out that Albert and New Brunswick's mayor, John Lynch, also owned the notorious toxic waste handling firm known as A to Z Chemical Company. Lynch was both part-owner and one of the corporation's officers. To make it complete, Fine testified that invoices clearly showed Sampson Tank hauling toxic waste from the A to Z firm (which was recently condemned) to Chelsea Terminal.

John Fine's testimony before this state subcommittee on the interlocking directorates and corporate veils used by organized crime figures and their associates in the toxic waste disposal industry was, in many ways, his last hurrah as a prosecutor. He was fired in the summer of 1980, and as far as prosecutions in New York were concerned, many of the most notorious dumpers undoubtedly breathed easier. Fine, however, was not yet finished as an investigator. The one New York State investigative committee which had shown interest, indeed commitment, to exploring the toxic waste issue was Senator Marino's Select Committee on Crime. John Fine was hired, on a temporary basis, by that committee as an investigator, and for another year pursued the organized crime dumpers. The committee, while not a part of law enforcement, did have the power of subpoena and a reputation for zealously investigating organized crime since the 1960s.

New York's Senate Select Committee on Crime was not exactly beginning from scratch when it hired John Fine. It had already started looking into the toxic waste problem in 1979, contacting Bill Carracino, John Fine (while he was still with the OCTF), and others who had knowledge of dumping in New York. In fact, the committee also hired Bill Grogan, on the same basis as Fine, when he retired from the Yonkers Police Department. By May, 1980, committee investigators were ready to hold the first in-depth state hearing on organized crime and toxic waste. Dramatically enough, it was in the midst of this hearing, which stretched over several months, that John Fine was fired. Fine was called as a witness scheduled to appear on July 8, 1980. Opening the morning session, Senator Marino announced that "Last Tuesday, July the 1st, while the Committee was conducting a public hearing into the illegal dumping of toxic waste in the Town of Ramapo, we were informed that Assistant Attorney General, John Fine, who headed the New York Metropolitan Region Office of the State Organized Crime Task Force, was fired from his job."

The beginning of the end for Fine came just a little earlier, when he was asked by his boss in the Organized Crime Task Force, Ralph Smith, whether or not he was talking with the New York State Investigation Committee, a state agency originally constituted to investigate organized crime and corruption. Smith was reportedly afraid that Fine was providing politically sensitive information on corruption to other state investigators. Perhaps at the request of other investigative agencies, Smith then asked him—so Fine testified—if the OCTF office was bugged. Fine answered with a question: "I asked Ralph Smith if he had participated in squelching the Orange County and Rockland County investigations." His answer, Fine testified, was "Yes." Smith then added, according to Fine, that "we wanted to stop the grand jury report too, but it had gone too far and we were afraid to stop it." Finally, on June 16, Smith reportedly made a surprise visit to Fine's office demanding to know if Fine was talking to investigators from Marino's Senate Select Committee on Crime. Fine refused to answer, and by the end of the month he was fired. He was given until the end of July to clean out his office. However, when Marino's committee subpoenaed his records, he was immediately locked out.

Of the many issues covered in this first Select Committee on Crime Hearing on Rockland County, most were concerned with politicians and their alleged influence on law enforcement and the activities at the Ramapo dump. One by one, the various people involved in the Ramapo affair, and the others mentioned before in Yonkers and Orange County, were called to give their versions of what had happened. Little new information was added to the existing record, but in John Fine's testimony on July 8, a new cast of characters was presented, which brought to the fore a number of insidious questions.

In an attempt to illustrate the "character of the unlawful conduct uncovered in Orange County," Fine played a tape recording of a conversation between the manager of an SCA facility and one of his drivers. SCA which stands for Service Corporation of America and is registered as SCA Services, Inc. is one of the three largest waste handling firms in the nation. One of the two individuals from SCA was cooperating with the investigation in Orange County and taped the conversation (which one has not been revealed):

> He must be doing all right. Whatever happened to ah, what the fuck was his name? Al.
> Big Al?
> Yeah, what was his last name? Bert? Albert? Al, Al, I can't remember his last name? Albert? Al, Al, I can't remember his last name.
> Brucio (phonetic)

What was it?

Brucio.

Whatever happened to him?

He's in his own business now.

Still? The honey wagons?

He's selling fucking drugs.

Really?

(unclear)

Does he do his shit legally or what?

I guess pretty much yeah.

Yeah? They're pretty strict I guess.

Yeah, you got to fucking be . . .

You got to what?

You can't fuck around like we used to.

What do you mean? As far as dumping shit anywhere?

Yeah. (unclear)

Used to, used to do some crazy shit huh?

Oh, man. . . .

What, right down the fucking hill there?

You know that little fucking lot on the side there?

Which one? There was a lot of little fucking,

Like ah, like when you first, pulled in the yard in the bottom
    there was like a empty lot there.

Where the old hospital is under the ground?

Yeah, yeah, yeah.

Yeah?

That fucking hospital there. You know how many fucking chem-
    icals we dumped down in that fucking hospital?

I have no idea.

Fucking,

Oh yeah?

Yeah.

Truckloads of this shit or what?

Oh yeah, a whole fucking load man.

It's right under the,

. . . get rid of the shit.

Yeah?

You don't know how long it took me and Jim to find a place. I
    said, Jim look at that fucking hole. That thing goes way the
    fuck down all ready. Yeah, yeah, yeah. So he backed over

there and run the fucking hose down to the fucking woods,
man. A whole fucking load man. Tell you some potent fucking shit man.

Yeah?

One minute (unclear) thing you ever see (unclear) made to
close that fucking business right down.

What kind of shit, what, what do you mean?

Chemicals.

I know chemicals, but I mean what, what's so bad that you
know, I mean the shit melt the rocks or what?

Acid, fucking corrosives, fucking dyes, and all kinds of shit,
man, I'm telling you.

Acids and corrosives? In that hospital?

Yeah. Fucking water, ah, main fucking ah, Harriman water
pump is right down the fucking across the street there.

Nobody ever checked it?

Well nobody I know. I don't know. Checked the water pump, I
guess. I guess they do check it. And that fucking, that water
well wasn't in, wasn't drilled through rock either. It was
fucking through gravel. It was through fucking sand and shit.

What do you mean? The one they're pumping on?

Yeah, that, that fucking ah,

That artesian well thing there?

Yeah.

That little red brick building?

Yeah. You know, if you could drill a well through rock or you
can drill a well through, you know, like just sand and,

Yeah, you don't have to go as deep.

Gravel and shit.

Yeah, right.

But that fucker wasn't through any solid rock.

So all the chemicals were flowin' right into the fucking thing?

Holy christ.

Holy christ.

Fucking Don came down there a couple of times and raised
hell about shit he'd seen (unclear) around that yard there.

But he never did anything?

No, he didn't.

Good old Don Hunter. Is he still there?

An yeah, I guess so. Jeff took, took care of him.

Oh yeah?

He took him there.

Kept the man happy.

Sure.

Paid him right the fuck off.

Yeah. He wouldn't say anything.

He's the kind of guy that wouldn't, you know.

We got, we got three fucking ah, three trucks down in Yonkers now. Fucking lease trucks, their own drivers.

What do you mean? Tractors?

Yeah.

Don Hunter was identified only as a public official in Orange County. Jeff was identified as Jeffrey Gaess, a proprietor of numerous toxic waste companies with ties not only to SCA but also to the organized crime figures who owned the Al Turi Landfill Corp. in Goshen, New York, and finally to the notorious Kin-Buc Landfill in New Jersey.

Going to Washington

A little over ten months after John Fine's testimony and firing, the House Subcommittee on Oversight and Investigations probed some of the SCA story during the course of a one-day hearing. By then, the chairman of the subcommittee was Representative John D. Dingell from Michigan. Congressional interest in SCA and related toxic waste and organized crime matters had been sparked considerably earlier than the May, 1981, hearing, however. Indeed, the Subcommittee on Oversight and Investigations held its first hearing devoted exclusively to organized crime and hazardous waste disposal on December 16, 1980, while still officially chaired by Bob Eckhardt of Texas. (In fact, Congressman Eckhardt had been defeated that past November in his bid for reelection, and chose not to attend the December hearing.) Both hearings focused on New Jersey. While the first of these sessions came more than eighteen months after the subcommittee's 1979 hearing, the members had not forgotten either their first probing questions about organized crime and toxic waste in New Jersey or the unsatisfactory response of New Jersey's officials.

One of the first moves made by the subcommittee in preparation of these new hearings had been to contact Detective Dirk Ottens. That initial contact was closed off when Bob Winter of Criminal Justice told Ottens he wasn't allowed to go to Washington to talk about anything. It seems the subcommittee's investigators had turned to New Jersey at that time because the state was supposedly moving vigorously ahead with a major investigation. Whether or not that was true, neither Ottens nor his partner, Jack Penney, had let up for a moment in pursuing their investigations. However, the peculiarity of investigating organized crime and illegal toxic waste disposal in New Jersey without help or encouragement was beginning to take its toll on both men.

The frustrations of Ottens and Penney were so great that one day in the summer of 1980, when they happened to be in Trenton, they decided to tell State Police Colonel Clinton L. Pagano what was going on. Before they could do that, though, their captain told them to write down their complaints and problems. Right then and there, he ordered them to sit down and write. They asked for permission to work on their statement at least overnight, which was grudgingly granted, and they returned to Newark, where they had a makeshift office, to prepare their report.

Back in Newark, Ottens and Penney documented their problems in investigating the toxic waste industry, pointing out the innumerable obstacles thrown in their path by the DEP and other agencies. They well knew that the standard operating procedures of the state police, in instances of criticisms of and complaints about other state agencies, called for action by the colonel. What they hadn't anticipated was that most of the action would be focused on them. It was skillfully done, with the end result that both detectives were left out in the cold. Their report disappeared in an endlessly trivial series of bureaucratic maneuvers, which effectively buried the questions and complaints raised by them.

The big chill came unexpectedly. The two men were sitting in their back-room office at the Turnpike station in Newark late in the afternoon on September 18 when a trooper came in and told them they had two visitors. Ottens walked out to the reception area, and the visitors identified themselves as congressional investigators. The investigators had not come to chat; they brought with them congressional subpoenas commanding all the detectives' records and their appearance as witnesses. Ottens told Penney to call their

superiors in the state police and tell them they had been subpoenaed. But it was now at least five o'clock and Penney was unable to reach any of them. While the detectives were gathering up
their records, including the summary to Colonel Pagano, Ottens
was asked where their secretary was. What secretary? was the answer. The one, the congressional investigators stated, written into
the grant.

The scene in the barracks was strange, to say the least. Other
troopers assigned to the station watched in stunned silence, unable
to believe what was going on. In the midst of this, Penney was
finally able to get in touch with their major, Anthony DiMassi.
Only Penney's end of the conversation could be heard, going
something like this:

"Yes sir, Major, this is Detective Penney here. Listen, we just
wanted to advise you that we have uh, two members of the U.S.
Congress here with subpoenas for all our records. Yes sir, Congress, sir. All our records and their subpoenas, and they've got
subpoenas for us to come down to Washington, too. Later, later
on. Well, the records? Yes, we keep our records here. This is our
office. Well, they already have them. Get them back, sir?"

With that, the congressional investigators stood up and reminded the detectives of congressional power and so on. Ottens
told them to calm down, the records were theirs now. And Penney
said into the phone: "We can't do that, they already have them."
Then he hung up and told Ottens they had to report to Trenton the
following morning.

The next morning Ottens and Penney reported to divisional
headquarters in Trenton. There, they were confronted by two
high-level state police officials and Edwin Stier in a very tense
meeting. It was clear to Ottens and Penney that there was deep
concern over what they might divulge in Washington about New
Jersey's inept investigation of toxic waste and organized crime. At
this meeting, Director Stier took the lead, reportedly stating that
they could destroy both him and the Division of Criminal Justice if
they talked about their leads on corruption. All that Stier had
worked for, all that he had built up, he said now was in jeopardy.
The apparent point of this meeting was to convince Ottens and
Penney to be as circumspect as possible when discussing New
Jersey's investigation in Washington.

One interpretation of exactly what Stier meant holds that the whole toxic waste investigation was itself grounded on an initial fraud, and this explained the missing secretary and other such inconsistencies. A reporter working on the case mentioned to several detectives that there were indications that Criminal Justice was padding the books on the grants it received from the EPA and the Law Enforcement Assistance Administration (LEAA). His allegations that the same people were on both grants, thereby allowing the state to collect double salaries, and of other fraudulent practices never saw print, however. The reporter was hustled out of the state from Newark Airport after he spotted what he believed to be contract killers.

When Ottens and Penney left for Washington a few days after this Trenton meeting, on September 24, 1980, they were accompanied by Major DiMassi. Congressman Eckhardt convened the interview by declaring the subcommittee was going into executive session. With that he left the room and Ottens and Penney were told to follow him. As they stood up and moved forward, so did the major, expecting to follow them into executive session. At this DiMassi was told he could not accompany the detectives; that this was an executive session, and he had to leave. He did so, but reportedly went storming around the offices slamming doors and being generally disruptive. As one witness described it, he was "bent way out of shape."

On the very day that Ottens, Penney, and the major left for the rendezvous in Washington, the state of New Jersey returned an important indictment against Duane Marine. The defendants were Duane Marine Salvage Corporation, trading as Duane Marine Corp.; Edward Lecarreaux, the current president; Ronald J. Coelho, a salesman for Duane Marine; Vincent S. Potestivo, the accounts receivable manager; and Peter Hyrcyshyn (known as Peter Harrison), the former president. According to the grand jury, Duane Marine had dumped about 500,000 gallons of chemical wastes into the waters off Perth Amboy, and more than 182,000 gallons of chemical wastes into the Edgeboro Landfill in the town of East Brunswick. If convicted, the total penalties for the corporation and the defendants would come to a possible 120 years in prison and fines of $1,446,000. Given the many questions raised by the entire Duane Marine investigation and its aftermath, it is important to note that Deputy Attorney General Sackowicz presented the case to the grand jury, and the law enforcement units which conducted the inquiry, according to the indictment, included the New Jersey Inter-Agency Hazardous Waste Task Force and the DEP.

When the indictment was made public, Attorney General John J. Degnan issued a press release which described the case against Duane Marine. The release quoted Edwin Stier, who had reported the 500,000 gallons dumped into the Perth Amboy sewer system and then out into the water, but had undercut the grand jury's estimate of dumping into the landfill by 100,000 gallons. According to Stier, "such investigations are lengthy and complex . . . in this case, 13 witnesses testified before the State Grand Jury, an additional 30 more witnesses were interviewed, voluminous records were examined by investigators and accountants and chemical tests were performed by the DEP." These conclusions, however, would not have been possible but for two actions by Ottens. The first was his insistence that the Duane Marine records be confiscated. The second was the timely and lucky action by Ottens and Penney to prevent those records from going back to Duane Marine in the summer of 1980.

By chance, Ottens and Penney had walked into the Division of Criminal Justice office where the Duane records were kept and asked one of the officers there if they were doing an audit. The startling answer was that the boxes were going back to Duane. Surprised and angered, the detectives started going through the records themselves. Within a very short time, they came up with a case of illegal stockpiling. In addition, they pointed out to the staff attorneys what else could be found in the records and what possibilities existed for prosecutions. Their intervention made it impossible to bury Duane Marine. Interestingly enough, Duane Marine burned down about two or three weeks after the time the records were supposed to have been returned. Finally, on June 5, 1983, *The New York Times* reported that the New Jersey Division of Criminal Justice had announced a recent plea bargain between the state and Duane Marine which resulted in the corporation pleading guilty to drastically reduced charges. Duane Marine paid a fine of $25,000.

The two detectives stayed in Washington for about three days testifying in executive session. The major left on the second day. They returned to New Jersey over the weekend and had to report to Trenton on Monday morning. From September 29 until November 21, 1980, with one exception, they did nothing but sit in a classroom at headquarters; eight hours a day, they sat. They were told this wasn't punishment, that the brass wanted them close by in case they needed them. Even though it wasn't officially punishment, the bizarre treatment brought forth a complaint from the State Troopers' Non-Commissioned Officers Association of New Jersey, Inc., Fraternal Order of Police Lodge 21. On November 6, the troopers' union unanimously passed an unusual resolution which supported the officers in their actions and concluded:

> Whereas, the superior officers, set over Detectives Sergeant Ottens and Penney in accordance with the rules and regulations of the Division of State Police, failed to respond to the United States House of Representatives Subcommittee on Oversight and Investigations in a timely fashion, which necessitated the issuance of a subpoena compelling the surrender of records and formal sworn testimony of the said Detectives . . .

> Whereas, Detectives Sergeant Ottens and Penney have not, since their testimony before the United States House of Representatives . . . been permitted to actively pursue their assigned responsibilities as members of T.W.I.P., namely the collection of tactical intelligence in the area of organized crime infiltration of the illegal disposal of toxic waste. . . .

The facts, the State Troopers' Association held, led inescapably to a resolution of unequivocal support for Ottens and Penney to Colonel Clinton L. Pagano, superintendent of state police. "Their actions," the resolution went on, "are in keeping with the high standards of the Division of State Police and reflect great credit upon themselves and the Division."

While the rank and file of troopers knew exactly what was happening to Ottens and Penney and why, their show of support had no discernible impact on those who could have rectified the outrage. In fact, all during that time when they sat classroom duty, they were approached by different officials in different ways, all trying to find out what they had said in Washington. They even ended up in front of the Attorney General, John J. Degnan, who pounded his desk to remind them he was their boss. Their answer was rhetorical: Where have you been up to now while all this was going on?

On December 10 they met once again with Attorney General Degnan, nine days before the public hearing would be held in Washington. He brought enormous pressure to bear on Ottens and Penney to say what had gone on in Washington. New Jersey officials were clearly afraid of what might be waiting for them before the House subcommittee. In desperation, they reportedly talked about making some cases on toxic waste, something, anything to take to Washington. The Attorney General and key state police and Criminal Justice officials even went so far as to call the congressional subcommittee, trying to get permission for Ottens and Penney to talk. The answer from Washington was fairly straightforward: To violate the rules of the executive session was to be in contempt of Congress.

Efforts at damage control did not end with the unsuccessful inquisition of Ottens and Penney. There was one other angle left to play. Among the members of the subcommittee was the lameduck congressman Andrew Maguire, of New Jersey. With Chairman Eckhardt not in attendance, Maguire was the ranking Democrat on the subcommittee. It apparently wasn't very difficult to convince Maguire to stick around Washington that December and chair the hearing. There wasn't much pretense involved in the maneuver. Maguire stated, it has been claimed, he was there to protect the reputation of both the state of New Jersey and the Attorney General. Some have speculated that the primary reason for protecting the Attorney General came from New Jersey's Governor Brendan Byrne, who favored Degnan as his party's nominee for Governor the following year. Whether that is accurate or not, Maguire certainly prevented the hearing from pursuing many of the most important issues. In addition, New Jersey officials told the subcommittee most of the specific cases they might want to cover were currently before various grand juries and, therefore, couldn't be discussed. When all was said and done, Ottens and Penney were called in and told by subcommittee staffers they'd like them to discuss only briefly organized crime and some of the ways that toxic waste is illegally disposed.

While there is little doubt that those with something to conceal succeeded, the very fact that damage control was necessary meant that much would nevertheless be revealed. For the public, more-over, a congressional hearing on organized crime and toxic waste was a notable event. Even if the full extent of organized crime's involvement would be hidden on December 16, enough would come out to indicate the need for more and more scrutiny, and for at least another public hearing in the following spring.

6

Controlling the Damage

WHEN CONGRESSMAN ANDREW MAGUIRE of New Jersey gaveled the December 16, 1980, hearing to order at ten o'clock in the morning, he announced that the subcommittee would be considering two matters: organized crime's involvement in toxic waste disposal, and "the operations of the Federal-State toxic waste strike force in New Jersey, a pioneer pilot program funded under EPA and LEAA grant money." He went on: "This is a pilot program which could well be a model for other States. In this regard, it is appropriate to commend New Jersey for its initiative and foresight in taking the lead." To make sure that New Jersey's position was crystal clear, Congressman Matthew J. Rinaldo, also of New Jersey (who earlier in 1979 had asked those embarrassing questions about toxic waste and organized crime in Elizabeth), stated: "I hope that today's hearing will end unfounded speculations about the New Jersey Inter-Agency Strike Force and provide guidance to the Federal Government and other States embarking on similar programs." Rinaldo added that he believed that New Jersey had only the best intentions in setting up the special strike force. What the unfounded speculations exactly were remained unsaid.

While it is true that the Washington subcommittee investigated the actions and activities of the New Jersey Strike Force, it was not really an all-out effort. Their investigators had more or less stumbled upon allegations of corruption and evidence of laxity in the state's efforts against illegal toxic waste disposal. Washington had thus become privy to information which was potentially very embarrassing to New Jersey. That caused the subcommittee to review more systematically New Jersey's work on illegal toxic waste dumping, and to ask the General Accounting Office to audit the financial records pertaining to New Jersey's grants from the EPA and LEAA. The questions raised by the investigative reporter who fled New Jersey had reached Washington. Nevertheless, Rinaldo's remarks were more a reflection of the anxiety in New Jersey political and Criminal Justice circles than a response to specific charges from the subcommittee.

This is not to denigrate the subcommittee, however. On the first question facing the subcommittee, it uncovered many of the costs and implications of the illicit disposal of toxic waste, and was beginning forcefully to confront the links between toxic waste and organized crime. At this particular point, though, before new leadership could arrive on the scene, and before it had much time to gather evidence adequately, the subcommittee was also controllable. The clear but unspoken function of the December hearing concerning New Jersey's official efforts against the toxic waste dumpers, therefore, was to deflect criticism and deny a proper investigation. This was damage control at work.

The first witness called that morning was Harold Kaufman, the FBI informant, who, Maguire made note, had to contact the subcommittee himself to offer assistance. The fact that Kaufman called the subcommittee apparently on his own initiative only one week prior to the hearing indicates something of the depth of the subcommittee's investigation of New Jersey. Kaufman's testimony was carefully controlled at this hearing, through an agreement between the subcommittee and New Jersey officials to restrict his discussion to matters currently under investigation in which he might be a witness.

Accompanying Kaufman to the hearing was Edwin Stier, who commented that Kaufman had been working with the FBI and New Jersey's Division of Criminal Justice for about a year and a half, and was instrumental in the indictments of the New Jersey Trade Waste Association and Duane Marine, which Stier called a major toxic waste prosecution. Before finishing his remarks, Stier reminded the subcommittee of his function. "During the course of Mr. Kaufman's testimony I will try not to interrupt the flow of his testimony. I think it is important that it have continuity. But according to our agreement, you have indicated you would give me the opportunity to indicate those areas that Mr. Kaufman might touch upon which would overlap with the details of some of the cases which are now pending in our State." Along with Stier, New

Jersey was represented by Deputy Attorney General Steven J. Madonna, in charge of the garbage investigation, and Deputy Attorney General Gregory Sackowicz, the leader of the inter-agency toxic waste task force that had developed the Duane Marine case.

Harold Kaufman: Witness for the People

Questioned initially by Congressman Gore, Kaufman described the structure of the garbage industry, noting that grievances over "property rights" were handled by organized crime in its typically violent way—beatings and killings. Within the first two or three minutes of his testimony, Kaufman spoke of two murders. One killing involved an individual who had encroached on the property rights of SCA. It was put on the record that SCA was one of the three largest toxic waste disposal firms in the nation, whose stock was traded on the New York Exchange. Other questions about organized crime, toxic waste, and the concept of "property rights" brought forth this statement from Kaufman: "There is an informal system in the sense where solid waste enters into it. I can't speak about any 100-percent chemical firm, but you got to understand there is multifacet firms, like SCA, BFI [Browning-Ferris Industries], Free Hold [sic] Carting, people like this that do multiwork, they do toxic and solid waste work. With these people, their property rights go right into the toxic." Asked what would happen if someone encroached on the property rights of such companies, Kaufman answered, "You get your legs broke; you get shot."

Congressman Maguire asked Kaufman if what he was saying was that organized crime presently controlled the solid waste industry and was scheming to do the same in toxic waste. Kaufman's reply was not quite on that point, but was nevertheless very revealing. He stated that the manifest system in New Jersey was nothing but a kind of public fraud. All it took in New Jersey to get a hazardous waste hauling license was $50 paid to the Public Utilities Commission. "They made every garbageman in New Jersey . . . hazardous waste haulers." There was no checking on the haulers' qualifications, their knowledge of toxic wastes, nor, indeed, anything else about them. As far as Duane Marine went, it was a complete and utter sham; it had no way of legally disposing of anything. But the first day the state's manifest system went into effect, Duane Marine received a license to operate as a toxic waste facility.

Clumsily, Maguire picked up where Gore had left off. "I want for a moment to pursue this question of the licensing process," he said. The following interesting exchange occurred:

> *Maguire:* As I understand it, if you haul waste in the State of New Jersey, you can get a license or you were able in the past to get a license. . . . Simply for $50, without an investigation.
>
> *Kaufman:* $50 to the DEP of New Jersey, and they sent you a sticker.
>
> *Maguire:* Which doesn't protect the public interest particularly effectively.
>
> *Kaufman:* Of course not.
>
> *Maguire:* Is that still the situation?
>
> *Kaufman:* To my knowledge, yes. As you know, Congressman, being from New Jersey, New Jersey is one of the few States where the public utilities commission controls the sanitation industry. The sanitation industry is treated like every other utility in New Jersey on paper. You can't raise a customer without going through the PUC. You can't do anything. We all know it is a fraud. It is a complete fraud because the company I was with, Statewide Environmental Contractors, raised 300 percent without blinking an eye.
>
> *Maguire:* Raised the prices they charged?
>
> *Kaufman:* Yes, because of property rights.
>
> *Maguire:* What about Duane Marine? What process was required there for licensing?
>
> *Kaufman:* Lecarreaux was a very good friend of Dr. Buchanan. That is the only reason I know he got a license.

Maguire then stopped his own line of questioning, stating that perhaps they were getting into an area they weren't supposed to. Congressman James Florio of New Jersey, who was attending the hearing as a member of the full committee, asked if Maguire would yield his time for a question. Meanwhile, Kaufman simply went on with his story about the president of Duane Marine, Eddie Lecarreaux, who, he said, "had no more right to be licensed than the man in the moon. Nobody checked our facility before we were licensed, because we didn't have a facility. Nobody checked Eddie's financial statement because Eddie owed everybody in the United States, including the government and the State of New Jersey, on taxes. He was financially shaky. He had no facility. Yet, we were one of the first companies to receive a temporary facility license." Finally, Florio was able to break in, asking whether this area should be covered. Edwin Stier then said that Kaufman was touching on an area that was presently before a state grand jury.

Naturally, we do not know what was before one of the New Jersey State grand juries at that particular time. But it would be surprising if Duane Marine was still one of the subjects being pursued. It was, after all, some two months since the Duane Marine indictment was returned. The indictment and accompanying press release had been issued on September 24.

Under the listing of overt acts committed in the execution of the conspiracy, number 7 in the indictment charged that Lecarreaux "did photocopy a letter of authorization signed by Dr. Ronald J. Buchanan, dated August 7, 1978, the said letter authorizing the Duane Marine Salvage Corp. to dispose of a certain type of industrial waste at any landfill registered to accept such waste." The eighth overt act also concerned Dr. Buchanan's August 7 letter, stating that a representative of Duane Marine gave a photocopy of the letter to someone, "said letter having been addressed to Ed Lecarreaux and signed by Ronald J. Buchanan, Ph.D., Chief, Bureau of Hazardous and Chemical Waste, said letter to be furnished to an agent of the Edgeboro Disposal Inc." The indictment then charges that a Duane Marine representative "did present to an agent of the Edgeboro Disposal Inc., photocopies" of the letter of authorization. What is entirely unclear from the indictment is whether Dr. Buchanan's letter merely authorized Duane Marine to dispose of one type of industrial waste only at so-called landfills registered to accept that type of industrial waste, or whether it authorized Duane Marine to dispose at the Edgeboro Landfill. The phrase, "said letter to be furnished to an agent of the Edgeboro Disposal Inc.," appears to imply the latter.

If that were the case, then there was something very strange about the second charge against Duane Marine. This held that the company dumped over 182,000 gallons of dangerous chemical wastes "to the injury and damage of the employees of the Edgeboro Disposal Inc., doing business as a solid waste facility. . . ."

Duane Marine, with the authorization from the DEP Bureau chief, did so at the Edgeboro Landfill and thereby broke the law. But perhaps Duane Marine was only allowed by Buchanan to dump a certain category of industrial waste at Edgeboro? The problem, therefore, is twofold: One, did Buchanan authorize Duane Marine to handle hazardous waste or only a certain category of industrial waste; and two, did he authorize Duane Marine to dispose of the material at any registered landfill or was Edgeboro (described in the indictment as only a solid waste facility) allowed by Buchanan to accept other than solid waste delivered by Duane Marine or one of its subcontractors? Also, if Duane Marine was only allowed to dispose of a certain category of industrial waste at Edgeboro, and had dumped other types, then why was that not one of the charges? In addition, if Buchanan and Lecarreaux were close friends, as Kaufman testified, then how likely is it that the Bureau chief was unaware of the very nature of Duane Marine's operation, unaware of what waste his friend's company was taking in? Duane Marine was a fraud from beginning to end, but one with this difference. It had some kind of letter of authorization from the chief of the Bureau of Hazardous and Chemical Waste, Department of Environmental Protection, Dr. Ronald J. Buchanan.

Some indication of the kinds of authorization Buchanan gave to hazardous waste haulers was provided later on when two letters of authorization that Buchanan wrote for the Chemical Control Corporation were entered as exhibits by the Oversight Subcommittee at its next hearing, in May, 1981. One of them may have been similar to the one given to Duane Marine. The first letter went on November 14, 1977 to Michael Dunay, a consultant to Chemical Control, and was fairly general. The second Buchanan letter, directed to Michael Colleton, an officer of Chemical Control was much more detailed. Written on June 12, 1978, it dealt with polystyrene and methyl methacrylate plastics, and noted that "solid polymeric plastic materials as described in your letter of May 15th may be disposed of at any landfill registered to accept industrial waste (I.D. 27)." Buchanan's permission, in this case, was bounded by three conditions, including one which warned that "an inspector from the Solid Waste Administration will be available to inspect such drums for disposal as deemed necessary by the Department." The subcommittee introduced these letters of authorization to Chemical Control because they were used by another party, Waste

Disposal, Inc., as authorization to take drums from Chemical Control to the MSLA landfill in Kearny, New Jersey.

Conditional and precise as these authorizations may have been, there was, unfortunately, no follow-up by the Solid Waste Administration or, indeed, anyone else. It seems that no one checked the Chemical Control drums to see if they contained only what Buchanan specified. Without the inspection of drums, of course, any letter of authorization to dump anything anywhere would create unlimited opportunity for fraud. Restraint would depend entirely on the good character of those in the business. In the case of Duane Marine, it is worth repeating Kaufman's assertion that Buchanan and Lecarreaux were friends. The reason that the Chemical Control letters were introduced by the subcommittee was because they were used as cover for indiscriminate toxic waste dumping. Duane Marine was no different. The major unexplored issues, therefore, concern Buchanan's intent. Was he aware of how his authorizations were being used, and if not why not?

In the original Duane Marine indictment, Buchanan was not named as a co-conspirator, not even an unindicted one. Returning then to the December, 1980, hearing, one wonders what Director Stier could have meant when he maintained that Kaufman was touching on issues currently before a grand jury. Buchanan was never charged in any future amended indictments of Duane Marine. Indeed, Buchanan was never a target of any New Jersey Grand Jury investigation that has ever surfaced. His conduct as Bureau chief never seems to have been questioned at all. Compounding this questionable behavior was the strange command from DEP to its field officers to stay away from Duane Marine. There is no evidence indicating that a grand jury was considering any of these matters, after its initial indictment of Duane Marine and its major officers. What Stier was referring to, therefore, remains a mystery, unless it was merely the reflex action of a damage control officer protecting the so-called integrity of a state agency.

Duane Marine was a very difficult topic to avoid, however. Congressman Norman F. Lent of New York brought attention back to it after the New Jersey officials harumphed their way past the Buchanan issue. He asked Kaufman for clarification on several points, including his impression that Duane Marine carted toxic waste. Kaufman corrected him by pointing out that Duane Marine "didn't cart . . . because of property rights." Duane Marine was a subcontractor acting as a receiving facility. The haulers were garbage companies which had permits to cart hazardous waste, and Duane Marine was the licensed end of the line. Duane Marine solicited business by giving the haulers a cut of their own profits and, apparently, instructing the haulers on how to inflate charges.

The Trouble with SCA

Before ending his testimony at that crucial December 16, 1980, hearing, Harold Kaufman returned to the subject of SCA. He was trying to explain just exactly what it means when garbage and toxic waste companies are one and the same. Kaufman pointed out that SCA had been expanding into many parts of the country during the 1970s by acquiring various independent garbage companies. Kaufman added that SCA had "some of the toughest organized crime companies in the world." SCA had both toxic and solid waste businesses, and was a company "born on the property rights concept." As far as Kaufman was concerned, SCA was an example of garbage racketeers taking over a large part of the toxic waste disposal industry.

The naming of SCA at the December hearing was only the prelude to a larger examination of that company later in the spring. During the last week in May 1981, SCA became the focus of the subcommittee's continuing work on toxic waste and organized crime. By that time the chairman of the subcommittee was Representative John D. Dingell from Michigan, and there were no New Jersey members left. The primary purpose of that hearing, Dingell stated, was to review Kaufman's testimony about SCA presented the past December and to give SCA an opportunity to respond. Dingell then added a sobering story: "Without inferring any connection between the two, it is relevant to this hearing, and of great concern to the subcommittee, to note that last December 22—6 days after Mr. Kaufman testified before this subcommittee—Mr. Crescent Roselle, general manager of Waste Disposal, Inc., one of SCA's largest New Jersey subsidiaries, was brutally murdered in what appeared to be a gangland-style execution." The Roselle homicide as well as two others supposedly linked to SCA matters—the murders of Alfred DiNardi and Gabriel San Felice—were rather prominently discussed during the course of this hearing and will be explored in detail in a later chapter.

What was established at this hearing was that SCA had grown in the fashion described by Kaufman in December. In contention were the claims that SCA's president, Thomas Viola, was an organized crime associate; that he and the SCA corporation were aware of and participated in illegally restraining trade in the waste industry through the "property rights" system; and, undoubtedly, the unspoken claim that SCA was nothing more than an organized crime conglomerate. Various law enforcement officers from New Jersey, including Lieutenant Colonel Justin Dintino of the New Jersey State Police, two sergeants from the State Police Intelligence Division, and Deputy Attorney General Madonna, all offered their opinions that it was inconceivable that SCA (and Viola) was unaware of "property rights" in the waste industry. Needless to say, Viola and the other SCA officers present at the hearing asserted the contrary. On "property rights," Viola stated: "I have no knowledge of the existence of any such system and can state categorically that SCA does not participate in it, if it does exist.

"To the best of my knowledge," Viola added, "no one in SCA has any connection with organized crime, and organized crime exercises no control or influence over SCA." He quickly added, however, that SCA had grown very rapidly by buying out more than 130 garbage companies, and so it was "conceivable that some of the employees who came with some of these companies may have committed crimes or even had contacts with organized crime." Viola also admitted that, as he put it, the past president "had unlawfully converted corporate funds." More detail on this affair was furnished by SCA's chairman of the board, John M. Fox, who accompanied Viola to the hearing and also testified. Fox, who became an outside director of SCA in 1977, stated that in mid-1975 it became known that SCA president Christopher P. Recklitis, and the company's founder, Burton Steir, had conspired to defraud SCA out of millions of dollars.

The Securities and Exchange Commission, in an investigation into SCA's affairs carried out in 1974, had accused Recklitis of diverting about $4 million of company money for his personal use. Joining him in this scheme was Burton Steir and SCA's Northeast regional controller, Nicholas Liakis. Another reported participant in the scheme was Anthony "Tony Bentro" Bentrovato, who was himself indicted in 1975 in a kickback case involving the Upstate New York Teamsters Pension Fund. Also looting pension fund money was Anthony "Tony Pro" Provenzano, one of the organized crime leaders of the Teamsters. Bentro and Provenzano were convicted of this charge in March, 1978. Apparently, Bentro was a substantial SCA stockholder, having sold a profitable garbage company to SCA in 1973 for $1.17 million worth of stock. Investigative reporter Robert Windrem found that Bentro and his brother had formed the company in 1969, and with the help of political contacts secured important municipal hauling contracts. With the aid of high Teamster officials, they also received extremely favorable labor deals.

Before Bentro sold the waste business to SCA, but well after negotiations had started, he moved into the offices of M & M Trading, which was controlled by Matthew Ianniello, discussed earlier and described by Windrem as New York's most important loan shark, "the gangster who arranged the murder of Joey Gallo at Umberto's Clam House in Little Italy." What Bentro did for Ianniello was to arrange gambling junkets for high-rollers to Caribbean casinos controlled by Ianniello, help in collecting gambling debts with mob enforcer Larry Paladino, and invest in many companies for both Ianniello and Anthony Provenzano. The Teamster Pension and Retirement Fund scam was discussed (and probably planned) at the M & M Trading office by Bentro, Ianniello, Ben Cohen, Provenzano, Jimmy Fiorillo (owner, as noted earlier, of a major New York garbage company), and Larry Paladino. Unknown to these individuals, however, another participant in the talks at M & M Trading was recording the conversation for the U.S. Justice Department. Federal authorities were running an undercover operation, code-named Cleveland, aimed at organized crime's control of the Teamsters Union, and had enrolled the individual as an informant.

The meeting took place in the summer of 1974, about a year after Bentro and SCA had made their deal. It is more than likely, therefore, the SCA fraud managed by Recklitis, Steir, and Liakis was part and parcel of even larger frauds involving Bentro, Provenzano, and Ianniello. It is also worth repeating the point that even though Viola and Fox were forthcoming in mentioning the fraud, they were adamant in denying any organized crime connection to SCA. They were willing to accept that perhaps one or two of the companies bought early on, in the scramble of expansion, had unsavory owners. But they were not willing (for good reason, no doubt) to disclose that the founder of SCA, and its president in 1975, mixed and mingled with notorious organized crime figures such as Ianniello and Provenzano. Yet this Bentro connection squarely places the very top leadership of SCA in the midst of organized crime–dominated intrigues, not simply corporate frauds, during that period.

The subcommittee investigators were well aware of some of these issues. That is probably why they introduced as exhibits, in the May, 1981, hearing record, portions of transcripts from the earlier Securities and Exchange Commission investigation of SCA in which Viola was questioned. He testified before the SEC about his family businesses, which included three corporations—Industrial Haulage, Intercity Service, and Avon Landfill—sold to or merged with SCA. Immediately after SCA's acquisition of them, Viola joined the board of directors on the recommendation of Burton Steir. In addition, Viola also became an SCA vice president in 1972. His duties as vice president centered on acquisitions primarily, but not exclusively, in New Jersey. Asked which companies he brought into the SCA fold, Viola stated: "IMPAC Incorporated, Delorenzo Paper Stock Company, Interstate Waste Removal Incorporated, A. A. Mastrangello, Incorporated, United Carting Company, Instant Disposal Incorporated, The Rozelli [sic] Companies, 4, 5 of them, those were in New Jersey. In New York State there was C & D Disposal, [and various companies located in Reno, Nevada, including] Reno Disposal Company." While vice president, Viola was also co-director and then director of what SCA called the Mid-Atlantic Region, which included New Jersey and the Philadelphia area. When Viola became president, Burton Steir was again his supporter.

It seems as though the SEC was attempting to establish that Viola was Steir's man, chosen by him to accept leadership positions in SCA including the presidency, all during the time Steir was looting the company. Could Viola have been so naive, the SEC seemed to be asking, as not to know what Steir, Recklitis, Liakis, Bentro, and others were doing? The congressional subcommittee was also making the important point that Viola was the one who brought into the SCA fold the two murdered waste entrepreneurs, Roselle and DiNardi.

The subcommittee's hammering of SCA in the spring of 1981 was not over yet. Congressman Gore went on to probe another

SCA subsidiary bought in 1972. This one was Tri-County Sanitation of Detroit, whose president was Nicholas Micelli. As far back
as 1963, Gore stated, Tri-County had been identified as an organized crime firm. A Detroit police inspector, Earl C. Miller, had
stated then that Tri-County Sanitation was run in Detroit by
Joseph Barbara, Jr., whose father was the host of the infamous
1957 organized crime meeting in Appalachian, New York. Barbara,
Jr., was also the son-in-law of Peter Vitale, one of two brothers
who were alleged to be among the leaders of Detroit organized
crime. It appears from Miller's testimony that the Detroit operation was a subsidiary of Tri-County Sanitation, incorporated in
New York. There is little doubt, however, that Tri-County activities in Detroit were run by organized crime, and that it quickly
became a dominant force in the waste disposal industry in the
Motor City. Nicholas Micelli, the president of Tri-County when it
joined SCA, was, like Barbara, Jr., also Peter Vitale's son-in-law.
Questions from the subcommittee to Viola about Tri-County were
answered with the refrain that this matter had been under the direction of Burton Steir, and that Micelli had left SCA in 1974.

In New Jersey, the SCA buying spree totaled twenty firms.
One of the most interesting was Gaess Environmental Service Corporation, although the subcommittee members paid no attention to
it. Perhaps they were unaware of the findings of the New York
State Senate Select Committee on Crime on Jeffrey R. Gaess and
especially his brother, Anthony D. Gaess. This committee had
found that their company, Gaess Environmental, was purchased by
the SCA–Earthline Division in 1977. Six years earlier, Gaess Environmental had been called Tony Gaess Service Corp. At that
time, its officers were Anthony D. Gaess, president, and
Christopher P. Recklitis, vice president. In approximately 1973,
therefore, Recklitis, who was very soon to become SCA's president, was in business with Anthony Gaess. As noted, this was just
around the time that Recklitis began conspiring to loot the SCA
treasury.

Other information gathered by New York State Senator Ralph
Marino's investigators indicated that Anthony Gaess was also an
associate of Richard Miele, who was believed to be the proprietor
of the firm known in the waste disposal trade as Modern Transportation. A chart prepared by the New Jersey DEP indicates that
Miele owned a portion of the MSLA landfill. MSLA, located in

Kearny, is the landfill in which huge amounts of toxic chemicals were dumped. Next to MSLA were two more landfills also reported to have been used by toxic dumpers, C. Egan & Sons Sanitary Landfill and the P.M. Landfill.

The procedure for dumping at MSLA was simple; trucks used gate number 2 on the site, which was reportedly opened by a guard who was paid for his service and told to keep quiet. Besides Miele, others with interests in MSLA included William and John Keegan, Joe Cassini, and the murdered Crescent "Chris" Roselle. Anthony Gaess and Chris Roselle, it turns out, had several common interests outside of MSLA, in which Gaess was represented, it is claimed, by Richard Miele. According to police intelligence reports compiled by detectives in Elizabeth, Anthony Gaess met with Roselle on a regular basis in order to show him how best to profit in handling chemicals. In these same intelligence reports, it is alleged that Gaess was "caught stealing accounts and running drums of toxic waste" into the infamous Kin-Buc Landfill.

For many concerned with toxic waste dumping and organized crime's involvement, the Gaesses' interests are undeservedly unknown. This is so despite the fact that their operations in toxic waste were very large. They hauled and disposed of toxic waste for some of the major petrochemical generators. Among their customers were: Reichhold Chemicals; Borden Chemical, a division of Borden, Inc.; Air Products & Chemicals; NL Chemicals Division; Refined-Onyx Division of the Polyurethane Specialties Co., of Kewanee Industries, a subsidiary of Gulf Oil; Process Chemical Division of Diamond Shamrock; Soda Products Division of Diamond Shamrock; Lederle Laboratories of American Cyanamid; Millmaster Onyx, a division of Gulf Oil; F & F Department of DuPont; Specialty Chemical Division and Plastics Division of Stauffer Chemical; Mobil Chemical, a division of Mobil Oil; and Pfizer, Inc.

The activities of the Gaess brothers escaped prolonged and intensive law enforcement attention until fairly recently. Anthony Gaess's allegedly illegal activities, his hauling contracts with various petrochemical giants, his business deals with associates like Miele of MSLA, with crooks like Recklitis, with the murdered Chris Roselle, and with many suspected organized crime figures have now made him a prime investigative target (see chapter 10 for details). Nevertheless, SCA took some pains to try to disassociate itself from Anthony Gaess, and thereby avoid significant financial liability.

Attorneys for SCA Services, SCA Service of Passaic, Inc., Earthline Company, and Anthony Gaess filed a legal brief in the spring of 1979 which denied that Gaess was the principal operating officer of Earthline, the SCA subsidiary that bought Gaess Environmental. This denial was made despite the fact that minutes from a special meeting of the board of directors of Scientific, Inc. (the owners of Kin-Buc Landfill) on June 30, 1975, held that "management has been investigating the feasibility of acquiring from SCA Services, Inc., the Gaess group which consists of SCA's liquid collection business." The Kin-Buc directors were especially interested, first because, as they stated, "the business was run by Tony Gaess aggressively with a view toward expansion"; also Gaess would be the ideal coordinator for Scientific's landfill (presumably Kin-Buc, one year before it was closed as an incredible hazard); and finally, Gaess would be excellent at coordinating their commercial collection operations. They were also interested in buying Gaess from SCA because they understood that the previous year's profits generated by the "Gaess group were $750,000." The reason why SCA was taking so much trouble in this matter was its fear of civil liability in the Kin-Buc case. The brief was filed in answer to a civil action brought by the U.S. Attorney for the District of New Jersey. This suit named Gaess, SCA Services, and nine others responsible for unsafe and improper methods used in handling and disposing into Kin-Buc millions of gallons of liquid waste, much of it highly toxic.

SCA may have been correct in asserting that Earthline was not a Gaess-run company, at least not until after Kin-Buc was shut down in 1976. Earthline did buy up Gaess Environmental the following year, 1977. But the more substantial point is that certain Gaess companies were SCA subsidiaries well before then. Otherwise, there wouldn't have been much point in Scientific's board holding meetings to discuss buying Gaess away from SCA. Gaess probably came on board with SCA when his partner, Recklitis, assumed office, although he may have kept one of his companies, Gaess Environmental, from SCA until 1977. Intriguingly, this kind of action was also taken by the murdered Chris Roselle, who sold all but one of his companies to SCA.

Trying to figure out all of the Gaesses' interests, however, is difficult, for the Gaess brothers seem to have been hidden owners or had substantial interests in several waste companies. For instance, New Jersey DEP records dealing with Gaess are cross-referenced with a firm called R & R Sanitation Service of Randolph, New Jersey, and R & R was in turn a trade name for Carl Gulick, Inc., an industrial waste hauler working out of Mt. Freedom, New Jersey. R & R Sanitation Service, and Carl Gulick, Inc., were both acquired by Thomas Viola for SCA some time in the early 1970s. The Gaess brothers may have had much more substantial involvement with SCA through these other companies than anyone has realized. This is a typical example of what John Fine has called the corporate veils and interlocking directorates characteristic of organized crime's control over the industry.

There is one last aspect of the relationship between Anthony Gaess and SCA that needs to be addressed in this corporate history. Anthony Gaess received a $140,000 loan from SCA in the form of "an unsecured note which is not interest bearing" on September 1, 1975. His payments were due at the rate of $14,000 per year for ten years, starting on September 1, 1976. At least one of the payments was deferred in lieu of Gaess's pledging 3,000 shares of SCA common stock as collateral for the unpaid settlement. This extremely handsome loan arrangement came, it might be noticed, shortly after Scientific Inc. began to discuss purchasing the Gaess interests.

During the May 1981 hearing, the SCA team spent a fair amount of time denouncing Harold Kaufman who was brought back as a witness by the subcommittee. At that time, Kaufman also faced some sharp questioning by Pennsylvania Congressman Marc L. Marks especially over his past record as a bank robber. Interestingly enough, the New Jersey law-enforcement representatives completely backed Kaufman, with Madonna stating that except for dates, "which Mr. Kaufman is not very good at handling, I have found him to be totally accurate." This support, however, raises an exceedingly important issue—the vast difference in tone, if not behavior, on the part of New Jersey officials between their actions in the December, 1980, hearing and the subsequent one in May, 1981. By the spring, New Jersey officials were quite outspoken when it came to SCA and allegations about organized crime and toxic waste dumping. In the winter of 1980, however, they had been, to put it mildly, much more circumspect, seemingly much more nervous.

Of course, the difference was probably caused by the shift in the subcommittee's interest and by the nature of the witnesses. In the spring, New Jersey didn't have to deal with Detectives Ottens and Penney testifying, nor with any confrontations involving spec- ulations and rumors about the Inter-Agency Hazardous Waste Task Force. That subject seemed to be closed, and the two detectives safely tucked away from the limelight. The forthrightness of New Jersey officials in the spring thus may have reflected their success at damage control in the winter; they may have felt that they were off the hook. Moreover, it is possible that they had some genuine interest in exposing SCA. One can never discount the complexities of law enforcement, and the fact that protection and exposure are so often deeply wrapped in unknown interests and complex ambi- guities. Certainly, New Jersey officials felt the necessity of support- ing Kaufman (and keeping him as tightly reined as possible), as he was, after all, their star witness in the trade waste prosecutions. And certainly there was no denying that Roselle had been mur- dered in organized crime style right after the winter hearing, and that he had been very much a part of SCA's operations. When all is said and done, however, the fundamental difference in the hear- ings was that the first was much more political than the second, which focused overwhelmingly on SCA. This second hearing sim- ply didn't demand damage control, as it never called into question the integrity of New Jersey's state agencies.

The Integrity of the State

Putting a lid on Duane Marine was not the only example—nor even the most significant—of the way in which New Jersey assidu- ously avoided sensitive areas in the December, 1980, hearing. New Jersey's unfortunate success in controlling the congressional hearing was most evident when the time came (and quickly went) for the Detectives Ottens and Penney to testify. Their entire testi- mony was over and done with in a matter of minutes. Additionally, most of the questions put to them were either on issues they per- sonally hadn't investigated, or were general and abstract in nature.

New Jersey's Congressman Rinaldo was very good at asking the unanswerable, and in phrasing his questions to make his customary pitch for the virtue of New Jersey. Rinaldo took almost as much time praising the state as he did asking questions of substance. And despite what every member of the subcommittee staff knew were the real facts, Rinaldo said boldly:

> As far as I am concerned—and I am sure that every member of the subcommittee and the subcommittee staff will agree with me—we have received excellent cooperation from the State police, in particular, the New Jersey Attorney General's Office, the Division of Criminal Justice, and everyone that the subcommittee sought to obtain information from.

Having made his point that New Jersey was doing a splendid job, he then turned to the harassed detectives and asked them several questions about the notorious Chemical Control Corporation. The bottom line, however, as Congressman Rinaldo either did or should have known, was that Ottens and Penney had never worked the Chemical Control investigation.

The only member of the subcommittee to try to develop new information in questioning the detectives was Congressman Gore. He moved the hearing, however temporarily, toward another area of significance by asking the detectives if they knew of "an interrelationship between fuel oil companies and the disposal of toxic waste." Detective Penney responded: "Yes, sir, we received information that this is another area of illegal disposal of flammable toxics. The methodology is such that the toxics, solvents or PCB's, are mixed with [fuel] oil." Penney commented that this brew was sold to public utilities, school systems, and hospitals.

Ottens, answering another question from Gore, described how he and Penney conducted their investigations. This prompted Gore to ask what organized crime "groups or families" were involved in toxic waste. Two crime syndicates were identified: Genovese/Tieri, and the DeCavalcante organized crime group. Penney then remarked, "We learned an individual was employed at a facility in the State as a public relations man with this company. He is closely aligned or associated with John Riggi, who is a documented member or an underboss of that family member group," meaning the DeCalvacante syndicate.

While not immediately apparent, the hearing had just reached a very critical stage. The facility Penney was talking about was Kit Enterprises, and it presented the state of New Jersey with some extremely sensitive problems. Gore was aware of this, but was hampered by the subcommittee's ground rules protecting New Jersey. Nevertheless, he was determined to get some information about Kit on the record, although he did not identify the facility by name. After Penney's statement, Gore asked a few questions on other matters, and then, seemingly quite out of the blue, said: "What about Jojo Ferrara?" Ottens answered that Ferrara was listed as the public relations man. Wasn't he, Gore asked, the person tied to John Riggi of the DeCalvacante syndicate? The answer given was yes, indeed. And that was as far as Gore could go with the detectives on the subject. Later on, however, the minority counsel, Claire Whitney, was able to get the name of the facility into the record.

At that point Edwin Stier, the director of Criminal Justice, was testifying before the subcommittee. Counsel Whitney wanted to know from Stier how the Division of Criminal Justice coordinated its handling of the Kit case with the state police. Whitney prefaced her remarks by noting that on January 4, 1980, in a Division of Criminal Justice quarterly report to the EPA (such reports were mandated under the grants given to New Jersey by the EPA, and also by LEAA), the project director, Bob Winter, had assured the EPA that a very close liaison was being implemented between Criminal Justice and the state police, which "will assure [a] free flow of information on the critical issue of organized crime infiltration in the toxic waste industry." In light of that statement, Whitney asked if the facts of the Kit case could possibly support Winter's claim. Before Stier answered, she recited some of the facts of the case, as the subcommittee "obtained them from your records": no doubt, some of which came from those originally subpoenaed by the subcommittee from Ottens and Penney.

On May 14, 1979, she pointed out, the Union County Prosecutor's Office filed a report which indicated dealings between Kit and Chemical Control. The report should have gone up the ladder in the Division of Criminal Justice. Furthermore, Whitney noted, although Criminal Justice formally opened an investigation into Kit five months later, Criminal Justice never appeared to coordinate its surveillances with the state police. In fact, Whitney stated,

Detective Sergeant Ottens was watching Kit both before and after Criminal Justice got involved, and he had stated there was no coordination between Criminal Justice and the state police.

Stier's response was that this was one of those unfortunate instances of a failure of communications. However, he added, this was only one case out of many, and the fact that information didn't flow quite as expeditiously as possible shouldn't be misinterpreted. New Jersey's state police superintendent, Colonel Clinton Pagano, then spoke up in defense of Stier and Criminal Justice, telling Whitney that one of Detective Ottens's reports wasn't sent to Criminal Justice because Ottens had included the name of one of his informants. Both Pagano and Stier attempted to explain away their agencies' botching of the Kit case. Stier's refrain was to look at the context; so much going on, so many cases, inevitably producing confusion. Pagano simply blamed Detective Ottens for poor reporting.

Counsel Whitney, however, was not satisfied. She pointed out that the public safety director of Elizabeth, New Jersey, had told Ottens and Penney of organized crime involvement with Kit as early as February, 1980. They reported this in early March, and yet Deputy Attorney General Sackowicz closed down the investigation on March 24, 1980. Stier replied that "the investigation was closed because no further logical leads appeared to be available to the investigators handling the investigation." To make sure she understood both Pagano and Stier, Whitney asked if they meant that there was never even enough evidence to call for a search warrant by the Division of Criminal Justice. She was told that was a correct interpretation, although she probably knew that it simply wasn't true. What made Kit Enterprises so sensitive was not only its indisputable dumping of toxic waste, nor that it had on the payroll a known organized crime figure, Jojo Ferrara, but that two former deputy attorney generals were part of the Kit family. It is likely that the latter issue was viewed within the Division of Criminal Justice as something critically dangerous, best left unexplored given the possible political consequences of exposure.

Investigating Kit

The Kit Enterprises site in Elizabeth, New Jersey, was leased from the Inmont Chemical Corporation through a firm known as

Tree Realty. Kit started some time in late 1977 or early 1978, according to police intelligence files. The original conspirators were Thomas F. Kitzi, Robert E. Gooding, and Joseph A. "Jojo" Ferrara. Both Robert Gooding and Thomas Kitzi were very familiar with toxic waste matters. Gooding had formerly been associated with Gaess Environmental Services. Kitzi was the founder of Vamp Chemical Resources of Sayerville and South Jersey, and of PCA Corporation of Avenel, New Jersey, which, along with Madison Industries of Old Bridge, New Jersey, was responsible for dumping about 3.2 million gallons of toxic waste into a pit that supposedly led to the Old Bridge sewer system. Surprisingly enough, the information on Kitzi's criminal activities with Vamp and PCA came from an amended indictment dealing with Madison Industries, which was handed down on December 3, 1980. This meant, of course, that Kitzi was already very well known as a major toxic waste dumper by the Inter-Agency Hazardous Waste Task Force which conducted the investigation, and raises even more forcefully the question of why, if not for reasons of political influence, Kit Enterprises was treated with kid gloves. To suggest, as Stier did, that there wasn't probable cause or enough evidence to issue a search warrant on Kit was absurd and unconscionable.

The fact of the matter is that Kit Enterprises was protected by officials in New Jersey until so much pressure was brought to bear that the case was reopened. The pressure came from two officers in Elizabeth: Detective Sergeant John Guslavage, and the director of Public Safety (Police Department) Joseph Brennan. By the summer of 1980, informants were reporting some strange activities at Kit to the Elizabeth officers. On June 20, one reported that Jojo Ferrara had allegedly received a payment of $100,000 for services. Ferrara, by the way, was a building inspector for the city of Elizabeth all during his employment by Kit Enterprises. Detective Guslavage's surveillance of Kit Enterprises started in earnest in the winter of 1980–81, and showed that Kit was bypassing the treatment plant and dumping directly into the Elizabeth sewer system. At the end of January, it was discovered that one of the carting companies allegedly delivering toxics to Kit was Freehold Carting, owned by Tom Blanshard who, in the recent past, was also a part-owner of the horribly contaminated Lone Pine Landfill. Some of the toxic waste brought to Kit by Freehold, it was alleged, was dumped into the sewer, while the rest was mixed with other material in a roll-off and taken to a landfill in Elizabeth.

In February, 1981, two tractor trailers from an outfit known as Hazardous Waste Disposal (HWD) located on Long Island, New York, were seen at Kit. HWD operated Long Island's largest chemical waste storage facility, which up to 1981 had shipped or received—according to the December, 1983, edition of *Waste Age* Magazine—approximately 2.6 million gallons of hazardous waste every year. One way that HWD got rid of the stuff, besides delivering it to Kit Enterprises, was to dispose of it down a storm drain in Farmingdale, New York. By the end of February, the detective watching Kit was himself rather chillingly informed that he was being watched by organized crime figures associated with John Albert and Joseph Lemmo. (Albert and Lemmo had earlier been arrested in Middlesex County for gambling and narcotics violations, as John Fine stated back in spring, 1980.)

The Division of Criminal Justice was informed on March 4, 1981, of the current investigation and asked to prepare a search warrant for Kit. The request was sent to John H. Stamler, the prosecutor for Union County in which Elizabeth is located. A few days later, the Elizabeth detective was notified, by an assistant prosecutor, that Stamler had ordered the office not to proceed with any investigation of Kit Enterprises. The reason given was that the Division of Criminal Justice and the Oversight Subcommittee were both moving on Kit. A check was made with Washington by the Elizabeth officer, and the answer came back that the subcommittee was not investigating Kit, although someone should. The Division of Criminal Justice had closed its so-called investigation of Kit almost a year earlier.

At the beginning of the second week in March, Guslavage searched the files of the Joint Meeting Sewerage Authority in Elizabeth to see if it had any record of Kit Enterprises using the sewer system. And, indeed, he found a report showing that certain public officials in the city of Elizabeth must have known that Kit was dumping down their sewers as Kit was paying a "surcharge" determined by the Joint Meeting for its use of Elizabeth sewers. In the same spirit as Greenberg, Grogan, Fine, Ottens, and a few others, Guslavage also took samples from the Elizabeth sewer at those times when he believed that Kit was flushing toxics. He dutifully filled mason jars, sealed them, and turned them over to either the Division of Criminal Justice or the DEP. The fate of Guslavage's samples paralleled those collected by Greenberg and Ottens; initially he was told they weren't good enough. Later, he would be told they had disappeared.

But Guslavage and his boss Brennan were relentless. They kept pressuring Criminal Justice, the County Prosecutor, the DEP, and any other agency which should have been minding the toxic shop. Finally, a meeting was held on March 12, 1981, with Guslavage, Deputy Attorney General Sackowicz, and a representative from the Union County Prosecutor's Office to discuss Kit. It ended with everything still up in the air. One week later, Guslavage was informed that as far as Sackowicz was concerned, "they didn't have a criminal violation at Kit." And, he added, no one would authorize a search warrant. Still Guslavage, with the support of his chief, pushed on.

Taking matters a bit further, Chief Brennan wrote to Attorney General James Zazzali (Zazzali had succeeded Degnan), in the last week of March, that the Elizabeth Police Department was experiencing problems and delays in its attempt to investigate Kit Enterprises. Brennan requested a meeting with the Attorney General. On April 10, 1981, a call to the Attorney General's Office about a response to Brennan's letter, which also included a request for a search warrant, brought forth this strange reply: The letter had never been received. Detective Guslavage, meanwhile, had also been trying to see the Attorney General. Apparently, he was told to leave it alone, that Zazzali wanted nothing to do with Kit Enterprises or with him. While both Brennan and Guslavage focused on the Attorney General, Edwin Stier had supposedly pushed for a meeting with them. During the second week of April, Brennan called Stier's office and left a message the gist of which was that he would only talk with the Attorney General.

By early May, the flawed samples Guslavage had taken from the sewer were reported missing by the DEP. Finally, realizing that no other agency was going to help, the Elizabeth Police Department issued eight summonses charging Kit Enterprises with violating several city ordinances. It was the last gasp; there was nothing else left to do except surrender, and that they wouldn't do. This action taken by the Elizabeth Police (the most they could do) did not close down Kit Enterprises. But, clearly, the actions and activities of Guslavage and Brennan produced quite a bit of heat within New Jersey. Ultimately, the Inter-Agency Hazardous Waste Task Force would indict Kit on a variety of charges that will be examined shortly. This indictment was handed down in the spring of 1983, almost two years after Elizabeth had issued the city summonses. In fact, the indictment came one year after Kit was closed. It wasn't, however, any official agency which actually closed it down. Apparently one of Tree Realty's representatives, a Mr. Mandelbaum, put a chain across the entrance to the property.

The strange events surrounding Kit Enterprises cannot be explained by focusing on the owner of record, Thomas Kitzi. As noted above, the Inter-Agency Hazardous Waste Task Force and other law enforcement agencies in New Jersey did not hesitate to investigate Kitzi in 1980, and again in 1981. On June 1, 1981, Kitzi suffered his second indictment, this time charged with dumping chemical wastes in the Sayreville, New Jersey, Municipal Landfill. The press release on this charge, from Attorney General Zazzali's office, held that Kitzi, working through his former company, Vamp Chemical Resources, had "paid certain individuals, who are not identified in the indictment, for permission to bury the drums at the landfill." It could never be argued, therefore, that the investigative failures were because Kitzi was being protected. Nevertheless, Kit Enterprises was protected or tolerated for quite some time.

The answer to the mystery of Kit can be pieced together from the reports of several informants gathered and compiled by very knowledgeable police detectives. Kit Enterprises was the scene of several intrigues. First of all, the original partners, Gooding and Kitzi, had stubbornly resisted the efforts of several large toxic waste disposal companies and entrepreneurs to buy them out. SCA, Browning-Ferris Industries, and Scientific, Inc., represented by Marvin Mahan, had all attempted to purchase Kit. Both Kitzi and especially Gooding resisted. A strategy was then worked out to force Gooding to resign. Tony Gaess allegedly went to Beatrice Tylucki, the director of Solid Waste for the DEP, and told her to get rid of Gooding on some pretense or another. Tylucki, in turn, supposedly involved Deputy Attorney General Sackowicz, whose job was to find something in Gooding's past record that would allow the DEP to pressure him to leave the company. Gooding left Kit soon after.

Replacing Gooding as one of the chief officers of Kit Enterprises was George Gregory, a former Deputy Attorney General. For a short period, Gregory reportedly ran the operation with Kitzi acting as the front man. Apparently, it was Gregory who had the right connections with certain DEP officials to make Kit virtually untouchable. One indication of how this was being played out came when Kit finally received its license as a toxic waste facility. Under Gooding and Kitzi, the business had had great difficulty in securing the necessary permits. But on April 23, 1979, after Gooding was out and Gregory in, Kit received permit #4251 issued by Beatrice Tylucki, according to records located in the Elizabeth Fire Department.

Not only did informants provide details about the intrigues said to be going on between Gregory and the DEP; they also reported that Gregory claimed to have influence with the Assistant U.S. Attorney from the Newark office who handled the Kin-Buc case and others for the federal government. The next maneuver in the Kit scene involved getting rid of Kitzi himself. It may have been planned all along, or it may have developed because Kitzi was too well known as a toxic waste dumper. In either case, Kitzi was soon indicted for his past activities with Vamp and other firms. The implication, from the informant reports, is that Kitzi was targeted in order to give Gregory—or perhaps others—full control of Kit Enterprises. One of the others may have been another former Deputy Attorney General, Mark Furst, who became Kit's legal counsel. In any event, Kitzi was out in 1981. Among those who apparently were left running the show were former deputy attorney generals and an important representative of organized crime, Jojo Ferrara.

Some of the Kit story surfaced in the spring of 1983, when an investigative reporter for Cable News Network, Peter Arnett, learned some of the details and interviewed Deputy Attorney General Steven Madonna. Questioned about the seeming lack of law enforcement zeal when it came to Kit Enterprises, Madonna promised that a major investigative breakthrough would be announced shortly. Madonna was right. On May 23, 1983, Attorney General Irwin I. Kimmelman (successor to Zazzali) announced the indictment of:

Kit Enterprises, Inc. (also known as Evergreen Environmental Industries, Inc.), George Gregory, an attorney and former vice president of Kit, William F. Addvensky, former corporate officer of Kit and operator of Intercity Tank Lines, Intercity Tank Lines, Inc., a waste oil hauling company, of Sayreville, Thomas P. Colicchio, Union County Corrections Officer and former Kit security guard, Joseph A. Ferrara, a Building Inspector Trainee for the City of Elizabeth, and an employee of Kit, Paul A. Francisco, former president and treasurer of Kit, and Robert Gooding, co-founder of Kit, . . .

There were over fifty counts in the indictment, with charges ranging from conspiracy, theft by deception and of services, tampering with public records and making false statements to the DEP, bribery, official misconduct, evading taxes, unlawful possession of a handgun, and the unlawful and illegal disposal of pollutants and hazardous waste.

Kit Enterprises had gathered toxic waste from some of the largest generators in the nation—including the Nestlé Company, Clairol, Coca-Cola, GATX Terminals, Continental Can, Cooper Chemical, C. J. Osborn Chemicals, Proctor & Gamble, Witco Chemical, and Pet, Inc.—and dumped it down a drain connected to the Elizabeth sewer system. This system fed into the Arthur Kill, described in the indictment as "an already much abused waterway." Various parts of the indictment confirmed the information provided by informants during the course of Guslavage's torturous and hampered investigation. For instance, he had been told back in February, 1981, as noted, that he was being watched while conducting surveillances on Kit. Count 36 of the indictment, which charges "Official Misconduct—Second Degree," states that Thomas Colicchio, a Union County corrections officer also employed by Kit, probably as a private security officer, had access to motor vehicle registration records in the Sheriff's Department. Colicchio passed information to Kit that certain cars around the property were unmarked police cars, thereby compromising and endangering Guslavage and his investigation. Other counts make it quite clear that George Gregory had primary responsibility for handling Kit's affairs with the DEP.

George Gregory, as might be expected, was not identified in the indictment as a former Deputy Attorney General. In addition, the other former Deputy Attorney General who was Kit's counsel, Mark Furst, was never mentioned, which may mean that his ac-

tivities were not as significant or criminal as the information alleged. One point is clear, however. Kit's activities were
widespread. The first count notes that the conspiracy was planned
and carried out in many different parts of New Jersey, and also in
Stamford, Connecticut, in Staten Island and other parts of New
York, and, lastly, in Nazareth and Philadelphia, Pennsylvania. The
conspirators were charged with pocketing over $1.6 million from
the dumping of toxic waste.

The fanfare associated with the long overdue Kit indictment,
played up in press releases and stories, cannot obscure the most
salient feature of Kit's history. There is no doubt that it was protected by various New Jersey law enforcement and regulatory officials for a critical period of time, during which it dumped about
13 million gallons of hazardous waste down the Elizabeth sewer
system.

New Jersey, like other states no doubt, walked many a tight-
rope when it came to the problems associated with toxic waste.
The irrefutable involvement of organized crime with the toxic
waste industry presented any number of threatening problems, not
the least of which involved danger to public health and the environment. But what appeared to be almost equally significant was
devising some strategy that would permit investigations and prosecutions to control the most egregious forms of toxic waste dumping, while avoiding the obvious political corruption. New Jersey
faced these problems more often than most states because it had
seized on the issue of illegal toxic waste dumping, either in order
to aggrandize its law enforcement agencies or because it realized
that it faced a severe problem over the generation and disposal of
toxic waste. Most likely, its rapid strides in securing federal money
for special task forces and related activities was some combination
of both. Also, the notoriety of Kin-Buc, Chemical Control, and several other sites and facilities had gone way beyond the confines of
its borders. Congressional attention, however, made it immeasura-
bly more difficult for New Jersey to carry out its strategy of selected and limited prosecution. Even the rather perfunctory survey
of the grants used to build the Inter-Agency Hazardous Waste Task
Force and related entities—hurriedly carried out by the GAO following the subcommittee's request—embarrassingly revealed
some "accounting errors," as they were called. The integrity of numerous state agencies was challenged from so many quarters that it

took a massive effort both to prosecute and cover up at the same time.

In New York, the strategy for most law enforcement agencies was a great deal simpler to follow than New Jersey's. The plan in the Empire State appears to have been no prosecutions at all. So tardy, if not delinquent, was law enforcement in New York that the Assistant U.S. Attorney assigned to head the primary investigation into toxic waste dumping was often unable to find the time to meet with investigators and to subpoena important records. The city's district attorneys appeared equally disinterested in the problem, even though so much of it was directed by New York–based criminal syndicates. And, however frustrating it was for Ottens, Guslavage, Penney, and Brennan, they weren't fired as John Fine had been. New York did nothing that came close to matching the positive work accomplished, against very heavy odds, by its neighbor. It did match New Jersey, however, in the seriousness of the corruption problem within its state and local agencies.

7

Landfills and the Politics of Waste

THE SIGNIFICANCE OF LANDFILLS for waste disposal businesses cannot be overestimated. In almost every wiretap of organized crime members involved in the waste business since the 1960s, the control of dumps is discussed. Even earlier, in both congressional and state testimony on the garbage industry, the domination of landfills was identified as one of the ways organized crime's waste companies muscled legitimate firms out of business while providing substantial profits for the owners. Sometimes, of course, organized crime firms, as well as those only marginally associated with organized crime, have even been aided in their domination by public officials. Instances can be found where legitimate landfill operators have been driven out of business by public agencies while horrendous dumps have been allowed to remain in operation. Such inequities provoked suspicion from those attempting to understand the pattern and logic of state regulation.

For instance in 1981, during a hearing on poisoned landfills before the House Subcommittee, this point was raised by Donald Jones, a refuse carter and landfill operator for twenty-eight years in New Jersey. Jones stated that his landfill, which had been constantly inspected by the DEP but never fined for leachate problems or any other violations, was closed on December 11, 1980, because it did not have an approved engineering design. He wondered about this in light of the DEP's actions toward several other much larger poisoned landfills, such as Global and Edgeboro, which also operated without approved engineering plans. Both of these, Jones added, were located in wetland areas adjacent to surface water flows. He wanted to know why DEP shut him down and not Global which, over the years, had been repeatedly fined for leachate violations, failing to provide adequate cover, dumping garbage into the water, receiving sludge contrary to regulations, and for accepting PCBs.

Jones went on to testify that in March, 1978, a health officer had asked the DEP to stop a New Jersey company from disposing of aluminum sludge which contained arsenic, lead, and other extremely toxic substances. The DEP ignored the health officer's advice and did not test the material. Rather, the DEP official who had been contacted by the health officer wrote in a letter to the company that "the above waste is considered nonhazardous and does not require the use of the New Jersey Special Waste Manifest Forms," thus giving its go-ahead for the waste to proceed to Edgeboro. All this is reminiscent of the approval letters written by Ronald Buchanan of the DEP for Chemical Control, allowing it to use Edgeboro and other landfills as long as "their papers were in order." Inside knowledge which was passed to the DEP claiming that the manifests were fraudulent was simply ignored.

Illicit landfill operations and official corruption go hand in hand. This is especially so when organized crime syndicates are involved in the daily operations of landfills. Law enforcement officers Grogan, Greenberg, and Fine became embroiled in the politics of landfills when they discovered illegal dumping in Clarkstown and then Ramapo. Before long, they were dealing with the criminal activities of Carmine Franco. Along the way, as the investigators pointed out, time and again they were prevented from moving ahead by various political figures. John Fine was fired. Detective Greenberg wasn't, but he was called a liar by Rockland County District Attorney Kenneth Gribetz during the summer of 1980, when the New York State Senate Select Committee on Crime held its contentious hearing on Rockland County.

District Attorney Gribetz's testimony at this hearing was interesting. His opening remarks contained the following declaration: "During the coming decade the resources and facilities of the New York State Police and the New York State Attorney General's Office must be bolstered in order to meet head on the problem of organized crime activity in the landfill industry and to continuously monitor the careful utilization of our landfill sites." And a little later in his testimony he added: "If we do not take immediate action on a uniform and statewide basis to ferret out official corruption and to root out organized crime activities involving the misuse of our landfills, we will have severe environmental, ecological, law enforcement and health problems throughout our State." Action was imperative, he concluded, otherwise organized crime would totally control the landfill industry.

Yet when questioned about Raymond Cimino and his links to organized crime, Gribetz said that "the term organized crime is probably the most loosely used term that there is in the State of New York." In answer to another question, he commented that "every county in the State of New York has a serious organized crime problem without exception dealing with carting and dumping." When asked specifically about the Sorgine arson and extortion case, Gribetz pontificated: "Again, without going into—it's easy to allege organized crime. It's a great word. It's also a meaningless word. . . ." Back and forth Gribetz went: organized crime was a menace, controlling carting, dumping, landfills, and politicians everywhere; and organized crime was meaningless, misused, and an absurd term, particularly when it was brought up in the context of Rockland County, in the arson of Sorgine's house, in the person of Carmine Franco.

For Gribetz, organized crime had meaning only when he used the term; Greenberg was a Republican liar out to ruin the Rockland County Democrats; and Ralph Smith, the man who fired John Fine, was an honest man. Since the Organized Crime Task Force investigation into toxic waste dumping in Rockland County was, in effect, taken over by Gribetz after Fine was dismissed, he was asked whether any witnesses had been brought before the grand jury. Gribetz responded: "At the present time it's the belief of the New York State Police that there is insufficient evidence to warrant the arrest of anybody." Toward the end of his less than enlightening testimony on Rockland County, Gribetz couldn't resist returning to his theme. The most important law enforcement problem in New York State going "unattended" was organized crime and official corruption, coming together in certain environmentally dangerous landfills. Realizing what that last statement actually meant, he hurriedly added that the problem really came about "through a lack of resources, simply not because of any wrongdoing by law enforcement officials or State officials."

There is no argument with Gribetz about the lack of resources. Indeed, there is no argument with his statement that organized crime and corrupt politicians acted together to create some of the most toxic landfills in the nation. The lack of resources was well established at the 1980 hearing through the testimony of Joseph Puchalik, a former regional solid waste engineer with the DEC. Puchalik was the DEC official responsible for the Ramapo dump, along with 120 other landfills that he alone worked. Puchalik's budget from the DEC in 1976 was $900 for travel expenses and $200 for equipment and supplies. At one point, Puchalik couldn't even afford the $24 necessary to give conservation officers litmus paper to determine if a truck was carrying a caustic or acid solution. Puchalik also noted that DEC personnel were hardly the type to deal with the organized crime people, "who are," as he said, "doing a number on the environment."

The end of the line for the Ramapo landfill came on New Year's Day, 1984. New York State Environmental Commissioner Henry G. Williams ordered the dump closed because he feared the possible contamination of drinking water. The current Town Supervisor argued that Ramapo still needed time to work out a long-term solution, but he was told that time had run out. The Ramapo dump was characterized as one of the worst in the state, and was reclassified as a hazardous waste site, eight years after Grogan and then Greenberg began to suspect that organized crime was "doing a number on the environment."

Managing the Public's Right to Know

Many governmental agencies are withholding vital information about toxic wastes from the public because they march to the tune of various private interests. What we spoke of earlier as "damage control" is partly an expression of the political manipulation of information. The less than forthright statements offered by New Jersey officials before the Congress in December, 1980, demonstrated how political considerations temper information. In New York, damage control in the form of misleading information—untimely and grudgingly released to the public—was something of an art form.

New York, of course, found it much easier to mislead than New Jersey did, because New York never bothered to put together any special investigating or prosecuting units as New Jersey had. New York, thus, never had to report on progress, never had to evaluate, never had to justify the use of federal funds. Once John Fine was fired, the state of New York never had to worry about the actions and activities of state organized crime task forces. Indeed, the firing must have been quite a message to other prosecutors and investigators who might have been unclear about priorities. With no concerted action, no one had to tremble at the thought of testifying before Congress, no one had to be afraid of anything. Clearly, New York officials had learned a lesson from Love Canal. They had waded through the public outcry, the terrible publicity, determined not to let it happen again. Other Love Canals, whether they actually existed or not, were not to be looked for.

One of the ways in which protection from bad publicity is assured is the constant manipulation of information. Managing information on toxic waste issues through manipulation has included the careful editing of material dealing with the manner in which toxics are handled and by whom, and how agencies have grossly mishandled environmental and health hazards. These kinds of activities need not be designed—although they often are—to cover particular criminal acts or groups of criminal conspirators. They may be done routinely as defensive acts to enable governmental agencies to gain time. It is clear to many people, for instance, that various "ad hoc" fact-finding bodies are constructed and sent on their missions in the hope that they will take their time in reporting on whatever problem they are formed to investigate, and that their findings will not be too unpalatable for those in positions of responsibility. Government needs time to work out what we may call its "posture" on large-scale problems.

In 1982, New York faced a crisis of sorts over the issue of toxic waste in New York City's landfills. The crisis was three-pronged, although all the elements were not distinctly related. First, the city was caught, through a judicious leak to a local newspaper, with an embarrassing report which indicated that toxic wastes were a much more severe problem in the municipal landfills than had previously been admitted. Second, the New York State Senate Select Committee on Crime held a hearing in the spring which produced undeniable testimony of toxic waste dumping on a massive scale into certain of the landfills. Along with the testimony came the admission that a key Department of Sanitation employee was paid off to allow the dumping. And, third, a company which provided cover (dirt) for at least two of New York's landfills was jointly owned by a notorious organized crime figure and a state senator. Any one of these issues was a potential public relations disaster for the city.

This last matter was the focus of a Washington investigation into the alleged organized crime associations of Secretary of Labor Raymond Donovan when he worked for the Schiavone Construction Corporation in New Jersey. The Washington investigators were not concerned that one of Schiavone's subcontractors had also contracted to supply dirt to the New York City Department of Sanitation. They were very interested, however, in the fact that the subcontracting firm was run by a mobster and what that might mean for Secretary Donovan. But it wasn't that simple for the city, which knew it had another landfill public relations problem on its hands. Beginning in the spring of 1982 and continuing through September, one event after another kept bringing various landfill questions back to public attention.

The political manipulation of environmental information concerning toxic waste in New York City's landfills—which lie in Staten Island, Brooklyn, Queens, and the Bronx like huge suppurating wounds—is one among many expressions of corruption plaguing New Yorkers when it comes to toxic waste. Four of the five counties that comprise New York City suffer from poisons which are in the landfills. To what degree is unknown. Those who live near these landfills, and others who pass by them on a regular basis, do not know what is brewing. Their lack of knowledge is by design.

On June 23, 1982, a study entitled "Health/Environmental Impact Assessment of the New York City Landfills" was leaked to the press. Six months later a second study, "New York City Landfill Assessment," was released. Both were prepared under the direction of the New York State Department of Environmental Conservation (DEC). The June document has been variously described as a working paper, interim report, or draft, while the December paper was written for public release. There is no question that the December report was a mere public relations effort on the part of the city and the DEC, intended to cover up the revelations of the earlier study. Both documents had more to do with political considerations than with public health and the environmental hazards of toxic wastes. Even the first study was itself commissioned as a stopgap measure to prevent a possible public outcry over the illegal dumping of toxic wastes at city landfills. Clearly enough, even its conclusions were politically unpalatable.

City Landfills and Public Health

On September 7, 1982, the Staten Island *Advance* reported that "Arsenic, mercury, lead and other toxic metals seeping out of three city garbage dumps might be accumulating in shellfish and killfish growing in Jamaica Bay, a state panel of landfill experts wrote in a recent unpublished report." The *Advance* was referring to a study conducted by an ad hoc group known as the New York City Landfill Assessment Team, composed of Earl H. Barcomb from the New York State Department of Environmental Conservation, Division of Solid Waste; Robert L. Collin from the Division of Water; and Wallace E. Sonntag representing the Division of Air.

The team was created after reported incidents of hazardous waste dumping at New York City landfills, at the request of the Department of Environmental Conservation's Region II regional director. Actually, the team investigated not only the city landfills but also the effect of the dumping on public health. Earlier, the New York City Health Department had maintained that toxic exposure from city landfills had not threatened public health. Mincing no words, the Landfill Assessment Team revealed that the original so-called study by the Department of Health was constructed on a data base that had significant deficiencies. They noted with astonishment that the report was only available in the form of a May 19, 1982, "verbal status briefing by a City Health Department representative." Additionally, there was no indication of when the City Health Department would issue its ultimate findings. Nevertheless, the team was verbally briefed and did have access to some preliminary data analysis.

With these limitations in mind, the Landfill Assessment Team wrote that the City Department of Health had committed analytical errors of the most elementary nature in its investigation of water quality, and its manner of taking and testing water samples. And the team was unable to find any data on the amounts of organic and inorganic toxic materials that had accumulated in the marine life and sediments near the landfills.

In a very small section of the report entitled "Adequacy of Existing Department of Sanitation's Sampling Programs," an enumeration of Sanitation's shoddy efforts at evaluating the toxicity of landfills is given. It points out even Sanitation has admitted in its own inquiry, "the number of monitor wells installed for this preliminary investigation is not adequate to determine if toxic substances are moving from the site as groundwater flows around the entire periphery of each of the four landfills." In addition, the record keeping by the Department of Sanitation of its analysis was so poor that the Assessment Team was unable to tell which log applied to which monitoring well, and at what depths the groundwater was sampled. All this meant that the area "most likely to show large concentrations of volatile chemicals (the water table surface) was never really sampled." It seems obvious that anyone relying on New York City's Departments of Sanitation and Health to determine the safety of city landfills and those neighborhoods near them could be in peril without realizing it.

Once it became clear that the earlier study was so deeply flawed and scientifically marred, the Assessment Team conducted its own analysis. Its analytical results showed unmistakably that the concentrations of arsenic, barium, chromium, lead, manganese, selenium, and phenols exceeded DEC groundwater standards in each one of the city landfills. It was also true that for some of the city landfill sites, the amounts of cadmium, chloride, copper, iron, mercury, zinc, ethylbenzene, and methylene chloride exceeded groundwater standards. After sampling surface water near the beleagured landfill areas, it found concentrations of mercury in excess of EPA surface salt water criteria. The Assessment Team made these discoveries in about a month's time.

The mistakes, the hesitant and faltering efforts, represent something more than scientific bungling. Officials in charge of city and state departments and agencies are, of course, anxious to establish that they are not responsible for either past deaths and diseases or current and future disasters. Not surprisingly, investigations conducted by those having a vested interest in the outcome of the probe reveal a public record of agency diligence and innocence. The primary function of public reports such as New York's December one is to beguile the public into believing that things are under control.

Even accepting the appalling bungling of the Health Department, it is still remarkable that other city agencies claimed to be unaware of these problems. The Assessment Team's reconstruction of how information was collected on the illegal dumping shows these agencies were hardly as innocently uninformed as they pretended to be.

The draft report states that early in May, 1982, testimony taken by State Senator Marino's Select Committee on Crime indicated that hazardous waste was being illegally dumped in New York City landfills. A driver-dispatcher employed by an outfit known as Hudson Oil Refining Co. testified that metal plating, lacquer, solvents, waste oil, and sludges had been disposed of at the major city landfills from May, 1974 until April, 1980. During the six years of dumping by Hudson Oil alone, the volumes of waste discarded ranged from 11,000 to 55,000 gallons per week in 1974 and upward of 50,000 gallons a night at one particular landfill in 1978. In addition, the Senate Select Committee revealed that Hudson had at some point moved its operations to Pennsylvania. In a court case in Pennsylvania which centered on Hudson's dumping into the Susquehanna River, it was admitted that other contaminants dumped by Hudson included cyanide, dichlorobenzene, dioctylphthalate, napthalene, ethylbenzene, toluene, xylene and alkyl phenols. The Assessment Team concluded there was every reason to believe that whatever Hudson dumped into the Susquehanna was also deposited in the New York City landfills.

The historical point was that until the Select Committee on Crime held its hearing in May, the city was simply uninformed. The problem with this view is that it was untrue. Senator Marino's committee had been delving into the problem of toxic wastes in New York City landfills and other places, such as Ramapo, for several years. It had held hearings on the problem since 1980, and according to staffers had been hampered, not aided, in its investigation by city agency after city agency. Only the accumulated pressure of innumerable revelations by the committee finally led to the DEC's political decision to form the Assessment Team. It may well be that the spring 1982 hearing was partially a device employed by the committee to shame the city and state into taking some action against Hudson Refining and other toxic waste dumpers. So, rather than the first step to awareness that the Assessment Team thought it was, the hearing was more accurately the final

step by the committee to have the landfills properly evaluated at
last.

The Select Committee's Investigation of City Landfills

To understand more fully the way in which the public record
was manipulated, we should note what was developed during the
May 6, 1982, Senate Select Committee on Crime's Hearing on
Hazardous Waste Dumping. Held in the Great Hall of the Cham-
ber of Commerce Building in Manhattan, the first witness was
Kenneth Mansfield, who worked for a firm known originally as
Northeast Oil. In the early to mid-1970s, his firm picked up waste
oil from industrial users and service stations and transported it to
its recycling plants. The hearing quickly established that Northeast
Oil had spread contaminated sludges and other toxic liquids on the
roads crisscrossing the city's landfills. This material often included
a combination of fuel oils, industrial oils with PCBs, and lube oils
from gas stations.

The states generating this waste were New Jersey, Connecticut, Massachusetts, Delaware, and, fittingly enough, New York. In
1976, the approximate volume of toxic wastes being dumped in the
landfills by Northeast was around 12,000 gallons a day. Northeast
also dumped waste on city property outside the landfills, in Long
Island City, in Brooklyn, and in Staten Island. The Brooklyn sites,
which were industrial properties, were being worked by the Sanitation Department. Because Mansfield's illegal dumping operation
was done at the same time as Sanitation worked, it suggested that
some sort of cooperative arrangement or financial understanding
had been reached between Northeast and Department of Sanitation officials.

The committee next turned to questioning Mansfield about another company called Newtown Refining, a firm composed primarily of the same individuals as Northeast Oil. Newtown had
received a New York City contract worth hundreds of thousands of
dollars to clean up a dump that the company itself had created.
The dump in question was located at College Point in the borough
of Queens. Newtown Refining also received a contract from the
state of New Jersey to clean up a lagoon of oil, oil sludges, and
other material that contained PCBs. Just as in the New York exam-

ple, it turned out that the creator of this lagoon was an oil company called Diamond Head which was owned by at least some of the principals of Newtown Refining. In the New Jersey case, it was pointed out that some of the oil picked up was dumped at Long Island City, some into New York City landfills, some taken to Massachusetts, and some simply pumped down a nearby sewer. The amount of toxic material in this particular affair was at least 1 million gallons. Concerning the so-called recycling facility at Long Island City, Mansfield testified that as of the hearing (May 6), it was closed and in the hands of a court-appointed trustee. Nevertheless, this did not make the approximately 300,000 gallons of toxic wastes disappear.

Having established to some extent the range of toxic dumping engaged in by Northeast Oil and other related concerns such as Newtown Refining and Diamond Head, the committee then questioned Mansfield about the routine followed by toxic dumpers who used city landfills. Mansfield stated in his opinion nobody "went directly on their own into a landfill"; the operation had to be cleared by "an official in the City of New York." In Mansfield's experience, the official was John Cassiliano, an employee of the Sanitation Department. The committee also questioned Cassiliano that day, but all he stated was that he had been with the Sanitation Department for twenty-eight years and that his last position was general superintendent of the Structural Division.

The committee confirmed at the May hearing that toxic waste dumping into city landfills had been going on for some time. Moreover, testimony indicated that illegal dumping on a grand scale was apparently sanctioned by at least one official in the Department of Sanitation. And, finally, other witnesses called by the committee stated that there were exceedingly deep divisions within the Department of Environmental Conservation over the issue of the city's landfills. For example, Samuel J. Kearing, Jr., who had been the regional counsel for the DEC's Region II, testified that the DEC was virtually impotent when dealing with the city and what he termed its wildly out-of-compliance landfills. On this subject, Kearing had written a letter to the compliance counsel of the DEC, which stated, among other things,

> . . . what troubles me most is that we have no credibility with the city. We have not enforced the law where the city is con-

cerned, and no one has any reason to believe that we ever will. This issue has demoralized the staff of our water program and has a strong negative influence across other programs as well. . . . We have an opportunity with the Fresh Kills matter to establish a new posture, to start acting like a regulatory agency in regard to the biggest single polluter in this region.

Fresh Kills was a city landfill on Staten Island with an extraordinary leachate problem.

Kearing sent this letter in August, 1980, and its ultimate effect was to cost him his job. The first response came from Terry Agriss, who was his supervisor and a regional director of the DEC in New York City. Agriss, according to Kearing, threatened him with an unsatisfactory personnel evaluation if he did not follow her instructions concerning the city's landfills. After this, the split between Kearing and various other officials within the DEC heightened. Kearing summarized the tensions in the following manner:

Well, what occurred was that I had a number of complaints about the way the enforcement process was being handled in the New York City region, and I was attempting for a period of almost two years to do something about it, and this letter on Fresh Kills was really part of the process. I was concerned that the policy of the agency, the explicit policy of the agency, was not to enforce the law against the City of New York. That subsequently became a tacit policy, and that I was being directed to do things that I felt were improper and indeed contrary to my—to my code of ethics which every attorney has to adhere to, and I wrote a letter to Commissioner Flacke about that finally in October of last year, October of '81 and . . . it was, I think worthy of a response.

Unfortunately for Kearing, the answer he received was a summons to appear in Albany before the first deputy commissioner of the DEC, Peter Lanahan, who told him that he had five weeks to get out of the agency. In addition, if Kearing agreed to leave voluntarily, Lanahan would give him a good letter of recommendation; otherwise he wouldn't. Kearing told Lanahan that he was a civil servant protected by law, and then went on to state that the DEC policy concerning New York City was both illegal and improper, and that as far as toxic and hazardous wastes were concerned, "the department simply does not have a coherent policy, that the net effect of the—of the hazardous waste program of the State of New York and the federal Environmental Protection Agency is just about zero."

Following this meeting, Kearing found out that he was to be fired on Christmas Eve. He subsequently told his supervisor that he would go to court if that happened. The DEC responded to Kearing's refusal to leave, and his determination to fight his imminent dismissal, by filing charges against him under Article 75 of the Civil Service Law. This meant, Kearing testified, that he was charged with "insubordination, refusal to prosecute four cases, and being nasty to Miss Agriss." When all was said and done, Kearing was not fired but moved from his post as DEC's regional counsel to the position of administrative law judge on Long Island for the DEC.

Prior to this maneuver, however, Kearing was charged with non-prosecution of certain cases by the DEC. On this issue Kearing testified that one case concerned the City Housing Authority. At the time the charges were filed against him, he had an offer from the Housing Authority to settle the case. Their representative agreed to spend $20 million and to clean up eighty-four incinerators. Kearing felt that the charge lacked substance.

Another case involved a company called J B Waste Oil. Kearing readily admitted that he refused to prosecute, but the circumstances surrounding the case presented a far different conclusion than the one suggested by the DEC. J B Waste Oil was supposed to be one of the best companies in the industry. The owner had the reputation for being the "most responsible guy" in waste oil. A small three-truck firm, company officials and Kearing were meeting to work out a DEC consent order so it could continue its business. Kearing was then informed that the DEC wanted to drive J B out of business. "At that point, I just threw up my hands. I mean I was going to bring a . . . legal action against the best one in the business when we were permitting the worst ones to operate under a consent order? And I just thought the whole thing was ridiculous, and I refused to do it."

The DEC's unhappy and unfair treatment of Kearing and J B Waste Oil paralleled the case of Donald Jones in his dealings with New Jersey's DEP. Both Jones and Kearing asked the same question, finding it incomprehensible that the worst companies were allowed to continue their practices while the best ones were constantly hounded by state environmental officers.

Public Relations versus Public Health

On December 1, 1982, the DEC issued its only public pronouncement on the city's landfills. The primary conclusion claimed that the city had acted swiftly and in the public interest over the issue of toxic dumping in its landfills. The fact is, however, that city and state regulatory agencies consistently betrayed the public interest and protected the toxic waste dumpers. Interestingly, the DEC classified this public report as an interim statement whose conclusions were not final. When problems are mentioned, they are presented obliquely: "The available data base does indicate adverse impacts to ground and surface waters," with a quick recanting: "it is important to note, however, that ground and surface waters in the vicinity of the landfills are not used as sources for public drinking water supplies." The impression created is that toxic leachate from the city landfills is not very significant because it does not directly and immediately affect public drinking water supplies.

It may well be that the purpose of information controlled by government is to satisfy bureaucratic needs, and the most important need is to prolong that period until an accounting is finally necessary. The structure of the information-gathering and reporting process in the hands of government is such that the process itself is typically so well hidden that it takes a major effort merely to locate the gatherers, let alone to evaluate their findings. More than this, the vocabulary employed by government to describe reports not originally designed for public consumption, such as "interim," may be seen as part of the corruption. The passage of time defuses both the public interest and the outrage. Everything becomes more manageable; responsibility is confused because the connections between events are lost.

The residents of New York and New Jersey are, of course, not unique in this. Connecticut's Department of Environmental Protection has recently reported on a company, Environmental Waste Removal, Inc., which has been accused of improperly disposing of toxic chemicals on its property in Waterbury. The report holds that there is little evidence to support the charges that have been made by "employees." But *New York Times* reporter Ralph Blumenthal stated that citizens' groups claimed the Department investigators looked in the wrong places. Additionally, an analysis completed by a consulting company hired by the Connecticut State's Attorney, "but never publicly released," found that the data was developed from an "inappropriate sampling method." And while current and former employees have told *New York Times* reporters "that they had participated in, or knew of, improper dumping of large quantities of hazardous waste taken in for treatment by the company," two of the key witnesses were never called for questioning by the state. When confronted with the fact that Environmental Waste Removal was still discharging excessive cyanide waste into the city treatment plant, Waterbury's chief industrial waste inspector remarked: "This is a concern to us."

There are other more insidious reasons why government should mislead the public about toxic waste rather than merely to gain time in which to develop a public relations angle. One is the covering up of crimes and criminals, because to do otherwise invites further investigation which may be uncontrollable and lead to embarrassing public corruption—the New Jersey dilemma. The strategy called for is the same in any of the cases: Do nothing for as long as you can, preferably forever.

It was always one of John Fine's contentions, for instance, that the DEC had made a conscious decision to cover up the most dangerous activities of the major toxic waste dumpers. From his perspective, he was convinced that the policymaking officers of the DEC always acted with malice aforethought. Perhaps his most telling example of this came when he testified about the Chelsea Terminal site on Staten Island. Fine stated he had contacted the New York State Department of Health and the DEC, eventually dealing with Kearing's nemesis, Terry Agriss. One of the problems on Staten Island around the Chelsea Terminal site was leachate running into the Arthur Kill waterway. Not only might there have been all sorts of toxic chemicals in the leachate, but during the course of the original investigation medical vials were found bobbing in the water. An investigator reached into one of the many corroded barrels and came out with "plastic bags that contained medical residue, the residue from hospital laboratories." Immediately, a toxicologist was sent for. Professor Milton Bastos, who was the head of the toxicology laboratory of New York's Office of the Medical Examiner, arrived with a geiger counter and determined that the medical wastes were emitting low levels of radioactivity. Fine then requested the DEC to test the Arthur Kill for radioactivity, but DEC Regional Director Agriss refused to authorize the tests. Fine told of an exchange between himself and Agriss. "You mean you don't want to know that any of these potentially radioactive wastes have been dumped?" he asked Agriss. He reported her answer as "No, the results would probably turn up to be radioactive and then I'll be under pressure to do something about it."

Dealing with Organized Crime

City and state officials were able to weather the storm coming from both the leaked "interim" report and the Marino committee's hearing. The December study was constructed to end what the city called irresponsible allegations and speculations. In addition, when John Cassiliano was indicted and eventually convicted for accepting bribes from toxic dumpers, the city used this case to prove it was on top of the situation. One might conclude, however, that it merely proved that once city officials were faced with the testimony from Marino's hearing, they had to do something. Moreover, they were given a participant in the conspiracy, Kenneth Mansfield, who had confessed publicly before the committee. His words could not be denied and he was looking for a chance to get a break by admitting all, including his bribing of Cassiliano. This revelation was not welcomed by certain powerful city officials.

There was no "squeeze" attempted during the Cassiliano prosecution, though hardly anyone believed that he was the only agent from the Department of Sanitation involved in the bribery scheme. Those most knowledgeable were sure that he was only one among many taking money. But local law enforcement was unwilling to pressure Cassiliano for information; no agency tried to pressure him to reveal who else was part of the payoff chain. Cassiliano was the beginning and end of Sanitation's corruption, and that was going to be that. This was so despite the fact that Harold Kaufman, who walked into FBI offices so many years before, had first-hand knowledge of high-level corruption in New York surrounding the waste industry. With Kaufman's information and Cassiliano's troubles, New York had an opportunity to open up the entire seamy affair; a chance to investigate vigorously and then prosecute the organized crime dumpers and those like Mansfield who belonged to no organized crime syndicate but operated within the ground rules established by organized crime. Perhaps even those politicians who aided and abetted their activities could have been identified and brought to justice. However, it was an opportunity that was either overlooked or deliberately buried.

Toxic waste produced a sort of double anxiety that spring for many New Yorkers. The first was that suffered by those who believed they were being poisoned but were unable to pin down the extent of the danger. The second plagued those responsible for the damage, who were afraid that they were losing control of the situation. It was bad enough that the public had become privy to the so-called interim report on the landfills. It was worse still that Senator Marino's committee was uncovering more and more evidence that the landfills were some sort of private preserve for the toxic dumpers and their friends in the Sanitation Department. Now, an even more threatening problem loomed.

Part of the new danger came in the spring when investigators for the Select Committee on Crime were led to believe that it would be fruitful to look into companies supplying cover for the landfills. Informants had stated that one way toxic waste was disposed of by organized crime companies was through saturating cover destined for landfills. Records of contracts in the files of the Department of Sanitation were reviewed, revealing that one of the primary companies supplying cover for the landfills was owned and operated by organized crime. Subsequent events did not conclusively prove that this particular company's dirt was saturated with chemicals before delivering it to the landfills, although there are still a number of unanswered questions about the possibility. Nevertheless, the city had contracted with an organized crime firm to furnish cover for the landfills, which in itself was very revealing.

What made this last issue so important was that it merged with the explosive investigation in Washington dealing with charges that the Secretary of Labor, Raymond Donovan, was tied to organized crime. These issues came together in the form of the JoPel Contracting & Trucking Corporation. It was JoPel that the Senate Select Committee's investigators had found in the Department of Sanitation's records; it was JoPel that was clearly a mob company; it was JoPel that had reportedly been allowing toxic waste saturation of its dirt before delivering it to city landfills; and it was JoPel's relationship to Secretary of Labor Donovan which, among other things, so intrigued Washington.

The issue of Donovan and organized crime had been serious enough to merit the appointment, on December 19, 1981, of a Special Prosecutor, Leon Silverman, to investigate allegations that Donovan and his former employer, Schiavone Construction, worked with organized crime. Substantively, the investigation was structured around the possibility that Donovan had lied during his confirmation hearing before the U.S. Senate. JoPel came into the picture, for Silverman, when it was discovered that the company had subcontracted work from Schiavone Construction, which had a large and profitable city construction project. The particular job JoPel performed, under its arrangement with Schiavone Construction, was the basis for the company to then contract with the Sanitation Department to provide landfill cover. The spring and summer of 1982 were therefore trying times for politicians not only from New York but right up to and including those in President Reagan's cabinet. Any number of reporters were laying odds that Donovan would be out by the fall: others were digging around picking over Schiavone Construction looking for mob ties that the Special Prosecutor might miss; and finally, some were working the JoPel angle, guessing that it might be the smoking gun in the Donovan case.

On May, 9, 1982, *New York Times* correspondent Michael Oreskes noted that the Special Prosecutor's initial investigation into Donovan had been expanded to cover allegations that Schiavone Construction dealt with Anthony "Tony Pro" Provenzano. In the same story, Oreskes reported that Special Prosecutor Silverman had reviewed FBI tapes of discussions "involving William Masselli, who is serving prison terms for drug violations and involvement in a hi-jacking ring." Masselli was further identified as a member of organized crime who was one of the owners of a trucking company employed by Schiavone Construction on the construction of a new subway line for New York. Although not identified in the story, that trucking company was JoPel.

Before much could be made about JoPel, the whole Donovan inquiry took on even more sinister tones. On June 15, 1982, the *New York Post* carried a story by Cy Egan headlined: "Witness in Donovan Probe Gunned Down." Reporter Egan stated that Fred Furino, a Teamster official missing since June 3, had been found shot to death and stuffed into the trunk of his car. Furino was supposedly a significant witness in the Donovan investigation because he "reportedly served as a sometime 'bagman' and 'picked up money' from Donovan for a New Jersey mobster." Among Furino's past and present organized crime associates were Salvatore Briguglio, murdered in 1978, and Provenzano. Both Briguglio and Provenzano had been prime suspects in the disappearance of Teamster boss Jimmy Hoffa. According to a *New York Daily News* story on the Furino murder, Furino was among those called before a Detroit federal grand jury investigating the Hoffa case in 1976. Reliable FBI sources have stated that Briguglio, allegedly Donovan's associate, was murdered right before he was to lead the FBI down the final path in the Hoffa case.

The Furino murder was enough for *Newsweek* magazine to headline its June 28 story, "Donovan: 'He's Got to Go.'"Commenting that Donovan was vacationing in Europe, *Newsweek* went on to report gossip gleaned from various high administration officials which indicated that Donovan's "already precarious position in the Reagan Cabinet was crumbling." The story quoted Republican Senator Orrin Hatch from Utah, chairman of the Senate's Labor Committee before which Donovan had testified during the confirmation process, who stated that Donovan should resign. Republican Robert Dole, chairing the very powerful Senate Finance Committee, appeared to agree with Hatch, said *Newsweek*.

Time magazine gave more detail on Donovan than the other publications in its June 28 story. It noted that Furino had been questioned, very intensively, by Silverman's staff and the special grand jury, especially about his alleged role in collecting payoffs from Donovan when he was vice president in charge of labor relations for Schiavone Construction. Other items in *Time*'s report included the fact that Frank Silbey, the chief investigator for the Senate Labor and Human Resources Committee, had been threatened with death unless he layed off the Donovan investigation. *Time* also reported allegations that Donovan associated with organized crime figure Phillip Moscato. And, it added, one of Donovan's associates could be heard on a wiretap talking with William Masselli, whom the magazine described as "an admitted Mafia member."

All this attention came to a head that summer for two reasons. One was, of course, the murder of Furino. The second was the anticipation of Special Prosecutor Silverman's report on the investigation, which was completed on June 25, 1982, but which was being reviewed before it would be made public.

Only a short time after all these stories with their very intense speculations were published, Silverman's report was out. Very carefully, Silverman enumerated the various charges made by several informants concerning Donovan and Schiavone Construction. Most of the information on Donovan came—as Silverman pointed out—from informants such as Ralph M. Picardo, a "former participant in the federal witness protection program whose admitted crimes include loansharking, fencing, labor racketeering and conspiracy to commit murder." Picardo claimed that Secretary of Labor Donovan, when he was vice president of Schiavone Construction, conspired with several organized crime figures including the late Salvatore Briguglio and Armand Faugno, and at least one crooked politician, William V. Musto, who had been the mayor of Union City, New Jersey, a state senator, and chairman of the New Jersey State Judiciary Committee. Musto was convicted in the early spring of 1982 of aiding a government contractor in a scheme to inflate certain construction costs on two federally funded projects in New Jersey, and then keeping a portion of the overcharges.

Picardo was interviewed several times by the FBI and others, including a Newark, New Jersey, Strike Force attorney, and two staff assistants from the Senate Labor Committee. On January 15, 1982, Picardo gave an account of his dealings with Schiavone Construction and Donovan. Basically, his charge was that Schiavone Construction had been paying off the mob for "labor peace," and that Donovan was one of those actually passing the money.

A very elaborate account of Donovan's alleged organized crime contacts and associates came from Giacomo (Jack) Napoli, described as a former federally protected witness dismissed from the Witness Protection Program because he continued his criminal activities. Silverman, who was put in touch with Napoli by an ABC Television producer, interviewed him a number of times in May 1982. Napoli claimed to have met Donovan on several occasions in

New Jersey and Florida, and maintained that Donovan had social and business relationships with some very infamous organized crime people. Among those he mentioned were John DiGilio, Joseph A. Zicarelli, Joseph Paterno, Salvatore Briguglio, Frank Basto, and especially Philip Moscato. Napoli also remarked that the entire leadership of Teamster Local 560, dominated by Anthony Provenzano, was "knowledgeable" of Donovan's association with Briguglio. After a great deal of searching, interviewing, and grand jury testimony, Silverman stated that there was no evidence to support any part of the Napoli story. Furthermore, Silverman suggested that Napoli might have concocted or colored his story in order to get back into the Federal Witness Protection Program.

The Scandal of JoPel

Silverman began that section of his report on William Masselli, the co-owner of JoPel Contracting & Trucking, by noting that Masselli had pleaded guilty to a number of serious charges, including a drug conspiracy, in 1981. Masselli also apparently admitted that he was a member of the "Genovese Mafia family." At Donovan's confirmation hearing following his nomination to Reagan's cabinet, he was asked by the Senate Labor Committee about Masselli. He admitted knowing Masselli but only "in passing, on the job site." He did not know, Donovan testified, that Masselli was a mob figure. As far as the Senate Labor Committee was concerned, Donovan's explanation was not enough to deny him confirmation as Secretary of Labor. The issue seemed over until *Time* magazine revived it on June 8, 1981, with a report that wiretaps of JoPel contained conversations between Donovan and Masselli. Nothing much happened until Silverman was appointed Special Prosecutor over seven months later. During the second week of January, 1982, staff members from the Senate Labor Committee shared with Silverman "serious reservations" about Masselli's ties to Schiavone Construction, which came about when JoPel was hired as a subcontractor on a project to build a new subway line in New York. Most helpfully, Schiavone gave JoPel a $200,000 start-up loan for its part of the project.

Special Prosecutor Silverman spent a great deal of time on the JoPel matter. His conclusion was that Secretary of Labor Donovan had not lied during his confirmation hearing about his passing association with William Masselli, and that he had little to do with either Schiavone Construction's deals with JoPel or any of the disputes that flowed from them. The upshot of the Special Prosecutor's investigation was the exoneration of Donovan, although, specifically in the JoPel case, Silverman made it clear that other Schiavone Construction officers might deserve closer scrutiny. Silverman noted that Richard Callaghan, senior vice president for Schiavone Construction, had used a Florida condominium owned by Masselli in the past. But as far as Secretary Donovan was concerned, the case seemed settled.

In New York, however, the JoPel matter was not by any means resolved. While Donovan was out of it, the city of New York still had to resolve its connection to JoPel. What had been simmering in Washington for so long had now become a potentially damaging scandal in New York. Just a few weeks after the Silverman report, *New York Daily News* reporter Marcia Kramer wrote that the city had paid JoPel over $500,000 for landfill cover which the city already owned. She noted that the cover was used by the city even though it was below the standards set for landfills. And, if anyone had missed the news, Kramer stated that JoPel was owned by a mobster and a state senator. Two days after Kramer's article, Mayor Edward I. Koch ordered the New York City Department of Investigation into the fray. Specifically, it was to investigate how and why JoPel was awarded two subcontracts from the Department of Sanitation. Before the Department could begin its work, Kramer wrote another story which revealed that the city also had contracted with a firm called Red Apple Equipment Corporation that was very closely linked with JoPel.

The Department of Investigation could not have worked much more than a month on this matter since its final report is dated September, 1982. In between the time the staff started and finished, probably the single most explosive event in the entire JoPel–Schiavone episode occurred. On August 25, 1982, William Masselli's son, Nat Masselli, was shot in the back of the head while sitting in his car, parked in the Bronx. The murder of Nat Masselli caused Special Prosecutor Silverman to reopen his investigation into Donovan. After a short time, however, Silverman announced that there seemed to be no connection between the Donovan affair and the murder.

This conclusion was not shared by prosecutors working the killing. Two suspects, Salvatore Odierno and Philip Buono, both identified as important organized crime figures, were quickly arrested in the case. Although Buono had worked for another Masselli company for many years, listed on the payroll as a salesman, Odierno had no known, direct relationship with the Massellis.

About a year later, Odierno was tried for the murder. Buono's case was separated from Odierno's and he was tried and convicted afterward. The prosecution's contention at the first trial, held in the State Supreme Court in the Bronx, was that Nat Masselli had been murdered by Odierno to end the federal investigation into Donovan and organized crime. Masselli was shot "to impede, obstruct and destroy the investigation into Mr. Raymond Donovan," Assistant District Attorney Martin L. Fisher stated in his summation. The Odierno case was decided on October 5, 1983. He was convicted of first-degree manslaughter, and acquitted on the charge of murder in the second degree. Clearly, the jury was convinced that he participated in the murder, but voted for the lesser charge because Odierno was not accused of firing the fatal shot. In addition, Selwynn Rabb of *The New York Times* reported that the jury believed Odierno had not intended to murder Masselli. It was apparently, they concluded, a meeting in Masselli's car which got out of hand.

While Silverman was unable to tie the Masselli murder to any of the allegations about Donovan, the city's Department of Investigation hardly found it worth mentioning in any detail in its JoPel report. As tightly drawn as a drum, the report nevertheless revealed a great deal. First, it affirmed that the Department of Sanitation had negotiated two contracts in 1980 for landfill cover at sites in Edgemere, Queens, and Fountain Avenue, Brooklyn. For its work in Queens, JoPel received $143,069; for Brooklyn, the price was $325,495. The Department of Investigation next noted that the dirt provided by JoPel had once belonged to the city, but it had surrendered ownership of the material under a contract in 1979 between Schiavone Construction and the New York City Transit Authority. In passing, the report stated that the city had the option of keeping the cover material and directing Schiavone Construction to bring it to one or more of the landfills, although, it hastened to point out, Schiavone Construction could then have charged the city for delivery.

When everything on this topic was analyzed, the Department of Investigation concluded that "we believe it unlikely that the City experienced a loss when it purchased the cover material. If the City did experience a loss it was not a substantial one." Then, seemingly to qualify its previous position, it added that the entire problem was very difficult to answer because the question of whether the city lost on its complicated deals with Schiavone Construction and JoPel resisted "the application of empirical data" as a result of the "number of alternative fact patterns that could have evolved and the principals and corporations who were involved in this matter, many of whom have been the subject of criminal investigations." It is, of course, quite unclear what that clumsy phrase—"alternative fact patterns"—means.

The Department of Investigation next turned to the quality of the cover JoPel delivered. The cover was not exactly what the contract called for. Failure to meet the contract requirement of a minimum 25 percent clay or silt content cost JoPel almost $8,000 in penalties. However, the exact same amount was later credited to JoPel for supposedly exceeding the contract requirements in other deliveries. The report stated that, in any case, all the cover delivered by JoPel exceeded the quality demanded by the New York State Conservation Rules and Regulations. How the Department of Investigation knew that was not discussed, since the only way to get that information was to analyze the material—and only the Department of Sanitation could have done that. But it was precisely the Department of Sanitation which was, if not under investigation, then surely under a dark cloud of suspicion. Nevertheless, the investigators clearly accepted Sanitation's word on the quality of the cover.

Actually, Sanitation engineers certified the cover by examining the excavation site, not the material delivered. Whether anything at all was added to the dirt taken from the excavation site was unknown to Sanitation. JoPel trucks were weighed at the landfills, but the material was not inspected before it was spread. JoPel could have trucked excavation dirt to a second location, had it saturated with toxic waste, and then carted it to Queens and Brooklyn. This, of course, gets right to the heart of the Senate Select Committee's informants' claims that JoPel was dumping cover saturated with toxic wastes and using a second site for that part of the operation. One is left with the Department of Sanitation's word that this did not happen.

The fascinating question of just who was behind JoPel was also addressed in the Department of Investigation report. The majority owner (51%) of JoPel was New York State Senator Joseph Galiber. William Pelligrino Masselli, who served as president of the company, owned 49 percent. The Department of Investigation stated that it was not unlawful for Galiber to have a financial interest in a firm contracting with the city. In addition, it was pointed out that although New York City could have tried to disqualify JoPel as a subcontractor on grounds of "irresponsibility," the report doubted the attempt would have worked. In fact, as Sanitation did not do a background check on JoPel, there was no reason for any agency to object. As far as the Department of Investigation was concerned, all this history was meaningless, but it did recommend that in the future the city should not do business with JoPel. It concluded the Department of Sanitation had done nothing wrong.

William P. Masselli had a criminal record that stretched back to 1958, when he was convicted of robbery in one case and kidnapping in another. His robbery conviction was subsequently overturned on appeal, and he was released from the Auburn Prison in 1964. (On this same matter, Special Prosecutor Silverman remarked that Masselli was incarcerated at the Clinton Correctional Facility from April 1958 until May 1962.) After his release, nothing much was heard about him until the U.S. Attorney's Office began an investigation into one of his companies in 1979. This probe determined that Pelligrino Masselli Meats was "the headquarters and nerve center for a sophisticated and highly organized hijacking, theft and stolen property ring." Masselli's meat plant was used as cover for the operation, and as a storage and distribution center for hijacked trucks and trailers. As part of the same investigation, Masselli was also indicted for conspiring to manufacture synthetic cocaine. He pleaded guilty to various charges in both cases and received a sentence of about seven years.

During the course of the federal investigation into Masselli Meats, information about Masselli's other criminal activities was also developed. One other scheme involved JoPel, which, in the winter of 1979, proposed to the Long Island Railroad that it be permitted to dispose of landfill on Railroad property. In order to influence the Railroad, William Masselli bribed Anthony Bacco, the head of the Railroad's Real Estate Department. Bacco pleaded guilty to mail fraud in federal court on June 27, 1980, and about seven months later was sentenced. Given the timing of the Bacco case, coming prior to JoPel's contracts with Sanitation, it could have proven highly embarrassing to the Department of Sanitation if it became public knowledge. But the proceedings were sealed by the court to protect the ongoing investigation into Masselli Meats. It was not until October 9, 1981, that the case became a matter of public record, well over a year after the Sanitation contracts with JoPel.

All this begs the question whether those officials in Sanitation and other city departments and agencies which dealt with JoPel were as uninformed as the Department of Investigation claimed. The likelihood of their knowing nothing about Masselli's mob connections, his past criminal record, is hardly credible. It is well to note that any reputable sociology of organized crime points out that racketeers are, contrary to the spirit of the report, typically well known. Their mob connections serve to advertise their ruthlessness, enhance their reputation, and help, not hinder, their ability to conduct business.

The very origins of JoPel reflect quite clearly how handy it is to be known as a gangster. Before JoPel came on the scene, another company known as Nargi Contracting, headed by Louis R. Nargi, subcontracted a job from Schiavone Construction. This job called for Nargi Contracting to haul dirt away from a Schiavone Construction job in the Bronx. For start-up money, Nargi borrowed $50,000 in cash from his good friend William Masselli. The work was more expensive than Nargi bargained for, and he borrowed additional money from Masselli after Schiavone Construction turned down his request for up-front operating funds. Nargi's second round of borrowing from Masselli was done more formally, with papers signed at an attorney's office in White Plains. Apparently, Nargi was able to finish the job with this infusion of Masselli money, because he next bid on another Schiavone Construction job located on Archer Avenue, Long Island City.

At this point, Masselli told Nargi that a Schiavone Construction official, Al Magrini, had notified him that the subcontractor on the new job had to be a minority company. In order for Schiavone Construction to secure federally funded projects, it reportedly had to give a certain amount of its subcontracts to minority companies.

This was the basis for JoPel. State Senator Joseph Galiber is black, and he and Masselli formed the company in order to take advantage of the federal requirement. It was, as Nargi stated to the FBI in 1980, a sham company set up merely as a device to circumvent the law. After a short time, Nargi was moved out of the business by JoPel. First, Nargi was supposed to be a silent partner; next, JoPel and Nargi Contracting were thoroughly mixed together; then Nargi became a salaried employee of JoPel, although both JoPel and Nargi Contracting had separate contracts from Schiavone Construction. Finally, in 1978, Nargi simply walked away from the business after an argument with William Masselli. The FBI memorandum states:

> Nargi advised that the reason he "walked away" from the business was because Masselli knows all sorts of dangerous people and that the risk was too great for him to object. . . . He knew that Masselli was a friend of Philip Buono whom Nargi knows was a "made guy" in the Mafia. He also knew that to fight a "made guy" meant danger to him since the word on the street is that, "made guys hurt people."

Certainly Nargi understood the commercial value of a reputation for violence, of being known as a member of organized crime. Nargi later recanted his statements to the FBI in an interview with the Special Prosecutor's staff on February 24, 1982, claiming that he had been mistaken. Probably another example of street wisdom in action. And, given what happened to Nat Masselli, Nargi was undoubtedly wise.

The tortured logic of the Department of Investigation's report became even more absurd as it reached its conclusion. While excusing all those in government who should have known that JoPel was nothing but a mob company with a state senator as its front, taking jobs from real minority businesses, the Department of Investigation still had to acknowledge that it was aware, "prior to the award of the two Sanitation contracts in 1980, that William Masselli was the subject of a federal investigation," that the investigation was "publicized by articles . . . which appeared in the *New York Times* beginning February 11, 1980," and that the articles also discussed Senator Galiber. Sanitation signed on with JoPel several months after *The New York Times* articles. Not even the Department of Investigation could claim that *New York Times* stories as recent as the winter of 1980 passed unnoticed by government officials. But its final report was concerned with absolving itself and Sanitation from any accusations of laxity, and, incredible as it may sound, restating its position that there were no grounds for denying JoPel its subcontracts.

The Power of the Dump

As we have already stressed, one of the keys to organized crime's control of waste businesses (both solid and toxic) has been its access to dump sites. Whoever controls the landfills controls a great deal. Clearly enough, organized crime figures representing major crime syndicates heavily involved in toxic waste disposal owned numerous private sites, leased or managed various municipal and township landfills, and bribed their way into others such as New York's. To protect the public from such outrages, there are agencies and departments which have the duty to prevent private interests from overwhelming the public weal. Whether or not JoPel dumped toxic waste, it is still a clear example of two elementary facts when it comes to the battle between public and private interests. Organized crime had the inside track with the Department of Sanitation, which ostensibly controlled city landfills. And, once that became common knowledge, other official departments did their level best to cover the scandal and protect both the image and the careers of civic offices and officers.

Even the Department of Investigation conceded in its discussion of New York's buying back its own dirt that "it strains credibility for government to hold out to taxpayers that their money is well spent ceding landfill cover and then purchasing it later, particularly when the Department of Sanitation represents as it did that it has a continuing need for cover material." The recognition of public credibility, however, did not sit well with the Department of Investigation when it considered other areas in the JoPel case and the role of State Senator Galiber. Essentially, it found nothing unlawful or even unethical in Galiber's conduct. There was also no comment on JoPel's dubious status as a minority company.

However, in comparison with the reporting on the toxicity of city landfills, the Department of Investigation's report on JoPel was a model of candor. Of course, there would have been no investigation of JoPel if not for the Donovan affair, the constant probing and prodding by the New York State Senate Select Committee on Crime, and the timely stories by Marcia Kramer of the *Daily News*. For the public to have to depend upon such serendipitous events in order to find out that it is being poisoned, that organized crime has managed such easy entry to landfills, that state agencies such as the DEC hide from problems, is absurd and outrageous.

Residents of New York and northern New Jersey are not the only ones to suffer these landfill crises. Congressional testimony is filled with examples from across the nation of landfills being laced with toxic waste and citizens in despair because state and federal officials seem unable or unwilling to do very much about this condition. Recently, KYW-TV of Philadelphia aired a program on some poisoned landfills in southern New Jersey and Pennsylvania. The report concentrated on landfills owned and operated by David Erlich and Richard Winn, two waste entrepreneurs attempting to expand their "trail of destruction." Winn, according to KYW, was the money man behind the operation, lining up banks to finance the landfill projects. Erlich took care of securing customers for the landfills and keeping watch on the daily operations. Most of Erlich's business ventures, it was reported, are veiled in secrecy, conducted from post office boxes. Although not yet finished, the investigation by KYW-TV into landfills run by Erlich and Winn has uncovered information allegedly linking them to organized crime. Whether this turns out to be the case, the gathering of this evidence, it should be noted, is being done by reporters and not by New Jersey's DEP or the Inter-Agency Task Force.

What was most upsetting to Pennsylvania residents was that after Erlich and Winn had already poisoned at least three landfills in southern New Jersey, they were permitted to open a new one in Pennsylvania located in Chester County. When the local residents in Chester County protested to the Pennsylvania Department of Environmental Resources (DER) in 1978, citing what had happened in New Jersey, they were told that this background of poisoning was irrelevant. Erlich and Winn were allowed to open their landfill. Investigating the past activities of the two, KYW found that they operated a dump known as the GEMS landfill in Gloucester Township, New Jersey, only minutes from Philadelphia via the Ben Franklin Bridge. The GEMS (which stands for

Gloucester Environmental Management Services) landfill, taken over by Erlich and Winn in 1975, has an exceptionally sordid past. Starting in 1976, the landfill was cited almost sixty times for violations. In 1980, over twenty toxic chemicals were finally identified in the site, including toluene, chloroform, and benzene. Eventually, the EPA found the Gloucester dump among the dozen worst hazardous waste sites in the nation.

It took many years for New Jersey's DEP finally to close the GEMS landfill. But, when it did, Erlich and Winn simply walked away much richer than before. Over the period from 1976 to 1980, Erlich's salary was about $300,000, while Winn made about $750,000. They also received large salaries totaling several hundreds of thousands of dollars from a subsidiary company which was supposed to provide the landfill with management services. "Holding the bag," as KYW put it, is Gloucester County, which owns the property. Erlich and Winn only leased it. Much the same situation prevails at other Erlich and Winn landfills such as one in Jackson Township, New Jersey, where a site known as BEMS (short for Burlington Environmental Management Services) has accumulated toxic poisons for years.

Despite this record of poisoning, Erlich and Winn are petitioning the Pennsylvania DER to enlarge their Chester County dump by a factor of four. As KYW pointed out, this would make the site "higher than William Penn's statue, atop Philadelphia's city hall." It appears that they have a good chance of getting approval, even though, "throughout the application process, they have resisted disclosing their track record in New Jersey to Pennsylvania environmental officials." They may well have resisted, but it is unclear why Pennsylvania has not taken the necessary steps to gather information. KYW-TV could find out that in their wake, Erlich and Winn have ruined numerous lives in New Jersey by constructing monstrously poisoned landfills. It is difficult to believe the DER didn't know what Erlich and Winn had done in the past and couldn't find out what they are currently about. It appears, then, that Pennsylvania's environmental officials, in this case anyhow, are playing the same game found in New York and New Jersey. Perhaps the pressure brought by television exposure will be enough to persuade Pennsylvania officials in the DER to change their inexplicable attitude that past behavior is irrelevant. Permitting the Chester dump to open in 1978 indicated a callous disregard for the public welfare. Allowing it to expand would be another slap in the face to the nearby residents.

The manipulation of public information goes hand in hand with other activities which mark the triumph of private interests over the public welfare when it comes to toxic waste disposal. Governmental deceit is only one part of the package. In addition to corruption, organized crime is prepared to threaten, beat, burn, and kill in order to maintain and extend its control in the waste industry. It represents, in fact, the violent workings of a secret government.

8

The Secret Government of Waste

IT ISN'T ONLY garbage and toxic chemicals that get dumped at landfills. Sometimes dead bodies are casually dropped off during the night. That is the account of a professional killer given recently in an interview while he drove through some of the most squalid sections of Newark and Kearny, New Jersey, in his very expensive foreign car. He explained he had been in the business for well over a decade and had murdered people in New York, New Jersey, Florida, and Chicago. His skills were contracted for by what he called the local Mafia in New York and New Jersey, as well as by Portuguese racketeers in Newark and Greek mobsters in Fort Lee, New Jersey. He had started out as a general purpose strong-arm man who enjoyed, as he put it, "busting someone in the head with a lead pipe." In the early 1960s, he became acquainted with an experienced professional killer who taught him about guns and how to kill efficiently and more or less dispassionately. Although he had begun his career in neighboring Kearny, it was not long before he had achieved some reknown in the Newark underworld.

Driving through Kearny, he commented that it was a favorite mob dumping ground for the dead. In fact, as he drove slowly over the access roads of the notorious MSLA landfill, operated by Richard Miele, William and John Keegan, and several others, and the C. Egan & Sons Sanitary Landfill, he remarked that mob killers routinely dumped bodies at both sites. What made them more attractive than many other landfills, in his estimation, was that massive doses of chemical wastes were also dumped there, meaning the bodies were destroyed faster and much more completely than would otherwise be the case. As he drove down a dirt road, he pointed out the owner of one of the landfills while commenting on the splendid view of New York City. With a wave of his hand toward the owner, who was standing to the side of the road seemingly watching some bulldozers, he recounted that this particular landfill operator was heavily "involved with the Mafia." Coolly, the man related that a number of times he himself had participated in murders and then disposed of the bodies in the Kearny dumps, "where they would be left in the back with the chemical shit and covered with a bulldozer." Sometimes, they put the body in a barrel first and then dumped it alongside numerous 55-gallon drums. MSLA also had an incinerator where bodies were cremated. It was, he remarked, "no big problem." From Kearny to Jersey City to Newark, he listed the landfills where he and others had placed their victims, and where toxic wastes were illegally but, for the killers, so handily dumped.

Landfills were not only perfect places to get rid of bodies, but were often the focus of intensely violent struggles between organized crime figures as they fought for their control. This happened in Rockland County, for example, when Eugene Sorgine's house was torched. The fierceness of this struggle over routes, stops, landfills and access to landfills, and other matters proved deadly as associations and organizations pitted themselves against one another.

Murder in Rockland County

At eleven-thirty at night on June 2, 1976, Natale Schettino's seventy-eight-year old mother-in-law, Caroline Nadel, heard noises outside the house where she lived with the Schettinos and her three grandchildren. Upon opening the front door of the Valley Cottage home to investigate, she was hit in the face, neck, and chest with a blast from a shotgun.

This particularly gruesome murder came after several other incidents involving Schettino's garbage business. A reporter for the local newspaper pieced together some of the story, concluding that the murder of Schettino's mother-in-law was only the latest act in a campaign of harassment against him. The gruff, one-armed Schettino had worked in Clarkstown for several years until 1973, when he and his partner were forced out. Three of their garbage trucks were blown up, and his partner and one of their workers were severely beaten with lead pipes. It was also reported that shortly before the murder, after reentering the business, Schettino had testified before the Clarkstown Sanitation Commission. He complained some garbagemen had banded together to form a monopoly and were trying to intimidate him.

The murder of Caroline Nadel remains unsolved, as are the other acts of violence experienced by Natale Schettino both before and after the killing. Not that there weren't suspects. The Rockland County Sheriff's Department—Greenberg and his colleagues—had investigated the Clarkstown incident and established that, in 1973, Schettino's company, Five Town Sanitation, had underbid its competition for a garbage contract with the Jamesway Stores. The competitor was Round Lake Sanitation, one of the companies the New York Senate Select Committee on Crime identified as controlled by the organized crime cabal of the Mongellis, Milos, and Gigantes. It was shortly after Five Town Sanitation began servicing the Jamesway route that the trouble began. Early one morning, three men stopped one of Schettino's trucks and beat the driver and his assistant. The assailants were identified as Louis J. Raymundo from Yonkers, Richard A. Barone from Bergenfield, New Jersey, and Angelo Michael Prisco, also from Yonkers. The sheriff ran a check on them and found Prisco had been "mentioned in a large scale narcotics case back in 1972, disposition unknown." It was also discovered that Prisco was "on wiretaps on organized crime figures in the New York City area."

What the sheriff's detectives did not know at the time was that the three suspects in the assault were members of a new criminal organization with very strong ties to the Genovese/Tieri crime syndicate. It wasn't until December 7, 1976, that the first unified intelligence report on this group was compiled, with information from the Drug Enforcement Administration, the New York State Police, the New York City Police Department, and the FBI. The group was known as the Purple Gang, and comprised a younger generation of professional criminals from the Pleasant Avenue–East Harlem section of Manhattan. (They were named, as many crime syndicates have been, by a journalist who was reminded of the violent Detroit bootlegging mob of the 1920s called the Purple Gang, after the purple polo shirts they wore.) This gang emerged in the early 1970s as a major one in the heroin trade,

which for several decades had been headquartered in its neighborhood. Many of these young men were related to prominent
organized crime figures, members of older, more traditional syndicates dealing in heroin, and had worked with the older generation
doing many of the menial jobs associated with the trade. However,
the younger group had become "so uncontrollable that the older
traffickers would attempt to avoid them socially in an effort to
evade the attention of law enforcement."

By the mid-1970s, the Purple Gang was noted for having "an
enormous capacity for violence, and involvement in numerous
homicides." Some were also notable for a decided "lack of respect
for other members of organized crime," considering many of the
old-timers to have grown fat and soft. Among the original twenty
members of the Purple Gang, it turned out, were Angelo Michael
Prisco and his brother, Pasquale. It was also clear in 1976 that
Richard Anthony Barone and Louis James Raymundo were part of
the Purple Gang. According to the intelligence report, the Purple
Gang beat Schettino's men at the request of either Mario Gigante
or Joseph Pagano, "a prior federal narcotic violator who originally
came from the Pleasant Avenue–East Harlem area and is now a
ranking member of the Genovese/Tieri organized crime family directing operations in the Rockland–Orange County area."

In any case, there is no doubt that Schettino's original Clarkstown operation was closed down by organized crime, and when he
attempted a kind of comeback a few years later, organized crime
marked him for death, murdering his mother-in-law by mistake.
The fact the original terror campaign against Schettino was carried
out by Purple Gang members certainly suggests that Mrs. Nadel's
murder may also have been one of their assignments. And, even
though the wrong person was killed, the right person undoubtedly
got the message. Beginning with the Schettino case, the use of the
Purple Gang by organized crime to control waste activities in the
New York–New Jersey area became increasingly frequent and included the murders of several major industry figures.

Murder and the Waste Industry

While battles over landfills were one of the causes of violence
in the waste industry, nothing was quite so inviting to violence as

violations of the property rights system. Year after year, beatings, murders, and arsons took place as competition was restrained. It mattered little whether those violating the illegal property rights system were mob firms or legitimate haulers, as Joseph "Joey Surprise" Feola found out in 1967. To step out of line was to invite violence, although there were usually a number of steps taken before one would be "whacked"—the term used by the killer conducting the tour of Kearny.

Gangland-style murders are now so commonplace they get little attention unless they involve someone of the stature of Jimmy Hoffa. But when the House Oversight Subcommittee was conducting its hearings, three particular murders received more scrutiny than most. Not surprisingly, little of the testimony about organized crime and its involvement with toxic waste disposal was as dramatic as the announcement by Congressman Dingell at the May, 1981, hearing that six days after the December hearing, Crescent "Chris" Roselle had been murdered. Now, three important waste entrepreneurs had been murdered, and officials wanted to know why.

Talk about murder in the waste industry was one of the themes explored at the May hearing, and the SCA officers were confronted with the brunt of questions that spring. There were two primary reasons why SCA had to suffer this uncomfortable scrutiny about the recent murders. First, when Harold Kaufman had testified in December, he had linked SCA with the murder of Alfred DiNardi. DiNardi's firm, Custom Disposal, was taking towns away from SCA (and others), which resulted in his murder, Kaufman said. The same condition was true, Kaufman added, in the murder of Gabriel San Felice, who headed a business known as Sano Carting. The second reason was, of course, the Roselle killing on December 22, 1981. At the time of Roselle's murder, he was the general manager of Waste Disposal, Inc., a major SCA subsidiary in New Jersey.

The endemic violence in the waste industry encompassed far more than the three supposed SCA-related homicides. Much more violence was committed than ever reported. Most individuals who suffered the milder forms of violence—the intimidation by threat, the late night phone calls warning of harm to come, the display of weapons, physical menacing, the occasional beating, the destruction of property—simply gave in, surrendering garbage routes, selling their business, acquiring new partners who invested nothing, signing leases for unnecessary equipment that was often non-existent, or, finally, just walking away. And, for all the violence and intimidation among various businesses in waste disposal, there was an equal amount against the customers. Those firms, for instance, that were unhappy with their carting service could do little. Those who tried endured the many forms of coercion routinely used in the waste business: garbage left to rot in front of stores, phony strikes called by mob-teamster locals aimed at disrupting business, telephone calls asking how the children are, and sometimes even physical assaults.

Most paid the price and went about their business. Extreme violence generally occurred in situations where mob firms competed with one another for territories; where racketeers failed to show respect for one another; where they cheated one another; where they chose not to respond, for one reason or another, to the dictates of illegal arbitration; and where they were suspected of informing. Most of the murder victims, therefore, were of organized crime members or their close associates. DiNardi, San Felice, and Roselle came from that inner circle of syndicate members and associates who knew exactly the dangers involved in their activities. Unfortunately for them, they must have believed that they were either more powerful or smarter than their counterparts.

The murders of Gabe San Felice, Alfred DiNardi, Chris Roselle, and several others share certain characteristics. Those characteristics and the personalities involved provide a window through which the secret government of waste can be seen and understood. Although most of the tumultuous relationships which marked the rise and fall of those in the waste industry are an extension of the constant fighting endemic in the garbage industry, it is good to remember that many of the individuals mentioned were also major entrepreneurs of toxic waste. They hauled and dumped toxics with the same gusto as residential and commercial garbage. They owned and controlled some of the largest landfills in the Northeast, landfills which were the site of indiscriminate toxic waste dumping. Some of them merged their businesses with those waste conglomerates, like SCA and Browning-Ferris, which have commanding positions in the field of toxic and hazardous waste disposal all across the nation. The secret government of waste, which is revealed in its most grotesque form in contract murder, covers all facets of the waste industry, including toxic waste disposal.

When Alfred DiNardi was murdered on June 4, 1976, in New York, it was alleged that at least some of his troubles came about because of his violations of property rights. His firm, Custom Disposal, was reported to have engaged in a bidding war with other carting companies owned by SCA. Immediately after he was shot, his own firm was taken over by Carmine Franco. And one of DiNardi's most financially important stops—the National Starch Co. in Plainfield, New Jersey, which reportedly paid $35,000 a month—was taken by Jersey Sanitation, owned by John Albert, another member of organized crime, and the Stamato family. For violating property rights, DiNardi was murdered and organized crime divided the spoils.

A representative of SCA testifying before Congress in May, 1981, claimed that DiNardi and SCA had only minor difficulties at most. In particular, he discussed one competitive situation between SCA's subsidiary, Waste Disposal, and DiNardi's firm, Custom Disposal. The competition was over a municipal garbage contract with the borough of Roselle Park, New Jersey. The SCA company had the contract in the past and was underbid by DiNardi. SCA then initiated a series of legal actions against Roselle Park and Custom Disposal to void the contract. SCA lost the first legal go-round, but later won at the appellate level. Sandwiched in between the first court's decision in favor of Custom Disposal and the voiding of the contract by the appellate division was the murder. SCA's conclusion from this series of events was that "it is simply incredible that a corporation which submits to legal processes to vindicate its claims, and is in the midst of doing so, would seek to murder its adversary."

The problems that DiNardi experienced were not tied only to SCA. He was also involved with Cooper Funding, the suspected loan-sharking firm of the waste industry. DiNardi, it is reported, owed around $200,000 to Cooper Funding. Informant information collected by law enforcement agents noted he had received his money through P.F.R.D., which had solicited about $300,000 from Cooper Funding. It is unclear whether DiNardi chose not to repay the money plus the enormous interest to P.F.R.D., or Cooper and P.F.R.D. were feuding and DiNardi was made an object lesson because of some internal mob dispute. In any case, his association with Cooper and P.F.R.D., probably in conjunction with his violations of property rights, was enough to get him shot three times, once in the head and once in each buttock, as he and a "female companion" waited for his car at the 20th Century Garage in midtown Manhattan.

Final evidence linking these murders to organized crime was provided by reporter Paul Meskill of the *New York Daily News*. He wrote that the Roselle, DiNardi, and San Felice murders must have been committed by what he called the "enforcement arm of the Genovese" syndicate, because the pistols used in the murders were bought by three New York mobsters in the summer of 1975 during a "gun-buying binge in South Florida." In fact, the pistols were bought by four members of the Purple Gang and were used to murder at least eight other mob associates from 1976 through 1980. The events and personalities involved in two of the most important killings, allegedly involving SCA, contribute further to our understanding of the secret government of waste.

The Murder of Gabriel San Felice

Gabriel "Gabe" San Felice, at the time of his death, was the secretary-agent of Sano Carting, a garbage company incorporated on March 9, 1966, and operating in Hoboken, Bayonne, Elizabeth, Jersey City, Union City, and Kearny, New Jersey. The company president was his wife. San Felice, who was only forty-two years old when he was murdered, had come out of Brooklyn, and had a fairly heavy criminal record. According to his application for a private carter's license from the New Jersey Public Utilities Commission, San Felice had been convicted of assault and battery in Brooklyn in 1957 and 1962. In 1963, still in Brooklyn, he was twice more convicted. His only prison time despite all these convictions amounted to eight months behind bars; this was for a violation of New York City's gun control law.

San Felice came to New Jersey from Brooklyn when he and his wife, the former Frances Lomangino, bought a garbage route in Newark. They named their company Sano Carting, and moved to Hazlet, New Jersey. The money for the purchase came from his wife's family, and she personally owned 15 percent of the stock in Sano Carting. The other officers and stockholders were Frances's father, Stephen Lomangino, who held 80 percent of the stock, and her brother, Paul, the vice president of Sano, who owned the remaining 5 percent. The Lomangino family, deeply involved in the sanitation business, probably bought the New Jersey firm to give their new in-law a business, to get him out of Brooklyn where he had experienced so much trouble with the law, and, finally, to extend their own activities beyond the city.

Stephen Lomangino had been in the waste disposal business since at least the 1940s. Apparently, he was only one of several members of the Lomangino family in private carting in New York at that time. Following the sensational congressional hearing into the garbage industry in New York of 1957, Joseph Lomangino, who was then doing business as Atomic Carting and Allied Carting Suffolk, was charged with conspiring to restrain trade. Not much happened to the vast number of private carters charged, although they were all enjoined from any further restraint-of-trade activities. But sixteen years later the Lomanginos had more trouble with the law. This time it was Joseph Lomangino, doing business as United Carting (also called, it seems, the 8201 15th Ave., Corp.) and Fred Lomangino from Lomangino Brothers Carting, who were among the targets of Brooklyn District Attorney Eugene Gold's 1974 investigation into the garbage industry.

The companies and their officers were indicted in the sweeping investigation of the Brooklyn Trade Waste Association. Once again, the charge against the carters was restraint of trade, and it added up to the familiar wrist slap and finger wagging. While Stephen Lomangino was not charged in either of the two major investigations of the waste industry, he was, reportedly, closely associated with Joseph Schipani, the garbage racketeer thought to be a part of the Genovese crime syndicate. San Felice's in-laws were both powerful in the sanitation industry and close to major organized crime figures. His murder, therefore, represents one of those extreme cases where arbitration by the mob failed to impress the naturally aggressive.

According to police investigations into the San Felice killing, there were several New Jersey carting companies associated with Sano and its owners which figured in a complicated and ultimately deteriorating series of relationships, finally ending with murder. Among the firms was Meadowbrook Carting, located in Iselin, New Jersey, and owned by John Pinto, who until recently was an officer in Browning-Ferris Industries, the second largest toxic and solid waste disposal company in the nation. Another company at odds with Sano was Haulaway, Inc., from Hoboken, whose president in 1978 was Joseph Scugoza. Two years earlier, on July 1, 1976, a part-owner of Haulaway, Vincent D. Capone, was also murdered. Newspaper accounts stated that he was associated with John DiGilio from the Genovese–Tieri crime syndicate, and was shot with weapons that came from the South Florida buying spree.

The end for San Felice came late in the afternoon on a spring day in 1978. He was in the midst of unloading one of his garbage trucks in an open field close by the infamous Global Landfill in Old Bridge, New Jersey, when he was shot twice in the head. His killers adopted a novel disguise and getaway. While San Felice worked close to the Global site, they were playing catch in a field nearby dressed in baseball uniforms. At some point when San Felice was facing away from the field, two men approached and shot him at point-blank range with a .32 caliber automatic handgun. They made their escape on ten-speed bicycles which were later recovered in a dumpster.

The Background to Murder

The beginning of the end for San Felice started about six years before. At that time Sano Carting had just purchased another garbage company and was beginning to expand. With the purchase, Sano moved to bid on contracts in the Bayshore area of New Jersey. But he was quickly told—allegedly by a representative of R.F. & M., a garbage business operating in the Holmdel and Madison Township area—that while he could service the route he had bought in Hazlet, he had better not attempt to work elsewhere. San Felice responded to this warning by writing a letter to the Public Utilities Commission complaining that his competitors were trying to keep him from bidding on municipal garbage contracts. The PUC sent his letter to the state police for investigation. Nothing positive came of this, however.

Years later, San Felice's widow, Frances San Felice, would believe it was this letter that set in motion the long chain of events which culminated in her husband's murder. So convinced was she, that within days of the killing she requested that the PUC destroy its copy. It would make no difference by then, of course, as copies of the letter had long before gone to a number of other state agencies. Basically, what the letter stated was that Chris Roselle had pressured a landfill owner into refusing San Felice its use. This alleged move by Roselle was meant to keep San Felice from competing with Roselle in Keyport, New Jersey. The landfill owner called San Felice at one point and told him that he wanted out of the dispute, that there were other people involved (by implication he meant New York organized crime people), that the fight involved more than he had thought. San Felice was unintimidated, however, and submitted additional bids on contracts in the Bayshore area.

He won the contract for Middletown Township, and in February, 1973, took the Matawan Boro contract as well. One of the defeated competitors was R.F. & M. In the fall of 1973, San Felice bid on the municipal contract in Keyport Boro, although his offer was not accepted. Just as the letter to the PUC had stated, Chris Roselle and Peter Marinaro of R.F. & M. and Waste Disposal, Inc., were extremely displeased with Sano's activities in areas once controlled exclusively by them. It is notable that SCA Services had acquired the assets of both Waste Disposal and R.F. & M. prior to the Keyport contract. SCA had closed the deal for the stock of Waste Disposal on May 10, 1973, and R.F. & M. on August 31, 1973. According to SCA's chairman of the board in 1981, John M. Fox, in his congressional testimony before the Oversight Subcommittee, Waste Disposal won the Keyport contract in 1973 only to lose it to Sano Carting during the next round of bidding in 1975, thus proving that active competition was a real part of the industry.

Fox's point that there was only healthy competition is contradicted by overt signs of displeasure with Sano Carting. First, in late 1973, two of San Felice's garbage trucks were vandalized. Next, San Felice was approached by representatives of Local 945 who attempted to organize his drivers. In the midst of these discussions and, indeed, arguments, San Felice became embroiled in a reportedly staged car accident with Flen Chestnut, an important Local 945 organizer. The following day, gravel was poured into the gas tanks of several of his trucks.

San Felice had had enough. He contacted Frank Caruso, "a personal friend" and member of the Genovese crime syndicate. It was time for San Felice to show he too had friends in the secret government. Caruso arranged a meeting between San Felice and 945's notorious business agent, Ernie Palmeri. San Felice, Caruso, and Palmeri met at the Union Hall in West Paterson, where San Felice was told he had only to allow some of his men into the union. A deal was struck which called for five out of fifteen Sano drivers to join 945; in return Sano would be left alone and allowed to bid on municipal contracts. The deal lasted only about six weeks, however, when Palmeri and Chestnut tried to pressure San Felice into expanding Sano's unionization. This necessitated another mob meeting, at which Caruso warned Palmeri to leave Sano alone.

Some time after Caruso seemed to have solved the problem, word got around that San Felice had lodged a complaint with the PUC. Someone, probably at the PUC, had leaked the news of San Felice's letter. Turning to the authorities was not something done in this business, especially if one was connected to the mob and expected help from his friends. San Felice was questioned closely by Caruso about the matter. Knowing he had committed a serious error, San Felice lied, assuring Caruso he had never written a letter to the PUC. Apparently satisfied, Caruso continued to support him in these internecine mob disputes.

In 1975, the situation once again heated up. First of all, Sano Carting bid for the Keyport job, as Fox testified, and won against SCA of New Jersey, Inc. Then a complicated deal involving the Raritan Arsenal in Edison evolved, which eventually brought Sano into further conflict. The Arsenal job had been awarded by the General Services Administration to a New York garbage firm that didn't have a New Jersey permit. Therefore, they arranged to have the stops serviced by the Allegro Brothers Rubbish Removal firm out of Secaucus. According to intelligence reports, Allegro was chased from the job by John Pinto of Meadowbrook Carting, who told them "the stop belonged to someone else." John Pinto—so Harold Kaufman later maintained—was a close associate of various organized crime figures and was in at least one business with Charles Macaluso prior to moving into the Browning-Ferris fold. Allegro faded from the scene, and the New York company contacted San Felice, asking him to do the job. He readily agreed.

Having beaten out SCA and taken the Arsenal job, San Felice was re-contacted by Local 945. In the interim, San Felice's primary protector, Caruso, had died of natural causes. Taking over many of Caruso's interests was the notorious Vinnie Mauro (or Morrow), Harold Kaufman's friend and associate. As far as San

Felice knew, Mauro was an important Genovese syndicate member with major investments in loan sharking and narcotics. He also reportedly believed Mauro had been involved in the murder of former gang boss Thomas Eboli. Still feeling threatened, San Felice started paying Mauro $300 a month for protection. In June, 1975, San Felice, Mauro, Palmeri, and San Felice's uncle, Frank Panza, held a meeting to discuss the entire situation. At this time, Palmeri demanded that all of Sano's men join Local 945, that San Felice give up his two new contracts and join the "protective association" being set up for New Jersey's waste entrepreneurs.

As expected, San Felice protested vehemently, pointing out that he was being victimized by Chris Roselle, who was taking away some of his contracts. Palmeri then became very angry and he and San Felice began exchanging sharp words. At one point Palmeri pointed at San Felice and told him he was a "dead man." San Felice replied that Palmeri had better watch his own back. The meeting then broke up with San Felice's turning to Mauro and his uncle, telling them he meant no disrespect. Nevertheless, San Felice believed Mauro had sold him out. And apparently he was right. It was reported that Mauro subsequently met with the head of the Genovese syndicate at the time, Frank Tieri, who told Mauro to "walk away from San Felice." Convinced he was a marked man as far as Palmeri was concerned, San Felice started to carry an automatic pistol.

There was no gunplay yet, however. Instead, the pressure from 945 increased. Pickets were placed around two of Sano's oldest customers, located in Kearny. Although the pickets didn't interfere with Sano trucks, other union drivers delivering to the companies refused to cross the line. San Felice was nothing if not tough, and he filed a complaint with the National Labor Relations Board (NLRB) in July, 1975. He and an attorney representing one of his customers attempted to get the Board to enjoin Local 945 from picketing. Shortly after their appearance before the NLRB, the pickets disappeared. The rest of the year passed fairly quietly.

With one year of relative peace over, the battle started again. In the summer of 1976, San Felice and Chris Roselle began fighting over bids on jobs in Keyport, Matawan Boro, and Matawan Township. San Felice had not run out of organized crime contacts, and turned to Philip Moscato, a friend of the family for over fifteen years. Originally from Hudson County, New Jersey, Moscato had moved to Florida, so San Felice and his wife went there to talk over their problems. San Felice explained the recurring dilemma he had with Palmeri and Local 945, and his fights with Chris Roselle. Moscato decided to call John DiGilio and have him arrange a meeting between Tino Fiumara and San Felice.

Following Moscato's wishes, Fiumara, DiGilio, and San Felice met and talked at a custom tailor shop in Secaucus. Although it didn't appear as though Fiumara was very sympathetic, he did arrange another conference with all the interested parties. Those attending the second meeting were reportedly Fiumara, DiGilio, John "Moose" Marone, Palmeri, Roselle, San Felice, Stephen Lomangino, and lastly Santo Sclasani, "who was a personal friend of Mr. Lomangino's and reputed to be a close friend of Frank 'Funzi' Tieri." Fiumara made the decisions at this meeting, calling for San Felice to give Roselle certain of his contracts. He then told San Felice that he was to report to Carmine Franco if he had any further problems.

That seemed to end the squabbles for the time being. But in early 1977, Sano Carting ran into financial difficulties; bills accumulated, drivers left, there were no funds to maintain the trucks, and Sano's service drastically declined. In a move to cut back, San Felice turned over more contracts to the SCA subsidiary, Waste Disposal. On September 8, 1977, officials from the borough of Keyport agreed that Waste Disposal could take over Sano's contract. Still, the financial slide for San Felice continued. Around November, 1977, the Internal Revenue Service reportedly claimed that San Felice owed over $25,000.

San Felice must have hit rock bottom by then, because he also stopped paying off loan shark Peter Palazotto from Brooklyn. Apparently, he had borrowed $20,000 from Palazotto as early as 1972. Half that sum had come from Vincent Buffa, Salvatore Profaci's brother-in-law. Profaci was the oldest of three sons of Joseph Profaci, one-time leader of his own crime syndicate, headquartered in Brooklyn with interests nationwide. Ranked with gangsters such as Vito Genovese, Joe Bonanno, and Carlo Gambino, Joe Profaci died in the early 1960s, and his syndicate was taken over by Joe Colombo, who was himself gunned down in 1971. According to the New York City Police Department, leadership of this syndicate then passed to Carmine Persico and Jerry Langella. The three Profaci brothers are important members. It seems San Felice paid back the capital and enormous interest owed to Buffa and Profaci, but was never able to repay Palazotto. In fact, from his original loan of $20,000, he ended up owing a total of around $190,000. San Felice paid Palazotto $1,000 a week for approximately two years, but it only covered the interest. With his business falling apart, he told Palazotto he wouldn't pay him any more. A fight broke out, and San Felice threw Palazotto out of his office.

For Gabe San Felice, everything had now turned very bleak. He couldn't even sell his residential garbage routes because of the squeeze of territorial restraints—other companies weren't "allowed" to expand. Two of his larger customers, upset with the irregularity of Sano's work, canceled their contracts and turned to Meadowbrook Carting, which was operated by John Pinto. Naturally, this too could not have happened unless it was sanctioned by the organized crime figures enforcing the property rights doctrine. Working with John Pinto in taking over Sano's routes was San Felice's old nemesis, Chris Roselle (allegedly Pinto's cousin), who supposedly was a secret part-owner of Meadowbrook. The Roselle–San Felice battles had once again reached a critical stage.

In order to help him resolve what he saw as the Roselle push to take over his routes, San Felice again called Moscato. A few days later, Moscato and Vincent Ravo appeared at the Sano office. Ravo reportedly worked for Moscato as his chief enforcer in a major loan-sharking operation. Moscato told San Felice that Ravo would now become his collector and would help him with his problems. (Ravo was arrested in the summer of 1978 and charged with killing Charles Lombardo, who had attempted to set up a rival loan-sharking operation.) Shortly after this, Moscato offered to buy out San Felice. What Moscato meant by buying out was to send down a crew of men to service the Sano stops, and to pay the San Felices a nominal weekly salary. Frances San Felice rejected the offer, even though Gabe was now willing to walk away from his troubles. With this offer rejected, Moscato turned his back on the San Felices. Time was rapidly running out on Gabe.

There were a few more attempts by both Gabe and Frances San Felice to sell part or all of the business. For instance, on May 25, 1978, a meeting was scheduled with Chris Roselle, Peter Marinaro, and John Pinto at the Waste Disposal office in Elizabeth. When only Frances showed up, however, the meeting was canceled, the men telling her that Gabe should have been there to discuss matters. Another meeting was arranged. Meanwhile, Gabe and Frances were also supposed to discuss selling Sano's residential routes with a representative from Golden Gate Carting, based in Elmhurst, New York. About an hour and a half before the scheduled May 31 meeting, Gabe San Felice was murdered.

SCA and Crescent "Chris" Roselle

Clearly, Chris Roselle was a deadly enemy in the estimation of Gabe San Felice, and probably in DiNardi's, too. For years Roselle had wrangled with San Felice and was probably responsible for a great deal of the anger and hostility directed at him. On December 22, 1980, at 5:18 P.M., the Elizabeth police dispatcher sent two officers to investigate a shooting close to the office of Waste Disposal. There they found the well-dressed body of Chris Roselle slumped over in the front seat of a late-model gold Cadillac. He had been shot at least three times. The County Medical Examiner removed two .22 caliber bullets from his neck and one .32 caliber bullet from his chest. The tumultuous life of Chris Roselle ended that clear evening at the age of sixty.

Ironically, the claim was soon made that Roselle had died because he too was competing with SCA. Unlike DiNardi and San Felice, however, Chris Roselle was the leader of a series of intertwined family businesses that had been bought by SCA in the early to mid-1970s. The merging of Roselle interests—including Waste Disposal, R. F. & M., Peter Roselle & Sons, Fareday & Meyer, and Roselle-Lippman—with SCA was marked almost from the very beginning by numerous disagreements. For instance, as early as August 13, 1974, SCA Chairman Burton Steir received a letter from Peter Iommetti, who had recently joined the SCA corporation. Iommetti wrote, ". . . for sometime now there has been meeting after meeting to resolve and finalize the acquisition of the Roselle Companies. An unhealthy atmosphere has been created between S.C.A. officers and Chris Roselle that should be quickly reversed. . . ." Steir's answer pointed to one of the basic problems between SCA and Chris Roselle: When SCA bought up the Roselle companies, it thought the deal included all Roselle firms, including one called White Brothers. SCA was mistaken, however, and Roselle held White Brothers out for his private ownership.

In the following year matters seemed to deteriorate even more dangerously. Burton Steir was convinced Chris Roselle was maneuvering to get his companies back from SCA for half what he had charged for them. Steir alerted SCA's officers to this Roselle plan and told them to be prepared to counter any sharp Roselle move. In the summer of 1975, SCA accountant Peter Casey, the brother of the current director of the CIA, prepared a memorandum at Steir's request detailing "those areas of corporate practice and procedures which are not being followed by any of the Roselle operating centers even after repeated requests to comply." Roselle refused, for example, to become part of the SCA payroll system and to participate in the company insurance program. That fall, Tom Viola, now SCA vice president and an old associate of Roselle's, wrote to Roselle complaining that Waste Disposal was "the only company in SCA which has consistently refused to comply" with various SCA programs. He added that as long as Roselle was the chief executive officer, he was responsible for implementing the programs.

Probably the most telling sign the Roselle/SCA merger was in trouble came in a memo written by Viola to Burton Steir, which noted: "On Wednesday evening, 11/19/75, Cres Roselle informed me that he was entering a joint venture, via White Brothers Inc., with La Fera Contracting Co., for the purpose of submitting a bid for refuse collection service in the City of Hoboken, N.J. I asked him why he did not consider SCA entering into the joint venture rather than White Brothers. He said he did not want to get SCA involved." There was further discussion between Viola and Roselle concerning a possible lawsuit initiated by Roselle against SCA. Apparently, Roselle believed SCA had bought his companies cheaply by illegally manipulating carting prices. But Roselle was not the only party considering a lawsuit. SCA was thinking of suing Roselle for competing in Hoboken, and then challenging the city of Hoboken in court if SCA's bid was turned down in favor of White Brothers.

Although it is unclear why he changed his plans, it appears Roselle did not go ahead with his joint venture. Nevertheless, the relationship between Chris Roselle and SCA continued to be notable for its rancor. There were constant reports, right to the end of Roselle's life, that he was competing against SCA for various garbage contracts. Once even Marvin Mahan of Scientific, Inc., accused him and SCA of hauling chemical wastes contrary to a partnership agreement between Mahan and SCA which restricted SCA's toxic waste business to Mahan's firm, Earthline.

During the last year of his life, Roselle became involved in a bitter dispute with several firms over garbage contracts in West Orange and Roselle Park, New Jersey. This put him at odds with Joseph C. Cassini, Jr., Richard Miele, and Bruce La Fera of La Fera Contracting. Instead of Roselle's teaming up with La Fera Contracting as he had told Viola he would, others had done so, starting another round of squabbling and fighting among New Jersey's garbage lords. The Miele–Cassini–La Fera interests were comingled in three companies: Maplewood Disposal, headed by Miele; the James Petrozello Company, run by Cassini; and finally, Disposamatic, owned and directed by Miele and La Fera.

Most of the fighting started when Roselle, using White Brothers, bid against the Miele–Cassini–La Fera firms. Cassini's company and Miele's had come together in a joint venture to bid for scavenger services in West Orange. In the dispute that followed, Maplewood Disposal's attorney informed the president of the Town Council that White Brothers "have not only impugned my client, but have also infected and cast doubt upon the bidding process." The attorney's letter added that a representative of White Brothers "made certain derogatory statements which reflected upon the integrity of my client, as well as that of James Petrozello Company, Inc." Much the same situation took place in 1980 in Roselle Park. There, Cassini's firm entered into a limited partnership with the Miele and La Fera company, Disposamatic. These contracts were not negligible. The one for Roselle Park called for a three-year total of over $544,000, and the year before, Petrozello and Disposamatic had negotiated a three-year contract with the city of Paterson for more than $6.3 million.

What made the anger more heated than usual may have been the fact that most of the principals had in the past worked together. The original Roselle firm, Peter Roselle & Sons, had been partners with both La Fera Contracting and James Petrozello Company in the early 1950s. In 1955, the Roselle company severed its partnership and bid against its former partners for contracts in East Orange, according to police intelligence reports. Also, Roselle, Miele, Cassini, and several others were partners in the MSLA landfill in Kearny.

Many of the people interviewed by detectives investigating the Roselle murder commented that Roselle and Joe Cassini had become bitter enemies in recent years. They were, one commented, "at each other's throats." Another described a tremendous argument between Chris Roselle and Joe Cassini over a dumping incident late in 1979. Apparently, the subject of the dispute was toxic chemical waste. Toxic waste containing PCBs was reportedly picked up at the Public Service Electric & Gas's facility in Newark and hauled by Roselle to MSLA—until Joe Cassini found out. Cassini was furious because he supposedly wanted the contract from PSE&G. Since he hadn't gotten it, he wasn't about to let Roselle use MSLA to get rid of the waste. Even though Roselle and Cassini were both part-owners of MSLA, Cassini could stop him from dumping toxic waste there as the Kearny landfill had no authorization to accept it. During the argument, one witness reported that several Cadillacs rolled up carrying suspected organized crime figures who intervened. When the reported arbitration was over, Roselle had the material removed and taken to another site. Allegedly, the new site was the water at the end of a pier near the utility's property.

In the last five years of his life Chris Roselle had angered many figures in the waste industry, not the least of which were his associates in SCA, MSLA, and his former associates in carting. It was also noted by Harold Kaufman in several interviews that Roselle had played a key role in the DiNardi and San Felice homicides, pushing for their deaths as the only way to stop them. He had gathered a fairly long list of enemies in the course of half a decade. When the end came, however, he too paid the full price for believing he was powerful, well protected, and clever. Somewhere along the line of his many disputes, one or more of his enemies decided to put an end to the innumerable problems they believed Roselle created.

The Killers

Chris Roselle became another example of the power of organized crime in the waste industry, a victim of the secret government. There is no more telling sign of government than its power to allocate resources, arbitrate disputes, and punish those it considers outlaws. That organized crime has performed all these tasks for so long is the mark its governance of the New York–New Jersey waste industry has overwhelmed various state agencies. It prospered, of course, in part because it was so successful in either penetrating or paralyzing various legitimate agencies.

Murder was the ultimate example of all this. What is most remarkable about the murders chronicled in the waste industry is that they were carried out by Genovese–Tieri syndicate members located in Hoboken, New Jersey, with weapons supplied by the Purple Gang, or by the Purple Gang itself. As early as the assault on Schettino's partner in 1973, there was every reason to believe this young group of killers had become a part of organized crime's enforcement arm for the waste industry in the region. But not even the murder of Schettino's mother-in-law was sufficient to cause the Rockland County District Attorney to investigate the Purple Gang.

The most complete summary of Purple Gang activities was compiled by the Treasury Department's Bureau of Alcohol, Tobacco and Firearms (ATF) and put into report form in July, 1979. The ATF noted four members of the Purple Gang—Charles Micieli, Frank Chierco, Ralph Amatto, and Frank John Viserto, Jr.—had purchased guns and silencers at nine gun shops in southern Florida in 1975. These particular weapons were then used in eight murders in New York and New Jersey. Most of the murders involved people far removed from the waste industry. Organized crime figures who were part of the secret government had a reach into many licit and illicit activities patrolled by killers. Waste was only one of their industries. The victims were members or associates of the Genovese–Tieri organized crime syndicate. When someone was to be killed, the contracts were given to either the Hoboken or the East Harlem killers. The Genovese–Tieri syndicate and the Purple Gang had entered into a deadly conspiracy.

The two organized crime figures suspected of issuing these contracts to the killers were John DiGilio and Tino Fiumara. DiGilio was a prime suspect in three of the murder conspiracies. It was also reported that DiGilio probably met with Frank Viserto, Jr., of the Purple Gang to discuss murder contracts and weapons. Fiumara was suspected for several reasons. He was known to be in contact with members of the Purple Gang, including Angelo and

Pasquale Prisco. Also, Fiumara and DiGilio were in almost daily contact with the Hoboken gang, which included Joseph Franklin Scarbrough and Thomas Principe. Supposedly, Principe was the "top contract killer" for the Genovese–Tieri syndicate, and his closest associate was Joseph Scarbrough, who was identified leaving the scene when Vincent Capone (Haulaway) was murdered. Of the eight murders analyzed by the ATF, it was believed that Scarbrough was the "possible killer of five . . . and that Scarbrough works for Principe."

Vincent Daniel Capone, shot to death on July 1, 1976, was the first known victim of this new murder conspiracy. In addition to his garbage business, Capone was a gambler and associate of John DiGilio. About six months later in New York, Frank Chin was shot five times in the head with the same weapon used to murder Capone. Chin was one of the premier electronic eavesdroppers in America, some of whose equipment was used to bug the office of John DiGilio's attorney. Two and a half weeks after Chin was murdered, another related killing took place in Queens, New York. Fifty-two-year-old Arthur Milgram, whose company, Automated Ticket Vending, had the exceptionally lucrative contract to manufacture New York State Lottery tickets, was shot to death on February 9, 1977. Automated Ticket Vending was owned by a company called Regency Associates, which included among its investors Frank John Viserto, Jr., and two other members of the Purple Gang.

The next significant victim in this killing spree was John Lardiere, who was on furlough from prison when he was gunned down. Prior to his sentence, Lardiere controlled a major section of the Newark waterfront and was the business agent for Local 945. He was shot with a .22 caliber pistol and a .38 Colt revolver. The .22 was traced back to Florida, where it had been bought by Purple Gang member Frank Chierco using the alias John Bruno. In between the Milgram and Lardiere killings, there was another one. "A small-time Brooklyn hood," Thomas Palermo, was found in the trunk of a car at Kennedy Airport shot to death with both .22 and .32 caliber pistols. Ballistic tests determined that the .22 was the same one used to murder Capone and Chin. In the fall of 1977, one of the Hoboken killers struck again. Gino Gallina, a former assistant district attorney in New York, was killed in Greenwich Village. After his service in the district attorney's office, Gallina had entered private practice and represented several important mobsters, including John DiGilio. ATF investigators also were convinced that the same two gangs worked together on the murder of Salvatore Briguglio on March 28, 1978. Briguglio was murdered because he knew too much about several other murders, including that of Jimmy Hoffa. The final killing discussed in the ATF report took place on November 1, 1978, when James Joseph Queli, Jr., was murdered in North Arlington, New Jersey. He, too, was killed with the same .22 caliber pistol as some of the others. Queli, it was believed, had attempted to "set up his own gambling operation in the Ironbound section of Newark, long a Fiumara stronghold."

The slayings of Alfred DiNardi and Gabe San Felice were not connected by the ATF to the murders committed by the Hoboken mob and the Purple Gang. Other investigators have connected them, however. It is believed, for instance, the .32 caliber used to murder San Felice came from the Purple Gang's cache and that there were other links between the 1976 DiNardi homicide and the Purple Gang. Roselle, of course, was murdered after the ATF report, but investigators appear convinced he was killed with Purple Gang guns. What few of the current investigators realize, though, is that Purple Gang members had been identified as "muscle" for the Genovese–Tieri syndicate in the garbage trade as early as 1973. Prior to the infamous Florida gun-buying spree, Prisco, Barone, and Raymundo had reportedly assaulted Schettino's partner and helper. That the Rockland County District Attorney didn't know or think it worthwhile to pursue the Purple Gang connection following the murder of Mrs. Nadel probably caused others to miss this important background information. In any case, it is a mistake to assume it was only after the Purple Gang bought eighty-six guns in Florida that they began to work with the Genovese–Tieri syndicate. It would be an even bigger mistake to assume the Purple Gang didn't start killing until then, either.

Although the Purple Gang often used .22 caliber pistols to do their killing, there was nothing magical about the weapon. It was just that certain killers preferred it. Purple Gang members used whatever they had around—.357 magnums, knives, shotguns, and machine guns, in addition to the small caliber weapons. They tortured and mutilated some victims and quickly dispatched others. What did appear to develop over time, however, was "contract swapping" with the Hoboken section of the Genovese–Tieri syndicate, a practice that seemed to follow the purchase of guns in South Florida. Killing for one another, however, did not come about because of the Purple Gang's supply of guns from South Florida. It came about because Purple Gang members had achieved a degree of eminence in organized crime, especially with the Genovese–Tieri syndicate.

The waste industry was ruled by a secret government which murdered whenever it felt necessary. That the murders of Vincent Capone, Alfred DiNardi, Gabe San Felice, and Chris Roselle can be traced back to the cabal discussed above reflected the killers' stupidity on the one hand, and their confidence on the other. That they chose to use weapons which could be traced, that they often used the same weapon for several murders, were actions dumb only in retrospect, however. This brazen behavior was also a measure of their confidence, their belief that they had little to fear from the criminal justice system. The members of the Purple Gang were aware that the bolder they were, the stronger would be their reputation for ruthlessness. And that, they knew—just as William Masselli did—always worked in favor of professional criminals.

Any student of civics knows government defines and enforces its own system of law. In all respects, organized crime did this effectively and fairly efficiently in the New York and New Jersey waste industry. It surely did these governmental tasks better than the various environmental, political, and criminal justice agencies did. In addition, organized crime's governance was a secret only from the general public. Certainly few in the industry were unaware of its power and control. Industry figures who acknowledge in private that the mob runs it are loath to express that opinion in public for a number of reasons. Congressional testimony by industry representatives, as well as the innumerable puff pieces designed by public relations outfits to reassure the public all is well in the waste industry, must be taken with much more than the proverbial grain of salt. The great fear on the part of the knowledgeable is that the secret government of waste is spreading its power farther and deeper than ever before, and that those who protest too much may also face the guns of organized crime. Indeed, all is far from well in the waste industry, as the families of the murdered know. Others know it too, including those who have been threatened, bullied, intimidated, and frightened by the mob. But the fear of organized crime's control of waste, particularly hazardous waste, may extend beyond those directly involved, as the citizens of Elizabeth, New Jersey, witnessed as they watched toxic fireballs rise over their homes on a spring evening in April, 1980.

9

The Chemical Control Nightmare

ELIZABETH'S BIGGEST FIRES occurred two hundred years apart. In 1780, the British burned the city in the midst of our war for independence, but it was rebuilt to become the county seat of Union County. Taking advantage of its location on Newark Bay, Staten Island Sound, and the Elizabeth River, as well as its proximity to Newark and New York City, Elizabeth grew as a busy port and industrial center. Soon it was a vital part of New Jersey's north central industrial shoreline of refineries, docks, factories, and various small businesses which provided employment for a growing population of working-class families that came to call Elizabeth home. The city's first great fire destroyed the entire settlement; its second one, on April 21, 1980, had that potential but did not succeed. While it is one thing to lose a city in a fight for freedom, self-determination, and justice, it is quite another thing to lose it to greed, crime, and corruption. Yet that would have been the case if the fire at the Chemical Control Corporation that April night had done what officials knew it was capable of, but prayed it would not do.

Shortly before 11 P.M., a series of explosions rocked the Chemical Control Corporation, located on South Front Street in the city's Elizabethport section. Although explosions and fires at this hazardous waste treatment facility were not unusual, local residents knew immediately there was something different about what they were hearing this spring evening. The frequency and resonance of the bursts, coupled with the fear many of them had living in the shadow of thousands of drums of toxic chemicals, drove people into the streets to look in the direction of the site. What they saw transfixed them. Against the night sky, flames were

245

leaping high into the air fed by chemicals which gave the fire shades of color few had seen before. Barrels were exploding with a violent intensity, sending shards of burning liquid in every direction. With each boom of some exploding substance, the fire seemed to travel to a new area, growing larger and more frightening.

Within minutes of their arrival, Elizabeth fire fighters called in a second alarm. Confronted by a fire raging out of control and already engulfing a sizable portion of Chemical Control's 2.2 acres, a problem bad enough in its own right, officials became even more concerned when they realized what might happen if the inferno spread. A high-pressure gasline ran only 600 feet from the site. A little farther away was a natural gas tank with a capacity of about 150 million cubic feet of liquid, as well as a number of 60,000-gallon propane gas tanks. Not far down South Front Street were gasoline storage tanks, each with a capacity in excess of 100,000 gallons.

Every fireman on the scene must have wondered what would happen if the flames reached these highly volatile materials. How much of Elizabeth would be destroyed if that happened? The only answer was to keep the fire from spreading in the direction of the explosive substances, or, for that matter, in the direction of the nearby residential area and the local neighborhood school. Soon, flames were shooting 150 feet into the air, and thick, foul-smelling smoke was rising above the scene. Everywhere 55-gallon drums were exploding, sometimes hurtling the lids into the air like a shot. The contents of the drums burned with a furious intensity, spreading the fire to other areas of the facility where even more drums were stacked. In fact, as many as 60,000 drums of hazardous chemicals, some highly explosive and most flammable, were stacked three, four, and even five deep on the grounds of Chemical Control and on the street outside the company's gate. Everywhere one turned, from the street to the Elizabeth River, drums were stacked waiting to explode. As the fire grew, a third alarm was sounded, bringing more men and equipment to the scene.

From South Front Street and from across the river on First Street, firemen poured water on the inferno. Deck guns were set up on the trucks, which could pump more water than the ordinary fire hoses. No amount of water seemed to do much good, though, as drums continued to burst and the fire spread in waves of strangely colored flames. At times the heat was so intense that water from the fire hoses vaporized in mid-air. Once, a group of barrels exploded with such velocity that a white ball of fire rose high into the air, emitting a searing blast of heat and causing firemen to seek refuge under their trucks. At approximately 11:20 P.M., the fourth alarm was turned in.

With the fourth alarm, other Union County Fire Departments went on alert and a fire boat was dispatched from New York City to battle the blaze from the Arthur Kill, the body of water separating New Jersey from Staten Island. About 250 firemen were now fighting the fire, which at points was leaping 300 feet into the air and spreading rapidly down South Front Street. The explosion of each new cluster of barrels launched fireball after fireball skyward, where they were swallowed up by the thick smoke hanging everywhere over the area. The intensity of the heat pushed the smoke high into the atmosphere and air currents began to move it in the direction of Staten Island.

Elizabeth fire officials knew shortly after arriving on the scene that this would be no ordinary fire. For some time they had been worried about the potential of explosion and fire at the Chemical Control Corporation, where perhaps as many as 50,000 drums of deadly chemicals were stored. But what they were confronted with this evening went even beyond their expectations and their fears. No one could make out what was burning to make the fire so ferocious and so quick to spread. Just what was causing the multicolored flames, the fireballs of searing heat, the mushroom clouds hanging over the port area, and the explosions that launched 55-gallon drums like rockets in every direction? Where were the fumes from these unknown substances going and what deadly damage might they cause to those who breathed them?

Elizabeth and New Jersey State officials began arriving on the scene shortly after midnight. Aside from residents of the immediate area, they decided there was no need to evacuate the city, primarily because the prevailing winds were pushing the fire's smoke and fumes away from Elizabeth and out over the water. Throughout the night they would confer on the scene and make new decisions as conditions changed and the situation warranted. Around 12:30 A.M., New Jersey officials contacted the New York City Police Department and warned of the possibility of toxic smoke drifting over Staten Island. Ironically, at that time the danger was probably greater for the residents of Staten Island than it was for those living in the area of Elizabeth.

Within a couple of hours, various New York City officials, including the mayor and police commissioner, set up a command post at the Holiday Inn on Staten Island. From that vantagepoint they kept abreast of developments in Elizabeth and discussed alternative courses of action, including the evacuation of all or part of the island. Because the information reaching the New York officials was unclear, the mayor and a number of his aides left Staten Island and drove to Elizabeth in order to evaluate the situation for themselves.

The fire continued to rage out of control and move relentlessly in the direction of the propane and natural gas storage tanks. Explosions continued to rock the area as huge clouds of acrid smoke were sucked into the atmosphere. Representatives of the Department of Environmental Protection who were now on the scene took air samples to determine what compounds were being emitted by the fire and inhaled by those in the area. What they found, of course, was not good news. Dangerously high levels of known toxics like benzene, chloroform, toluene, and other chlorinated hydrocarbons were in the air that night. In addition, the millions of gallons of water poured onto the fire mixed with various chemicals and flowed from the site into the Elizabeth River. Samples of the river water contained, among other things, pesticides that had been banned because they were considered carcinogenic.

For three hours now the fire had been burning uncontrollably with no end in sight. The flames no longer leaped from barrel to barrel but spread to entire clusters of drums, causing them to explode with resounding booms and flashes of fire that made the night sky white. Firemen became increasingly uneasy about containing the inferno, and about the hot ash and even acid falling on them from the heavy clouds of smoke. Everywhere, fire fighters were experiencing difficulty breathing and some were getting sick from the nauseating sweet smell of chemicals that permeated the area. And, all the while, the fire continued to gulp the hazardous chemicals and spit out strangely colored flames and explosions that vibrated windows blocks away.

Water was running everywhere, and sometimes even it was burning. Although fought from virtually all sides, the flames continued to spread southward toward the city of Linden. Tanks of alcohol at the nearby Apel Chemical Company were steaming as firemen poured water on them to keep them cool. Elizabethport itself was threatened.

As the police continued to evacuate those living within a few blocks of the fire, state and city officials debated a further course of action. To evacuate the entire port area, they decided, would take the National Guard, and there was no time for it to mobilize. Furthermore, air samples taken by the DEP convinced them an evacuation was not necessary at that time. Because the wind had shifted and the clouds of toxic smoke were now drifting out to sea, no large populations appeared to be in immediate danger. On this basis, local residents were told to stay indoors with their windows closed. It was also decided to ask local school officials to cancel classes for the day in order to keep children off the streets and protected from whatever harmful elements were in the air.

At last, the herculean efforts of the fire fighters paid off. As the fire reached the boundaries of the Chemical Control site, it seemed to lose its momentum and slowly begin to wane. By four o'clock in the morning fire officials knew they were no longer fighting a losing battle, though the fire was far from being out. For five hours more the hundreds of firemen continued to work at a feverish pitch, pouring countless gallons of water on flames that stubbornly refused to be smothered. By nine o'clock on April 22, the fire was declared under control. But for four more days the remaining drums and other debris would continue to smolder.

When New York's Mayor Koch and his aides arrived in Elizabeth and conferred with New Jersey officials, they too decided against immediate evacuation, but to make plans for that possibility if the need arose. They were encouraged by the shift in the direction of the wind and by the fact the fire was burning with such intensity that the heat itself seemed to be consuming some of the toxic fumes that would ordinarily be a danger to human health. In addition, they also realized the difficulty of evacuation, especially in the wee hours of the morning when the tens of thousands of Staten Island residents were asleep and unable to hear radio and television bulletins. Like their New Jersey counterparts, however, they decided to urge Staten Island residents to stay indoors during the day and asked that the schools be kept closed.

How bad was the Chemical Control fire? Journalist David Weinberg, writing in the August 1980 *New Jersey Monthly*, offers

an apt description and summary of what happened and what might
have happened that night in Elizabeth:

> The fire had been awful, but it was nothing compared to what
> could have happened. What could have happened that night on
> South Front Street is a scene nobody likes to think about, and
> few people in the DEP like to talk about. The fire could have
> made the jump over to Chevron and set all of the port on fire.
> The toxic fumes that were up so high in the air could have
> come down to earth and hurt or killed 250 firemen and hun-
> dreds of other people around the area. What could have hap-
> pened is a fire that consumed the entire city. We could have
> lost Elizabeth.

The same reaction was echoed by Elizabeth's health director,
John N. Surmay, who concluded that "we were within a hair's
breadth of disaster." If the fire had not burned as intensely as it
did, it is possible that more toxic fumes would have been released
by the blaze. If the wind had been blowing in a different direction,
it is likely that tens of thousands of people would have been affected by toxic smoke. If any number of other factors had been
slightly different, the Chemical Control fire might have become
one of the nation's worst disasters, entirely manmade and completely avoidable.

That is not to say, however, that there were no consequences of
the holocaust. A number of firemen were sick for days after the
event, complaining of appetite loss, headaches, and nausea. Many
received chemical burns. People living in Elizabeth and Staten Island experienced some of the same symptoms as the firemen, presumably as a result of breathing the air during and after the fire.
Some were treated for throat and lung irritations. According to a
citizens' group health survey taken about three months after the
fire, nearly one hundred residents of the area around Chemical
Control suffered from rashes, sore throats, chest pains, headaches,
or burning eyes. At least two lawsuits have been filed on behalf of
Elizabeth and Staten Island residents who claim they have suffered
from the effects of the fire. But the ultimate effects of the inferno at
Chemical Control may not be known for years, until the long-term
health consequences of the toxicants released that night have had
an opportunity to reap their damage on the bodies of those who
were close enough to be affected.

How It All Began

The story of the Chemical Control Corporation is much more than that of one gigantic fire which raged for ten hours. It is more than the story of a possible disaster of unimaginable proportions. It is more than the story of a toxic waste facility that had stockpiled tens of thousands of drums of dangerous chemicals in the heart of a major population center. In addition, it is the story of what is wrong with a large part of the hazardous waste disposal industry, and of the state's inability to control that dangerous business, which threatens the public welfare. The story of Chemical Control contains all the unlawful and perilous features that characterize so much of the industry. Some may see it as a caricature, where every element is exaggerated because they come together in the same story. Maybe so, but Chemical Control did happen, and its illustration of midnight dumping, of organized crime's takeover, and of official bumbling, ineptitude, and possibly extraordinary venality did take place.

The Chemical Control Corporation was founded by William Carracino, a resident of nearby Union. After a stint in the Navy, Carracino hauled coal for a number of years in the 1950s until he got into the business of hauling chemicals. About 1960, he began handling chemicals going to landfills, including the infamous Kin-Buc facility in Edison Township. Even though there were few restrictions on dumping chemicals in sanitary landfills in those days, Kin-Buc and its operator, Marvin Mahan, were in the process of making New Jersey's largest waste disposal site a definite threat to public health. Carracino learned a great deal from Kin-Buc and Mahan, however, and soon became a master of the complexities and deceptions involved in disposing of hazardous chemicals. An aggressive, self-assured, sometimes cocky man, he taught himself the properties of chemicals and their dangers, as well as techniques for disposing of them. By 1968, he was ready to strike out on his own, deciding he wanted to start a facility to treat hazardous chemicals rather than simply dumping them into the ground.

Carracino purchased a site on the Elizabeth waterfront that had once been the home of the Abbott Barrel Company. Naming his new firm The Chemical Waste Disposal Company, he began to make contact with local chemical and pharmaceutical companies, offering to haul and dispose of their waste. After all, with thousands of such companies located in the area, and with disposal costs ranging from $50 to $200 a drum, the potential for profit was substantial. And although some of the wastes would have to be buried in landfills, the treatment and reclamation of others would not only be a contribution to the industry, but had the potential of even magnifying profits. Within two years business was prospering and Carracino decided to expand.

In order to recover some valuable chemicals more efficiently and to dispose of useless by-products, Carracino needed a thin film evaporator and an incinerator. Purchasing these items was beyond his financial means, so he approached numerous banks in New Jersey and New York seeking the capital needed to enlarge his operation. Although he tried for a number of months to raise a million dollars, he was unsuccessful and eventually approached a private party for the loan. As a result of a recommendation from a New York banker, Carracino contacted Michael Colleton and two brothers, Robert and Charles Day, who owned and operated Northeast Pollution Control Company, which had just become a public corporation. Northeast Pollution was a small corporation that built and installed scrubbers, a pollution control device used in the incineration of garbage. After a series of negotiations lasting until the middle of 1971, Carracino's Chemical Waste Disposal Company merged with Northeast Pollution, and a new firm, Chemical Control Corporation, was formed as a subsidiary of Northeast Pollution. Under terms of the agreement, all the assets and liabilities of the old company were transferred to the new corporation, with Northeast Pollution owning 81 percent of Chemical Control's stock.

Now, with the help of Colleton and Robert and Charles Day, Carracino got his equipment, although the incinerator turned out to be used and in need of considerable work. Final purchase of the incinerator was to occur when a certificate to operate it was granted by the New Jersey Department of Environmental Protection. Although it failed its first test because it lacked an adequate scrubber, a new scrubber allowed it to be certified in May, 1972. Shortly thereafter, having passed the state's air-quality tests, the Chemical Control Corporation was given a five-year permit to operate its incinerator. That may have been the last good thing to happen at the site of South Front Street in Elizabeth.

Since the merger of his company with Northeast Pollution, Carracino had retained control of the day-to-day operation of the business, overseeing the technical aspects of chemical disposal and supervising the eleven employees. Colleton and the Day brothers, over at Northeast Pollution's Brooklyn office, took care of the company's financial matters and maintained all the records. Although this arrangement sometimes made Carracino nervous, he had no choice in the matter, and business was increasing as news of the new incinerator began to spread around the state and beyond. Because this was the only incinerator in the New York metropolitan area handling chemical wastes, and only one of two in the entire state of New Jersey, business boomed. In fact, chemical wastes began to arrive from Connecticut, New York, and Pennsylvania, as well as from some of the largest corporations operating in New Jersey.

Soon after the incinerator was certified, Colleton told Carracino that he had some bad news for him: Northeast Pollution had filed for bankruptcy in New York. Among a variety of other debts, the company owed a great deal of money to the Internal Revenue Service, which might very well seize Chemical Control as an asset of Northeast Pollution. As it turned out, that did not happen. Chemical Control was permitted to continue to operate while the parent company was in Chapter 11 of the Bankruptcy Code. Financial difficulties were common now, however, as Colleton and the Day brothers became more active in the management of the company in their quest for money to relieve their financial problems. According to Carracino, that was the turning point for the company and the end of his dream of creating a model recycling plant. He claims that it was Northeast Pollution Control and its officers that forced him to change his policies and engage in dangerous and sometimes illegal disposal activities. At one time, Colleton allegedly reprimanded Carracino for successfully controlling a fire at the facility, claiming the fire insurance would have gotten them out of their financial troubles.

Whether Carracino's claims are true or not, it is certainly the case that the company's operation began to shift markedly around this time. The incinerator became very noisy and often belched out black smoke, sometimes dropping a coat of ash on everything in the neighborhood. Barrels of chemicals, now beginning to pile up on the site, often leaked and sometimes the waste ran into the Elizabeth River. Neighbors complained to city and state officials, but complaining didn't seem to bring much response or change in the company's operation. During this period, the Elizabeth Fire Department recorded twenty-five separate incidents of rule infraction or dangerous conditions, ranging from leaking drums to small fires on the site. Sometimes the city issued summonses. In 1973, the company was caught dumping chemicals into the Elizabeth River and fined $12,000.

Ironically, while all this was happening, business continued to improve. The company accepted for incineration and processing large amounts of solvents, degreasers, acids, and other flammable wastes generated by industry and even by the federal government. When wastes could not be burned or recovered, they were shipped to landfills, generally in Rhode Island. At some point during this period, the company even began to accept explosives like dynamite and nitroglycerin, as well as various suffocating gases.

As the incinerator's efficiency decreased, Carracino reportedly started to burn the wastes at night, when darkness hid the amount of smoke. But no amount of deception could keep the smell out of the air of Elizabethport or help area residents now being bothered more frequently by nose and throat irritations and stinging eyes. Neighbors complained constantly to Carracino, who became increasingly defensive and short-tempered. Carracino maintains that he could not afford to fix the incinerator because his partners were draining the company of its profits. Others, including reporter David Weinberg, paint a somewhat different picture, claiming Carracino himself was spending great sums of money on his personal life. In any case, it was clear that Carracino and his company were in need of cash and willing to do almost anything to get it.

By 1976, conditions at the facility were getting out of hand. The inefficient and sporadic operations of the incinerator necessitated the stockpiling of thousands of drums. While the DEP estimated no more than nine thousand drums could be stored at the site in a safe manner, several times that number were now scattered about the yard and in the building. A number of the drums were rusting badly, and their contents leaking onto the ground. Sometimes the escaping chemicals would form colored puddles of liquid about the yard or drain into the Elizabeth River. In the midst of all this, however, the Chemical Control Corporation bid for a job being offered by the Federal Food and Drug Administration and was awarded the contract. It appears that 500,000 cans of Bon Vivant Vichyssoise had become bacterially contaminated and had to be destroyed. Chemical Control did the job and was even praised by the federal agency as "a model of recycling waste disposal." Few of Carracino's neighbors would have believed that.

In spite of all the complaints and the obvious mismanagement of the wastes which Chemical Control was allegedly treating or incinerating, the state of New Jersey did virtually nothing to stop or even modify the company's practices. Apparently, the DEP's Division of Environmental Quality never even ordered a stack test to see what pollutants were being emitted by Carracino's incinerator. Routine checks consisted of an inspector's looking at the incinerator and deciding there was no problem. Although state law required the operator of a chemical waste incinerator to furnish the DEP with an engineering plan for his equipment, Carracino never did and was never requested to do so by the state. One report alleges that state officials ignored Carracino's violations because they feared he would abandon the site and leave the state with the task of cleaning it up. In addition, since the only other licensed incinerator was in South Jersey, they allegedly feared any action on their part might close down Chemical Control and deprive generators of an important disposal facility. Hence, they concluded that Chemical Control's small and inefficient incinerator was better than nothing, even though it was poisoning the air and making life miserable for those who lived and worked in the Elizabethport section of the city.

In August, 1976, Carracino borrowed a considerable amount of money and used it to take the Chemical Control Corporation out of bankruptcy. Despite his making these arrangements on his own with money that he had secured, Northeast Pollution and Michael Colleton still remained the owners of 81 percent of the company. Although Carracino hoped this action would shake him loose of his partners, it did little more than free him and the company of court scrutiny. Colleton and the Day brothers still remained in the background, in need of cash and holding the ultimate power in the corporation.

Other problems were plaguing Carracino about this time as well. For reasons he could not comprehend, drums of chemicals, sometimes entire trailerloads of them, were disappearing from the

Chemical Control Corporation. Although he reported these thefts to the police, no one was ever apprehended and the strange disappearances remained a mystery. A mystery, that is, until the drums were found abandoned under highway overpasses and the trailers parked in various spots around the city.

It is possible, as some charge, the thefts never really occurred, but were part of Carracino's plan to cover up his midnight dumping activities. If the abandoned toxic chemicals were found and traced back to his facility, he was covered because he had reported them to the police as thefts. On the other hand, if they were never found or never traced back to him, he would be rid of a substantial quantity of drums he had no way of handling. But those were not the only cases of illegal dumping ultimately charged to Carracino. Much more damaging was the caper his employees carried out on Delancey Street in Newark.

In early 1977, Carracino and his company were under surveillance by the State Attorney General's Office because of their suspicions of his involvement in illegal toxic waste dumping at various sites in New Jersey. Armed with a camera, the investigators photographed a tanker being loaded with toxic chemicals at the Chemical Control site and then driven to Delancey Street, a residential avenue in Newark. Proceeding to the end of the street, the tanker unloaded its 5,000 gallons of liquid into dirt previously excavated by Carracino who, not surprisingly, was not the owner of the property. Several hours later, Carracino's workers dumped a load of trash and garbage on top of the toxic chemicals and, using a front-end loader, mixed it with the previously saturated dirt. The dangerous mixture was then loaded into a truck and taken to a sanitary landfill where it was deposited. Unfortunately for Carracino, the entire operation was recorded in pictures taken by members of the surveillance team, one of whom was overcome by fumes as the tanker was unloading its contents and had to be hospitalized.

By September, 1977, Carracino and several of his employees were indicted for their midnight dumping. More significantly, he was also forced out of the Chemical Control Corporation in a series of bizarre events resulting in the takeover of the company by a known organized crime figure. Early one morning in September, Michael Colleton visited Carracino in his Chemical Control office and after a brief discussion asked him to sign a business document.

Under questioning from Jeremiah McKenna of the New York State Senate Select Committee on Crime, Carracino describes what happened next:

> *Mr. Carracino:* The next thing was that Mr. Colleton walked out five minutes later and six people came in.
>
> *Mr. McKenna:* Did you recognize any of them?
>
> *Mr. Carracino:* I recognized John Albert and John Collins. The other four guys, I didn't know who they were. And Michael Colleton, as well, with them.
>
> *Mr. McKenna:* Was anything said to you?
>
> *Mr. Carracino:* What was said to me was that the men and John Albert were going to run the company. Do as they tell you and you'll get your money back. You do as they tell you and everything will be all right. I asked to talk to Mr. Colleton alone and they went out. I told Mike that I was not going to go for the deal, that I didn't have to have anything to do with them. That these people, they were the mob. And I told him I was going home. At that point the door to my car was kicked in and John Albert told me to get out. I called Jack Water and told him they were taking papers out of my car. Mr. Water came down and he saw these other four guys stealing papers out of my car. At this point Albert walked over to my car with one guy and slammed me against the car and showed me a gun and said, "Do you want it now or later?" The other fellow put his foot on the bumper and rolled up his pants leg and there was a gun tucked in his sock. They told me not to come back, to stay out of the chemical business and stay out of South Front Street, away from Chemical Control.

In the midst of this wild exchange, Carracino was informed that he was being replaced as the operator of Chemical Control because Albert and his associates knew how to dump chemicals and get rid of them better than he could. Carracino said he would have none of it, and gathered as many papers as he could and left the premises. Some law enforcement officials apparently believe Albert was behind Carracino the whole time he operated, a charge that Carracino vehemently denies. What relationship existed between John Albert, an alleged syndicate member with interests in a number of New Jersey garbage companies, and Michael Colleton and the Day brothers has never been established, either. Were, for example, the majority stockholders in Chemical Control really looking for more effective management and turned to Albert for his expertise in the hazardous waste disposal field? Or did Albert and his partner, Eugene Conlon, have a prior relationship with Colleton and the Day brothers in Northeast Pollution? Whether the relationship was old or new, the fact is that together they seized complete control of Carracino's company and added it to the list of those hazardous waste disposal firms controlled by representatives of organized crime.

The excitable and quick-tempered Carracino was not going to take his ouster at gunpoint lying down. While removing some of his personal property from the site, he and employees of a towing company were once again run off by one of Albert's henchmen who showed them a gun. Carracino then called a number of his former customers and advised them not to deal with the new operators of Chemical Control because they would not dispose of the chemicals properly. Next, he went to the Fire Prevention Bureau of the Elizabeth Fire Department and told them that Colleton and Albert would burn the place down for the insurance. He even went so far as to draw the firemen a map of the site, indicating what hazardous chemicals were there and where they were stored on the property. He wasn't finished yet, however. From there he called State Senator Anthony Russo, and with his wife visited the office of Congressman Matthew Rinaldo. In each case he explained that the company had been seized by the mob and predicted that they would load it up with chemicals and burn it down. He warned people would get killed as a result of what he knew they were going to do. He was heard sympathetically, but told there was little that the senator or congressman could do about the situation. Why, they each asked, didn't he go to the police with his story?

Carracino didn't trust the local police. From long experience, he knew that they considered him a sleazy operator and would probably take whatever he had to say with some amount of skepticism. In addition, there was always the possibility the police had organized crime ties themselves, and whatever he said to them would be fed right back to Albert, Conlon, and their associates. He did, however, have more confidence in the State Division of Criminal Justice, and arranged a meeting with a representative of that office. He told him what he had told the others, and warned of the possible consequences of having a facility like Chemical Control in the hands of unscrupulous hoodlums. Once again, he was listened to politely and assured that the Department would look into the matter. One can only imagine Carracino's disgust when, some time later, John Albert repeated to him the nature of his discussion with the Division of Criminal Justice representative.

For the remainder of the year, Carracino was unemployed and did little more than stay around his home. In February, 1978, he went to trial on charges of illegally dumping hazardous wastes. After a spirited defensive in which he claimed he had been framed, he was convicted on three counts of illegal dumping and sentenced to a two- to three-year prison term. The Chemical Control Corporation was also fined $75,000. Although the jury was apparently unmoved by Carracino's claim that the stolen drums and trucks were related to the takeover of his company by known mob figures, somebody evidently heard what he was saying. Shortly thereafter, his wife received a phone call at their home telling her their teenage daughter had been burned by acid. After a period of considerable anguish, the Carracinos discovered the call was a hoax and their daughter had not been harmed. The following day, however, another anonymous caller told Carracino his daughter would actually have acid thrown on her if he continued to talk about the takeover of his company. On the advice of his attorney, he reported these incidents to the Union Police and to the State Division of Criminal Justice.

Carracino's bad luck continued. Less than a month later, he was called to testify before a state grand jury investigating the unlawful dumping of toxic wastes in New Jersey. By now, of course, it was common knowledge he had a great deal of information on the subject and should be able to provide state investigators with information permitting them to secure indictments. On the day he was to testify, both of his legs were broken in what Carracino claimed was a freak accident. According to him, he came upon a wrecked tractor trailer and decided to stop and help get it back on the road. In the process of trying to right the trailer, he slipped and the trailer fell on top of him. Instead of testifying before the grand jury, he spent the next thirty days in the hospital.

What actually happened to Carracino remains something of a mystery, although he has never changed his story about the "accident." Nevertheless, others have cast doubt on his story, claiming his accident was a warning from the mob to keep his mouth shut. One source maintains John Albert himself broke Carracino's legs to keep him quiet. Whatever the real story is, the fact remains Carracino's eventual testimony before the grand jury apparently revealed little and was not particularly helpful. Although more candid revelations about illegal dumping and those involved in the dirty business would ultimately be offered by Carracino, for now he would bide his time.

Under Mob Control

When John Albert and his associate, Eugene Conlon, seized control of Carracino's company, they were no strangers to the toxic waste disposal business. In fact, Albert had an interest in perhaps as many as a dozen other disposal firms, and appeared to be expanding his empire as quickly as possible. With the closing of the Kin-Buc Landfill the year before, waste haulers had been deprived of their major dump site and were now searching for alternative facilities. Carracino's business had been improving since the landfill's closing, but Colleton and Albert apparently thought the potential was even greater. Because the facility had an incinerator, enormous quantities of waste could be accepted under the pretense they would be burned. But since the incinerator's capacity was far short of what would be required and because it didn't work very well anyhow, the wastes would be stockpiled or dumped at little cost. Hence, the opportunity for profit was great and, if Carracino was correct, a convenient fire at some point in the future would reduce the inventory and allow them to collect a substantial amount of fire insurance. Chemical Control was a not insignificant addition to the mob's list of waste companies run by John Albert.

By the time he came to Chemical Control, Albert was well known to New Jersey police officials and the FBI as a member of the Genovese–Tieri crime syndicate of New York City. Then headed by its acting boss, Philip Lombardo, this criminal organization, which traced its early leadership back to Vito Genovese and even Lucky Luciano, was known to control the carting industry in the area through its association with Local 945 of the Teamsters Union. Albert's career in organized crime was tied closely to the garbage business, particularly the disposal of hazardous chemical wastes. For a number of years, he had shown a knack for putting together companies engaged in every kind of unsafe practice but making huge profits.

Albert's particular talent was organizing firms with overlapping and interlocking directorates, often designed solely to confuse those who might investigate his activities. According to John Fine, "In many cases they weren't even incorporated. They picked a name out of the air, stuck it on their company and when the state would say, 'Well, now, wait a minute you're not permitted, we're going to cite you in violation, you must clean up,' they changed the name, moved the barrels, when nobody was looking, and dumped them unlawfully." Among others, Albert was a principal in and directed A to Z Chemical Company, J & B Disposal Service, Jersey Sanitation, Sampson Tank Cleaning Company, Gibraltar Tank Company, Hudson-Jersey Sanitation, American Collectors, and Frank Stamato & Company. In practically every one of these companies, the cast of characters was the same: Albert and Conlon joined by a small group of partners. In Jersey Sanitation, as we mentioned earlier, Albert and Conlon each held 25 percent of the ownership while the remaining 50 percent was divided among members of the George Katz and Frank Stamato families. Frank Stamato and his two sons, Patsy and Frank, Jr., along with George Katz were directors of J & B Disposal as well. The Stamatos also supplied waste equipment to Albert's various firms through a company known as Commercial Resources.

Albert ran Sampson Tank Cleaning Company with another associate, Bernie Gordon, who served as vice president. Apparently it was Mr. Gordon who arranged, through a representative of the Teamsters Union, to provide West Milford, New Jersey, with free oil to be put on dirt roads for dust control. Unfortunately, the supposed gift was merely a ploy to get rid of harmful wastes, since the free oil contained large amounts of PCBs which ultimately had to be removed from the county roads. On another occasion, Sampson Tank Cleaning was paid $48,000 by Jersey City to remove some eight hundred drums of chemicals abandoned on the city's pier. Although the city paid for the drums to be disposed of properly, they were later found stockpiled at the Chemical Control Company.

By 1977, the forty-two-year-old Albert, whose history of arrests went far beyond waste disposal activities, was riding high in the toxic chemical field. During that summer, he called FBI informant Harold Kaufman and asked if he and his boss at Duane Marine would be interested in joining an association. He announced, "I'm forming an association of toxic waste." The two Duane Marine officers, themselves tightly affiliated with organized crime and engaging in blatant illegal disposal practices, indicated that they would be interested, and met with Albert to discuss the possibilities. Albert proposed that the association be organized just as the solid waste associations were, the principal feature being property rights. Everyone would gain, he claimed, and no one would lose since his proposed system would abolish any pretenses of competition within the field. When Kaufman was asked at a hearing by Congressman Albert Gore how the property rights would be enforced and by whom, he answered.

Mr. Kaufman: Albert said he had the okay, so I—well, his rabbis, his mentors, let's call them mentors, his mentors were Vinnie Morrow and Joe Beck in New York.

Mr. Gore: Well, now, when you say mentor, is that—you use the word "rabbi," is that a new word to describe a mini-godfather of some sort?

Mr. Kaufman: Well, I don't know if you would call them godfathers, but these were the ones of the enforcers of the garbage industry for organized crime. Before Vinnie Morrow and Joe Beck, there was a guy called Frank Caruso. He died. These two gentlemen, Vinnie Morrow and Joe Beck—Beck's dead, now—Morrow took over from him when he died. And they were the enforcers of the industry. They were the ones that actually were the rabbis of, I'd say, 40 to 50 firms that I know of my own knowledge. And one of the firms was Jersey Sanitation, Johnny Albert.

Mr. Gore: Now, among the chemical waste haulers in New Jersey, has an informal system of property rights in fact evolved?

Mr. Kaufman: There is an informal system in the sense where solid waste enters into it. I can't speak about any 100 percent chemical firm, but you got to understand there is multi-facet firms, like SCA, BFI, Free Hold Carting, poeple like this that do multi work, they do toxic and solid waste work. With these people, their property rights go into the toxic.

Mr. Gore? And there is an informal agreement that no one goes after the property rights that a company has on toxic waste?

Mr. Kaufman: It is not in writing, but it is not informal; you better not.

Although the Joe Beck referred to in Kaufman's testimony was dead by the time the informer told his story, he was very much alive during the period when Albert was setting up his waste empire and directing the operations of the Chemical Control Corporation. The person in question was really Joseph Lapi considered by the police to be an "elder statesman" of the New York syndicate. Lapi, whose quiet and soft-spoken demeanor stood in direct contrast to his lengthy police record, owned a fish store in New York's Fulton Fish Market. Often seen at the Chemical Control site, Lapi apparently had a financial interest in the operation and, according to some, may even have been a partner in the company. Whether Lapi was acting solely for himself or for others in the syndicate as well, Albert showed him great respect and gave him business reports at each of their meetings. According to Albert's driver and bodyguard, who testified against him at one of his subsequent trials, Albert's weekly reports to Lapi concerned the chemical business and how each of his companies was doing. At each meeting, Albert gave Lapi an envelope containing several thousand dollars. Sometimes other individuals were present at these meetings, including Frank Vispisiano, a reputed organized crime hit man. Like Lapi, he too received money from Chemical Control, once cashing three corporation checks at Lapi's New York fish market.

By 1978, Albert and his organized crime associates were firmly entrenched at Chemical Control. Michael Colleton and the Day brothers had obviously slipped into the background and the firm's management now rested completely in the hands of Albert and Eugene Conlon. Under their direction, the stockpile of drums grew worse, the incinerator was an even greater irritant in the neighborhood, and investigators were getting worried that the amount of illegal and dangerous dumping was increasing. Organized crime figures from New York and New Jersey were frequent visitors at the site, and were obviously involved in various business transactions with John Albert. In spite of all this, however, an astonishing thing happened that year: the Federal Drug Enforcement Administration (DEA) used Chemical Control on at least three occasions to dispose of discarded pharmaceuticals and other drugs. In April, a trailer truck filled with barbiturates and tranquilizers was brought to the site for disposal. In October, a large amount of "precursor" chemicals used to make illicit narcotics was delivered to the site, and in December another load of outdated tranquilizers arrived. In all three cases, federal agents claimed they witnessed the destruction of all drugs delivered each time. Amazingly, the agency claimed it was unaware the owners and operators of Chemical Control had any criminal connections.

Questions have been raised, however, about the complete destruction of all drugs delivered to the site by the DEA. In May, 1979, Dr. Glenn Paulson of the State Department of Environmental Protection said the authorities had found various drugs at the Chemical Control site, including narcotics, steroids, and other pharmaceuticals. Another report from an undercover state investigator claimed that bales of marijuana were found in the loft of a Chemical Control building when state officials searched the premises less than a year after the federal agency used the facility. Interestingly, records show the precursor chemicals were destroyed by the company without charge, a remarkable example of charity by a group of men otherwise interested in making a profit at any cost.

The DEA's use of Chemical Control became even more puzzling when John Albert was arrested and indicted in July of 1980 on charges that he and several associates financed an illegal drug laboratory in Plainfield, New Jersey. After an extensive local investigation, code-named Operation Jigsaw, Albert and others, including Joseph Lemmo, the owner of Edison Disposal Company and another alleged organized crime figure, were charged with gambling and the manufacture of amphetamines. These charges against someone who only a short time before was entrusted with the destruction of truckloads of drugs and drug-related substances makes one wonder how the DEA was fooled so easily.

The DEP's first decisive action against Chemical Control occurred in March, 1978, when the agency went to court seeking a consent order against the company. The court order instructed Chemical Control to reduce its inventory by one thousand drums a month and to eliminate the entire quantity within two years; to submit a monthly report to the court of wastes treated and disposed of; to accept only wastes that could be destroyed within sixty days; to remove all leaking drums and saturated soil which might leach into the Elizabeth River; and lastly, to construct a fence around the property. Surprisingly, the court order did not shut down Chemical Control, but merely required the inventory be reduced and new shipments of chemicals be treated or removed within two months of their arrival. As one observer points out, "The owners were allowed to go on doing business as usual, even though at this point environmental officials had every reason to know how poorly the incinerator was working."

The order posed little problem for Albert and Conlon, who went on doing business as usual. When they were not ignoring the administrative order, they moved their drums to other sites they were operating or dumped them illegally, often out of state in New York or Massachusetts. One place to which drums were sometimes moved was the A to Z Chemical Resource Recovery Company of New Brunswick, New Jersey. A to Z, apparently owned by Albert, Conlon, and John Vispisiano, the brother of Frank, operated for some two years without a permit, though the state of New Jersey was considering their application. While this did not prevent them from putting drums on the Triangle Road property in New Brunswick, the lack of a state license was the subject of frequent conversations between Albert and Joe Lapi. Again, Albert's former driver testified he overheard the two men speak frequently of the new facility as another Chemical Control.

When drums were not being stockpiled at Chemical Control or moved from one Albert site to another, they were often dumped across the water in Staten Island and in Massachusetts. By now, barrels were being moved among the various companies so rapidly it was difficult to know where they had originated and which of Albert's many companies were doing the out-of-state dumping. After some period of operation, he was finally indicted in Massachusetts in 1980, charged with dumping over two thousand barrels of waste in Plymouth County. In addition to the dumping, the indictments also tell of the intimidation of witnesses and the fire bombing of the automobile of one witness against the New Jersey dumpers.

Although DEP inspections increased after the court order, little was done for the remainder of that year. Chemical Control officers submitted reports showing the drum inventory was being reduced, but no one could see any real physical change. A September DEP inspection revealed approximately 25,000 to 30,000 drums stored on the site, covering the entire outside area of the property. The report also noted that drums were piled in the buildings and no work on the perimeter fence had started yet, even though the court order was now six months old. Two months later, a report submitted to the DEP by the Hazards Research Corporation indicated that "the overall disaster potential for the facility must be rated as substantial." This report also placed the number of drums somewhere between 30,000 and 39,000, and indicated the probability of chemical interaction on this site was overwhelming. The consultant's report concluded that the "public welfare demands that the clean-up proceed with all possible speed. . . ."

Before the Fire

Between 1975 and January, 1979, the DEP inspected Chemical Control thirty-one times. Over time, the deterioration in the site and its operation began to be reflected in the inspectors' reports. Although no deficiencies were noted in 1976, a year later the inspector noted that about 26,000 drums were stored on the site. Fourteen months later, the report revealed that so many drums were stacked everywhere that a walkway was no longer visible. Finally, in early January, 1979, the inspector wrote that he observed a smoldering fire being extinguished by several men and that leaks were observed throughout the yard, which was completely covered with drums full of chemicals. That appeared to be enough, even for the very tolerant Department of Environmental Protection. Within days, the Department was in court again asking for an injunction to prohibit the accumulation of more drums and forcing Chemical Control to clean up its site. The order, issued by Judge Harold Ackerman, instructed Chemical Control to stop accepting more waste and to remove 12,000 drums from the property immediately, particularly those that were leaking. The owners of Chemical Control were also ordered to prevent further discharges of waste materials into the lands or waters of the state and to install additional fire-fighting equipment. The injunction placed the responsibility for cleaning up the site squarely on the owners and operators of the facility, under the direction of the DEP. But the agents of organized crime and their accomplices saw no profit in that.

Fearful of the possibility of a deliberately set fire, and wanting to prevent an unauthorized increase in the number of drums on the site, the DEP posted twenty-four-hour security at Chemical Control. The agency staff members assigned to watch the facility soon became concerned for their own safety, however. Just days after the security program started, they submitted a memorandum to their superiors complaining of the potential dangers at the site and that the Department was not paying enough attention to their health and well-being. Their dissension did not last long enough though, since the program was discontinued for budgetary reasons only three weeks after it began.

It soon became apparent Chemical Control was not going to clean itself up. After much stalling and delaying by the company, the DEP got the message and returned to court on March 8, 1979, asking that the company be placed in receivership and that full responsibility for the clean-up be turned over to them. Judge Ackerman readily complied.

The state's seizure of Chemical Control was bad news for John Albert. Not only had a lucrative source of profit dried up, but the files at Chemical Control were full of documents which might serve as incriminating evidence against him and his other enterprises if discovered by state investigators. Since the site was again under guard, retrieving them would be difficult but certainly not impossible if the right techniques were used. To accomplish this task, Albert dispatched an employee, Richard Pirmann, to Chemical Control to steal all the files he could carry out. Pirmann did precisely that by climbing over some barrels and sneaking in the back door. Once inside, he took everything he thought might link Albert and New Jersey Sanitation to the Chemical Control operation. Back in Albert's office at Jersey Sanitation, the two of them systematically went through the documents destroying anything that might be embarrassing or tie Albert and his enterprises to illegal activities. Fortunately for them, their job was finished when someone called to say that Pirmann had been seen and the files had to be returned. Since Albert now saw no problem with this, he invited the caller to come down and pick them up at his convenience. The identity of this messenger has never been revealed.

A little more than a decade after the company was founded and some nineteen months after William Carracino was run off the property at gunpoint, Chemical Control shut its doors as a hazardous waste treatment facility. After ten years of a malfunctioning incinerator, environmental pollution, midnight dumping, stockpiling drums, and organized crime takeover, the state of New Jersey finally decided to take decisive action. Even though the 1976 Resource Conservation and Recovery Act would have permitted the state to define Chemical Control as an imminent hazard years earlier, it had neglected to do so, waiting instead for the problem to grow absolutely desperate. In the last nineteen months alone, under the direction of Albert and Conlon, somewhere between 14,000 and 20,000 drums of toxic chemicals had been added to the 20,000 left behind by Carracino. Now, thousands of these drums had corroded and were leaking badly. Worse yet, no one knew exactly what the drums contained, although everyone was quite sure that deadly chemicals were represented among them. Quite obviously, cleaning up Chemical Control would be no easy task, although few expected it to prove as difficult as it actually turned out to be.

Immediately after assuming control of the company, the DEP contacted four major waste hauling and disposal firms and requested they submit proposals for the clean-up of Chemical Control. Although each submitted bids indicating the entire job could be completed for less than $6 million, the final contract was negotiated and signed with a company that didn't even submit a proposal. Coastal Services, Incorporated, of Linden, New Jersey, was given the job without a formal bid, ostensibly because it was also cleaning up other toxic waste sites in the state at the same time. Coastal was to identify the chemicals stored on the property, repack those drums that were leaking and other items that could not be shipped as they were found, and clear the site so would no longer be a danger to the public welfare. Coastal Services began its clean-up in April, 1979.

In the weeks that followed, South Front Street was a busy place around the Chemical Control site. In addition to Coastal employees, federal and state officials searched the premises attempting to decide what was stored there and how it should be handled. Soon after the takeover, Commissioner Daniel O'Hern of the New Jersey DEP held a meeting of concerned agency representatives to discuss plans and procedures for the clean-up. State health officials reported to a stunned audience that they had found enough chemical poisons and pesticides to provide a lethal dose to all the residents of Staten Island and Lower Manhattan in the event of a fire that could not be controlled immediately. Protective measures for the clean-up workers were also discussed, as well as enlisting the help of the United States Army to remove some of the explosives that would not be handled by the Federal Bureau of Alcohol, Tobacco and Firearms. Although this agency had already removed quantities of picric acid, nitroglycerin, and other explosives, there were still more the Army's Technical Escort Unit could handle better.

For the next year, Coastal employees worked at the site, placing leaking drums and packages of laboratory wastes into containers for disposal. At all times, the DEP had an on-scene coordinator and several other representatives available at the site to work with Coastal Services. But those working and living around the area and concerned policemen and firemen who knew the site was supposedly being cleaned were mystified by what they saw. At times, new drums of chemical wastes were actually being delivered to the facility in spite of Judge Ackerman's court order, and although there always seemed to be much movement of drums onto and off the grounds, the numbers never seemed to diminish. In fact, there were those who were convinced that the number of drums was actually increasing. And, amazingly, they were right.

In testimony before the New York State Senate Select Committee on Crime, John Fine explained what happened. When asked by Senator Ralph J. Marino if the number of drums on the Chemical Control site actually increased during the period in question, the following exchange took place:

Mr. Fine: Thousands more.
Senator Marino: During this period who was in control of the site?
Mr. Fine: State of New Jersey, Department of Environmental Protection, New Jersey's Department of Criminal Justice, the Attorney General's office and they had a contract with

Coastal Services and Peabody Testing, to undertake to clean
up the site and test the chemicals.

Senator Marino: Can you tell us why there was a build-up
while the State of New Jersey controlled the site?

Mr. Fine: I do know this, witnesses told us that Coastal Services was under mandate to clean Bourne Chemicals, so the
contractor brought the barrels of poison onto the site, building them up. They were taking them from other areas they
were paid to clean up.

Senator Marino: Are you saying then, Coastal, who was paid to
clean up this particular site, was actually building up more
containers on this site from other sources?

Mr. Fine: That is correct.

Senator Marino: Do you know what sources they were getting
containers from?

Mr. Fine: One of the company's name was Bourne, B-O-U-R-
N-E, maybe a half or a block further down Front Street, in
Elizabeth. At that time Coastal Services had perhaps a million gallons in bulk tanks stored on the Bourne property and
they had to get rid of it.

Much later, at the end of 1983, John Fine's charges were substantiated by New Jersey Attorney General Irwin I. Kimmelman,
whose department revealed that thousands of drums were moved
onto the site during the period of alleged clean-up. Although some
observers believe as many as 20,000 to 30,000 new barrels of toxic
wastes were placed on the site, the Department of Criminal Justice
concluded the number was only "about 5,700 drums." After what
officials claimed was an exhaustive investigation, they were unable
to show that any crime had been committed. Claiming there was
no evidence of anyone's taking money, Criminal Justice Director
Donald R. Bensole said, "There is no more investigation. It is time
to write the obituary."

Although New Jersey investigators could not find anyone who
took money for allowing the additional drums to be dumped at
Chemical Control, there was a great deal of money to be made. As
Herb Jaffe of the Newark *Star-Ledger* points out, generators were
paying up to $100 a drum in 1979 to have their toxic wastes dis-
posed of illegally. If, as the Attorney General's final report claims,
5,700 drums were added, they would have been worth $1.7 mil-

lion. And, as others claim, the actual figure was closer to 30,000 drums, then a staggering $9 million was to be made by the deception. Since the investigation is now officially closed, what happened during that twelve-month period when Coastal Services was being paid by the state to clean up the site remains a mystery.

What is even more surprising is that Coastal's stockpiling was not detected earlier. Although the DEP on-site supervisors complained about Coastal and the way it was doing its job, there is no evidence they ever warned anyone of what was happening. Perhaps one reason was that the state DEP was doing the same thing itself, authorizing the acceptance of several trailerloads of drums shipped to Chemical Control from other sites. Whether the result of corruption or ineptitude, the fact of the matter is that a festering situation was made even worse with the help of a state agency charged with protecting the public welfare.

Early in April, 1980, one of the on-site inspectors, Ed Faille, called Bill Carracino to ask for his help. Apparently, a very bad odor was permeating the area and no one could quite identify what it was. The smell was sickening, he claimed, but Coastal's testing of the contents of the barrels on the site did not reveal anything that would cause such an offensive odor. On Carracino's advice, Faille went to the area in question and, taking off his mask, took a deep breath. He quickly returned to the telephone and informed Carracino it was a sweet smell and it made him want to throw up. When Carracino heard this, he told Faille he had a serious problem on his hands and he better find it quickly. The former owner of the chemical waste treatment plant, as a self-educated expert on properties of toxic substances, knew from Faille's description that a powerful and deadly compound was emitting its fumes into the air down in Elizabethport.

Carracino went immediately to police headquarters and spoke to Chief Joe Brennan, a long-time foe of toxic waste dumpers. Brennan had been dissatisfied with Coastal's lack of progress but had been instructed to leave the situation alone since it was the state's problem. Now, however, hearing that toxic fumes were present at the site, he advised Carracino to go to Chemical Control and see if he could locate the source of the dangerous odor. Along with several Elizabeth authorities, Carracino did just that, but was turned away at the gate. The Coastal employee in charge would not allow him to inspect the grounds he once owned. Even without

Carracino, Ed Faille and Coastal employees found the white powder he told them to look for. Analysis showed that the barrel in
question contained DECP, a highly toxic pesticide that can cause
death. The revelation proved to be embarrassing for Coastal Services, since its officials had already charged the state for supposedly analyzing the contents of all the barrels on the site. If this
had been done, why didn't they know a number of deteriorating
drums contained DECP? In addition, the Elizabeth police now
began to voice stronger complaints about the nature and progress
of the clean-up. DEP officials even began giving serious consideration to changing clean-up contractors.

Before a decision could be made, the fire occurred. No one
knows exactly how it started, but those close to the case believe it
was torched. The New Jersey State Police investigation, which
went on for nearly four years, concluded little more than it was a
fire of "suspicious origin." Whether or not the fire was deliberately
set, it seems reasonable to conclude with David Weinberg that it
"couldn't have happened without a State Department of Environmental Protection that was unwilling or unable to use the law to
regulate the Chemical Control Corporation." The same may also
be said for that agency's relationship with Coastal Services and its
failure to clean the site, instead making it even worse.

How bad was the Chemical Control site at the time of the fire?
That seems impossible to determine in retrospect, given the con-
flicting estimates in numerous official reports. On the one hand,
Coastal Services said it removed 8,200 drums and billed the state
for $1.9 million. On the other hand, the DEP concluded there
were 60,000 drums on the property the night of the fire, some
26,000 more than when Coastal began its alleged clean-up. Somewhere in between these two extreme estimates is the Attorney
General's conclusion that 5,700 drums were added during the year
the site was under Coastal's control. In any case, the fact remains
that thousands of tons of toxic waste fed the fire that Monday night
in April, 1980.

Cleaning Up the Mess

Immediately after the fire, Coastal Services was relieved of any
further responsibility in the Chemical Control clean-up. Instead,

the director of the Hazard Management Program in the DEP selected several clean-up contractors from a list of seventeen previously approved. The entire list was made up of contractors recommended by on-scene coordinators who had monitored their previous work and judged it to be of high quality. The major clean-up contractors were O. H. Materials Company of Ohio, New England Pollution Control of Connecticut, Rollins Environmental Services of New Jersey, and Cecos International, a company with which the state had previously signed a three-year contract to apply to any clean-up needed in New Jersey. In addition, numerous subcontractors were also used to get the job finished as quickly as possible.

Thus began the state's second effort to clean up Chemical Control. As before, DEP officials were assigned to supervise the job and contractors were instructed to work around the clock under a "state of emergency" order. No expense would be spared to do the job and do it right this time. And, apparently, no expense was spared. Over the next fourteen months, the New Jersey Spill Compensation Fund paid the contractors over $26 million for their work at Chemical Control. And still the clean-up remained unfinished. Work ceased because the state ran out of money.

Concerned by the long delay in cleaning up this environmental and health hazard, and suspicious because the DEP refused to allow him to examine the fiscal records of the clean-up project, Herb Jaffe convinced the State Treasurer's Office to allow him access to their records. What Jaffe found was another DEP-related scandal of mismanagement and ineptitude, which he detailed in a series of twelve articles appearing in the Star-Ledger in 1982. As a result of this public scrutiny, both state and independent audits were performed, confirming Jaffe's original assessment of the clean-up program.

Aided by a fellow reporter trained as an accountant, Jaffe spent four weeks examining the files of the New Jersey Spill Compensation Fund. He found ripoffs everywhere, large and small, in all phases of the work. Exactly how much the state misspent is impossible to calculate because of inadequate record keeping and even missing documents, but it appears safe to conclude the amount totaled millions. How could this happen after DEP's previous experience? In one sense the answer is simple: When an ineffective and inefficient public agency is charged with supervising profit-oriented private contractors in a business characterized by fraud and deceit, the contractors will take advantage of every opportunity they can get away with to maximize their earnings. Such seems to have been the case once again at Chemical Control.

Jaffe found that hundreds of truckloads of contaminated waste were recorded as weighing one amount when they left the Elizabeth site but another amount at the disposal sites at Niagara Falls, New York, and Williamsburg, Ohio. Ideally, of course, the weights were to match, but records showed all of the trucks leaving Chemical Control weighed 35,000 pounds but ended up in New York and Ohio weighing anywhere from 28,000 to 46,000 pounds. Strangely, of the many manifests Jaffe examined, none indicated the loads taken to the Cecos facilities weighed 35,000 pounds on arrival. Even stranger, no DEP official was present at the Ohio and New York weigh-ins, even though these amounts were used to bill the state for services rendered. On many occasions Cecos International billed the state for the removal of contaminated soil at $100 a ton when, in actuality, the load consisted of contaminated brick and fire debris contracted for removal at $50 a ton. Jaffe's evidence showed hundreds of tons of waste were misbilled in this way.

The state was also charged huge sums to support the round-the-clock work schedule. Because of this, the average laborer earned close to $2,500 a week, with foremen and supervisors usually collecting a weekly wage of more than $3,000. It was not unusual for professionals, such as chemists, engineers, and microbiologists, to be paid a week's salary of $3,500. These huge salaries were largely the result of overtime pay, since many workers put in eighty hours or more each week. It is difficult to know what the scores of workers did throughout the night, however, since DEP on-site supervisors did not work more than twelve hours a day, leaving the private contractors unsupervised for half the time they were being paid premium rates. Oftentimes, state coordinators would sign work reports for days they did not work at the site.

Other abuses cited by Jaffe included free lunches and payments as high as $75 an hour for employees while they ate and even loafed on the job; freight charges indiscriminately raised from time to time over the clean-up period; equipment rented by the day that stood idle for weeks; 15 to 30 percent cost overrides to the major contractors for services performed by subcontractors; and a host of slipshod management policies which ended up costing the state millions. Most important, though, were the environmental abuses committed by the contractors and tolerated by the state's environmental protection agency. On one occasion, employees of O. H. Materials were caught punching holes into drums and allowing the contents to run onto the ground. According to an on-site supervisor's daily log, the practice continued even after they were instructed to stop. On numerous occasions, trucks hauling waste out of Chemical Control were stopped on the highways of different states because their contents were leaking. At one time, the state of Ohio seriously considered barring all trucks coming from the New Jersey waste site. At other times, drums fell from trucks as they were being hauled from the site. All in all, no one is quite sure what environmental and health damage may have been done by the transportation of more than 100 million pounds of contaminated soil, bricks, and fire debris from Elizabeth to the various dump sites.

The $26 million cost of the Chemical Control clean-up almost bankrupted the state's Spill Compensation Fund. With very little federal money available for the project, the state was forced to bear virtually the entire cost. Various state officials have promised the remaining clean-up will be completed "as soon as possible," but the residents of Elizabethport continue to wait. Former DEP Commissioner Jerry English acknowledged the clean-up was taking an inordinately long time, stating, "We had hoped to have a park on the site by now. Maybe I'm too impatient." Although one would have to question the wisdom of placing a park on the ground where thousands of drums leaking deadly chemicals once stood, one certainly could not accuse Commissioner English of being too impatient. Instead, the "patience" and incompetence of her agency was undeniably a major factor in this latest toxic waste scandal, just as it had been a factor in the supposed pre-fire clean-up.

The Department of Justice seemed to concur in this judgment. In a report issued after the *Star-Ledger*'s revelations, the Department said: "The dependence of the Division of Hazard Management upon the veracity of the contractors for supporting documentation and the lack of an independent record-keeping system maintained by the division created the atmosphere for fraud . . ." Attorney General Kimmelman followed that up by declaring, "There is no doubt that there was gross mismanagement

on the part of public employees during the clean-up." But Kimmelman further stated that here too, as with the first clean-up, no
crime could be proved. Although none of the investigation was
ever brought to a grand jury for possible indictments, the state's
chief law enforcement officers were willing to chalk up the entire
bungled affair to bad management, even though it cost the taxpayers unknown millions of dollars and to this day continues to
endanger their health. In a 1984 editorial, the *Star-Ledger* comments on this final phase of the Chemical Control saga:

> Removal of the lethal waste from the Chemical Control prop-
> erty has been going on for five years under DEP supervision.
> The costly job is still not completed. The ineptitude and extrav-
> agance of the DEP in this life-and-death matter have badly
> shaken public confidence in the Department and the key of-
> ficials who were in charge. Many of the individuals responsible
> for the administrative nightmare are still on the state payroll,
> still making decisions in toxic waste disposal.

The Chemical Control Corporation no longer exists. Its former
location on South Front Street in Elizabethport is a grim, barren
piece of land containing only a few visible remnants of days gone
by. Trailers containing hazardous waste are still lined up at the site
waiting to be transported elsewhere. "No Trespassing" signs hang
on the fence, warning visitors not to enter. Neighbors are still
bitter about what happened to them because of Chemical Control,
blaming William Carracino, John Albert, and the state of New
Jersey for the disruption and torment of their lives. None of them
expects a park to be built where the drums once stood.

William Carracino served a short prison sentence and then returned to the trucking business, although he no longer hauls hazardous wastes. In 1979, he began working with the New Jersey
State Police and the New York State Senate Select Committee on
Crime, assisting in waste dumping investigations. He has also appeared voluntarily before various governmental groups inquiring
into the illegal hazardous waste disposal business and has been an
important grand jury witness several times. His information has
played a key role in investigations of illegal disposal practices in
New Jersey, New York, and Pennsylvania.

John Albert continues to operate a number of New Jersey waste
hauling firms, including those that deal in toxic chemical wastes.

Like many organized crime figures, he appears to be immune from any effective action by law enforcement to remove him from the business of crime. Equipped with the best legal counsel and strategically placed political connections, indictments seldom lead to convictions and convictions seldom result in substantial prison sentences. Even worse is the realization that John Albert and his takeover of Chemical Control is the story of only one mobster and one hazardous waste facility.

In its brief, twelve-year history, the Chemical Control Corporation went from bad to worse as it changed from a careless, sometimes illegal operation to one completely controlled by representatives of organized crime. While these changes took place, so did the conditions found at the company's site, as the stockpiling of drums increased and the incidence of blatant illegal dumping grew larger. The record of Chemical Control would be bad enough if it ended there, but unfortunately it doesn't. Compounding these already tragic events was the conduct of the state agency responsible for protecting the citizens and their environment as well as that of licensed private contractors responsible for the clean-up. Their contributions of gross mismanagement, professional ineptitude, fiscal irresponsibility, and perhaps fraud, make the story of Chemical Control even more frightening.

Was Chemical Control an isolated case, particular to the unique circumstances of New Jersey and the New York metropolitan area? To what extent is this story being repeated throughout the nation? The conditions that spawned Chemical Control exist elsewhere in the country, and it is more than probable new Chemical Controls are now festering in a number of states. Where the next potential for disaster is located is anybody's guess.

10

Across the Nation and Beyond

IN FEBRUARY, 1983, the Permanent Subcommittee on Investigations (PSI) of the U.S. Senate Committee on Governmental Affairs held hearings in Washington, D.C., on the nature and extent of organized crime in the mid-Atlantic region of the country. Amid testimony on outlaw motorcycle gangs, union racketeering, narcotics distribution, and mob killings, members of the subcommittee also heard testimony on organized crime's role in the toxic waste disposal industry. Research findings on illegal toxic waste disposal were presented; in addition, Jeremiah McKenna, chief counsel of the New York State Senate Select Committee on Crime, explained the group's pathbreaking role in the investigation of unlawful disposal activities.

McKenna and others discussed the basis of organized crime's involvement in toxic waste and the ways in which dangerous chemicals were being systematically disposed of in an unlawful fashion. Most of the cases cited came from the New York–New Jersey area, principally because at the time those two states were in the forefront of investigating illegal disposal practices. Because of the well-established tradition of investigating organized crime in the Northeast, and the large amount of toxic substances generated in the area, more was known about the organized crime/toxic waste link in that region than in others. Understandably, this raised some question about the extent of such activity and whether or not it was a problem found elsewhere in the country.

Committee members were assured, however, that this was a national problem, and the activities described were not particular to New York and New Jersey. Witnesses indicated that available evidence showed mob involvement in the waste disposal industry increasing in a number of states, particularly in the Sunbelt where industrial expansion was creating new opportunities for waste entrepreneurs. In many such areas, both the solid and hazardous waste industries were being infiltrated by representatives of New Jersey–New York crime syndicates. Some states had unknowingly become the dumping ground for wastes being hauled by mob-related firms. McKenna pointed out that John Albert was caught dumping in three states and that New York investigators had followed the trail of toxic dumpers from New York to dump sites in Indiana. Sometimes, waste cargo bound for out-of-state sites never got there. If all of the PCBs supposedly delivered to a licensed treatment facility in Alabama arrived at the time specified on the manifests, McKenna asserted that trucks "would have jammed every road in the state of Alabama, because there is no way all that PCB oil could have arrived in Alabama during that period of time." His conclusion was that many truckers simply dumped their cargoes at convenient places between the point of pick up and the Alabama treatment facility. Since PCBs supposedly were shipped to Alabama from all over the nation, it would mean that the dozens of states in between shared the problem of illegal dumping practices.

Following these hearings, the PSI sent a questionnaire to each state's Attorney General asking them to respond to several questions regarding illegal waste disposal. Specifically, they were asked to indicate the number of reports they had received of organized crime's involvement in toxic waste disposal. Although the results of the survey were not surprising, the subcommittee's interpretation of them was.

Calming Fears

Overall, sixteen states indicated they had received one or more reports of organized crime involvement. Most of those states had followed up the reports with an investigation, and in half of the jurisdictions the reports had actually resulted in convictions. Information on organized crime and toxic waste came primarily from states in the Northeast, mid-Atlantic, and upper Midwest. The remaining thirty-four states reported no knowledge of such involvement, even though a number of them indicated there

had been illegal disposal activities. Among those states reporting
no organized crime involvement was New York, which certainly
must have come as some surprise to John Fine and the New York
State Senate Select Committee.

On the basis of this information, the Permanent Subcommittee
on Investigations concluded organized crime's involvement was
less significant than expected. After acknowledging any amount of
organized crime activity in the area of hazardous waste disposal
must be regarded as a serious matter, the staff summary issued by
the subcommittee concluded that "in the past several years a sort
of mythology, fueled by supposition and false assumptions, has
built up around the role of traditional organized crime and hazardous waste." While the solid waste industry is influenced by organized crime in many areas of the country, the summary claimed
the same influence is not present in the hazardous waste industry.
Then, as a sort of afterthought, it asserted that "most state officials
emphasize that they simply do not have enough information to
make firm statements about organized crime's role in hazardous
waste disposal. . . ." Strangely, the admission by state officials that
they lacked sufficient knowledge to offer definitive answers to the
subcommittee's queries did not prevent the subcommittee staff
from labeling the relationship "mythology" and "less significant
than expected." One might conclude that this Senate panel wanted
to put everyone's mind at ease in spite of the information gathered
from the states.

How insignificant is the problem according to the PSI survey?
Even the flawed information reveals that reports of organized
crime's involvement in toxic waste disposal had been received in
32 percent of the states. Since it is quite obvious that New York
should also be included in that list, one-third of our states, including the largest and most industrialized, appear to be experiencing
the problem. This is all the more significant when one realizes few
states have actually looked for the relationship, or even know what
to look for. Quite clearly, those states reporting no organized crime
activity in this area do so principally because the relationship has
not been explored through aggressive investigations. In personal
correspondence with the attorney generals and chief environmental officers of a number of states, this theme is stated over and
over. Repeatedly, these officials commented that they simply do
not know what the situation is in their states, that no one has really

investigated the possibility. A typical case of this sort is Louisiana. Attorney General William A. Guste, Jr., is quoted as saying, "I want to know how far organized crime has gotten in the illicit transportation and dumping of hazardous wastes. I'm sure it is right here in Louisiana from reports I have received about midnight dumping. I have no proof at all but I have a gut feeling."

The Attorney General has good reason for his gut feeling. Louisiana is among the leading producers of hazardous wastes and has a powerful organized crime syndicate operating within the state. Since most of the characteristics which lead to the organized crime and toxic waste relationship in the Northeast are also found in Louisiana, there is ample cause to suspect the linkage occurs in that state as well. Regardless of this and the Attorney General's sincere concern, he reports: "I would like a thorough investigation made but don't have the resources to do it in my own office." Unfortunately, no one else in the state is doing it either.

Even in states which have investigative units devoted to hazardous waste issues, problems abound. In general, the units are small and usually of very recent origin, having only limited experience in this new and special kind of policing. A typical example is the Illinois Hazardous Waste Investigations Unit, a division of the Illinois Department of Law Enforcement. According to its coordinator, Commander Gary L. Long, the limited resources available to this unit have made it necessary for it to function in a reactive role. Instead of targeting potential violations and suspected dumpers, this small unit has had to respond to situations as they become known, usually because of some crisis circumstance. Long readily admits rumors and allegations of organized crime involvement in toxic waste disposal have not been investigated thoroughly because of a lack of funds, equipment, personnel, and training. If that is the case in Illinois, which has gone further than many states in setting up a specialized investigative unit, one can only imagine what the situation is like in those states which have so far paid little or no attention to the issues related to illegal dumping.

A National Dilemma

The New Jersey–New York investigations revealed extensive illegal dumping activities had been going on for quite some time in Connecticut, Massachusetts, and Rhode Island. Often with the consent of local organized crime figures, wastes were hauled to these states for disposal by any means possible. In addition, extensive use was made of eastern Pennsylvania as a dump site, particularly the beautiful Pocono Mountain region.

In April, 1983, a number of drums of dangerous chemicals were unearthed on a three-acre site in Pocono Summit, Pennsylvania, in the heart of a popular summer and winter resort area. The drums were stored on land owned by Herman Martens. Martens, the co-owner of the Mount Airy Lodge, agreed to accept the drums on the understanding they contained soap residue which he possibly could use for laundry purposes at his lodge. When it was discovered that the barrels contained a pasty substance rather than soap powder, Martens allegedly had the delivery stopped and asked that the drums be removed. Four years later, when this had not been done, he paid a New Jersey waste hauler $35,000 to remove some of them, although what the hauler did with them remains unclear. By the early 1980s, the illnesses of at least three persons and the contamination of a number of wells had been linked to the Pocono Summit disposal site.

Interest in this case heightened when Herman Martens was found to have been associated with the late Crescent Roselle, who had owned a small Pocono lodge himself and had been one of the alleged dumpers in the area. Roselle was the brother-in-law of Martens's brother, a Mount Airy employee and a friend of the family. According to Elizabeth, New Jersey, police intelligence reports, it was Roselle's associate Anthony Gaess who told waste haulers about the availability of the Pocono Summit site. At least six firms transported waste to the site, and, according to one informant, to other Pocono sites as well. The informant, who eventually passed a lie detector test administered by Pennsylvania authorities, claimed that hundreds of barrels of toxic wastes were buried under the golf course at the Mount Airy Lodge, placed there while it was under construction. Although the golf course was never excavated, authorities claim they have been unable to substantiate the informant's charge.

From the hills of Pennsylvania to the sun-drenched deserts of the Southwest, organized crime is making its influence felt in both the solid and hazardous waste industries. Although sometimes the initial thrust is directly into hazardous waste activities, more often the organized crime pattern is to move from solid waste into the hazardous area, just as it did in the New York–New Jersey region. Not surprisingly, these activities may be found where the need exists and there is money to be made. In a recent interview, FBI informant Harold Kaufman described one way in which organized crime spreads its influence and establishes its control in a region: "New York is pouring out into the southwest sunbelt because of the influx of industry and they are worried sick in New Mexico and Arizona and New York garbage companies are buying in there like it's going out of style."

Although Kaufman's observations appear to be correct, it is also true that persons with ties to organized crime in other areas of the country are also moving to the great Southwest. In Arizona, for example, the EPA issued a license to Chemcon Inc. to operate a toxic waste treatment plant in the Phoenix area. According to the *Arizona Republic*, one of the officers and directors of the firm is Louis M. Sarko, an alleged associate of organized crime figures in Detroit. Both Michigan and Arizona law enforcement officials claimed that Sarko was associated with Anthony and Vito Giacalone, both identified by a former Detroit police commissioner as organized crime leaders in that city. Anthony Giacalone, the brother with whom Sarko appeared to be friendliest, has a police record stretching back twenty-five years charging tax evasion, extortion, loan sharking, and bribing a police officer. Interestingly, it was Anthony Giacalone with whom Jimmy Hoffa was supposedly going to meet on the day he disappeared in 1975.

Louis Sarko's interest in waste can also be traced to his Michigan roots. As far back as 1968, he attempted to build an $18 million incinerator in Detroit but was denied the necessary permit because of his alleged connections. Although Sarko claimed that his company, Incinerator, Inc., was not related to the Detroit syndicate and that Giacalone did not have a hidden interest in it, the Detroit Common Council voted to deny him a construction permit. Subsequently, the sixty-nine-year-old Sarko pleaded guilty to a tax fraud indictment which included his filing false corporate and personal federal income tax returns. Sarko's son, Allen, a vice president of Chemcon was accused of bribing a labor union official in order to exempt one of his firms from contributing to the union's health fund.

Upon moving to Arizona, Louis Sarko, two of his sons, and a stepbrother purchased a twenty-three acre site for nearly $1 million. Despite the shady past of the property owners and company officials, and their longstanding involvement with known organized crime operators, the EPA gave its approval to the proposed treatment plant after a public hearing which no one attended. Later, officials learned the lack of attendance resulted from the meeting's being advertised in a newspaper which did not service the area of the proposed plant site. Strangely, police investigators could never discover the identity of the EPA employee who placed the notice for the public meeting in a distant newspaper.

Several years earlier, police in the neighboring state of New Mexico became suspicious of a New York mob's influence in their state when they arrested two New Yorkers in a stolen garbage truck. The truck, which had been stolen in Lindenhurst, New York, and apparently driven cross-country to New Mexico, was being used in a local business by Peter Marcello and Benjamin Dante. Marcello was a former part-owner of a New York area waste company, which he ran with his relative and partner, Joseph Petrizzo, a waste hauler believed to be the hidden power behind two garbage associations on Long Island. For at least two years, Marcello had been traveling back and forth between New Mexico and New York while attempting to establish himself in the Albuquerque garbage industry. At the time, New Mexico authorities noted he was putting pressure on local carting companies to buy them out or to frighten them out of business. Marcello's efforts to control garbage hauling were centered in the Rio Rancho area, a rapidly growing suburb north of Albuquerque. When arrested in the stolen truck, Benjamin Dante was listed as an employee of Marcello who had moved to New Mexico with him to work in the garbage industry.

New York police intelligence reports reflect the belief that Marcello's A-1 Disposal Company was the first of a series of solid waste companies started or taken over by representatives of New York interests. A few years later, Marcello sold his company to Joseph Capone, Jr., and Gary Curreri, also transplanted New Yorkers interested in going into the garbage business in Albuquerque. Capone's father had long been active in private waste carting in Brooklyn and at one time had been an active member of the Brooklyn Trade Waste Association. A New York police intelligence report asserts that young Capone and Curreri were sent to New Mexico by Nicholas Stilo, an associate of Joseph Pagano who was identified as a member of the Genovese crime group and operator of a carting firm in Westchester County.

Shortly after purchasing Marcello's firm, Capone and Curreri changed its name to A-1 Carting Services, the same name used by Nick Ratteni for one of his firms in Westchester County, New York. It is interesting to note that Ratteni was Joe Pagano's boss in the Genovese/Tieri crime organization. Eventually, Marcello's associate Benjamin Dante formed his own company with two partners. Since the late 1970s, a number of other New York waste company operators have moved in and out of New Mexico with regularity, or as informant Harold Kaufman said, "Buying in there like it's going out of style."

If police intelligence reports are correct that "Stilo . . . told associates in New York that he had gone to New Mexico to arrange for the take over of carting firms . . . and to control carting operations," there is no reason to believe these firms would deal only with solid waste. Since Albuquerque industry and defense installations generate toxic wastes which must be moved and disposed of, New Mexico waste companies would view the opportunity to haul hazardous wastes as another occasion to enhance their profits. The likelihood is increased by the barren nature of much of New Mexico's landscape, which provides an excellent opportunity for undetected dumping. In addition, the Sandoval County Landfill just north of the Albuquerque city limits, a vast but poorly supervised site, has apparently been receiving unauthorized liquid wastes in recent years. Local officials are becoming increasingly concerned about this situation. Not surprisingly, the state of New Mexico reported to the Permanent Subcommittee on Investigations it knew of no organized crime involvement in illegal hazardous waste disposal within the state.

Persons associated with organized crime have also followed the sun to Florida, where a pattern of infiltration similar to that seen in New Mexico has been taking place for a number of years. In a special 1973 report, the Florida Department of Law Enforcement expressed concern about the possibility of organized crime's infiltrating and monopolizing the garbage and recycling industry. At that time, it identified individuals and firms with mob connections operating in several counties, particularly Dade, Palm Beach, and

Pasco. Of special interest to law enforcement was Industrial Waste Service to Miami, operated by Albert and Jack Casagrande; Naranja Sanitation Service and its officers, Daniel and Thomas Larataro, sons of Joseph Larataro, an alleged member of the old New York Lucchese crime syndicate; and Packed Sanitation Service and its secretary-treasurer, Joseph Pelose. Prior to moving to Florida, Pelose owned and operated Rex Carting in New York and was an associate of Nick Ratteni and numerous other felons identified as organized criminals.

The national web of organized crime companies in the waste business was reflected in the report's discussion of the Dade County activities of John Valianos, president of International Dense Fog Corporation of San Francisco. Valianos had been trying to sell Dade County officials the services of his garbage compacting company, a California corporation. Local law enforcement authorities were suspicious of Valianos because of his previous association with a firm known as Arizona Bio-chemical, thought to be backed by Carlos Marcello, a powerful New Orleans crime boss, and with Total Waste Systems, another New York company with suspected organized crime connections.

In nearby Palm Beach County, officials were concerned with the activities of Phillip Moreno and William Baron, also known as William Barroni. By 1973, Mareno and Baron had already been involved with numerous garbage companies in the county and with waste collection activities in at least two other Florida counties. According to police reports, Moreno and Baron decided to move to Florida about the time a New York grand jury was starting an investigation of bookmaking activities.

While officials in Palm Beach and Dade counties were concerned with the apparent takeover of the local garbage industry, authorities in Pasco County were also hearing reports of violence and sabotage of garbage equipment. According to the Florida Department of Law Enforcement, two companies, the West Pasco Disposal Company and Community Disposal Services, were at the center of these problems. Although the firms had different officers and were ostensibly unrelated, both were controlled by Joseph Messina and his brother Salvatore. The Messinas, who had once been in the garbage business in Ohio and who also had business interests in their native New York, owned several firms in the New Port Richey, Florida, area, including a restaurant. The brothers' organized crime connections seemed to be through James Failla of the Gambino crime organization.

By the late 1970s, the number of mob-connected garbage companies and operators had increased, and so had their control of the industry. Led by Vincenzo "Jimmie" Acquafredda, the owner of a company which he had purchased from the Messinas, garbage operators in Pasco and Pinellas counties attempted to form an organization to control the business in the way operators had previously controlled it in places like New York and New Jersey. Through the property rights system, bid rigging, and the use of violence and intimidation to achieve their goals, these waste haulers were well on their way toward replicating the traditional pattern of criminal domination of the waste industry.

Out of these collusive arrangements, the Westcoast Cartman's Association was formed, eventually becoming the Suncoast Contractors Association. Agreeing to operate under "New York rules," cooperating garbage contractors escalated their prices and dictated the terms of their service, knowing full well they were protected under the terms of "property rights." On at least one occasion, Jimmie Acquafredda and an associate physically assaulted and beat a rival garbage collector in order to extort money from him for Association "dues" and to acquire an interest in his business. In addition to everything else, members of the Association were also charged with cheating the local waste resource recovery plant by altering the certified weight of their trucks so as to lower the dump fees paid for using the county facility.

After a four-year undercover FBI investigation code-named Operation Cold Water, twelve men were indicted by a federal grand jury on March 31, 1982, charged with attempting to take over the garbage collection business on Florida's west coast. According to the federal indictment, those charged represented a variety of organized crime syndicates, including those bearing the names Lucchese, Gambino, Bonnano, and one representing what was called the "Chicago Outfit." Also indicted was Santo Trafficante, Jr., leader of a very powerful organized crime group thought to control many of Florida's rackets. It was charged the indicted figures met with Trafficante in order to secure his permission to operate in his "territory." Although all twelve of those indicted were charged with conspiring to control the garbage industry, a number of them were also charged with other offenses, including gambling, prostitution, bribery, drug distribution, and even bank robbery. For permitting representatives of other organized crime groups to engage in these criminal activities on Florida's west coast, Trafficante was charged with receiving a percentage of the profit from their businesses.

As in New Mexico, there is no direct evidence linking Florida garbage companies controlled by organized criminals, often receiving orders directly from superiors in the New York metropolitan area, with the illegal disposal of hazardous waste. At the same time, there is also no evidence indicating anybody has ever looked for such a connection. Since those same criminal organizations and individuals who direct certain Florida operations have made exorbitant profits by including hazardous chemicals among the wastes which they collect and dispose of in New York and New Jersey, it is likely that they're doing the same thing in the Sunshine State. As the state continues to grow and industrialize, the amount of hazardous waste generated in Florida increases yearly. With no state licensed treatment facility, the cost of legitimate disposal is obviously high, further increasing the likelihood that haulers, drawn to quick and easy profits, will do in Florida what they have done elsewhere.

The role of organized crime in the toxic waste disposal business in most other cities and states also must await further investigation. Although it is known organized crime is the power behind the solid waste business in a number of places, neither federal nor state authorities have yet conducted investigations to probe the backgrounds and affiliations of those who operate hazardous waste disposal firms. Many still claim there appears to be insufficient evidence to warrant in-depth probes, and surely the PSI report provides no alert.

Even a recent EPA report entitled *Risks Associated with Environmental Investigations*, which notes a Chicago informant in a hazardous waste disposal case was told a $5,000 contract on his life would actually be carried out if he continued to talk with authorities, has had little effect. This same report talks of fire bombings, shootings, and of at least one illegal dumper also being a narcotics dealer. Still, few states, and certainly not the federal government, have done much about this type of illegal dumping.

While state enforcement agencies might be excused for their lack of experience and limited jurisdiction, it is difficult to understand why federal investigative agencies have also done so little. Yet they are not well equipped to do the job, either. As one federal official commented, "To really get at the big guys, where there's political corruption and organized crime, you need full criminal enforcement powers." And federal officers charged with enforcing environmental laws did not have such powers until mid-1984. "Currently, we are not equipped to investigate the involvement of organized crime in the hazardous waste industry. That is the type of investigation that would require full law enforcement authority," admitted Peter Beeson, the EPA's associate enforcement counsel, in a 1983 statement. Given the lack of investigative experience and authority at both the state and federal levels, it is perhaps surprising so much has already been learned about the hazardous waste activities of criminal organizations generally shrouded in secrecy.

The Big Firms

In addition to mob-controlled waste firms based in particular cities and states, organized crime figures have also infiltrated a number of national corporations, in some cases actually controlling their operations. Cooper Funding, which we examined earlier, was little more than an organized crime loan-sharking operation, providing fraudulent equipment leases for a number of companies affiliated with criminal syndicates. Although based in New York, it arranged loans for waste firms in at least nine states and the District of Columbia. Run by persons with known organized crime affiliations, Cooper secured loans from some of America's largest banks based on nonexistent or grossly overvalued equipment. In this way it serviced friendly solid and toxic waste firms while spreading organized crime's influence in the industry across the nation.

Cooper Funding was a mob-conceived, -organized, and -operated company. Yet there are many other national firms involved directly in waste collection and disposal which appear to have links to organized crime. Among this group are the country's three largest waste companies—Waste Management, Inc., Browning-Ferris Industries, and SCA Services. That each of these companies has ties to individuals and groups with criminal records is not surprising, since each expanded by absorbing a number of local firms and allowing the former owners to continue as corporate employees. As we saw in New Jersey, these local waste companies were often linked to organized crime figures who did not hesitate to use past business tactics on behalf of their new employer. Although the parent companies have repeatedly denied mob connections, it is difficult to deny they have benefited from their questionable affiliations. The participation of all three national firms in local trade waste associations, their retention of many local managers of marginal character and reputation, and their continued quest for expansion and profit at nearly any cost make their protests and denials suspect at best.

In addition, each of the three companies has blemishes on its record that raise the suspicions of those concerned about the precise role played by organized crime groups and affiliated individuals in national waste activities. Waste Management, Inc., headquartered in Oak Brook, Illinois, has been cited on numerous occasions for violations of the federal anti-trust laws. On one occasion, it was charged with restraint of trade in attempting to monopolize the private carting business in Chicago, activities strikingly similar to those of waste companies in the New York and New Jersey areas dominated by organized crime. In fact, through its acquisition of literally dozens of carting companies across the country, Waste Management created monopolies in many locations.

A significant portion of Waste Management's recent growth has come from its expansion in the area of toxic waste disposal. Viewing this as a profitable area in the 1970s, the company began to develop facilities for handling chemical wastes all over the country. Through the absorption of existing companies as well as the expansion of its current holdings, Waste Management quickly became the largest hazardous waste handler in the United States. By 1980, the company had set up eight specific disposal operations around the country, each having a fairly sophisticated laboratory equipped to analyze the chemicals destined for disposal.

When Waste Management, Inc. came to New York in an attempt to secure a contract for building the Oyster Bay, Long Island, solid waste disposal system, questions began to be raised about its operation. One of the items discovered linked Waste Management to Cooper Funding. Allegedly, Mel Cooper, the notorious front man for organized crime's loan-shark operation, negotiated a substantial loan for Waste Management with the Chemical Bank of New York in the mid-1970s. Why a company whose gross revenues in 1980 were over $800 million, which operated nation-wide, as well as in Canada, South America, and Saudi Arabia, worked with Mel Cooper as a loan broker is puzzling and un-known. Nevertheless, the possibility that it did, whether wittingly or not, means that organized crime's largest loan-sharking opera-tion in the waste industry enjoyed a financial relationship with America's largest toxic and solid waste disposal company. This, coupled with Waste Management's phenomenal growth through the 1970s, appears to be sufficient reason to wonder what, if any, influence organized crime has had on the development and current operation of this important corporation.

Browning-Ferris Industries (BFI) of Houston, Texas, the na-tion's second largest hazardous waste handler, grew the same way as Waste Management and thus has an equally spotty background. Describing itself as "the largest publicly held company engaged primarily in the collection, processing, recovery, and disposal of solid and liquid wastes" in the nation, BFI operates in thirty-six states and has assets in excess of $415 million. This corporate giant disposes of its chemical and hazardous wastes at a number of sites located around the country, including landfills, deep injection wells, and secure storage facilities. Yet with all these locations available for the supposed safe disposal of hazardous materials, BFI's record hardly stands out as a model for the industry to emu-late.

Unfortunately, the national stature of this company has not pre-vented it from acting like so many other illegal and dangerous dumpers of hazardous wastes. During the year 1979, for example, the company was cited in some thirty-three cases of "alleged viola-tions of water, air, and land protection laws." Perhaps the most famous of these cases involved BFI's supplying various Texas users with waste oil containing large amounts of nitrobenzene and cyanide for use on dirt roads. Investigation revealed that waste oil was routinely mixed with dangerous chemicals and offered free of charge as a dust suppressant. On one occasion, when a BFI em-ployee complained of this practice, he was fired. Between 1976 and 1979, as much as 900,000 gallons of contaminated oil was spread on Texas roads, reaping a considerable profit for the company. Unfor-tunately for BFI, the quick and easy profits realized from disposing of hazardous wastes on Texas roads was ultimately spent by the company to clean up the damage it had caused.

But the contamination of dirt roads with toxic chemicals was only one of BFI's questionable practices. Testimony before a congressional hearing revealed that the company billed for services not performed, was unable to account for large amounts of material it was paid to dispose of, and subcontracted with at least one firm of very questionable integrity. In May of 1980, Browning-Ferris Industries of Georgia, Inc., was indicted along with a number of other waste firms for a price-fixing conspiracy. Although acquitted, an official of New Jersey's BFI operation was named by witnesses as an active participant in the New Jersey Trade Waste Association's attempts to restrain trade and implement the property rights system. These few examples of BFI's suspicious and often overtly illegal behavior should come as no surprise, however, given the manner in which the company grew and the persons who were thus placed in positions of corporate responsibility.

Nowhere is this more evident than in the case of John Pinto. For a number of years, this former waste hauler served as a regional vice president of Browning-Ferris Industries. Although he had been a partner of Charles Macaluso and involved with a number of supposed mob-related waste companies, BFI employed him to represent its interests in New Jersey and other eastern areas. According to Harold Kaufman, Pinto was the force behind many of BFI's local acquisitions and was influential in determining the operating policies of these local subsidiaries. Unfortunately, BFI officials now refuse to discuss the exact responsibilities that Pinto had while employed by them.

We have already seen how this same technique of expansion has worked for SCA Services. Now the nation's third largest waste hauler, it was the fastest growing company during the 1970s and early 1980s. Today, SCA operates in well over thirty states and scores of communities, hauling and disposing of both solid and hazardous wastes. Since this company's organized crime connections have been discussed earlier in some detail, suffice it to say the operation continues to be the subject of suspicion and concern. In various state and federal investigations, SCA has been accused of attempting to intimidate competitive waste haulers and of being involved in the murders of San Felice and Roselle. Outside the East Coast area, SCA Services of Georgia was indicted in 1980 for participating in a price-fixing conspiracy. Subsequently, Congressman Albert Gore wondered whether a company "that can be so tolerant and comfortable with organized crime in one state can be trusted to avoid such contacts" elsewhere. The answer apparently is no. In February, 1984, an SCA representative with organized crime connections was indicted in Philadelphia for bribery, bid rigging, and mail fraud.

Waste Management, Browning-Ferris, and SCA Services are all national waste disposal firms with suspicious ties to various organized crime groups and figures which have played a prominent role in the refuse industry. Although no one has accused these firms of being organized crime operations, and each has vigorously denied all allegations linking it to mob figures and activities, available evidence demands their very close scrutiny. Only when the investigative spotlight has been focused on these firms can the true extent, if any, of organized crime's infiltration be known.

Such was the case with the Sanitas Service Corporation. In the early 1970s, this national sanitation company, engaged in both solid and hazardous waste hauling and disposal, grew rapidly by attempting to absorb local haulers and monopolize landfills. By 1975, following the classic garbage industry expansion pattern, Sanitas had subsidiaries in some twenty states, Puerto Rico, and the Virgin Islands. In many cases, local firms were bought out with Sanitas stock, which, during the period of acquisitions, was generally represented as being worth between $10 and $12 a share. When the value of the stock was not sufficient to convince local owners to merge with Sanitas, threats of violence were used to intimidate them.

Once Sanitas settled in an area, its technique was to try to drive other independent operators out of business by securing garbage contracts with extremely low bids. As competitors lost necessary business, they would agree to sell out to Sanitas or close their doors entirely. This, coupled with the company's deliberate attempt to secure and control local landfills, often gave it a virtual waste monopoly in various areas of the country. At one time, Sanitas's operation in Marion County, Indiana, including the city of Indianapolis, comprised four of the five major landfills and two-thirds of the private trash collection companies. In Dade County, Florida, the company allegedly used strong-arm tactics to gain control of the area's largest landfill.

Sanitas's rapid growth and methods of operation were accompanied by allegations of organized crime connections. In at least four states—Michigan, Florida, Connecticut, and Indiana—the company was accused of being connected to Chicago and Las Vegas mob figures. As a result of such charges and of the company's highly suspicious business practices, the Securities and Exchange Commission (SEC) began an investigation in 1973. At that time, the company stock was suspended from trading on the American Stock Exchange.

By 1975, with its investigation completed, the SEC filed charges against Sanitas and several of its officers, charging fraud and other securities violations. Named in the charge in addition to the company was its chairman, David Weintraub; two executive vice presidents, A. Theodore Barron and Abraham Weintraub; and former company president Alan R. Carp. In addition to a number of other improprieties, the SEC investigation revealed a Boston firm owned by Barron, ATB Enterprises, Inc., served as a vehicle through which Sanitas made illegal payoffs and kickbacks which were labeled as fees for such services as consulting, subcontracting, and dumping.

According to the SEC, Barron "distributed such funds as political contributions, payments to local politicians, bribes in order to obtain contracts, payments for use of private dump sites, kickbacks to receive lower dumping fees and other similar purposes." Allegedly, these activities took place in at least six cities and Puerto Rico. The bribes and kickbacks amounted to more than $1.2 million. Although the SEC failed to trace most of these funds, payments made by Sanitas in Boston and Indianapolis showed a pattern of illegality undoubtedly repeated in other cities around the country.

Testimony included in the SEC report revealed Sanitas secured a Boston dumping contract after making substantial political contributions on at least four occasions. A. Theodore Barron testified that he twice made cash payments of $5,000 to Mayor Kevin White, whose office denied the charges. In addition, other testimony showed that Sanitas paid $18,000 a month in kickbacks. The company's former president and chief financial officer, Alan Carp, remarked that most of these cash payments were "made at various dumps, the major portion of which was at the Chelsea dump, and it was paid to the operator, either the guy at the gate or the guy that ran the bulldozer." Apparently, the recipients kept the money for themselves, and charged the company a lower fee per load; they also allowed hazardous wastes to be dumped at these sites. Furthermore, cash payments were made for the use of an illegal dump near Wayland, Massachusetts, operated at the time by Barron's brother-in-law.

Because the SEC did not possess criminal jurisdiction, its investigators turned over the evidence they had uncovered to the Justice Department. For unexplained reasons, the U.S. Attorney's Office in Boston showed surprisingly little interest in the case, failing to initiate any prosecution. Although the Deputy U.S. Attorney handling the Sanitas case went into private practice with the lawyer representing Theodore Barron soon after the investigation died, all suggestions of impropriety have been denied by the Justice Department. Like their colleagues elsewhere in the waste disposal business, Sanitas officials were permitted to violate a variety of laws, including the illegal disposal of hazardous waste, with impunity.

The Indianapolis *Star* exposé of the Sanitas operation in Indiana revealed the company used "muscle" to take over local waste and landfill operations and paid substantial retainers to a number of local politicians. According to David Weintraub, the payments were to "keep the politicians happy . . . keep them off our backs." Obviously it worked, since Sanitas ran local affairs with a virtual free hand for a number of years. The *Star* reported that at one time a local organized crime figure, Norman Z. Flick, was involved in a number of secret meetings where control of the local landfills was discussed with various city and county officials. Flick also met often with a city employee who apparently served as a landfill inspector. Although these activities were highly suspicious, there is no evidence that local authorities ever learned the precise nature of Flick's role in local waste operations or why he met with garbage dump supervisors.

As a result of the SEC investigation and investor lawsuits, Sanitas underwent reorganization in 1975, changing its management and divesting itself of many of its subsidiaries. Local companies not sold back to their original owners were bought by another national firm, Waste Resources Corporation of Philadelphia. The big losers were apparently those businessmen who received stock for merging with Sanitas. In Marion County alone, the Indianapolis *Star* estimated that local businessmen lost up to $2 million as a result of the Sanitas stock fraud. Other losers appeared to be those police personnel who took seriously the need to investigate the corrupt dealings of this company. In Indianapolis, a police detective who spearheaded the investigation of Sanitas's dealings with local political figures was assigned to walking a beat because he apparently went too far. Even worse happened to the director of a team policing program in Hartford, Connecticut, where Sanitas was also under investigation. J. Andrew Ditzhazy claimed he resigned under pressure when questions he raised about the company angered local police officials. According to Ditzhazy, "The bottom line is, when I looked into Sanitas, I found attorneys, prominent citizens, and people involved with the governmental structure of Hartford also involved with Sanitas." It is ironic this national waste hauler involved in so many shady practices was able to lead such a charmed life when it came to both Department of Justice and local investigations.

To one degree or another, it is safe to conclude that each of the national firms we have mentioned has been touched by the tradition of illegality in the waste disposal business. Some firms, like Cooper Funding, seem to have strong and deep roots in organized crime affairs, while others, like the national waste haulers we have discussed, appear to have looser affiliations with mob figures and syndicate operations. Nevertheless, in each case a link does exist, raising concern about the extent and nature of illegal toxic waste disposal. The role of organized crime in the solid and hazardous waste business within cities and states across the nation, as well as within the operations of various national firms, makes this more than just a regional problem. Although known links between the criminal element and industry are more intense in some areas, clearly it is a problem of national scope. In fact, in recent years it has even become a problem of international scope. Both the national and the international nature of waste disposal operations can be seen in the workings of the company known as Modern Transportation.

The Dirty Business of Sludge

Located in Kearny, New Jersey, Modern Transportation's influence has been felt far beyond that small town since its incorporation in 1972. Although it has had various company officers, principal interest in the firm is owned by Richard Miele, a member of a family with extensive holdings in the New Jersey garbage industry. Through his father, brothers, uncles, and cousins, the forty-seven-year-old Miele has been involved in the waste industry for his entire adult life and has become a prominent member of the trade. In addition to Modern Transportation, he has owned all or part of several other waste firms and landfill operations. Included among his holdings has been a part ownership of the infamous MSLA landfill and the Disposomatic Corporation. In these and other ventures, he included among his business associates people like Crescent Roselle, Joseph Cassini, Bruce LaFera, and Tony Gaess. Several of the firms in which Miele has had an interest, and associates with whom he has done business, have allegedly strong ties with organized crime operations and have been involved in the illegal and dangerous disposal of hazardous wastes. In addition, Gaess has a long history of illegal chemical waste disposal and is alleged to have taught many garbage haulers the intricacies of chemical dumping. He, too, has been associated with a number of persons accused of having organized crime ties.

Soon after its incorporation, Modern Transportation grew to be one of New Jersey's largest waste hauling and disposal facilities. Although the firm had other interests, such as the transfer and shipment of coal, it was in the area of hazardous waste disposal that it expanded most aggressively, becoming the largest of the state's eighteen licensed disposal facilities. Manifest records on file with the New Jersey DEP show Modern Transportation handled over half of all toxic wastes reported disposed of in the state in 1978, and one-third of all such wastes in 1980. In addition, Modern Transportation owned a number of barges used for the ocean dumping of sewerage sludge. As sludge haulers, Modern had contracts with several East Coast cities, including Philadelphia. Throughout the 1970s as a toxic waste disposal facility and as a hauler and disposer of sludge, this firm operated on a regional basis, serving waste generators and communities on the East Coast and the mid-Atlantic region of the nation.

By the end of the decade, however, Modern's operations began to be questioned. A doctoral dissertation written by Anne Kruger at Princeton University raised serious questions about Modern's practices. Using manifests to track the flow of toxic wastes for the year 1979, Kruger concluded: "The Modern Transportation chemical treatment facility processed 49 percent of the manifested wastes received by facilities in the northeast region [of New Jersey], but where the residues and waste water from the facility went is not clear . . . only .08 percent of the manifested wastes received were shipped out with a manifest." By 1980, the New Jersey DEP also became concerned. From April through June of that year officials monitored the firm, discovering that between 37,000 and 50,000 gallons of toxic waste was accepted illegally each day. If this practice took place over the entire year—and the DEP had no reason to believe it did not—Modern Transportation may have been accepting as much as 12 million gallons of hazardous waste each year which it could not account for. The 1980 manifests also revealed that millions of pounds of oil and oil sludges were accepted by the company that year as well. However, Modern was not licensed to treat organic substances such as oil and oil sludges. Where the illegally accepted toxic substances went is anybody's guess, although the head of the state's Hazardous Waste Enforcement Program, Edward J. Londres, was quoted as saying, "There are only three places it can go, based on the equipment we know to exist at Modern Transportation's facility in Kearny—the ocean, sewers, or landfills." As a result of this investigation, the state DEP issued a cease and desist order and fined the firm $20,000.

At about the same time this was going on, Modern Transportation's principal owner and executive manager, Richard Miele, was having other legal problems. Beginning in October, 1980, a federal grand jury initiated an investigation of Miele and several New Jersey public officials for a supposed kickback scheme which permitted Modern Transportation to receive favorable treatment in the awarding of municipal sewerage contracts. The investigation did not result in indictments for mail fraud, extortion, and bribery against those suspected because important evidence was destroyed. Instead, the grand jury indicted Richard Miele because he allegedly "did knowingly, willfully and corruptly endeavor to influence, obstruct and impede the due administration of justice by destroying, mutilating, and altering documents material to the investigation being conducted by the United States Grand Jury for the District of New Jersey. . . ." After the usual amount of plea bargaining and horse trading, the United States Attorney agreed to allow Miele to plead guilty to aiding and abetting in the preparation of a false corporate tax return. As a result, all charges related to the kickback scheme were dismissed by the federal court. Shortly thereafter, Miele was sentenced to three years probation and a $5,000 fine.

While Miele and Modern Transportation were engaging in a number of illegal activities, they were also initiating an innovative and supposedly safe plan for disposing of huge quantities of sludge, or processed sewerage. In 1972, Congress passed legislation calling for an end to the ocean dumping of sludge by 1980. Philadelphia, like many other large cities, was producing a great deal of this waste, dumping approximately 125 million pounds a year into the Atlantic Ocean. Modern Transportation hauled much of the city's sludge out to sea, and stood to lose a considerable amount of business if the ocean shipments had to be halted. Faced with this potential loss, Miele and an associate came up with an alternative plan for the sludge.

Instead of dumping it into the ocean or landfills, the most conventional method of disposal, why not take advantage of the nutrient value of the waste and use it as fertilizer? Although one would not want to use it to grow fruits and vegetables even after it had been processed, sewerage waste could be used to revegetate strip-mined land being reclaimed. Hence, Miele and an associate, Douglas E. Murray, the head of a New Jersey construction company, proposed this use of Philadelphia's sludge. Everyone agreed that it was a promising idea and worth a try.

The idea was also intriguing from another angle. Recent legislation had made strip mine operators responsible for restoring the land once the mining was completed. This not only meant replacing the layers of soil as they were removed, but also reestablishing the land's original contours and replacing the vegetation through a process of seeding and fertilizing. To guarantee this was done adequately, mine operators had to place considerable sums of money in escrow, controlled by the state until it was satisfied the restoration had taken place and ground cover was reestablished. Only then would the funds placed in escrow be released to the owners and operators. Therefore, anything that would hasten the growth of ground cover and provide cheap, healthful nutrients for it was a money-saving blessing. Miele's plan won the support of Philadelphia officials who wanted to get rid of their sludge and was also endorsed by authorities in strip-mined areas of Pennsylvania who wanted to see local land restored.

At this point, Miele turned for backing to SCA Chemical Services and his friend Tony Gaess. SCA Services had previously purchased a number of Gaess's companies and had recently acquired, through its Earthline Division, Gaess Environmental Company, his last major holding. Gaess had been employed by SCA for some time, and through his knowledge of the waste disposal business and his friendship with several SCA officers, had become a valued employee. He apparently had little trouble convincing SCA officials to join Miele in this venture and to make him the company's representative in the new enterprise. In this way, the Modern Earthline Company was formed, with Modern Transportation and the Earthline Division of SCA Services each holding 50 percent of the partnership. Douglas Murray became president of the new firm, but it seemed clear from the outset that Richard Miele and Tony Gaess were in charge.

In 1977, without formal bidding, the city of Philadelphia awarded a $600,000 contract to Modern Earthline to explore the sludge hauling idea. At the time, city officials claimed Modern Earthline was the only company with the experience and know-how to handle the job. A plan was developed to truck the city's sludge to strip mines in Somerset County, Pennsylvania, and an apparently sound method of disposal was begun. In both 1978 and 1979, the company received additional contracts from the city to continue the hauling operation and to develop further sites in Somerset County. In those two years, a total of $1.8 million in contracts was awarded to Modern Earthline by the city without formal competitive bidding.

In 1980, however, under the administration of the new mayor, William Green, the city demanded its sludge hauling contracts be awarded on the basis of formal sealed bids. This time, Modern Earthline was not as lucky as it had been previously. Markim, Inc., won the bid with a price of $26 a ton, compared to Modern Earthline's bid of $32.50 a ton. But, unexpectedly, Markim withdrew its bid and the acting Water Commissioner, Kenneth Zitomer, threw all bids out, claiming the city would have problems if Modern Earthline did not get the contract, since it was the only firm planning to use local subcontractors. In the new round of bidding, Modern Earthline lowered its price to $31.94 while Markim increased its bid to $38 a ton. Obviously, Modern Earthline won the contract. Later the next year, when the city combined the hauling and management contracts into one, the only bidder was Modern Resources, Incorporated, a firm affiliated with Modern Earthline and for which Miele and Gaess served as principal officers. The new contract covered a five-year period at a cost of more than $26 million. Once again, the merchants of waste demonstrated that big money could be made from hauling and disposing of society's sewerage.

Encouraged by the Philadelphia experiment, a number of other cities became interested in the new use of sewerage sludge. Before long, Modern Earthline set up a Maryland division and began working with officials in the city of Baltimore on a plan to truck its sludge to Garrett County in western Maryland. There, as in Somerset County, Pennsylvania, the idea was to spread tons of the waste on strip-mined areas to enhance the reclamation project. Before the proposal could be approved, however, local opposition in Garrett County forced the city of Baltimore to abandon the plan. Although Maryland opponents of the sludge distribution idea were obviously motivated by many factors, the toxic nature of the Baltimore sludge may well have been one of them. Even though all urban sewerage contains some level of heavy metals as the result of local industries' using the sewer system, Baltimore sludge contained a higher level of such toxic substances than that of many other municipalities. Sludge containing heavy metals or any other toxic substances poses a particular danger when it is used to enhance the growth of grass, shrubs, and trees.

By early 1982, it became apparent that Modern Earthline was acting in the tradition of its parent company, Modern Transportation. Alerted by the curious circumstances surrounding the 1980 Philadelphia sludge contracts and Miele's 1981 indictment for paying off municipal officials in New Jersey, authorities began to probe Modern Earthline's dealings in both Baltimore and Philadelphia. In Baltimore, they found the president of the City Council, Walter S. Orlinsky, had accepted a $10,000 bribe to help Modern Earthline obtain the city's sludge hauling contract. Orlinsky apparently introduced company officials to representatives of the city and advanced their case in whatever ways he could. He eventually pleaded guilty and testified against company president Douglas Murray, who was found guilty of six counts of bribery and one count of conspiracy.

On February 29, 1984, the action moved to Philadelphia, where a federal grand jury indicted Miele, Gaess, Murray, and three others for allegedly defrauding the city of Philadelphia of $1.55 million. Ironically, the indictment charged the group had not only cheated the city but had also defrauded their partner, SCA Services, by withholding some $500,000 in payments that rightfully belonged to the Boston corporation. Allegedly, Modern Transportation had won Philadelphia's 1980 sludge hauling contract by bribing its competitor, Markim Inc., to withdraw. The indictment charged that Murray, Miele, and Gaess met with Markim's management in a Philadelphia steakhouse after the first set of bids was opened and revealed. The Modern Earthline officials supposedly agreed to pay Markim $4.90 per ton of sludge hauled out of Philadelphia. For withdrawing its bid, Markim would receive a bribe of about $70,000 a month. When Markim agreed to this arrangement, Modern Earthline was assured of receiving the contract at a cost of $5 per ton above the original Markim bid.

In their statements to the press, federal authorities revealed the Markim representatives had been persuaded to go along with the offer from Modern Earthline because of the substantial amount of the bribe and explicit threats of physical violence if they didn't. Once they secured the contract, Modern Earthline officials instructed a trucking company hauling the sludge to Somerset County to bill Modern Earthline for more than the actual cost of transportation. The inflated cost was reported to SCA, and the difference between that and the actual amount paid for hauling was used to support the Markim payoff and to enrich Modern Earthline officials. The indictment charged that Miele, Gaess, Murray, and a company accountant, also part of the scheme, pocketed a half million dollars that rightfully belonged to SCA Chemical Services.

From accepting illegal hazardous wastes in New Jersey to sludge frauds in Maryland and Pennsylvania, Modern Transportation's record as a corrupt, criminal waste firm has grown over the years. It is no wonder, then, authorities have become concerned about the company's involvement in two recent attempts to send hazardous waste abroad. In each case, friendly foreign governments have protested these activities, to the embarrassment of the U.S. State Department. But as the volume of hazardous wastes increases and as domestic disposal becomes more expensive, plans

like those involving Modern Transportation will undoubtedly pro-
liferate.

Under Caribbean Skies

In 1981, Jay C. Roderick and Larry Tinker, the operators of
Scotts Trucking of Atlanta, Georgia, conceived a plan to build an
incinerator on a small deserted island in the Caribbean, and to
burn hazardous wastes shipped there by American companies.
With the help of a representative in the Caribbean, Henry Beal,
the plan began to take shape. Beal proposed that the incinerator be
built on Dog Island, a small piece of land off the British-controlled
island of Anguilla. Wastes would be barged first from American
ports to St. Martin, where they would be stored until they could
be disposed of on nearby Dog Island. Beal assured Tinker as well
as the international office of the EPA that he had the full approval
and cooperation of the government of Anguilla and of Dog Island's
owner, the Anguilla Development Corporation and its major stock-
holder, Jerry Gumbs. In fact, in a letter to Tinker dated December
15, 1981, Beal specified that it would be a "three venture business," with their sharing the venture with the Anguilla Development Company as well as the Anguilla government. Beal was so
sure of the arrangements he invited EPA officials to contact authorities on both St. Martin and Anguilla, as well as the owner of
Dog Island, to confirm their willingness to participate in his plan.
The idea appeared so intoxicating to him he even offered EPA officials the use of his island, called Fourchu, as another site for the
disposal of American-generated hazardous waste.

Back in the United States, Roderick and Tinker needed help in
procuring large quantities of waste for shipment to the island and
with the hauling itself. They turned to Modern Transportation,
Richard Miele, and the president of his firm, Richard Albers. Apparently, the original idea was for Modern to ship the waste from
the ports of Newark, New Jersey, and Southport, North Carolina.
In addition, it would serve as the agent for the Roderick and Tinker holding company, procuring contracts with industrial generators for use of the uninhabited island. In a conversation with an
EPA official, Tinker indicated Dow Chemical was among the firms
interested in using the Dog Island plan, as well as several firms in
Puerto Rico.

Soon, however, Modern's role in the scheme changed. Instead of doing the hauling, the company would act only as the agent for the plan, procuring the waste contracts. Shortly thereafter, Tinker reported that Miele and Albers might bow out altogether, since they supposedly believed that Tinker's price for disposal was too high. If they withdrew, Tinker felt confident he could strike another deal with Richard Miele's brother, Dennis, the operator of Applied Technology of Toms River, New Jersey. Dennis Miele reportedly disposed of toxic waste for about forty companies, and at the time was looking for a new facility to replace a South Carolina site that had recently been closed.

As these negotiations were going on, the EPA notified the British government of the plan to use part of its self-governing dependency of Anguilla for toxic waste disposal. The reaction was quick and surprising. The British governor of Anguilla notified the U.S. State Department he had not authorized the shipment of hazardous waste to Dog Island and had no plans to do so under any circumstances. Later, Jerry Gumbs's son told EPA's Office of International Activities that his father "had never authorized Dog Island to be used for a waste disposal area. . . ." Strangely, the positions of both the governor of Anguilla and Mr. Gumbs must have changed radically in a very short time, or Henry Beal misrepresented their positions, perhaps feeling confident no one would bother to check.

About six months after the British governor had said no to the use of Dog Island as a hazardous waste facility, a supertanker was spotted anchored a short distance off the coast of the island. The British sent a small patrol boat to investigate and, in rough seas, communicated with the tanker captain without boarding the vessel. He informed the naval officers that he had picked up his cargo in New Jersey and was bound for New Orleans, but was having engine trouble which was now repaired. Unfortunately, the naval officers did not inquire further about the ship's cargo or what it was doing so close to Dog Island and so far from New Orleans. Within hours of this encounter, the tanker left the area.

Back in Anguilla, British officials became highly suspicious and demanded the United States investigate the presence of the tanker in their waters. An FBI investigation revealed the ship was of Swedish registry, owned by the Johnson Chemstar Company, and was apparently bound for undetermined ports in the

Caribbean. When FBI agents out of San Juan flew over Dog Island and the water around it, and later visited the island itself, they could find no evidence of hazardous waste in the area or that any work had ever been done to construct an incinerator on this exceedingly small patch of land.

Since the British governor's veto of the plan and the sighting of the strange ship in area waters, American officials have no knowledge of any further activity involving Dog Island or plans to use it as a waste treatment site. Obviously, the original plans had created a political controversy on the island of Anguilla and had served as a source of embarrassment to local officials. Fortunately, through cooperation with the U.S. State Department and the EPA, the plan to turn Dog Island into a reef of poison seems to be currently thwarted. As for Modern Transportation, the end of the Dog Island scheme probably meant it could now spend more time on plans to export PCBs to Honduras.

When Maxwell Cobb, the president of American Electric Corporation of Jacksonville, Florida, signed a 1981 contract with the Department of Defense to dispose of PCBs, he saw a very prosperous future, for himself and his company. For a number of years, PCBs had been used as a coolant in electrical transformers, but the danger associated with such use was causing military installations to get rid of such transformers. When bids were called for, American Electric won the million-dollar contract and agreed to transport and dispose of PCBs and PCB-laden oil from some twenty-five military bases. Once collected, the PCBs would be shipped for incineration to Honduras, with all transport arrangements handled by Modern Transportation.

The beauty of the plan really lay in the Honduran incineration of the wastes. Not only could these be burned without regard to EPA regulations, but they would be burned to generate electricity to power a saw mill. The saw mill to be run by the imported PCBs was on the 33,000-acre mahogany plantation owned by a retired Venezuelan admiral, then living in the United States. Cobb planned to make a substantial profit for hauling the PCBs away from defense installations; he would also provide cheap fuel for the milling of mahogany in Honduras. Even more, the plan called for him to market the mahogany lumber when it was imported into the United States. Seemingly, no one would lose in these various deals.

Unfortunately for American Electric and Modern Transportation, there was a flaw in the plan. Under the Toxic Substances Control Act, PCBs are regulated and their movement in or out of the country is controlled by the EPA. According to an EPA official, "Since May 1980, PCBs may not be exported or imported for disposal unless the United States and the other country have entered into a Memorandum of Understanding (MOU) which establishes mutually agreed upon criteria for the storage, transportation, and disposal of PCB's." As a result of this policy, American Electric had to petition the EPA for a waiver of the export ban. To bolster its request for an exception, the company submitted several supporting documents, including a resolution signed by the Honduran Minister of the Economy accepting the PCBs. Believing the documentation to be in order, the EPA requested that State Department officials in Honduras ask the government to negotiate an MOU as required by American law. After a great deal of consideration, the Honduran government decided not to allow PCBs to be imported into its country.

The announcement of the government's decision was quickly followed by the Minister of the Economy's claim that his signature on the statement supporting the use of PCBs was a forgery. Indeed, he claimed the entire statement was false and he had never seen it, much less signed it. The government of Honduras hastily announced a criminal investigation was being initiated. In due course, the investigation revealed the minister's statement was typed on authentic letterhead from his office, apparently stolen by a contact working for the ministry who was mysteriously killed in southern Mexico.

Back in the United States, American Electric's petition to export PCBs was rejected by the EPA, and little more came of the attempted fraud. Since only a copy of the Minister of the Economy's forged statement had been submitted by the EPA, the Justice Department did not believe further action against American Electric could be sustained without producing the original document. Nevertheless, American Electric's troubles were far from over. PCBs had been piling up at its Jacksonville facility waiting for a disposal opportunity that would now never come. As the Honduran deal collapsed, American Electric and its officials began looking for ways to dispose of the accumulated PCBs. One way existed close by, in the form of the Dickerson Asphalt Company.

This unsuspecting firm bought substantial quantities of what it thought was simple waste oil used to heat asphalt. Little did it know that the waste oil sold to it by American Electric contained two thousand times the danger level of PCBs. The asphalt company is now suing both American Electric and the Defense Department.

On another occasion, American Electric indicated on a required manifest that PCBs picked up from military bases were being sent to a disposal site in Greensboro, Alabama. Investigation revealed the site was an attractive antebellum home on Main Street of that small city. When told barrels of PCBs were supposedly shipped to that address, the woman answering the door replied, "It didn't come here. I know it because I never go anywhere but the grocery store and the doctor's office." The woman denying her home was a PCB disposal site was Margaret Hamm, the wife of Michael Hamm, Maxwell Cobb's partner in American Electric.

In October, 1983, Maxwell Cobb and Michael Hamm were indicted on twenty-four counts of defrauding the U.S. Department of Defense by sending it manifests alleging that their PCBs were being disposed of safely and properly. How they were disposed of, other than in the waste oil sold to the local asphalt firm, remains a mystery. What remained on the grounds of American Electric's facility in Jacksonville was destroyed by a suspicious fire in early 1984. In a situation strikingly similar to that of New Jersey's Chemical Control Corporation, news media reported the Jacksonville fire burned throughout the night and local officials were concerned about the pollution of the city sewer system and nearby waterways by millions of gallons of PCB-contaminated water.

Given the past success of federal and state prosecutions of toxic waste cases, it came as little surprise eight months later when Cobb and Hamm were found not guilty by a federal court jury. Claiming they were "two responsible businessmen caught in a trap of government ineptitude and pressure," their lawyers portrayed the EPA as a totally inefficient agency attempting to enforce vague and unclear regulations. Apparently the jury accepted those characterizations of both the defendants and the federal efforts to control PCB disposal.

Although these attempts to export hazardous wastes to Dog Island and Honduras were unsuccessful, they represent only a fraction of the activities of enterprising waste entrepreneurs on the international scene. There are indications that substantial amounts of dangerous waste are being shipped abroad each year, particularly to neighbors of the United States in the western hemisphere. Canada, Mexico, and Haiti are countries to which shipments have definitely been made, although it is hard to know the volume and nature of the waste exported. There are rumors of a great deal more waste dumping in the Caribbean, but evidence is difficult to acquire since there is no effective policing of waste shipments out of U.S. ports. The potential is there to be exploited, as more and more waste is generated and dumping within the United States becomes more expensive. Jacob Scherr of the Natural Resource Defense Council has pointed out that "American waste generators have been searching overseas for countries poor enough, desperate enough to become America's dumping grounds." As this search goes on, waste haulers and disposers who are associated with organized crime are likely to be in the forefront of the effort.

Whether within the United States or outside its borders, the role of organized crime in the illegal disposal of hazardous wastes is hard to assess. Where law enforcement personnel or investigative reporters have looked, they have found outright involvement or circumstances remarkably like those existing where organized crime domination is a fact. The problem is, however, that mob involvement in the waste disposal business has not been the subject of law enforcement investigations in most parts of the country. Unless and until that is done, it is both misleading and dangerous to conclude that organized crime's role in waste disposal is not a national issue. On the contrary, minimal investigative efforts indicate it is not only a national problem but an international one as well.

11

The Failure of Enforcement

THE ENFORCEMENT RECORD against toxic waste dumpers is not nearly as strong as the enforcement record was against bootleggers during Prohibition. Then, of course, speakeasies flourished and mobsters became wealthy. Nevertheless, more significant prosecutions took place against the purveyors of booze than have taken place against toxic waste dumpers. Naturally, many have claimed that the paltry record reflects the newness of RCRA and toxic waste disposal investigations. It is, however, eight years since RCRA became law, and surely the public has had a right to timely and effective enforcement. Instead, most observers agree the enforcement record is a disgrace.

Many dumpers have been encouraged by just those agencies whose mission is first and foremost protecting the public welfare. Various state departments of environmental protection and public utility commissions, when faced with the problem of regulating and policing facilities, haulers, and landfills, have chosen to permit harmful, even illegal practices because they believe no other reasonable choice exists. Where is all the garbage going to go, they ask, if they close down a landfill? Who is going to pay to clean up landfills known to be poisoned and the many more suspected, they wonder? It is such a monstrous headache that their inclination is to avoid as much trouble as possible.

Moreover, behind all these decisions are powerful economic and political forces constantly pressuring regulatory agencies to be, as they put it, "reasonable." Work with us, say the lobbyists for the chemical as well as the waste disposal industries, and we can take care of the problems, avoiding onerous regulations and pointless prosecutions which only bring bad publicity. Within this context, toxic waste dumpers have had an almost open invitation to continue their activities.

Enforcement failures occur for three reasons—a regulatory policy of minimal compliance which has marked both the Carter and the Reagan administrations' efforts in dealing with toxic waste disposal, encouraged by the mistaken belief that states should take the lead in enforcement; political and law enforcement corruption and cronyism, which knows no particular political boundary and has certainly been a feature well documented at the state and local level and deeply suspected at the federal level as well; and finally, a surprising level of ineptitude which characterizes much of the official intelligence-gathering and investigative processes. These three factors feed upon one another. Corruption in New York or New Jersey within the state environmental agencies mixes with or is covered up by ineptitude in surveying the problem and vigorously enforcing the laws, and together they mingle with state and federal environmental policies that are designed to serve the major generators of toxic waste.

Blame It on the States

State inaction would have been much more difficult to engineer, of course, if it didn't match in many ways the EPA's stance. It has been federal policy to build a world of environmental regulation dealing with toxic waste disposal, and then to have the regulations enforced by the states. Actually, as government officials have admitted privately, few sophisticated observers believed for a minute the states could or would be able vigorously to enforce environmental laws dealing with toxic waste disposal. This call for devolution to state authorities was primarily a sop to the states righters in Congress, to those concerned with the growth of the regulatory state, and also a convenience for federal officials who could blame non-enforcement on the states.

It has long been recognized that toxic waste dumpers are aware that accountability virtually stops at the state line, no matter how much talk there is of federal legislation. Hence they are as pleased with devolution as the most ardent anti-federalist. They know that within states there is, as the New York State Senate Select Committee on Crime put it, more often than not a "benign attitude towards the hazardous waste industry." So benign, in fact, that it is much more arduous to get a license to cut hair or drive a cab in most states than to be licensed to haul or store toxic waste. Moreover, sophisticated toxic waste haulers and disposers know how to beat the state systems of control and regulation with ease. The New York committee reported on some of the ways this may be done, such as naming fake out-of-state disposal sites on state waste manifests, and transferring toxic waste cargoes from hauler to hauler and site to site using trucks registered to several different corporations located in different states. State regulatory and enforcement agencies are ill equipped to control such practices even when they are disposed to do so.

A graphic example of what states are up against was provided by the many interests and intrigues of Russell Mahler, one of the individuals investigated by the New York committee as it pursued toxic waste dumping in New York's landfills. Mahler's activities, encompassing a wide geographical area and many different companies, operated in New York City; Syracuse, New York; Farmingdale, New York; Ontario and Quebec, Canada; Pittston, Pennsylvania; Bridgeport, Connecticut; and several spots in Massachusetts and northern New Jersey. His companies included Newtown Oil Refining, Hudson Oil, Northeast Oil Service, Anchor Oil, Newtown Refining, Hudson Oil Refining, Edgewater Terminal, P.S.C. Resources, Sea Lion Corporation, Diamond Head Refining, Ag-MET Oil Service, Skies Oil Service, and Tammy's Oil Service. Mahler was also the sole owner of the Portland Holding Company, which owned, among many companies, Polar Industries and the Casco Equipment Corporation. The latter, with another company, Winslow Leasing, was engaged in leasing trucks to yet another Mahler firm, Oil Transfer Corp.

Some of Mahler's confusing movements were attributable to state investigations or potentially threatening monitoring activities. For example, he diverted activities from Syracuse to Pennsylvania when it became more difficult to get away with dumping various carcinogens down the Syracuse sewers. His New York City activities picked up when Pennsylvania, Connecticut, and Massachusetts began investigations. Because of these state probes, Mahler merged most of his companies into Quanta Resources Corporation. Instead of becoming a corporate officer whose name would appear on company records, he carefully became Quanta's chief salesman.

The New York Department of Environmental Conservation then signed a consent order with Quanta which allowed it to operate without a permit and stipulated it would not be liable for any violations by its predecessor companies. What finally brought Quanta down was an ABC-TV news documentary on contaminated fuel oil. But Mahler's case was not unique. He realized as others did that corporate veils, interstate and even international activities made it extraordinarily difficult for any single state to stop him. The fact that he was able to cut attractive deals with state regulatory bodies was also telling.

Mahler, and many others like him, realized they had the best of both worlds: states that couldn't or wouldn't do the job, and a burgeoning federal policy witlessly based on state enforcement. The slow motion of federal rulemakers was also seen by environmental criminals to work to their advantage. Even federal officials anxious to move ahead with the plan to cut and run, leaving states to hold the enforcement bag, had to admit that before the states could propose their own programs, the EPA had to promulgate the necessary guidelines—the rules and procedures which at a minimum states would have to endorse in their own programs of toxic waste control. The EPA moved with glacial speed. Almost imperceptibly it moved to comply with congressional wishes embodied in the deeply flawed law called RCRA. Goaded, scolded, and sued, the EPA grudgingly developed the rules and regulations that would govern the hazardous waste disposal industry. Once constructed, this framework would, it was imagined or cynically stated, provide states with the basis for enforcement. Hand in glove, the states and the EPA would together implement a "cradle to grave" security system for the disposal of toxic waste. As it was originally envisioned, the regulatory paper trail would ensure that no significant amount of hazardous waste could be missed and, therefore, illegally disposed.

Far from this promising future, state enforcement has become even more suspect than before. In New York, for instance, Maurice D. Hinchey, chairman of the New York State Assembly's Environmental Conservation Committee, recently accused Governor Mario Cuomo of failing to enforce laws against toxic waste dumpers. Hinchey noted firms can "pollute with impunity," because New York had failed to provide necessary funds for enforcement and had even cut back the enforcement staff. This meant that four out of five municipal landfills and transfer stations were operating illegally, and the licensing of toxic waste haulers was eight years behind. Only about one-tenth of the state's landfills had permits and the number of individuals monitoring landfills had dropped from sixty-eight to fourteen. In answer to Hinchey's charges, New York's Environmental Commissioner, Henry G. Williams, blamed the previous administration, Hugh Carey's, for ignoring the enforcement of landfill regulations. If New York is a proper example, the belief that states can handle a manifest system in a competent manner, let alone an enforcement program expected to have a major impact on toxic waste dumping, is absurd. Equally ridiculous, but worth examining, is the claim that a "cradle to grave" system of manifests will provide a tracking mechanism that will prevent illegal disposal.

A Manifest Failure

The first line in the regulatory scheme that was supposed to guarantee safe disposal was the manifest system. The strategy was this: Once a proper paper trail was put into operation, both generators and haulers would comply with the rules and regulations because they faced the prospect of being audited and investigated. Manifests are the official records of hazardous waste transactions; they show if firms are, on paper, complying with the law. The system would only work to deter lawbreakers as long as the principals believed someone, somewhere, would check. Generators, haulers, and waste disposers had to be convinced some agency would routinely gather the manifests and scrutinize them to make sure each was properly licensed, and most important, that the paper trail was accurate.

Despite the fact that the first logical step in this system of law enforcement would be the monitoring of manifests, the confirming of the written record, none of this checking was routinely done. For the most part, manifests sat in the files of the generators. Gathering information through the use of manifests as primary intelligence documents was virtually nonexistent. One reason given by both federal and EPA officials for not using manifests for intelligence was the sheer volume of paperwork involved. It is true that checking all manifests would be prohibitively burdensome, but devising a system of random checks along with follow-up investigations would not. Some of those inclined to cheat might be deterred, knowing their records and practices were subject to agency scrutiny by the luck of the draw.

The first official body to utilize the manifests for intelligence-gathering was the House Oversight Subcommittee, which got into the business of surveying the nation's waste problem because the EPA wouldn't or couldn't. The subcommittee realized as early as 1978 that it couldn't count on the EPA to survey the problem properly. So, in the fall of 1979, on the basis of manifests examined, the subcommittee published the first national study of waste disposal sites, stating it had to do so because the "EPA was not acting with dispatch" to collect the information. The members of the subcommittee were convinced the EPA couldn't possibly "propose a rational hazardous waste regulatory program" without knowing how much toxic waste was generated, who was hauling it, where it had gone, and where it was still going. Once the survey was completed, the subcommittee gave the results to the EPA, recommending it undertake a comprehensive national inventory of disposal sites and conduct investigations of all haulers identified in the survey as carting wastes to locations unknown to the generators. But it was wishful thinking on the part of the subcommittee members to imagine, if they really did, that the EPA would take the hint and begin to tackle the intelligence problem seriously. Although the recommended national survey was undertaken, it, like most of the Agency's surveys, has been criticized because of slipshod methods which typically result in underestimating public hazards.

Congress, of course, recognized early on that the EPA was footdragging on toxic waste disposal. Several hearings were held in the latter part of the 1970s, which established that the EPA was hardly mindful of the need for timely action. During the Carter years, the head of the EPA was Douglas M. Costle, who testified on some aspects of the issue before the House Oversight Subcommittee in the late spring of 1979. Costle appeared several months after the subcommittee had quizzed the assistant administrator, Tom Jorling, about what the EPA was doing, which the subcommittee felt wasn't very much. The EPA had changed, Costle reported; it was now calling hazardous waste a top priority, and investigations and actions against hazardous waste sites presenting imminent hazards were to be a top enforcement priority.

In order to carry this out, the EPA was establishing a National Hazardous Waste Enforcement Task Force and a National Hazardous Waste Site Investigation and Response Unit, both to be located in Washington, D.C. Similar units were to be set up in the regional offices. When these structures were in place, the EPA would then systematically work at discovery and investigation leading to effective enforcement. This more muscular approach, Costle noted, would be staffed by about one hundred EPA people, who would work exclusively on enforcement and site investigations. Costle also stated there was a great deal of activity currently going on within the EPA and the Department of Justice as they worked together on "seven civil or criminal actions against parties responsible for imminent hazards." Moreover, the EPA was recruiting law enforcement–trained specialists for special investigating units.

Various congressmen asked Costle to give them a time frame when the rules, regulations, and new investigative and enforcement structures would be in place and effective. Costle indicated that the earliest point the regulatory program would become legally effective would be the summer of 1980. After that, actual effectiveness would depend upon the available resources at the federal and state levels. At that juncture, it was pointed out that economic pressures from the President and the Office of Management and Budget made it unlikely the EPA would receive the necessary funding to put the whole program into action. The testimony quite obviously demonstrated it would take the whole of the Carter Administration even to begin to implement RCRA.

There is no denying Congress, the administration, and the EPA all recognized the magnitude of the problem and the steps necessary to bring it under control. There is also no denying those steps were not implemented or else starved of the funding needed to make them effective. It wasn't until July 13, 1982, long after Costle and the other Carter appointees were gone, that the EPA issued its final standards for hazardous waste disposal sites. They were announced by EPA Administrator Anne Gorsuch (soon to be married and assume the last name Burford), appointed by President Reagan when his administration took command.

The first phase of enforcement, all agreed, was an intelligence-gathering system. What seemed to go unrecognized by the EPA and the Department of Justice, however, was that data from manifests provided the baseline for intelligence. Before the EPA concocted the federal model, several states had theirs in place. New Jersey, for one, had what was called a special waste manifest, which had to be filled out by the waste generator, the waste hauler, and a representative of the waste facility. What could have been done through a systematic scrutiny of manifests was displayed by the House Oversight Subcommittee which, again, was almost the only body that took intelligence-gathering as a serious issue.

In the December, 1980, hearing focusing on the many problems in New Jersey, Congressman Albert Gore stated that "one way to beat the New Jersey manifest system is to certify the chemical waste is being disposed of out-of-state at a special waste facility." The subcommittee did its own investigation, matching material gathered in its site survey with some of New Jersey's special waste manifests. It showed that "since August, 1978, major industrial companies, such as Koppers, Inc., in one case Exxon, Union Chemical Co. in the State of New Jersey certified that over 270,000 gallons of chemical waste were delivered to an out-of-state facility in Wilmington, Del., named Capital Recovery." The problem with Capital Recovery, Gore remarked, was it didn't exist; it was nothing more than a paper corporation. Supposedly located in downtown Wilmington, this phantom toxic waste facility had no offices, no phone, nothing but an address. The point the subcommittee was making concerned the ease with which any single state manifest system could be hoodwinked. The subcommittee was thus providing both an example of fraud and a way to gather intelligence and investigate.

What happened with Capital Recovery, however, is an indication of how little attention was being paid to either the particular example or the more general point. Despite the attention given to this phantom company by the House Subcommittee and the fact three of the fraudulent manifests were entered into the record, no federal law enforcement agencies appeared to notice. Capital Recovery was passed over in silence by the EPA and by the Department of Justice.

Almost three years later, in the spring of 1983, reporter Joe Trento of the Wilmington *News Journal* blasted the lack of enforcement and investigation in a revealing story. Trento found a New Jersey hauler had dumped pesticides, acids, and other toxic wastes at three Delaware landfills after stating they would be treated at the nonexistent Capital Recovery facility. The hauler was Olav Gromann, from Holmdel, New Jersey, who was under investigation by New Jersey authorities for supposedly running "an unlicensed toxic incinerator and for allegedly clogging the sewers of Elizabeth, N.J., with dangerous chemical wastes." The matter of Capital Recovery and Olav Gromann was much more substantial than just the phony facility, however. Trento interviewed Jonathan Berg, the head of enforcement for New Jersey's DEP, who stated several Fortune 500 companies dealt with Gromann because "he was cheaper and because he met the state's legal requirements on paper." Berg was obviously implying some of New Jersey's major generators of toxic waste were aware Gromann was a dumper.

Other information about Gromann had been developed by Detective Dirk Ottens before he was removed from toxic waste investigations. Ottens had conducted surveillances on Gromann's operation in New Jersey and turned over to the House Subcommittee information that Gromann's firm, Home Dell Construction, "illegally acquired contaminated generator fuel from New Jersey's largest utility company, Public Service Electric & Gas Co., mixed it with home heating oil and sold it to wholesalers at 40 cents a gallon." One of Gromann's drivers, interviewed by Trento, confessed he had hauled PCB-contaminated waste oil from PSE&G to a terminal in northern New Jersey, where it was mixed with home heating oil and sold through a "pipeline" set up by organized crime. A PSE&G spokesman, Neal Brown, admitted the utility had contracted with Gromann and then added he had a New Jersey license to haul toxic waste.

The state of Delaware, according to Trento, was totally remiss: "Information generated in the congressional investigation was forwarded to New Jersey and Delaware for follow-up action, but Delaware never attempted to charge or prosecute any company or individual." The extent of Delaware's action was a letter written by the state's acting solid waste administrator to Capital Recovery (it was returned unopened) and the assignment of an investigator. The investigator concluded that because the company didn't exist, it couldn't be engaged in any illegal dumping. In fact, the company had existed in 1978 when it was incorporated in Delaware. The following year it was dissolved by the state when it failed to pay its taxes. Capital Recovery had existed, then, although the toxic waste facility never did.

For law enforcement, the fact someone (actually Gromann) had incorporated the company should have been the first step in an investigation of a conspiracy to engage in fraud, at the very least. And, given that the case involved interstate matters, federal agencies could have assumed jurisdiction. It seems, however, the federal authorities were uninterested in Gromann's activities. The last word on Gromann from New Jersey was that he was out of business and would be tried on state charges in October, 1984. Federal authorities, it was reported, had nothing to say about either Gromann or Capital Recovery.

An enforcement strategy based on the systematic scrutiny of manifests (and other survey material derived from the House Subcommittee and the General Accounting Office, which is the investigative arm of Congress) was ignored. The consequences of failing to routinely gather intelligence were again made clear in the fall of 1983, when it was determined that "Fifty-one out of 65 licensed hazardous waste dumps that were checked in two states this year were violating the Federal laws under which they received their permits." As part of an interim report, the General Accounting Office found neither the EPA nor the states were checking the sites.

Congressman James J. Florio commented that the laws and regulations were being ignored by the operators because they were not enforced by the regulators. Florio and Congressman Norman F. Lent announced they would introduce an amendment to RCRA which would require the operators of dumps to certify their compliance with federal requirements. Fraud in the certification would allow for criminal prosecution. What Florio and Lent failed to add, though, was that someone would have to inspect the sites to determine fraud. And that was the original problem—the failure to check the sites. In the same way they failed systematically to check manifests, federal authorities failed to gather intelligence through periodic site investigations. Congressman Florio's remark that it was insufficient to pass a law and then simply expect it to be respected could well stand for the entire enforcement issue when dealing with toxic waste disposal. Laws without enforcement mean nothing; enforcement without intelligence is grossly inadequate.

The Reagan Administration

During the Carter Administration the EPA moved at a snail's pace. Perhaps some of the slow motion was caused by the wooing of several key EPA officers working in the hazardous waste field by the disposal conglomerate Waste Management, Inc. But however slowly the EPA moved in those years, it was moving forward. Under the Reagan Administration, at least during the time Anne Gorsuch Burford was in charge of the EPA, it appeared to move backward.

Perhaps it was only poetic justice that the downfall of Anne Burford and the industry representatives appointed to key staff positions in the EPA came about as the result of toxic waste. When the Reagan Administration assumed office, it began to implement the President's view that there is too much governmental regulation of all aspects of the free enterprise system and that environmental problems are grossly exaggerated. President Reagan once said, in fact, most pollution resulted from vegetation and the EPA had already received more money than it could use effectively. As chief executive, he quickly appointed to high offices within the Environmental Protection Agency persons who shared his philosophy and were thus disinclined to take aggressive action on ecological problems.

Placing their commitment to economic recovery and industrial growth ahead of environmental protection, Burford—who had virtually no previous experience with environmental issues—and her politically appointed associates, most with backgrounds in industries that had vested interests in EPA regulations, began a program of "regulatory reform." This meant little more than stripping the Agency of its ability to demand compliance with existing legislation. Within a year, the message from EPA was loud and clear: Industry did not have much to worry about from an administration that did not plan to enforce the law. The administration's feelings about the environment were further reflected in the EPA's operating budget. In each fiscal year since 1980, the Agency's budget has decreased, with the most significant drops coming after the Reagan-Burford team took control. Between fiscal years 1981 and 1982, total budget outlays dropped some $227 million, with a nearly $175 million decrease slated for the next year. The Agency's hazardous waste program experienced the phenomenal budget drop of over $55 million. This decrease occurred, of course, at a time when the production of hazardous wastes was at a record high level in the nation and the Agency director herself referred to the situation as a "ticking time bomb."

The policy of environmental inaction was also seen in the EPA's administration of the new Superfund, the special program designed to clean up toxic waste sites as quickly as possible. Although Congress appropriated $78 million for this clean-up in 1981, the EPA spent only $8 million of that allocation. Again in fiscal year 1982, the $71.1 million spent was far less than the $169.6 million appropriated. The EPA's reluctance to use its appropriations was certainly not the result of there being no job to do. The Agency itself had identified some 14,000 toxic waste sites in need of clean-up, and had further broken the list down to sites classified as the most dangerous in the country. Apparently, knowing where the dangerous chemicals were and having the funds to start cleaning them up were not enough for those officials running the EPA. The Agency continued to move at a snail's pace while toxic wastes continued to poison the land and water and threaten the health of countless communities.

Over the course of the first year and a half of the Burford EPA, enforcement was gutted. This despite the continuing threat posed by organized crime's penetration of the toxic waste industry, which was well known in Washington by that time, and the encouragement to lawbreakers that a weak enforcement program provided. One way for officials to sink or stall any federal program is to tie it up through bureaucratic means. What Burford did to the barely emerging program of civil enforcement was to subject it to continual reorganizations. These left it spinning through a series of bewildering moves until both policies and personnel were dizzy.

She started in June, 1981, by abolishing the EPA's Office of Enforcement, moving its primary components to different parts of the Agency, and then creating the Office of Legal and Enforcement Counsel, which was to report directly to her. This initial reorganization was followed by another in September and another in December. These had the net effect of separating the technical staff from the legal enforcement staff, a prior arrangement designed explicitly to address the unique enforcement problems associated with hazardous waste disposal cases, which demand "case development teams" composed equally of legal and technical personnel.

On December 19, 1981, the top EPA officials finally provided enforcement guidelines to both regional and headquarters staff. But before these could be implemented, they too were changed on February 26, 1982. Inevitably, all this produced endless confusion, and the ridiculous position noted by congressional investigators, that "while the Enforcement Counsel had the total responsibility for litigation and Justice Department liaison, control over the timeliness of the enforcement process, and the responsibility for evaluating enforcement results" he "did not have anyone in the regions, where enforcement cases are generated, working for or reporting directly to his office."

These changes in the structure of the EPA were mirrored by changes in personnel. The original associate administrator for Legal and Enforcement Counsel resigned the post two months after appointment. Burford appointed EPA General Counsel Robert Perry to the job on March 26, 1982. Perry would serve in both positions. About two weeks later, the Enforcement Counsel announced his resignation. If this wasn't enough to completely paralyze enforcement, Perry appointed a task force whose charge was to evaluate the reorganization of the Office of Legal and Enforcement Counsel and to review the recently mandated regional enforcement procedures and policies. Although there didn't seem to be much to evaluate or review, the regions dutifully went about their new tasks.

The resignation of key personnel in enforcement was the direct result of prior Burford decisions and produced a flurry of publicity. Philip Shabecoff of *The New York Times* noted that Burford had stripped her enforcement chief, William A. Sullivan, Jr., of all his independent powers, requiring him to obtain the approval of Perry before making any enforcement decisions. Sullivan was known, Shabecoff wrote, as a strong advocate of enforcement. Congressman Toby Moffett, a Democrat from Connecticut and the chairman of the Environment Subcommittee of the House Government Operations Committee, was quoted as saying: "The EPA's latest enforcement power shift is nothing more than a cynical charade to cover up the agency's almost total failure to enforce the law." Moffett also claimed Sullivan was to be the EPA's scapegoat for its enforcement failures. Sullivan's dilemma was interpreted by some in the EPA as well as others outside the Agency as an unmistakable signal that legal action would be contemplated only as a last resort by the Agency when it came to illegal disposers of toxic waste.

It wasn't until the summer of 1982 that the final word was reached on the administration of EPA's civil enforcement program. By then, the entire package put forth by the Enforcement Counsel in the winter of 1981–82 had been completely revoked. The House Oversight Subcommittee reported the year's delay by the EPA in finalizing its policies and procedures indicated "mismanagement, disregard, or indifference by top agency officials regarding their enforcement responsibilities." The turmoil caused by the delay and the way in which policy was formulated resulted, as might be expected, in few enforcement cases.

Although the situation was quite bad on the civil enforcement side of the EPA, things were no better in the criminal enforcement program. One mark of how bad it was there can be seen in staffing. It had long been recognized that the EPA needed "tough law enforcement investigators; investigators with training comparable to that of the IRS, the Customs agents, and the FBI." Yet during the first couple of years of Burford's leadership, virtually nothing was done to recruit any investigators. When she came to the Agency, it had a grand total of four criminal investigators. Three were in the Philadelphia regional office and one sat in Washington. Preparations to augment this tiny staff were started in the summer of 1981, when an Office of Criminal Enforcement staffed with at least twenty-five investigators was planned.

Ever mindful of Congress and publicity, Burford "approved a centrally-controlled criminal enforcement program and authorized hiring the additional investigators" just before the House Subcommittee held hearings on November 18, 1981. That allowed the EPA to claim at the hearings that it was truly concerned with criminal enforcement and the proof was in the recently approved expansion. The Enforcement Counsel at the time testified that "We are interviewing and getting them hired." Whatever may have been the expectation, however, as of the spring of 1982 no additional criminal investigators were hired. The EPA had not even advertised the positions by then, and the Enforcement Counsel was more than premature when he stated that the EPA was interviewing people for the job.

The House Oversight Subcommittee demanded an explanation from the EPA. In response, the EPA claimed it had a problem of overlap between the responsibilities of EPA's Inspector General and those of the criminal enforcement office. The subcommittee found this explanation "incredible since the Inspector General's office does not conduct investigations of substantive issues in environmental cases." Nevertheless, this maneuver was used by the EPA to stall the staffing of the criminal enforcement program for almost a year after the allocation of funds.

EPA's lack of criminal investigators was a very serious issue, no matter what the top administrators might have thought. It was serious enough for the FBI to conclude an agreement with the Agency which called for the Bureau to investigate thirty toxic waste cases a year. The only problem with this was the EPA couldn't manage to fill the FBI's quota. The agreement was reached in July, 1981, and over a year later, in November, 1982, only ten cases had been referred to the FBI. The lack of referrals bore no reference to the actual number of cases either known or suspected, but instead reflected a policy of noncompliance with the law which characterized the attitude of top EPA officials. This finally caused the House Oversight Subcommittee to recommend that the FBI implement its own program on toxic waste disposal violations instead of relying on referrals from the EPA.

Along with the damage to enforcement personnel and policies, Burford attacked one of the Agency's primary information-gathering techniques. In the spring of 1982 the EPA moved to suspend the regulation which required generators of toxic waste to file reports on their activities with the Agency. Speaking for the EPA on this important change was the director of the Office of Solid Waste, Gary N. Dietrich. He stated the EPA did not believe it was efficient to receive reports from 11,000 toxic waste producers. Instead, it was the EPA's intention to mail questionnaires on toxic waste disposal to a tiny fraction of the waste generators and only one-fifth of the disposal companies; in subsequent years the Agency intended to solicit information from 10 percent of the generators. The potential impact of this proposal was quickly pointed out by the EPA's chief in-house critic, Hugh Kaufman, who worked as an assistant to the director of hazardous site control. Kaufman stated that the proposal's adoption would mean the end of the Agency's mechanism of obtaining information on "midnight dumping" of toxic wastes. Perhaps the thinking at the top was that a drastic reduction in the flow of information would somehow justify the lack of enforcement. Under the Carter Administration the EPA's methods for gathering intelligence were confused, haphazard, and deeply flawed; under Reagan, the Agency was hostile to the entire process.

The reluctance to gather intelligence and engage in enforcement clearly showed the EPA had been captured by just those forces it was supposed to monitor. From one administration to the next, the substantive difference was the ever-increasing boldness with which the Agency protected the special interests. It wasn't that these weren't protected under the Carter Administration, but the style and degree of protection had now changed. Reagan's EPA was philosophically inclined to find regulation distasteful and crass enough to cater publicly to the polluters. For instance, the EPA's Inspector General reported that in December, 1981, Burford "privately promised a small oil refinery that it would not be penalized if it violated Federal lead standards." The company, located in New Mexico, had asked for an EPA waiver because it was financially strapped. Burford's response was that a waiver wasn't practical. Instead, she told company officials that the Agency simply would not enforce the regulations. In her defense it was pointed out that the EPA was considering changing the regulations on lead content in gasoline. Considering changes, however, was a far cry from making changes. Burford said: "I did not intend to authorize or encourage people to break the law."

The lead issue was small beer compared to what Burford did in the winter of 1982. This time the controversy dealt with toxic waste in landfills. Under RCRA there was a prohibition on placing barrels containing toxic liquid waste in landfills. Burford suspended the ban for a period of ninety days and proposed revoking it forever. Even though the EPA admitted the drums would eventually corrode and leak their toxic contents, it maintained the rules and regulations were "too extreme for real-world application" and far too expensive for industry. Urging this major change in environmental policy were the Chemical Manufacturers Association and the lobbying organization for the waste disposal industry.

An immediate firestorm of protest erupted. Environmental groups and congressional committees charged that Burford and the EPA were catering to the most regressive forces producing and handling toxic wastes. So much criticism was leveled that in three weeks the EPA changed its proposal. Instead, it established an interim regulation, which banned "the burial of drums containing toxic liquids in observable quantities." What those quantities would be—crucial information for any community adjacent to toxic landfills and any whose drinking supply was influenced by leachate—was unknowable because the rule addressed visibility, not quantity. The meaning of the new rule was, quite obviously, Out of sight, out of control.

In between the time the ban was lifted and the amended regulation proposed, critics speculated that millions of gallons of dangerous toxic wastes were landfilled. It was reported that several major toxic waste disposal companies, in anticipation of Burford's action, had stockpiled thousands of barrels eagerly awaiting the signal from Washington. Once given, they were reported to have moved swiftly into many landfills, expecially in Colorado and other western states, and dumped some of the most toxic substances they had. One of the companies alleged to have taken quick advantage of the EPA's new rule was Chemical Waste Management, Inc., a subsidiary of Waste Management. Chemical Waste Management did more than move quickly in Colorado, however. According to Congressman Florio, the company kept "two sets of books to conceal leaking at a Colorado landfill." Florio had found an EPA report which asserted the dual bookkeeping and the motive of concealment, and he then noted that after the report, the EPA nevertheless awarded $7.7 million to Chemical Waste Management to clean up a toxic waste site in Indiana. One way or another, Florio implied, toxic waste disposal companies would have their way.

The Scandal in Washington

Although EPA officials were working to slow down the Agency's enforcement activities, public support for environmental laws remained strong. According to a March 6, 1983, *New York Times* article, "Recent public opinion polls almost unanimously indicate overwhelming support for continued strong enforcement of those laws, even at the cost of loss of job or other economic sacrifice." Hence, while the public was demanding protection and the enforcement of those laws it defined as giving it that security, officials in the executive branch of the federal government were ignoring the public's desire. Apparently, profits could not be made if the nation's environmental agency did its job.

While environmental groups and professional staff members of the EPA were highly critical of the policies and inaction of the President's political appointees, several key congressional committees became increasingly interested in the Agency's failure to utilize the Superfund as the Congress had originally intended. Although $1.6 billion had been collected for the clean-up purpose, work had been completed at only five sites by the end of 1982. In October of that year, Representative John D. Dingell, chairman of the House Commerce and Energy Investigations Subcommittee, initiated an investigation of the EPA's management of the Superfund program and issued a subpoena for documents related to the work of the fund. One month later, a similar investigation was started by the House Public Works Investigations Subcommittee, chaired by Representative Elliott Levitas, who also subpoenaed EPA documents needed for review of the Agency's work. Almost simultaneously, additional probes were launched by other House subcommittees and by the Senate's Environment and Public Works Committee. As each committee announced its intention to review the EPA and its operations, the public learned of new charges of conflict of interest, poor management, political favoritism, employee harassment, and undue influence on Agency decisions by members of the chemical industry. The investigating committees made it clear they planned to take a hard look at what had been going on in the EPA for the past two years.

Even Washington insiders were surprised at what happened next. On November 30, President Reagan claimed many of the documents subpoenaed by the various congressional committees were protected by executive privilege, and he instructed Mrs. Burford not to provide the subpoenaed material. The President contended that he invoked executive privilege because the documents were "enforcement sensitive," meaning apparently that they were related to ongoing EPA investigations. Nevertheless, amid the charges and rumors revolving around the Agency, new cover-up charges were quickly raised, and critics, remembering the Watergate scandals of only a decade earlier, dubbed the new controversy "Sewergate." Reacting quickly, the Levitas subcommittee voted to cite Burford for contempt of Congress, and six days later, the full House adopted the committee's recommendation. For refusing to deliver the subpoenaed documents, Anne Burford thus became the highest ranking executive branch official ever charged with contempt of Congress. By virtue of the vote, the U.S. Attorney for the District of Columbia was compelled to present the case to a federal grand jury for prosecution, even though the U.S. Justice Department attempted to prevent such action.

When two paper shredders were delivered to the Environmental Protection Agency, critics assumed the worst, and key members of Congress demanded that Agency heads begin to roll. On February 2, 1983, Anne Burford attempted to comply by delivering the head of Rita Lavelle, the administrator in charge of the toxic waste clean-up program. Lavelle, a California crony of several White House staffers, came to the EPA position from the Aerojet-General Corporation, where she had been communications director for two of its subsidiaries. Although her lack of previous experience with environmental issues was in keeping with that of other Reagan appointees, her connection with Aerojet-General raised some eyebrows since that company was a major contributor of hazardous wastes to the Stringfellow Acid Pits near Riverside, California, known as "the Love Canal of the West." At the time, Lavelle's division was engaged in negotiations with a variety of companies which had contributed to the Stringfellow site in order to determine liability for the necessary clean-up. Lavelle had been a controversial administrator from the very beginning of her tenure, being accused by staff members of reluctance to take action against environmental polluters and being too political in her management of the Superfund.

In a letter to the Justice Department, Burford asked it to review the possibility that Lavelle "may have engaged in an ex-parte communication" with a company which the Agency was then suing in order to force it to clean up waste it had dumped into Lake Michigan. Two days later, Burford demanded that Lavelle resign, even preparing a letter of resignation for her in advance. Lavelle refused and vowed to take her case to the White House, where she assumed friends like Presidential Counselor Edwin Meese would save her job. But that was not to be. A few days later President Reagan fired her. In subsequent testimony before various congressional committees, Rita Lavelle was questioned extensively about charges that she had used the Superfund for political purposes and had been far too cozy with representatives of polluting industries. Even though she denied these charges, some of her testimony conflicted with evidence which had been uncovered by congressional

investigators, and she was soon indicted for perjury. Near the end
of 1983, she was convicted of having lied under oath before congressional committees.

While debate over the right of the President to withhold documents from Congress raged in early 1983, criticism of Anne Burford's direction of the EPA was also mounting. She had long been
the target of stinging attacks by environmental groups who objected to her unwillingness to enforce the laws while reducing the
Agency's role in protecting the environment. Now, however, criticism came also from a variety of other sources, including members
of the Republican Party who had once supported her. Four days
after the President said he had "full confidence" in Burford and
that she could remain at the EPA as "long as she wants to," she
resigned as the nation's chief environmental officer. With Burford's
resignation and growing suspicions on the part of the American
public, the President soon backed down and agreed to release all
the EPA documents requested by Congress. Along with Burford, a
number of other top officials at the EPA also resigned or were
forced out by the White House. Hence, routine investigations
which had begun quietly in late 1981 resulted in a massive shake-
up of EPA officials, not to mention a constitutional confrontation
between the President and the House of Representatives as well.

After the ouster of Burford and her aides, congressional sources
demanded an investigation by the Justice Department into a
number of allegations that had been made against them. Following
a six-month probe, the Justice Department report cleared all of
them of any criminal wrongdoing, stating no basis could be found
for charges which ranged from perjury and conflict of interest to
arranging for sweetheart deals with industry and politically manipulating the Superfund. But the report did not satisfy congressional
critics. Representative John Dingell charged: "While the Department of Justice may have concluded that certain conduct did not
reach the level of criminal behavior, it is clear that former EPA
officials violated the public trust by mismanagement, conflict of interest abuses, and the misuse of health and safety programs for
political purposes." Representative James Scheuer called the report "a transparently political document more geared to protecting
the administration's version of the EPA controversies than aggressively pursuing allegations of wrongdoing." Although further
congressional action was promised, it appears most members of

Congress, and even the Reagan Administration, were just happy to get Burford and her associates out of the EPA and to restore once again some measure of credibility to that important Agency.

How much damage had been done to the nation's environmental program in the slightly more than two years of EPA mismanagement and non-enforcement under Burford? And, more to the point, to what extent was Burford only the instrument of those above her dictating policies? On this point, Rita Lavelle was quoted in *Newsweek* magazine as stating, "I thought I was carrying out . . . the President's direction." Whatever the case, the damage may have been a tragic and profound setback for the environmental movement. According to a former EPA official in the Carter Administration, "We have lost the decade of the eighties. Even assuming a new president is elected in 1984 who is deeply dedicated to the environment and gives it top priority, it will be 1990 before we get it back to where we were." But even that goal may be unrealistic if the President and the Congress do not take environmental law enforcement more seriously.

Initiating Enforcement

Despite the EPA's paltry past record of criminal enforcement, a glimmer of hope has recently emerged. In May, 1982, the EPA created a Criminal Enforcement Division to supplement the Civil Division. Curiously, since the very beginning of the EPA, the enforcement of environmental laws had concentrated almost exclusively on civil and administrative cases. Although it was clear by the late 1970s that the civil enforcement programs were not particularly effective and waste dumpers and other polluters often wrote off the cost of legal judgments against them as business expenses, the EPA was very hesitant to develop a criminal case capacity to help ensure compliance. To a large extent, this probably resulted because EPA legal personnel had little or no criminal experience, coming primarily from civil law backgrounds. Their frame of reference, coupled with the Agency's traditional friendliness with the industrial community, seemed to mediate against any serious consideration of enforcing compliance in the courts.

The EPA's laxity and inefficiency are reflected in only thirty-seven criminal referrals to the Justice Department during fiscal years 1979 and 1980. Three and four years, respectively, after passage of RCRA, and at the time when illegal dumping was expanding all over the nation, fewer than twenty cases a year were sent for criminal prosecution. Even worse is the fact that 62 percent of those cases were declined by the Justice Department because they were so poorly developed. Clearly, from this point, the Agency had nowhere to go but up.

Even though the enforcement philosophy did not change among the politically appointed officials of the Reagan-Burford EPA, dedicated professional staff members continued to work for an increased effort in the criminal prosecution of illegal hazardous waste disposers. This, coupled with congressional pressure, eventually led to the Criminal Enforcement Division and a new framework for the development of such cases. Although experienced criminal investigators were not recruited and hired when EPA officials had said they would be, by October, 1982, twenty-three investigators were staffing field offices in five cities across the country. Spread far too thinly—with only five investigators covering the entire Southeast and southern parts of the country, stretching from Georgia to New Mexico—these environmental cops nevertheless represent an important first step in the Agency's attempt to enforce the nation's environmental laws.

Although the new Criminal Enforcement Division is concerned with more than violations of hazardous waste laws, violations of those laws do occupy a significant portion of the Division's attention. As a result, action taken against hazardous waste dumpers by the federal government has increased, even though it is far short of what appears to be needed to prevent or slow down illegal disposal practices. In 1983, EPA's active criminal case docket included about eighty cases that involved violations of hazardous waste laws. In addition, indictments were obtained in some fourteen cases involving thirty-eight corporate and individual defendants, as many defendants as were indicted in the four previous years combined. With this new aggressive attitude, and the recruitment of lawyers and investigators with a criminal law background and orientation, the problem of poor case preparation and subsequent rejection by the Justice Department seems to have diminished.

Nevertheless, these achievements mark only meager beginnings. Significant problems continue to exist, making enforcement extremely difficult and sometimes futile. In spite of the enormous environmental and human damage that may be caused by the illegal disposal of hazardous chemical wastes, most statutes designed to control these practices impose only misdemeanor sanctions, generally light fines that may be defined as little more than the cost of doing business or, very infrequently, the possibility of a short jail sentence. Some states have learned the lesson faster than the federal government and have created tougher laws designed to be effective deterrents. In Pennsylvania, for example, a maximum fine of $500,000 or a year in jail may now be imposed upon individuals convicted of illegal waste dumping.

The consequence of environmental statutes imposing only misdemeanor sanctions is that law enforcement agencies and prosecuting offices tend to view them as less important than the seemingly more serious felonies. This is directly related to the EPA's relationship with the Justice Department. Until recently, the EPA relied upon the FBI for help in investigating illegal dumping activities. With no experience in this area and an already overextended caseload, the Bureau was—and continues to be—reluctant to become involved in such investigations. When it has joined investigations, usually at the urging of other federal offices, it has been interested in developing and building its cases around those provisions of RCRA which provide for felony sanctions. Hence, mail fraud and filing false statements, both possible charges when manifests are involved, are generally the grounds upon which the FBI will try to develop illegal waste dumping cases.

The misdemeanor status of so many hazardous waste statutes also meant they were assigned a low priority when sent to the Justice Department for prosecution. Faced with a number of cases, prosecuting officers would understandably focus on those thought to be most serious, the ones which could result in the harshest penalties. Even though this problem continues to exist, it has been eased somewhat in recent years by the creation of the Environmental Crimes Unit within the Lands Division of the Justice Department. This unit has been staffed by attorneys who have both environmental and criminal law backgrounds and who are encouraged to place a high priority on cases involving the disposal of hazardous wastes. Unfortunately, the unit is small; coupled with the limited amount of cases an EPA investigative staff of only twenty-three can develop, the number of prosecutions is limited and will remain so until these conditions change.

Given this modest level of staffing and the original intention of
RCRA to turn its implementation back to the states, it would appear that additional law enforcement efforts must be made at the
state level. Although some states have developed specialized environmental investigative units, they remain quite rare and generally inexperienced. States like New Jersey, Pennsylvania, and
Illinois have developed investigative and prosecuting divisions spe-
cializing in waste disposal problems, but other states with equally
serious problems continue to leave such efforts to their local or
state police departments, with the rare prosecution handled by an
Assistant Attorney General who knows little about hazardous
wastes.

The problem is compounded even further when organized
crime figures and firms are involved in illegal disposal practices.
Local investigative units have little knowledge of or experience
with organized crime operations, particularly in the field of toxic
waste dumping. Investigating firms that use intricate techniques of
disposal and are protected by corporate veils and complex business
relationships is difficult for the most experienced police officers and
prosecutors. In cases of illegal hazardous waste dumping, coordinating other members of the investigating team whose orientation
is far removed from policing and law enforcement compounds the
difficulty. Chemists, toxicologists, and environmental officers are
only some of the specialists needed to investigate cases of dumping and develop the evidence required in court to ensure successful prosecution. The federal effort is quite limited and must
rely upon local enforcement, but few jurisdictions are capable of
doing the job.

Under these conditions, and given the effects and consequences of toxic waste dumping, it is totally unrealistic to expect
states to be effective in enforcing hazardous waste laws. Lacking
manpower and sophistication in enforcement and detection techniques, states are faced with the additional problem of having their
jurisdiction end at the boundary of the next state. Leachate,
groundwater, streams, and rivers do not respect these political
boundaries and may carry deadly contents from one state to another. When that occurs, the state government may find itself
helpless in enforcing laws designed to protect the land, water, and
residents within its jurisdiction. Such cases are truly federal problems, and should be controlled by federal enforcement agencies

with the necessary resources to keep the nation safe from those who would despoil it. Expecting local governments to enforce hazardous waste laws appears to be a sure way of permitting illegal and hazardous dumping to continue with little or no interference.

Enforcement is weak and the penalties for those few caught and successfully prosecuted are mild. Even though so many federal and state hazardous waste statutes define dumping and related behavior as misdemeanors, most of these statutes do provide for some term of imprisonment for those who are found guilty. In addition, some statutes that are related to the act of illegal toxic waste disposal are defined as felonies in the federal law and even in some state codes, and thus provide for the possibility of at least modest prison sentences. Nevertheless, a survey of those few cases that result in the conviction of individuals at both the local and the federal levels indicates the courts are reluctant to impose prison sentences upon those who are found guilty. In 1983, for example, periods of incarceration were imposed upon only four of the seventeen individual defendants convicted of violating federal environmental laws.

The record of state courts is not much better. The typical punishments are fines, probation, and suspended sentences, with polluters only rarely spending any time behind bars. For various reasons, it appears that judges have yet to define hazardous waste dumping as a very serious criminal offense, apparently perceiving it instead as another type of white-collar crime similar to offenses like fair trade violations and bid rigging. Criminal courts have never taken those offenses very seriously, often viewing them as a normal part of the free enterprise system. As long as courts continue to hold illegal waste disposal as just another form of business crime, the best intentions and the hardest work of the enforcement agencies will be in vain.

Dumping and Shooting

While the courts often treat toxic waste dumpers as businessmen who commit an occasional oversight, the investigative staff of the EPA's Criminal Enforcement Division has learned differently. Since beginning their work in October, 1982, these investigators have encountered arsons, assaults, shootings, threats, and other forms of violence. Fortunately, these circumstances were anticipated when the twenty-three special agents were recruited from approximately three hundred applicants. At that time, the description of the position stated: "Suspected violators are often highly organized crime groups whose criminal activities are interwoven with legitimate business activities. Assignments often involve large scale searches and seizures which may be performed under hazardous and potentially dangerous conditions . . . investigations involve the utilization of undercover agents and surveillances which require the penetration of close knit groups over extended periods of time." Those who read that description should have known what they were in for. Not surprisingly, the people hired had a minimum of five years previous experience in either federal or state law enforcement agencies. Their experience, plus additional training at the Federal Law Enforcement Training Center, helped to create a highly professional investigative staff, capable of developing cases that would stand up in court.

One problem remained, however. In spite of the government's apparent good intentions, it failed to provide the EPA's criminal investigators with law enforcement powers until the late spring of 1984. That had been the intention of the Carter Administration officials who originally proposed the investigative staff, but by the time the Division was implemented in October, 1982, the Reagan Justice Department and Office of Management and Budget had different ideas. They believed that a proliferation of law enforcement powers within the federal bureaucracy was dangerous, and that EPA investigators should use other agencies like the Federal Marshal's Office and the FBI when law enforcement powers were needed. But Congressman John Dingell said at a December, 1983, hearing of his Subcommittee on Oversight and Investigations: "That means they cannot stop a truck to check its manifest, they cannot prevent ongoing illegal activity, they cannot arrest violators, they cannot possess a weapon to protect themselves, and they cannot execute search warrants." Despite the administration's opposition to extending law enforcement power to these investigators, William Ruckelshaus, the new (and former) administrator of the EPA, has concluded that law enforcement powers are needed. At Ruckelshaus's swearing-in ceremony, two months after the resignation of the discredited Anne Burford, President Reagan singled out vigorous enforcement of the nation's environmental laws as one of the top priority areas for the EPA. Nevertheless, the Justice Department had failed to honor Ruckelshaus's request promptly, raising in the minds of some observers doubts about the President's actual commitment to enforcement.

Why EPA investigators should have law enforcement powers was discussed at some length at recent Dingell committee hearings. In a chilling statement, Steven J. Madonna, Deputy Attorney General in charge of New Jersey's Environment Prosecution Section, warned that

> if it is a serious attempt to investigate the waste industry, and I say the waste industry advisedly because I don't think that up front you can make a decision as to whether or not it is the solid waste industry or the hazardous waste industry—I don't think that you can get involved in a criminal investigation in this area without being armed and having full authority. . . . I make this statement, Mr. Chairman, because I believe that the waste industry is probably one of the most violent industries that exists in the country today . . . there have been murders, threats, assaults, arsons, intimidations. It seems to be unfortunately a way of life in that industry. I am not talking about the day-to-day collector, but the type of controls imposed are such that in fact organized crime plays a significant role in that industry.

From around the country, incidents of actual and potential risk associated with environmental investigations were cited. One EPA investigator discovered a "car stripping" operation while attempting to conduct interviews relating to a probe, and another was shot at while taking samples from property next to a suspected waste facility. On other occasions, EPA employees were forced from sites at gunpoint, assaulted by a suspected waste hauler, threatened with physical violence if they continued their work, and even menaced at knifepoint. At one time, an EPA inspector was told that "guys with jobs like yours can get shot." Murder and strong-arm tactics are, of course, traditional mob instruments of power and control, to be expected when criminal syndicates dominate an industry. To investigate toxic waste dumpers under these conditions without law enforcement powers, including the authority to carry a weapon and defend oneself, was ridiculous and dangerous.

In addition, the lack of law enforcement powers by EPA investigators was also frustrating, especially when it interfered with their doing their job. On one occasion, an EPA investigator witnessed a truck deliberately leaking PCBs onto a highway between Portland and Seattle. Because the investigator did not have the authority to stop the truck and had to wait until a sheriff's deputy was summoned, some fifty miles of highway were contaminated. Ironically, the same lack of authority to stop or detain trucks also prevented EPA investigators from checking manifests of shipments of hazardous waste without being accompanied by other law enforcement personnel. Again, when search warrants needed to be executed, outside police agencies had to be brought into the investigation and asked for cooperation, often given only at the convenience of the other agency and not necessarily coordinated with the requirements of the investigation.

The Justice Department's delay in granting such authority was consistent with its cautious and tentative approach to the illegal disposal of hazardous waste, and particularly to the role of organized crime in that business. This attitude is illustrated in the following exchange between Representative Dingell and F. Henry Habnicht, an Assistant Attorney General for Land and Natural Resources:

> *Mr. Dingell:* This committee has records which we have certified to you folks; in fact, we had some of the witnesses off the Department of Justice's protected witness list who appeared before us, as well as officials of the FBI, testifying about that fact, about organized crime's penetration into the hazardous waste and solid waste industry.
>
> *Mr. Habnicht:* We are interested in pursuing that.
>
> *Mr. Dingell:* This is a record that now is, I would say, about two and a half years old, and you heard Mr. Madonna and Mr. Welkes [Pennsylvania Assistant Attorney General in charge of hazardous waste investigations and prosecutions] both testify that in their experience organized crime is involved in the hazardous waste business.

Mr. Habnicht responded to Congressman Dingell by changing the subject.

Where Do We Go from Here?

With over 150 million metric tons of hazardous waste produced each year in the United States, we must question the future direction of statutes designed to protect the land, water, and human health. Not only is effective enforcement difficult, but it is sometimes viewed with ambivalence, not just by illegal dumpers but also by government officials and businessmen. Some businessmen believe they cannot comply with the nation's environmental laws, or more precisely, to comply would simply be too expensive. According to Alexander F. Giacco, the chairman, president, and chief executive officer of Hercules, Inc. in Delaware, "When you're in the chemical industry and you're facing a litigious society, you . . . face the possibility of almost a bankruptcy over something that you had almost no control over, something that happened years ago and something that you can't define even today." Since the mid-1970s, when more stringent controls were placed on the dangerous and indiscriminate disposal of toxic wastes, a number of business executives (including Hercules, Inc.'s, chief) and even some government officials have warned that industry might retaliate by moving its plants outside the United States. By so doing, it would avoid American environmental laws and, ostensibly, operate with impunity in locations that do not care about the environmental and health effects of companies producing hazardous wastes.

Of course, such moves would also rob the nation of tens of thousands of jobs, sometimes spitefully referred to as the price people will have to pay if they insist upon a healthy environment. It is difficult to know how serious these threats are, or what role other factors play in deciding where to locate an industrial plant; but a study by the Conservation Foundation, an environmental research foundation, does indicate that some organic chemical producing companies have shifted their operations overseas. In addition, the study points out that environmental regulations have curtailed some new plant construction and even disrupted the production of a few highly toxic, dangerous, or carcinogenic products. Although these are indicative of the obvious economic repercussions of environmental law enforcement, they must be weighed against the possibilities that exist without meaningful enforcement.

Perhaps this can best be done by looking at the consequences of rampant and untrammeled industrialization without effective controls in a foreign location which some American industries might find attractive. Cubato, Brazil, is the home of twenty-four petrochemical factories, which help make it that nation's most polluted town, with some 800 tons of toxic gases poured into the atmosphere every day. In fact, the air pollution is so severe that authorities do not even attempt to measure it since the instruments cannot withstand the corrosion. The residents of Cubato, now Latin America's most important petrochemical complex, have had a lethal red rain fall upon them for the past twenty-five years, killing all vegetation in the area and spreading numerous ailments among them. Children die by the thousands in what is known as "the Valley of Death," the area where the impoverished live within the industrial zone. The city also holds what must be the world record for number of children born with total or partial absence of a brain. Is this where American industries want to go to escape environmental regulations and maximize their profits?

It is unlikely our future will ever be as bleak as Cubato's, although we are sitting on ticking time bombs which grow more dangerous as our waste production continues to increase and our laws remain weak and ineffectively enforced. Under these conditions, the future will hold serious problems for our nation unless the toxic waste issue is taken seriously and made an important national priority. One step in that direction is simply to enforce the laws as they now exist. As we have seen, this is not always the case; in fact, it may more often be the exception than the rule.

Another step in the direction of more effective enforcement is to increase the penalties for illegal waste dumping. This is beginning to happen in some jurisdictions, but it is nonetheless necessary for the federal government to take the lead in this regard and to upgrade misdemeanor statutes to the felony level. Rather than taking the easy way out, plea-bargaining or negotiating settlements, federal agencies charged with enforcing waste dumping laws must let it be known that violators will be treated as serious criminals.

One way in which this may be done quickly and effectively is to use the Racketeer Influenced and Corrupt Organization Act (RICO) in prosecuting dumpers. A part of the Organized Crime Control Act of 1970, RICO defines racketeering as involvement in two or more acts which are prohibited by federal and state statutes. Thus, if a "pattern" of organized crime activity can be shown, a convicted individual is subject to twenty years in prison and a $25,000 fine. More importantly, however, those convicted are also required to forfeit any interest in businesses which are in violation of RICO. Plainly speaking, this means that waste haulers who are convicted of racketeering under the RICO Act may be forced to forfeit their business to the U.S. government. This appears to be a much more powerful penalty, capable of true deterrence, than the threat of a simple fine or suspended sentence. For some reason, prosecuting dumpers under RICO has been used only once, although Justice Department officials indicate that they are now giving more consideration to using the act in cases of this type.

Even though dumpers are the focus of most waste disposal laws, generators of toxic chemicals must also assume a greater burden of responsibility for their safe management. Generators may no longer claim ignorance of what their haulers do or how they dispose of toxics, since the manifest system now provides them with a way of checking on the work of their agents. This is seldom done by manufacturers. But the increasing trend of holding manufacturers responsible for their products may force them to pay more attention to those with whom they do business. Like the producers of asbestos and Agent Orange, who had no direct links with persons ultimately hurt by their products, manufacturers of chemicals that produce harmful wastes which are then improperly discarded in the future may find themselves subject to frequent and expensive lawsuits.

And, if nothing else works, the government may be forced in the future to impose rigid controls on the production of those goods that create dangerous wastes. It is entirely conceivable that the EPA of the next decade will limit industrial production to those commodities that generate only manageable waste. Drastic as such action might seem, it may be necessary if we are not capable of controlling the problem soon. If this does occur, many aspects of our lifestyle will have to change, and conveniences to which we have grown accustomed may become prohibitively expensive. But in either case all of us will have to pay, either with money in the short run or human health in the future.

Organized crime did not create America's hazardous waste problem, but mobsters in the business of dumping toxics for huge profits have contributed to it. Organized crime figures have played an important role in structuring the industry into something violent and corrupt, unworthy of the implicit trust an industrial nation must place in it. Their presence in the waste disposal industry has endangered the nation's land and water, and clearly threatens to overwhelm any effort at control. The toxic waste racket is fast making victims of us all.

The Cast

ACQUAFREDDA, VINCENZO "JIMMIE": Florida garbage collector who attempted to muscle operators in Pasco and Pinellas counties into a protective trade association.

ADELSTEIN, BERNARD: Leader of Teamsters' Local 813 and a close associate of many organized-crime figures in New York's private sanitation industry.

ALAMO TRANSPORTATION: New Jersey State Police undercover trucking operation established to investigate organized crime on the Jersey City waterfront.

ALBERT, JOHN: Reputed organized-crime figure; owner of several waste-hauling firms; seized control of Chemical Control Corporation at gunpoint.

BROWNING-FERRIS INDUSTRIES: Nation's second-largest hazardous-waste handler accused on numerous occasions of pollution, price-fixing, and cooperating with organized-crime figures in the waste industry.

BUCHANAN, RONALD J.: Chief of the Bureau of Hazardous Waste in New Jersey's Department of Environmental Protection.

BURFORD, ANNE GORSUCH: President Reagan's choice to head the Environmental Protection Agency; resigned under fire in 1983.

CAPONE, VINCENT D.: Waste hauler from New Jersey, associated with John DiGilio; murdered in 1976.

CARRACINO, WILLIAM: Founder of Chemical Control Corporation who lost company to organized crime; later furnished important information to state and federal investigators.

CASSILIANO, JOHN: Corrupt employee of New York City's Department of Sanitation; took bribes to allow toxic waste dumpers into municipal landfills.

CASSINI, JOE: Partner in the notorious MSLA Landfill in Kearny, New Jersey, with Richard Miele and Chris Roselle.

CHELSEA TERMINAL: Phony toxic-waste facility located on Staten Island, New York; illegally accepted millions of gallons of chemical waste.

CHEMICAL CONTROL CORPORATION: Elizabeth, New Jersey, hazardous-waste-disposal facility started by William Carracino; taken over by organized crime associate John Albert in 1977; destroyed by spectacular fire in 1980.

CIMINO, RAYMOND: Waste hauler from Yonkers, New York; associate of organized crime figure Joseph Zingaro.

COBB, MAXWELL: President of American Electric Corporation of Jacksonville, Florida, with Defense Department contract to dispose of PCBs; attempted to send toxic waste to Honduras for incineration.

COOPER FUNDING, LTD.: Organized-crime-backed equipment-leasing operation; run by Mel Cooper; front for mob loan-sharking in the waste industry.

DELANEY, ROBERT: New Jersey State Police detective who went undercover in Alamo Transportation; surfaced three years later as key witness for the state against organized crime.

DiGILIO, JOHN: New Jersey organized-crime figure; member of the Genovese crime syndicate and leader of a gang based in Hoboken, New Jersey.

DiNARDI, ALFRED: Owner of a waste-carting company in competition with SCA Services and others in northern New Jersey; murdered in 1976.

DINGELL, JOHN D.: Congressman from Michigan; chairman of the House Subcommittee on Oversight and Investigations, which probed organized crime's links to the toxic-waste industry.

DUANE MARINE SALVAGE CORPORATION: Toxic-waste-disposal firm located in Perth Amboy, New Jersey; engaged in numerous illegal dumping techniques, including flushing hazardous chemicals into the city's sewer system.

FAILLA, JAMES "JIMMY BROWN": One of the organized crime figures in charge of the Gambino crime syndicate's waste businesses and interests.

FERRARA, JOSEPH "JOJO": Associate of organized-crime figure John Riggi; employed at Kit Enterprises, a toxic-waste facility in Elizabeth, New Jersey.

FINE, JOHN: Former organized-crime prosecutor in New York; among the first to recognize organized crime's involvement in toxic waste; fired from his post in 1980.

FIUMARA, TINO: Member of the Genovese crime syndicate active in toxic-waste matters; convicted of racketeering in 1979 as a result of the Alamo Transportation undercover operation.

GAESS, ANTHONY D.: Waste entrepreneur whose companies were purchased by SCA Services, Inc.; mentor of many of the most notorious illegal dumpers.

GORE, ALBERT: Tennessee congressman actively involved in congressional investigations of toxic-waste disposal; member of House Subcommittee on Oversight and Investigations.

GREENBERG, STANLEY: Deputy sheriff in Rockland County, New York; vigorously investigated organized crime's control of landfills and waste companies.

GREGORY, GEORGE: Former New Jersey deputy attorney general; became one of the directors of the notorious Kit Enterprises.

GRIBETZ, KENNETH: Rockland County district attorney; accused of failing to investigate toxic-waste dumping and organized-crime involvement.

GROGAN, WILLIAM "BILL": Yonkers detective whose early investigative work uncovered mobsters' control of waste-hauling companies and landfills.

GUSLAVAGE, JOHN "GUS": Elizabeth police detective whose investigation of Kit Enterprises, in the face of constant political harassment, ultimately led to Kit's conviction.

HOOKER CHEMICAL CORPORATION: Niagara Falls, New York, firm largely responsible for the disposal of toxic wastes in the Love Canal and the eventual pollution of a large residential area of the city.

IANNIELLO, MATTHEW: One of the major leaders of the Genovese crime syndicate; owner of Dutchess Sanitation, an influential waste company; organized-crime controller of Manhattan topless bars.

KAUFMAN, HAROLD: Former professional criminal turned FBI informant; largely responsible for providing an inside view of the waste industry's links to crime syndicates.

KELLY, PATRICK: Businessman who became undercover agent; ran the Alamo Transportation sting operation.

KIN-BUC LANDFILL: Notorious Edison Township, New Jersey, dump site where toxic wastes were discarded until 1976; closed by the state when it contaminated the Raritan River.

KIT ENTERPRISES: Fradulent toxic-waste facility protected for years by state politicians.

KITZI, THOMAS F.: Well-known toxic-waste dumper, owner of Kit Enterprises and several other toxic-waste disposal firms.

LAPI, JOSEPH "JOE BECK": Elder statesman of New York crime syndicate; received regular payoffs from Chemical Control Corporation after organized-crime takeover.

LAVELLE, RITA: EPA administrator in charge of the Superfund program; allowed political considerations to influence decisions on Superfund cleanup projects; fired by President Reagan.

LECARREAUX, ED: President of Duane Marine Salvage Corporation.

LOMBARDOZZI, CARMINE: Major organized-crime leader from the Gambino crime syndicate with interests in loan-sharking.

MACALUSO, CHARLES: President of Statewide Environmental Contractors and key figure in the New Jersey Trade Waste Association; convicted of bribing public officials.

MCKENNA, JEREMIAH: Counsel to the New York Senate Select Committee on Crime; director of many investigations into illegal chemical dumping.

MADONNA, STEVEN J.: Deputy attorney general in charge of New Jersey's Inter-Agency Hazardous Waste Task Force.

MAHLER, RUSSELL: Owner of numerous waste-oil companies; specialist in the illegal mixing of toxic waste with fuel oil.

MARINO, RALPH: New York state senator, chairman of the Select Committee on Crime.

MAURO, VINCENT "VINNIE MORROW": Genovese crime syndicate member; had interests in loan-sharking and narcotics.

MIELE, RICHARD: President of Modern Transportation; co-owner of MSLA Landfill; partner in sludge-disposal firm convicted of bribing public officials.

MODERN EARTHLINE COMPANY: Partnership between Modern Transportation and the Earthline Division of SCA Services; disposed of sewerage sludge by spreading it on strip-mined areas of Pennsylvania and Maryland.

MODERN TRANSPORTATION COMPANY: Waste-hauling and disposal firm owned by Richard Miele; involved in Philadelphia sludge-disposal scheme as well as attempts to transport hazardous wastes abroad.

MSLA LANDFILL: Dump in Kearny, New Jersey, owned by Richard Miele, Joe Cassini, and others, which has been used for chemical-waste disposal.

NEW JERSEY INTER-AGENCY HAZARDOUS WASTE TASK FORCE: Special investigative unit funded by the EPA and the Department of Justice.

NEW YORK STATE SENATE SELECT COMMITTEE ON CRIME: Created to investigate organized crime; in the forefront of the battle against illegal toxic-waste dumping.

OTTENS, RICHARD "DIRK": New Jersey State Police sergeant; led investigations with partner, Jack Penney, into numerous mob-connected toxic-waste-disposal firms.

PALMERI, ERNEST: Organized crime leader of Teamsters Local 945; involved in bank scams and union corruption.

PINTO, JOHN: Former regional vice-president of Browning-Ferris Industries; associated with illegal waste haulers.

RATTENI, NICK: Long-standing organized-crime figure; owner of large private sanitation company; very influential in sanitation industry.

RECKLITIS, CHRISTOPHER P.: President of SCA Services in the early 1970s; defrauded the company out of millions of dollars along with Burton Steir.

ROSELLE, CRESCENT "CHRIS": Partner in MSLA; owner of several solid- and toxic-waste companies sold to SCA Services; murdered in 1980.

RESOURCE CONSERVATION AND RECOVERY ACT (RCRA): Federal legislation passed in 1976 setting standards for hazardous-waste hauling and disposal.

SACKOWICZ, GREGORY: New Jersey deputy attorney general in charge of toxic-waste investigations.

SAN FELICE, GABRIEL "GABE": Owner of a waste-hauling business, Sano Carting; constantly in trouble for attempting to compete with other haulers; murdered in 1978.

SCA SERVICES, INC.: Nation's third-largest waste-disposal company; expanded greatly by buying local hauling companies; the subject of intensive congressional scrutiny for possible ties to organized crime.

SCHIPANI, JOSEPH: Member of the Genovese crime syndicate; one-time officer in the Brooklyn Trade Waste Association.

SERRATELLI, JOHN: Corrupt official of Teamsters' Local 945; involved in extortion and kickbacks; disappeared in 1959.

SQUILLANTE, VINCENT "JIMMIE": Organizer of trade associations in the private sanitation industry in New York and suburban counties; organized-crime figure representing the interests of his godfather, Albert Anastasia; disappeared in 1960.

STATEWIDE ENVIRONMENTAL CONTRACTORS: Waste company owned by Charles Macaluso; employer of FBI informant Harold Kaufman.

STEIR, BURTON: Founder of SCA Services; conspired with Recklitis in a scheme to steal millions of dollars from the company; promoter of Thomas Viola as SCA corporate officer.

STIER, EDWIN: Former director of New Jersey's Division of Criminal Justice.

SUPERFUND ACT: Federal legislation designed to assist in the cleanup of hazardous-waste sites.

TRAFFICANTE, SANTO, JR.: Leader of powerful Florida-based organized-crime syndicate; received a regular payoff from West Florida organized-crime figures engaged in waste-disposal activities.

VIOLA, THOMAS: President of SCA Services in the late 1970s; protégé of SCA founder Burton Steir; resigned following congressional hearings linking SCA to organized crime.

WASTE MANAGEMENT, INC.: Headquartered in Oak Brook, Illinois, the largest hazardous-waste handler in the United States; has been charged with restraint of trade and violations of pollution laws.

ZINGARO, JOSEPH: Organized-crime associate of Nick Ratteni and James Failla; represents Gambino syndicate in New York area waste activities.

Suggested Readings

ABC News, *20/20* transcript (December 17, 1981), "Deadly Chemicals, Deadly Oil."

Alan A. Block (1983), "Organized Crime and Toxic Waste: A Summary," in U.S. Senate, Permanent Subcommittee on Investigations, *Profile of Organized Crime; Mid-Atlantic Region* (Government Printing Office).

Alan A. Block and Frank R. Scarpitti (1983), "Defining Illegal Hazardous Waste Disposal: White-Collar or Organized Crime," in Gordon P. Waldo, ed., *Career Criminals* (Sage).

Michael Brown (1980), "Drums of Death," *Audubon,* July: 120–133.

Michael Brown, *Laying Waste: The Poisoning of America by Toxic Chemicals* (Pantheon Books).

Douglas M. Costle (1982), "Environmental Regulation and Regulatory Reform," *Washington Law Review,* 57: 409–432.

Robert J. Delaney (1981), Statement in U.S. Senate, Permanent Subcommittee on Investigations, *Hearing* (Government Printing Office).

Samuel S. Epstein, Lester O. Brown, and Carl Pope (1982) *Hazardous Waste in America* (Sierra Club Books).

John Fine (1980–81), "Toxic Waste Dangers," *Water Spectrum,* Winter: 23–30.

Irene Kiefer (1979), "The Problems Caused by Dumping Hazardous Wastes," *SciQuest,* April: 16–22.

Kevin Krajick (1981), "Toxic Waste Is Big Business for the Mob," *Police Magazine,* May: 18–20.

Kevin Krajick (1981), "When Will Police Discover the Toxic Time Bomb?" *Police Magazine,* May: 6–17.

KYW-TV News, Channel 3, Philadelphia (November 30, 1983), "Trashed for Cash."

Jeremiah B. McKenna (1983), "Organized Crime in the Toxic Waste Disposal Industry," U.S. Senate, Permanent Subcommittee on Investigations, *Profile of Organized Crime: Mid-Atlantic Region* (Government Printing Office).

Joseph Mancini (1981), "The Dirty Business of Garbage," *Attenzione*, June: 56–61.

Ralph J. Marino (1982), "Case History of a Toxic Waste Dumper: The Manipulation of the State Department of Environmental Conservation and the Consequences of Non-Enforcement," *A Report* by the Select Committee on Crime (New York, N.Y.)

Ralph Nader, Ronald Brownstein, and John Richard (1981), *Who's Poisoning America: Corporate Polluters and Their Victims in the Chemical Age* (Sierra Club Books).

National Association of Attorneys General (1979), Summary of Speeches to the Environmental Control and Organized Crime Control Seminars, *Organized Crime Control: Special Report*.

New Jersey Senate, Committee Created Under Senate Resolution No. 4 (1958) and Reconstituted Under Senate Resolution No. 3 (1959) to Investigate the Cost of Garbage Collection and Disposal (1959), *Hearing* (Trenton).

New Jersey Special Legislative Commission (1969), *Public Hearing to Investigate Certain Problems Relating to Solid Waste Disposal* (Trenton).

New Jersey Superior Court, *State of New Jersey v. New Jersey Trade Waste Association, Hudson County Sanitation Association, et al., Indictment,* State Grand Jury Number SGJ66-80-8.

New York City Department of Investigation (1982), "Investigation into the Department of Sanitation's Award of Two Landfill Cover Contracts to Perez-Interboro Asphalt Co. Inc., Contractor, JoPel Contracting & Trucking Corp., Subcontractor, for the Edgemere Landfill, Queens, and the Fountain Avenue Landfill, Brooklyn (New York, N.Y.).

New York City Police Department (1983), *Report on Organized Crime in New York City to the U.S. Senate Committee on the Judiciary* (New York, N.Y.).

New York State County Court: Rockland County (1979), *Report by the Special Grand Jury for Investigations into Organized Criminal Activities of the County of Rockland*.

New York State Senate, Select Committee on Crime (1981), *An Investigation into Illegal Hazardous Waste Disposal on Long Island: Interim Report* (New York, N.Y.).

New York State Senate, Select Committee on Crime (1980), *Investigation into the Involvement of Organized Crime in Hazardous Waste Dumping: Hearing* (New York, N.Y.).

New York State Senate, Select Committee on Crime (1981), *A Public Hearing on the Hazardous Waste Industry and Its Effects on Long Island* (New York, N.Y.).

New York State Senate, Select Committee on Crime (1982), *A Public Hearing on Hazardous Waste Dumping in New York City* (New York, N.Y.).

New York State, Standing Committee on Environmental Conservation, Standing Committee on Health, Subcommittee on Toxic and Hazardous Substances (1980) *Joint Hearing* (Albany, New York).

J. J. Peirce and P. A. Vesilind, eds. (1981), *Hazardous Waste Management* (Ann Arbor Science).

R. B. Pojasek, ed. (1980), *Toxic and Hazardous Waste Disposal* (Ann Arbor Science).

Peter Reuter (nd), "Conspiracy Among the Many: A Study of Racketeers as Cartel Organizers" (The Rand Corp.)

E. S. Savas (1977), *The Organization and Efficiency of Solid Waste Collection* (D. C. Heath).

Sierra Club (1982), *Poisons in the Water* (Natural Heritage Report No. 5).

Leon Silverman (1982), *Report of the Special Prosecutor*, United States Court of Appeals for the District of Columbia Circuit.

T. L. Sweeney et al., eds. (1982), *Hazardous Waste Management for the 80s* (Ann Arbor Science).

U.S. Environmental Protection Agency (1980), *Everybody's Problem: Hazardous Waste* (Government Printing Office).

U.S. Environmental Protection Agency (1983), *National Survey of Hazardous Waste Generators and Treatment, Storage, and Disposal Facilities Regulated Under RCRA in 1981* (Government Printing Office).

U.S. House, Committee on Energy and Commerce (1982), *Hazardous Waste Enforcement* (Government Printing Office).

U.S. House, Subcommittee on Health and the Environment and Subcommittee on Transportation and Commerce of the Committee on Interstate and Foreign Commerce (1980), joint hearings on *Hazardous Waste and Drinking Water* (Government Printing Office).

U.S. House, Subcommittee on Oversight and Investigations of the Committee on Energy and Commerce (1981), *Hazardous Waste Matters: A Case Study of Landfill Sites: Hearing* (Government Printing Office).

U.S. House, Subcommittee on Oversight and Investigations of the Committee on Energy and Commerce (1983), *Law Enforcement Authority for the Environmental Protection Agency's Criminal Investigators: Hearing* (Government Printing Office).

U.S. House, Subcommittee on Oversight and Investigations of the Committee on Energy and Commerce (1981), *Organized Crime Links to the Waste Disposal Industry: Hearing* (Government Printing Office).

U.S. House, Subcommittee on Oversight and Investigations of the Committee on Interstate and Foreign Commerce (1979), *Hazardous Waste Disposal: Hearing* (Government Printing Office).

U.S. House, Subcommittee on Oversight and Investigations of the Committee on Interstate and Foreign Commerce (1980), *Organized Crime and Hazardous Waste Disposal: Hearing* (Government Printing Office).

U.S. House, Subcommittee on Oversight and Investigations of the Committee on Interstate and Foreign Commerce (1978), *Resource Conservation and Recovery Act: Hearing* (Government Printing Office).

U.S. House, Subcommittee on Oversight and Investigations of the Committee on Interstate and Foreign Commerce (1979), *Waste Disposal Site Survey* (Government Printing Office).

U.S. House, Subcommittee on Transportation and Commerce of the Committee on Interstate and Foreign Commerce

(1980), *Hazardous Waste Disposal: Our Number One Environmental Problem* (Government Printing Office).

U.S. Senate, Select Committee on Improper Activities in the Labor or Management Field (1957), *Investigation of Improper Activities in the Labor or Management Field* (Government Printing Office).

U.S. Senate, Subcommittee on Oversight of Government Management of the Committee on Governmental Affairs (1979) *Hazardous Waste Management and the Resource Conservation and Recovery Act: Hearing* (Government Printing Office).

U.S. Senate, Subcommittee on Oversight of Government Management of the Committee on Governmental Affairs (1980) *Report on Hazardous Waste Management and the Implementation of the Resource Conservation and Recovery Act* (Government Printing Office).

"U S. Underworld Linked to Illegal Toxic Waste Disposal," (1981), *AMBIO* 10: 189–190.

Nicholas R. Vasile, Intelligence Analyst, Newark Strike Force (1977), "Organized Crime in New Jersey: A Survey Report" (Trenton).

David Weinberg (1980), "We Almost Lost Elizabeth," *New Jersey Monthly,* August: 35–39, 97–109.

Georgina Wilheim (1981), "The Regulation of Hazardous Waste Disposal: Cleaning the Augean Stables with a Flood of Regulations," *Rutgers Law Review* 33: 906–972.

Robert Windrem (1978), "The Mob Comes to Wall Street," *Village Voice,* November 13: 17–24.

Index

INDEX